FINDING WISDOM IN

EAST ASIAN CLASSICS

1 Diagram of the Supreme Ultimate

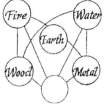

○ This represents the Supreme Ultimate and the Indeterminate. That is [it gives rise to] yin and yang, but this indicates that in its fundamental substance there is no admixture of yin and yang.

◉ This represents how ○ moves and produces yang, quiesces and produces yin. The ○ in the center represents their fundamental substance. ☽ is the root of ☾; ☾ is the root of ☽.

⋈ This represents how yang by its change and yin by its union therewith produces water, fire, wood, metal and earth.

☿ represents how the Indeterminate and yin and yang and the Five Elements wondrously unite and are without separation.

○ This represents how by the transformations of material force Ch'ien becomes the male and K'un becomes the female.

Male and female each have their own natures, but are the one Supreme Ultimate.

○ This represents how all things evolve and are produced by transformations of form.

Each thing has its own nature but all are the one Supreme Ultimate.

Yang ... Yin

Action ... Quiet

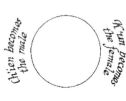

Ch'ien becomes the male

K'un becomes the female

The production and transformation of all creatures

FINDING WISDOM IN
EAST ASIAN CLASSICS

Edited by Wm. Theodore de Bary

COLUMBIA UNIVERSITY PRESS   *New York*

COLUMBIA UNIVERSITY PRESS

Publishers Since 1893

NEW YORK   CHICHESTER, WEST SUSSEX

cup.columbia.edu

Copyright © 2011 Columbia University Press

All rights reserved

Library of Congress Cataloging-in-Publication Data
Finding wisdom in East Asian classics / edited by Wm. Theodore de Bary.

p.   cm.

Includes index.

ISBN 978-0-231-15396-6 (cloth : alk. paper — ISBN 978-0-231-15397-3
(pbk. : alk. paper) — ISBN 978-0-231-52719-4 (ebook)

1. East Asian literature—History and criticism.   2. Wisdom in literature.   3. Best
books—East Asia.   4. Canon (Literature)   I. De Bary, William Theodore, 1919–

PL493.F56 2011

895—dc22

2010053572

References to Internet Web sites (URLs) were accurate at the time of writing. Neither the author nor Columbia University Press is responsible for URLs that may have expired or changed since the manuscript was prepared.

The frontispiece (p.ii) shows Zhou Dunyi's *Diagram of the Supreme Ultimate*, with the *Diagram of the Study of the Mind* (*Diagram of the Study of the Heart-and-Mind*) on page x. The diagrams are discussed on pages 336 and 348 and are from Michael Kalton's *To Become a Sage* (New York: Columbia University Press, 1988), 39 and 161.

To Irene Bloom

Anne Whitney Olin Professor of Asian and Middle Eastern Studies at Barnard College, 1989–2002. An outstanding scholar, inspiring teacher, and beautiful friend to all who knew her at Barnard and Columbia.

CONTENTS

Preface. The Great "Civilized" Conversation: Cases in Point
Wm. Theodore de Bary   xi

1.   Asian Classics as the Great Books of the East
     Wm. Theodore de Bary   1

2.   Asia in the Core Curriculum
     Wm. Theodore de Bary   30

3.   Why We Read the *Analects* of Confucius
     Wm. Theodore de Bary   44

4.   Mencius
     Irene Bloom   57

5.   Laozi
     Franciscus Verellen   72

6.   Zhuangzi
     Paul Contino   80

7.   Xunzi
     Wm. Theodore de Bary   93

8.   *The Lotus Sūtra*
     Wing-tsit Chan   110

9.   *The Teaching of Vimalakīrti*
         Robert A. F. Thurman   120

10(A).   The *Platform Sūtra* of the Sixth Patriarch
         Philip Yampolsky   128

10(B).   The *Platform Sūtra* as a Chinese Classic
         Wm. Theodore de Bary   136

11.   Tang Poetry: A Return to Basics
         Burton Watson   149

12.   *Journey to the West*
         C. T. Hsia   159

13.   *A Dream of Red Mansions*
         C. T. Hsia   174

14.   Zhu Xi and the Four Books
         Wm. Theodore de Bary   187

15.   *Waiting for the Dawn*: Huang Zongxi's Critique of the
         Chinese Dynastic System
         Wm. Theodore de Bary   199

16(A).   *The Tale of Genji* as a Japanese and World Classic
         Haruo Shirane   209

16(B).   Passion and Poignancy in *The Tale of Genji*
         Wm. Theodore de Bary   220

17.   *The Pillow Book*
         Wm. Theodore de Bary   231

18.   Kamo no Chōmei's "An Account of My Hut"
         Paul Anderer   241

19.   *The Tale of the Heike*
         Paul Varley   248

20(A).   Kenkō's *Essays in Idleness*
         Donald Keene   257

20(B).   Kenkō and Montaigne in Tandem
         James Mirollo   265

21(A).   The Poetry of Matsuo Bashō
          Haruo Shirane   275

21(B).   Matsuo Bashō
          Donald Keene   287

22.   Chikamatsu
          Donald Keene   301

23.   Saikaku's *Five Women Who Loved Love*
          Wm. Theodore de Bary   310

24.   Kaibara Ekken's *Precepts for Daily Life in Japan*
          Mary Evelyn Tucker   321

25.   The Contemporary Meaning of T'oegye's *Ten Diagrams on
          Sage Learning*
          Michael C. Kalton   335

26.   *The Memoirs of Lady Hyegyŏng*
          JaHyun Kim Haboush   352

27.   *The Song of the Faithful Wife Ch'unhyang*
          Rachel E. Chung   365

28.   Reading and Teaching *The Tale of Kieu*
          Conrad Schirokauer   376

         Index   389

8 Diagram of the Study of the Mind

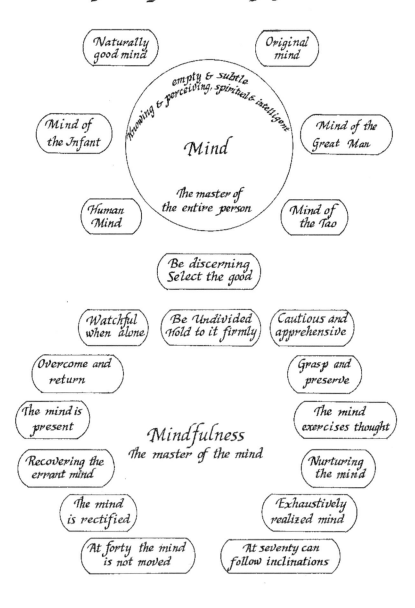

Naturally good mind

Original mind

Mind of the Infant

empty & subtle
knowing & perceiving, spiritual & intelligent

Mind

The master of the entire person

Mind of the Great Man

Human Mind

Mind of the Tao

Be discerning
Select the good

Watchful when alone

Be Undivided
Hold to it firmly

Cautious and apprehensive

Overcome and return

Grasp and preserve

The mind is present

The mind exercises thought

Recovering the errant mind

Mindfulness
The master of the mind

Nurturing the mind

The mind is rectified

Exhaustively realized mind

At forty the mind is not moved

At seventy can follow inclinations

The Great "Civilized" Conversation: Cases in Point

Wm. Theodore de Bary

T HOSE FAMILIAR WITH the early history of the movement at Columbia identified with the Honors Course of John Erskine (1879–1951) and "The Classics of the Western World," known later in Chicago and St. John's as the "Great Books Program," will recall how its early advocates, including, among others, Mark Van Doren and Stringfellow Barr, referred to the dialogue among the great writers and thinkers as "The Great Conversation." They thought of it as the great minds speaking to each other over the centuries about the perennial issues of human life and society. Contrary to those who misperceived the process as one of handing down fixed, eternal truths, for them it was a vital process of reengaging with questions that had continued to have human relevance, age after age. One could not afford to ignore what had earlier been said about those issues, because civilization depended on building upon the lessons of the past. Thus tradition, like civilization, continued to grow. It was cumulating and cumulative, not fixed.

Not all of the issues engaged in this conversation had to do with civilization and society—some religious issues might go beyond that—but sustaining the conversation itself required a civilized life, a willingness to show a decent respect for what others have learned or thought for themselves, what others have valued or held dear. Indeed, it was an appreciation for human life as it has been lived.

In the earlier phases of this movement, the conversation remained largely within the Western tradition and was closely tied to the question of how classics, originally expressed in the classical languages of the West, especially Latin and Greek, could survive in the modern vernacular as part of a classical education. But it was easily assumed that translation into the vernacular was possible because of the continuity of both language and culture into the later period. Such continuity in cultural values overrode historical change. As we shall see, this was largely (but not entirely) true of the major Asian traditions as well. They too had long-standing traditions of a Great Conversation, as later writers spoke to and reappropriated their own classics—and thus engaged with the great minds of the past.

It was not, however, a matter simply of conserving received tradition. It was, as the word "conversation" suggests, the present speaking to the past in its own voice, actively repossessing and renewing the classics in modern terms that spoke to contemporary concerns as well. In other words, these traditions had within themselves the capacity for reexamination and self-renewal.

In modern times, this meant reflecting on the classics in a way that responded to the new cultural situation in which modern writers found themselves. By the eighteenth century at least, Western writers recognized that Asian traditions had classic thinkers who spoke to the same issues and concerns, though perhaps in somewhat different terms. Thus Enlightenment thinkers began to speak to the thinkers of classical China as well as to Western classics, and the New England Transcendentalists spoke also to philosophers of ancient India. Benjamin Franklin, at the founding of the American Philosophical Society, dedicated it to the study of Chinese as well as Western philosophy. All this had an effect on early twentieth-century writers such as W. B. Yeats, Ezra Pound, T. S. Eliot, and many others. But as of the twentieth century, though the most creative minds were already extending the Great Conversation to Asia, it had as yet little effect on Western education at the basic level. Asian classics did not become part of the Great Books program. They were not among Mortimer Adler's "Hundred Great Books," nor did his "Hundred Great Ideas" include any Asian concepts.

Another limitation on the inclusion of Asian classics in the Great Conversation as conducted in the modern West was the tendency to focus the conversation on the classic writers of the Asian traditions, but not as part of a continuing conversation over time that matured well beyond ancient times. Thus Ezra Pound thought he could directly engage with the Confucian classics and even translate them himself with minimal Sinological expertise. Sometimes he succeeded brilliantly in intuiting and appropriating them for his own poetic purposes, but this falls well short of explaining what the *Analects* or *Great Learning* had meant to later Chinese, Japanese, and Korean civilizations. In other words, it was more of an extension of Pound's own culture, his own exploratory venture into the past idealizing Confucianism, than it was a substantial engagement with Chinese culture or civilization in its mature forms.

The time has come, however, for us to extend the conversation to twenty-first-century education in ways that do justice to Asian classics not just as museum pieces but as part of the historical process of the emerging world civilization. Given the domination of education today by economic and technological forces—the same forces that drive world business—this will not be an easy thing to do. Indeed, the preservation of any humanities education at all is problematic now anywhere in the world. I have written elsewhere about the crisis in East Asian education as modern universities have found it difficult to sustain the reading of even their own classics in the undergraduate curriculum.[1] But the reasons for it are the same as those that militate against any classical education at all, even in the West. For the most part, Chinese or Japanese classics are read only by a few students majoring in classics departments. Meanwhile, most students want to concentrate on economics, science, and technology, and for these English is the relevant language. Thus the problem for Asian education is little different from that in the West: how to sustain any place at all for the humanities in the curriculum. It is a global problem and everywhere raises the question: can traditional humanistic learning be sustained as part of a new global culture, which would otherwise be dominated simply by the market and technology?

In *Confucian Tradition and Global Education* (2006), I cited the difficulties that New Asia College, supposedly a bridgehead of Confucian culture into the modern world, was experiencing in trying to sustain the study of the Confucian classics. Let me now cite a similar case nearer "home" (even though today it is a question what one still can call "home," educationally speaking). It comes from a publication you may know of, *Inside Academe*, which speaks for an organization dedicated to upholding academic standards and traditional values in American education. In its summer 2007 issue, *Inside Academe* had an article entitled "Where's the Bard?" reporting on a

---

1.   See my *Confucian Tradition and Global Education* (Hong Kong: Chinese University Press of Hong Kong, 2006).

new survey, headlined as "The Vanishing Bard," of more than seventy universities, which reported that only fifteen among them require their English majors to take a course on Shakespeare. Instead, it says, "English majors are being offered an astonishing array of courses on popular culture, children's literature, sociology, and politics."

The article goes on to cite a long list of American publications, from *USA Today* to *The New Republic*, which regarded these survey results as significant. I doubt that many of us familiar with college education in the United States will consider this news. But for those concerned with how traditional humanistic learning stands in today's curriculum, the real significance of the report lies in its narrow focus on what is happening in English departments, to English majors—an academic vested interest—and it resembles what is happening to their counterpart departments in East Asia: the erosion in the study of their own classics, as upwardly mobile students choose to study English in its role as the lingua franca of the twenty-first century. What adds to the irony in this case is that, before this, educated East Asians in the nineteenth and twentieth centuries had already come to admire Shakespeare as a world classic.

For traditionalists of almost any stripe, it would be a matter of concern that Shakespeare was being put on the shelf, unstudied, in any English department, but the reason for it is something antecedent to the state of the English major. If there is no place for the humanities in a globalized market for education, then even English majors will turn away from so great a figure as Shakespeare and toward whatever finds favor in the current media or marketplace.

My point is that mere conservatism—holding to an old line that has long since been overrun—will not avail today unless we can establish a place for local tradition in a global humanism that has something to say about what values might direct and control rampant technologization and a runaway market economy. Put in such global terms, the magnitude of the problem may seem overwhelming: how can one deal with the problem locally except in the larger context of global education? On the other hand, how can one get a handle on something so massive and complex as global education? If we have to think globally (as the saying goes), how can we act locally to work our way toward that goal? The answer, it seems to me, is that even if we have to work within the limits of what is practicable in our local situation, we can begin the process of sharing our goals and experiences on a wider scale, so that the resources of the larger scholarly and educational community can be brought to bear upon, and be availed of, on behalf of beneficial, incremental change.

One way to get at this is to share our views on what has been considered "classic" in the major mature traditions of the civilized world and discuss how these can best be incorporated into our pooled educational resources—to put it simply, to make these resources available in a form that can be adapted to local systems. Thereby one might hope to establish some kind of working consensus in the same way that the United Nations established a consensus on human rights in its Universal Declaration of 1948. The Universal Declaration did not effectively become "law," but it did set an international standard that few could disagree with and that almost all the world's states formally "ratified," however much or little they actually complied with it. Activists, always a minority, at least had a standard they could invoke in working toward its implementation. Fortunately, the English text of the declaration had the benefit of multicultural consultation and was less culture bound than would otherwise have been the case. Something like that should be done to establish "Classics for an Emerging World."

Let us compare our situation to that of American education a century ago. No sooner had President Eliot of Harvard set up his Five-Foot Shelf of Classics than he went over to a system of free electives, which meant that students were free to ignore the Five-Foot Shelf. Columbia responded by making its "Classics of the Western World" a required Humanities course (a core course for all undergraduates). The Chicago version of this was dubbed "General Education," with the idea of its being intended for students in general, young or old, elite or popular (as the Columbia program itself had been). But "generality" was its undoing when general education at Harvard succumbed to diverse academic interests and disciplines—to "ways of knowing" (among other methodologies), which could lead anywhere. The "core" of the classics earlier had been "ways of living," that is, what the "Good Life" could mean in human terms, but this was premised on what it meant to be human. "Ways of knowing" was one aspect of this, but only one. Without a core of central human concerns, Ways of Knowing could lead to a diffuse unboundedness, out on the so-called cutting edge of knowledge.

The "elective" character of even general education at Harvard was congenial to the free market that has dominated almost all aspects of cultural life in the past century, and it has benefited from the affluence—the great range of choices—that free enterprise has afforded the better classes, based on the pervasive assumption of unlimited growth and expansion. Education in the twenty-first century, however, without the luxuries of bubble-market prosperity, will find itself constrained to make choices within much stricter limits. Choices are still there to be made, but just as the economy

will have to live with much less exploitation of natural and human resources, society will have to make harder choices and give up some of the
freedom our affluence has afforded in order to preserve other values judged
more essential. Education will have to do the same: make judgments as to
what is most essential. Without closing the door on intellectual growth, we
will have to prepare people to make qualitative judgments as to what is most
conducive in the longer run to the good life and as to what human goods are
sustainable.

In light of the foregoing, we do not presume to start from a preconceived
definition of the canonical values, which is then projected out and super-
imposed on other cultures. Rather, we proceed inductively to examine what
other traditions have considered classic, and from this empirical base we
develop criteria, both old and new, that may contribute to an enlarged conception of the humanities. Such a view of the canon may still be thought of
as a working, contestable construct for educational purposes.

Here we aim to address two main questions. What is the place of Asia
in the humanities curriculum today, and how may classics of the major Asian
traditions illustrate the values and genres honored in those traditions? In
chapter 1, a rather full list of classic works—by no means a fixed or complete
canon—is given. From this larger list a few examples are taken, representing the four East Asian traditions, and discussed in brief interpretive essays
intended to introduce them to the general reader. Here two points should
be kept in mind. First, we have not always chosen the best-known works,
because much has already been written about them, but have instead often
picked ones less known or at least less accessible to the average reader. Second, the essays are aimed at the nonspecialist. We have not striven for originality of interpretation—though some of that appears in these pages—but
rather for what is most central and commonly understood about these works
in their own tradition: what it is that has made them classics by general consensus over the centuries and what it is that can still speak to us most directly
today.

The present volume represents an updating of the earlier *Approaches
to the Oriental Classics* (1959) and reproduces a few of the essays originally
published therein. For the most part, however, its contents are new. They
either address the new educational challenges of the early twenty-first century or offer fresh approaches to the individual classics that always invite
reexamination and in that process win renewed appreciation. In the case
of some major classics capable of sustaining more than one interpretation,

two complimentary essays are included by different authors. To make room for these, we are publishing them in a volume limited to traditional East Asian classics. Volumes to follow will deal with other Asian traditions.

In these interpretive essays, reference is occasionally made to pertinent works beside the classics themselves, but no full bibliography is provided. For this latter purpose, readers may well have recourse to the Internet.

This book draws on the collective efforts and experience of many members of our staff over the years. Among them, the editor wishes particularly to recognize the longstanding and very distinguished service of Ainslie Embree, John Meskill, Irene Bloom, and Shang Wei.

FINDING WISDOM IN

EAST ASIAN CLASSICS

ASIAN CLASSICS AS THE GREAT BOOKS OF THE EAST

Wm. Theodore de Bary

T HE ASIAN CLASSICS may not be included in the "Hundred Great
Books" or the "Hundred Great Ideas"[1] today, but the idea of books so
challenging to the mind, so close to the human heart, and of such impressive depth or stature as to command the attention of generation after generation is certainly not confined to the Western world. Each of the major
Asian civilizations has had its canonical texts and literary classics. Significant differences appear, however, in the way that the classic canon is
defined—by whom, for what audience, for what purposes, and in what form.
To Muhammad, "the people of the book" was an important concept for lo-
cating the spiritual roots of Islam in an earlier prophetic tradition and for
affirming a common religious ground in the Bible among Jews, Christians,
and Muslims.[2] Yet it is by no means clear that the books of the Old Testament, or such of the New as he in any way recognized, were thought to be
essential reading for his own followers, let alone for the other "people of the
book." Anyone who today reads the great Muslim philosophers and theologians would know that they, no less than St. Augustine and St. Thomas, engaged in significant dialogue with the Greek philosophers and were long
ago party to the "Great Conversation" that Mark Van Doren, Lyman Bryson,
and Jacques Barzun used to talk about at Columbia and on CBS radio.
Though the contributions of Islamic philosophers were rarely acknowledged
in the discussion that Bryson held on CBS's Sunday morning "Invitation
to Learning," in 1978 a published series on Western spirituality recognized

that they do indeed belong in this company.[3] Here too, however, it is doubt-ful that in the Muslim world itself the writings of Plato and Aristotle would have been thought essential reading for any but the scholarly few who stud-ied Al-Ghazālī, Avicenna, Averroes, or Ibn Khaldūn.

Hindus had their own sacred scriptures, some lines of which would be on the lips of pious Indians, but for the most part these texts were consid-ered the sacred preserve of learned pandits, not to be read—much less dis-cussed—by the faithful. Among the latter, oral texts had far more currency than written. In China too there were the classics of the Confucian tradi-tion, but again they were the property principally of a learned elite, though Daoist works such as the *Laozi* and *Zhuangzi* also figured in cultivated dis-course among the literati and thus in a sense qualified as great books even if not as canonical literature.

In Japan, eminent Buddhist monks such as Saichō and Kūkai in the ninth century advanced the idea that, for those who would occupy positions of social as well as clerical importance, a proper training should include the reading of at least some Confucian classics, together with the major scrip-tures of Mahāyāna Buddhism. So assiduously cultivated in Heian Japan was this classical study that even court ladies such as Murasaki Shikibu and Sei Shōnagon, great writers in the vernacular Japanese literature of the elev-enth century, had themselves read the major Confucian classics along with the monumental Chinese histories and leading Tang poets, and they would have disdained as uncouth and illiterate anyone who had not done the same. Important later writers in Japan as diverse as the monk-essayist Kenkō in the fourteenth century, the teacher of military science Yamaga Sokō in the seventeenth century, and the great nativist scholar Motoori Norinaga in the eighteenth all had read the classic Confucian and Daoist texts as part of their mixed cultural inheritance, whether or not they identified themselves with either of the traditions from which these works derived. Thus the latter were read by non-Chinese too as great books that commanded attention even when not compelling assent.

In this respect, the Japanese (along with the Koreans and Vietnamese, who shared the same Confucian, Daoist, and Buddhist literature) may have been more accustomed to multicultural learning than some other Asian peoples who rarely recognized as classics the major works of traditions other than their own. As a general rule, certainly, the traditions transmitting these texts were apt to be socially circumscribed and more or less culture bound within the limits of a common "classical" literature. As religions, their appeal might be more universal, but in the transmission of texts they stood out as high classical traditions—"great traditions" for the few rather than little traditions shared in by the many. Their "great books" were most often scriptures preserved and read by particular religious communities or classics cherished by the bearers of high culture. A main reason for this lay in the fact that most classics and scriptures were preserved in difficult classical or sacred languages, and even popular works in the vernacular tended over time to become inaccessible, because spoken tongues, more subject to change (being less fixed and disciplined than classical languages), tend toward their own kind of obsolescence. The recognized "classics" of popular fiction too, as well as philosophical and religious dialogues in the vernacular (such as Zen dialogues or Neo-Confucian "recorded conversations"), could be so studded with colloquialisms as to present special difficulties for readers of a later age.

One can hardly exaggerate the persistence and pervasiveness of this problem in communication. Modern writers sometimes assume that the restricted readership of classical literature in Asian societies is mainly attributable to an exclusivity or possessiveness on the part of the custodians of the high tradition. Their monopoly of learning, it is supposed, gave them a vested interest in preserving sacred knowledge as something precious, recondite, and out of the ordinary man's reach. The Confucian literati, one is told, both jealously guarded the purity and reveled in the complexity of a written language the masses were not supposed to touch. Buddhist monks of Heian Japan, historians often say or imply, deliberately mystified religious learning so as to insure their own dominance over credulous masses.

Such imputations are not without some basis, as for instance in the case of the Confucian literati in fifteenth-century Korea who resisted the development and use of a new alphabet for their native language because it would compete for attention with Chinese language and literature—an argument not unmixed with the concern of some to maintain their own privileged position as dispensers of the Chinese classical tradition. Yet there are contrary cases. For example, the leading Japanese monk Kūkai, himself a spokesman for the so-called Esoteric School of Buddhism, advocated public schooling in the ninth century, and Zhu Xi, the great Neo-Confucian philosopher of the twelfth century, was a strong advocate of universal education through public schools. Zhu devoted himself to editing and simplifying the classics with a view to making them more understandable for ordinary persons. Since other leading Neo-Confucians after Zhu Xi took up this cause in their writings, the limited success of their efforts must have been due to factors other than the lack of good intentions. Chief among these were probably (1) the perception of peasants in a predominantly agrarian society that learning yielded few economic benefits unless one could convert it into official position or status and (2) the government's lack of interest in the matter beyond the needs of bureaucratic recruitment. In such circumstances, for those with little leisure to dispose of, the difficulties of mastering the great books in classical languages might not seem worth the costs.

In some ways Zhu Xi, as an educator trying to reach beyond his immediate scholarly audience, was the Mortimer Adler of his time, but he would probably have thought a reading list of One Hundred Great Books too ambitious. His goal was to reach the aspiring youth of every village and hamlet in China, for which he recommended a shorter list: a program based on the Confucian Four Books and his own compact anthology of Song-dynasty thought, *Reflections on Things at Hand* (*Jin-si-lu*). Zhu's competition in those days, the Chan (Zen) masters, were offering enlightenment at no cost in terms of reading, and Zen painters even portrayed sages tearing up the scriptures. Too much booklearning was already seen as injurious to the health, and Zhu Xi himself, as well as his Neo-Confucian predecessors, favored the careful reading of a few books, as well as reflection over them and discussion with others, instead of a superficial acquaintance with many. Hence he was modest in his initial demands, trying to keep his reading program simple and within people's means and capabilities.

In his efforts along this line, Zhu very early reached the Aspen phase of his Great Books movement, when snippets and selections would often have to serve in place of whole books if the reading was to be done by other than scholars. Two of his Four Books, in fact, were selected short chapters from the classic *Record of Rites*: "The Great Learning" and "The Mean." These he further revised and edited in order to make the texts more coherent, systematic, and integral—shaping them according to what, in his mind, the classic form must have been.

Zhu Xi also had his rough equivalent of Aspen in sylvan retreats such as the historic White Deer Grotto near Mount Lu, at the deep bend in the Yangzi River, where he conducted colloquia on the Confucian classics for his students and other literati of the day. But so concerned was he with the larger educational needs of his society and with developing a cradle-to-grave approach for the individual that he even directed the compilation of a preparatory text called the *Elementary Learning* (*Xiao xue*), as a guide to the training of the young before they took up the Four Books and Five Classics.

For all of these efforts at providing a Reader's Digest of the Confucian classics, Zhu never attempted to translate his scriptures into a Vulgate. Even the *Elementary Learning* was composed of so many excerpts in classical Chinese that it would serve better as a teacher's manual than as a student's primer. Followed or accompanied by the Four Books and then by the Five Classics, it became part of the standard classical curriculum throughout East Asia and had a remarkable diffusion for premodern times, yet it remained constrained by the severe limits that the classical Chinese language imposed on its adaptability to popular audiences and changing times. In China, this system lasted down to 1905, when the pressure to adopt Western scientific learning led to the scrapping of Zhu's humanistic core curriculum based on the Chinese classics.

Half a world away and by a curious historical coincidence, at about the same time that Chinese classical learning was being abandoned, American college education was being cut loose from its old moorings in classical studies. At what was sometimes called the new "Acropolis on the Hudson," which Columbia presidents Seth Low and Nicholas Murray Butler were erecting on Morningside Heights in the early decades of this century, the old language requirements in Greek and Latin, along with the reading of the classics in the original, were giving way to a new educational approach. John Erskine, following George Woodberry, championed the idea that all the benefits of a liberal education in the classics need not be lost even if Greek and Latin were no longer obligatory, provided that undergraduates could read and discuss the classics in translation. This was the germ of Erskine's Honors course, first offered just after World War I, out of which grew the later Great Books movement.

When purists objected that something of these classics would be lost by reading them in translation, Erskine countered by asking how many readers of the Bible in his day felt able, or found it necessary, to read the Good Book in its original languages. If that rhetorical question answered itself in Erskine's favor, it was at least partly because his largely WASP audience (a convenient example, by the way, of a colloquialism that may well, a century or so from now, require a footnote to make it understood) was so accustomed to reading and appreciating the Bible in the King James version that they would no doubt have thought something would be lost by reading it in the original.

What Erskine at least implied, if he did not actually say as much, was that great books could be read like the Good Book—that the principal measure of a great book was its having something to say so universal, so perennial, and so personal that it could speak to the human individual even through the medium of translation. Strict logic or hermeneutic method might resist an argument so circular, considering how readily one could be persuaded of a book's greatness if what one most wished to believe could be read into it through translation. As a practical matter, however, and for public purposes, some process of consensus among translators and readers has decided what would be thought sufficiently meaningful and of lasting value to be worth everybody's effort. In this way, enough such books have been made available in translation so that there are plenty for the individual to choose from on his or her own terms.

If great books were to be read for something of the deep meaning found in the Good Book, something too of a missionary zeal went into propagating the Great Books idea. Its advocates brought to the new movement a depth of conviction and evangelical zeal rarely seen in academic enterprises. The original locale may have been the classroom, but the spread of the Great Books program well beyond the halls of academe had something of the old-time religion about it, as if the religious roots of the early Ivy League foundations had taken on new life in the liberal, cosmopolitan atmosphere of New York, later to be transplanted to Chicago, Annapolis, Aspen, or wherever the populist spirit and new technology—rather than a stuffy traditionalism—might carry it.

An essential feature of the new movement was its insistence on the discussion method. The Honors course, as a colloquium, reasserted not only the primacy of the classics but also the importance of reading the classics for what they had to say about life as a whole, combining ideas and value judgments that were increasingly, in Erskine's day, becoming pigeonholed in one or another academic compartment. The discussion method rejected the idea that all learning should be presented in lectures, as specialized subjects taught by authoritative scholars to receptive—but largely passive—students. This latter method had become almost universal with the eclipse of classical education, but Erskine and his followers led a counterrevolution in American education to reassert the kind of intimate, personal engagement of teachers and students that has become increasingly recognized as a necessary antidote to the impersonality and passive ingestion so typical of large lecture classes.

Lionel Trilling once observed that the transition at Columbia from the old-style classical education for gentlemen of the Hudson Valley to the new liberal education was accompanied by a demographic shift toward the assimilation of bright young members of New York's immigrant populations—especially Jewish, Irish, and Italian—into the educated class. Trilling did not himself mention it, so far as I know, but the published memoirs of Diana Trilling suggest to me that there was in this process a strong admixture of New York Jewish intellectuality, with its legacy of Talmudic discourse from the ghettoes of Europe. That intense speculative and probing mode of discourse could well, it has seemed to me, have entered into the Great Conversation over the Great Books at that particular time in our cultural history. In any case, I shall continue in this belief for more anecdotal reasons than it is appropriate to recite here, where I am dealing with the Great Books of the East rather than with the good news of the Great Books as carried by the apostles to the Midwest.

What was then newly depicted as a great conversation over the ages, among the great minds and in the great writings of all time, was not the less real for having been discovered in the twentieth century by teachers and students who converted it into something quite timely and immediate. It was a learning method appropriate to the discussion of classics now no longer read as classical-language texts for well-bred gentlemen but as the new "Great Books." Later these were to be defined and literally packaged by Robert Hutchins and Mortimer Adler as the "Hundred Great Books," in fulfillment of their modern function in democratic education.

When the distinguished British classicist Gilbert Murray wrote in 1938 about liberalism in the modern world, he chose to term it "liberality" in order not to identify it solely with the "liberalism" of contemporary Whig politics but to associate it with a broader, more long-standing tradition of liberal humanism coming down from Greece and Rome. The latter he saw as having a universal mission, taking a particular form in modern times as the bearers of this honored tradition sought to share it with a larger world. In this sense, they were conservatives as well as liberals, and of this combination Murray said: "The object of conservatism is to save the social order. The object of liberality is to bring that order a little nearer to what . . . the judgment of a free man—free from selfishness, free from passion, free from prejudice—would require, and by that very change to save it more effectively."[4] The classically educated gentleman and humanist was seen by Murray as the product of a leisured and in some ways privileged class, working "to extend its own privileges to wider and wider circles," aiming at "freedom of thought and discussion, and equally pursuing the free exercise of individual conscience and promotion of the common good."[5]

Perhaps one could compare it, in everyday experience, to the way in which the handclasp or handshake as a form of greeting has evolved from the gesture of gentlemen in a more courtly Western age. Originally, it signified openness and a meeting on equal terms of persons who shared the same aristocratic traditions of personal honor and good breeding; now it has become a nearly universal gesture of friendship and greeting shared equally among persons of almost every class, culture, social system, or ideology.

Something of that spirit, it seems to me, is to be found in the Great Books movement that arose at the same time in America, aiming to conserve as well as to extend the same humanistic tradition through new forms of liberal education. As Murray's book was being written, the faculty of Columbia College, under the leadership of distinguished teachers who had already converted Erskine's Honors course into a two-year upper college "colloquium," was transforming this program into a required general-education course for freshmen, instituted under the title of Humanities A in 1937. It was an extension of the same process ten years later that led to the inauguration of a course in Oriental Humanities, dealing with what is here called the Great Books of the East.

Erskine's original idea, as he explained the Honors Course, was nothing very grand:

The ideas underlying the course were simple. It was thought that any fairly intelligent person could read with profit any book (except, of course, highly specialized science) which had once made its way to fame among general readers. Even without the introductory study which usually precedes our acquaintance with classics in these various fields, any reader, it was thought, can discover, and enjoy the substance which has made such books remembered. It was thought, also, that a weekly discussion of the reading, such an exchange of ideas as might occur in any group which had read an interesting book, would be more illuminating than a lecture. It was thought, also, that the result of such reading and discussion over a period of two years would be a rich mass of literary information, ideas and principles, even emotions.[6]

Erskine was well aware that such a procedure challenged prevalent scholarly conceptions concerning proper methods of serious study. In the same essay quoted above, written as a preface to a reading list for the Colloquium, he argued:

> Many scholars might object to certain implications in such a reading list as this. They might think that if we read, without assistance, Homer and the Greeks, Virgil and the other Romans, Dante and the other men of the Middle Ages, we shall probably get a false idea of each period, and we may even misunderstand the individual book. To a certain extent this is true. Undoubtedly we get a better historical approach to anything that is old if we have the time to study its environment and its associations. But in art it is not the history of a masterpiece which makes it famous so much as qualities of permanent interest. It is precisely those qualities which we recognize first when we take up an old book without prejudice, and read it as intelligently as we can, looking for what seems to concern our times. I personally would go rather far in protest against the exclusively historical approach to literature, or any other art. . . . As a matter of fact, the literature which grows up around a famous book is often composed less because the book needs the aid of interpretation than because it has inspired admiration, and man likes to express his affection. We all write essays about our favorite authors. It is well, however, if the world reads the favorite author, and mercifully forgets the baggage with which our approval has burdened his reputation.   (12–13)

Erskine's claims bespoke his confidence in the intrinsic value of the works themselves and their ability to speak directly to the individual about human life in the broadest terms. An artist and musician himself, as well as a critic, he distinguished this kind of reading from anything which would serve as an introduction to "different fields of knowledge." "It is the critic," he said, "not the artist, who invents distinct fields of knowledge. In life, these fields all overlap. . . . Great books read simply and sensibly are an introduction to the whole of life; it is the completeness of their outlook which makes them great" (18).

When I said above that this meant reading a great book as if it were, in a way, the Good Book, that connection was suggested by the manner in which these "Classics of the Western World" were recommended for a larger audience by the American Library Association, which published Erskine's Honors list for general use in 1927. A second edition in 1934 carried an introductory essay on "Sharing in the Good Books" by Everett Dean Martin of the People's Institute of New York, who went so far as to distinguish this kind of reading from any kind of "popularization," "uplift enterprise," or even "education" that aimed only at utilitarian goals or social advancement. "Self-improvement is a praiseworthy aim. The pursuit of knowledge is the noblest of quests. But all depends upon the spirit with which one enters upon this adventure." These were books "to be enjoyed for their own sake," he said, part of the temple of learning of which the reader might judge for himself, on reading them, whether "when the temple is done there is 'never a door to get in to the God'" (17–18).

Yet Martin, though representing the so-called People's Institute of New York (at Cooper Union, where promising scholars like Adler and Barzun got their first experience of teaching to general audiences), also spoke for the old amateur ideal of gentlemanly learning against the increasing specialization of scholarship and its technical, analytic method, which tended to make the "good books" less naturally enjoyable and meaningful.

> Doubtless the average reader does not turn to the masterpieces of literature because he imagines that such books were written by professionals for professional students and are not for such as he. Critics and commentators and pedantic instructors commonly give this impression of literature. They have sought to appropriate it to themselves. They have placed about it their own barricades of interpretation and have obscured it with historical and biographical irrelevancies. They have sought to reduce reading to a technique and have thus taken the joy out of it.
>
> The literature which human experience has found to be most valuable is not the output of professional educators. It is amateur and was written as a labor of love. This fact cannot be too strongly emphasized. Most of the great books of the world were written by laymen for laymen. It is important that one read such books and not be content with books about books. . . . [This] often comes as something of a revelation to people when they first discover that they may read the originals and form their independent judgments. The original is always more interesting. It is better reading. If one has time for only a few books, let him confine his reading to the greatest. There are many

commentaries: but the book itself, the original, is something that has happened only once in human history and he who lives through the experience of reading it will never afterwards be quite the same.

(19–20)

Today, more than seventy years later, one can marvel at the ease with which Martin separates the layman from the professional while deploring the substitution of vulgar popularization by second-rate scholars for direct access to the great minds of the past. He does not equate "lay" with "popular" but conceives of the layman rather as the true spiritual heir of the great humanists. Striking too is the ease with which he speaks of reading his "good books" in the "original," though this could only have been in translation. He is hardly mindful, it seems, of what "original" had meant a few decades earlier to the defenders of reading the classics in the original language. That battle was now over, and the "good books" in translation had emerged victorious. Martin, no less than the apostles of the "great books," could testify himself to a vital truth of his own and others' experience as readers and teachers—the natural stimulation and exhilaration of mind that came from making contact with the great minds of the past and being powerfully challenged by them—even in translation.

Parenthetically, if I may return momentarily to the Confucian tradition, this view was shared by the great Neo-Confucian teachers like Zhu Xi and Wang Yang-ming, who kept insisting on the importance of the individual's making his first reading a direct contact with the classics in the original text. For this to be done, of course, required that some kind of gloss accompany it, and Zhu Xi, digesting and refining earlier commentaries, provided a concise new one for this purpose. Yet it is significant that he too, while recognizing the need for this kind of "translation" into the current idiom, insisted on everyone's confronting the original by himself. No doubt this reflected the persistence of an earlier oral tradition, which almost everywhere in Asia saw memorization and recitation of the text as the way to achieve a personal appropriation of the classics or scriptures. Ironically, in modern times it was this traditional practice of memorization and recitation, this making of the classic a part of oneself, which struck uninformed Western observers as mere rote learning—a meaningless process that could not but be stultifying for the individual.

Meanwhile, as this traditional reading practice was being attacked in China, a modernized version of Zhu Xi's approach to personal appropriation of the classics was being recreated in New York. No doubt, in Everett Dean Martin's case, this phenomenon exhibited the perennial truth that "each generation chooses its own ancestors," asserting its independence by reaching back to the classics over the heads of its immediate predecessors. Yet at Columbia there proved to be more to it than that. A generation later, when the Humanities A course was subjected to reexamination, its position remained secure. A blue-ribbon committee chaired by the historian Fritz Stern was asked to undertake a thoroughgoing critique of the "great books" course, simply as a matter of curriculum review. This was during the 1967–1968 school year, a time when endemic student protest might well have been thought a spur to change. In fact, however, the Stern Committee could find no signs of dissatisfaction with the course among either students or staff, and even when it proposed the most modest revisions, the committee's suggestions were met with almost total rejection. No other required course in living memory has enjoyed such powerful, perennial support from students, faculty, and alumni. Obviously, the experience spoken of by Erskine and Martin was not a momentary enthusiasm.

In Erskine's day and for some time thereafter, the term "great books" was not well established at Columbia, and the further idea of a "Hundred Great Books" must have been a special revelation from on high to Dr. Adler or later Dr. Hutchins. Erskine himself disavowed any claim to having defined, in his list, any fixed number of such classics. In the direct successor to the Honors course, known in the thirties as "The Colloquium on Important Books," the works read were referred to as classics, important books, or major works, but only occasionally as "great books." Even Mark Van Doren made sparing reference to the term in his *Liberal Education*, published in 1943, and not often enough for it to appear in the index.

The terminological issue is not itself important, but a syllabus for the Colloquium first prepared in 1927 by J. B. Brebner (representing a stellar staff that included Mortimer Adler, Jacques Barzun, Irwin Edman, Moses Hadas, Richard McKeon, Lionel Trilling, Rexford Guy Tugwell, Mark Van Doren, and Raymond Weaver, among other distinguished scholars and teachers) was entitled "Classics of the Western World." More significant than the word "classics" is the fact that even prior to the establishment of the required Humanities A, its advocates and collaborators were conscious of the parochial limits of the Columbia program at that time. I can testify myself to the feeling among prominent leaders of the College faculty in the late 1930s that something needed to be done about expanding the horizons of the general-education program, including both the older Contemporary Civilization course and Humanities A, so as to bring Asia into the picture. Perhaps the most significant aspect of this progressive ferment was that it arose among scholars and teachers who had no professional interest in Orientalism but who certainly exhibited the kind of intellectual breadth and educational zeal that Gilbert Murray would have appreciated as liberal.

It is true that what Murray saw as the world mission of liberal humanism could appear to others as only cultural imperialism in Sunday dress. In this view, classical Orientalism too would be seen not as progressive scholarship but only as the intellectual vanguard of the Western assault on other cultures. Yet in actual fact, as matters stood at Columbia in those times, classical Orientalism was in serious decline, if not almost defunct. It had no articulate spokesmen among the College faculty, and since its fortunes had been closely tied to biblical studies, Semitic languages, and the old language requirements, it had few vested interests left to defend or assert once the new liberal education had taken over.

The advocates of the new Oriental Studies program were amateur types, liberal-minded gentlemen who took education, and not just their own scholarly research, seriously. Typical of them were Van Doren himself; his colleague Raymond Weaver, an authority on Herman Melville with a deep appreciation of Japanese literature; Burdette Kinne, an instructor in French with a passion for everything Chinese; and Harry J. Carman, a professor of American history and a New York State dirt farmer who wanted to see Asian civilizations brought into the Contemporary Civilization program.

When the first experimental Oriental Humanities course was set up in 1947, about as soon after World War II as one could have mounted such a venture, the lead was taken by such scholars as Moses Hadas, the Greek classicist; Herbert Deane, a political scientist specializing in Harold Laski and St. Augustine; James Gutmann, in German philosophy; and Charles Frankel, the philosopher of Western liberalism. Naturally enough, on putting together the reading list for their first Oriental Colloquium (as it was initially called) Deane and Hadas consulted specialists on the Columbia faculty more learned than themselves in the several traditions to be included within the scope of the course. From the start, however, the reading and discussion of the Oriental classics were to be guided by the principles of the earlier Honors course, as stated by Erskine above, and not by the

kind of textual scholarship that had long dominated the classical Orientalism of the nineteenth and early twentieth centuries.

The course's distinctive character arose in large measure from the fact
that it was conceived as part of a liberal education (later to be called by
some "general education") and was designed to supplement a core curriculum already set in place for the first two undergraduate years. In this program, priority had already been given to the study of Western civilization
and the "classics of the Western World" (as the Erskine/Brebner syllabus
put it). This is a fact I cite not to raise the issue of cultural bounds or to question the established educational priorities—which would take us beyond
our purpose here—but simply as a historical given in this case (and obviously a given also for the Great Books program). In practice, our experience
has shown this sequence to entail no disadvantage, since students come to
the new course as a natural next stage in their core curriculum, already familiar with the ground rules of the reading-discussion method and prepared to take an active part in a discourse well underway. It did mean, however, that the choice of Asian classics would, in turn, be governed by the
same high degree of selectivity as in the Western case and further still by
the need to exercise this selectivity with respect to several major Asian traditions at once—indeed, all that might be included in the so-called non-
Western world. In other words, it demanded a rare combination of both
breadth and selectivity, which was much in contrast to the kind of specialized study that traditional Orientalism had favored; it went beyond even
what advocates of the Hundred Great Books—for all their high standards
of selectivity—would have suspected was necessary.

Exercising this selectivity in the multicultural East was far more difficult
than it had been within the bounds of the more unified Western tradition.
There was an added complication in that though the "East" had something
like "great books," it had nothing like the Great Books of the East. The latter
is a Western idea, both in seeing the East as one and in imagining that there
had been a common tradition shared by the peoples of this "East." Each of
the major Asian traditions tended to see itself as the center of the civilized
world and to look inward—spiritually and culturally—toward that center
rather than outward on the world or on one another. The famous "Sacred
Books of the East," as published at Oxford, was a Western invention. It
sprang from the minds of nineteenth-century scholars in Europe as their
intellectual horizons reached out along with the West's expansion into Asia.
"Asia," a geographical designation, represented no common culture or moral

bond among the peoples of that continent until, in modern times, a new unity was found in their common reaction to that same expansionism.

There being no common tradition in Asia to define the Great Books of the East, a reading list had to be constructed synthetically out of largely separate and discrete traditions—a construction made all the more difficult and delicate, in the absence of any Eastern canon, by the risk that the very process of its devising might be contaminated by Western preconceptions. Instead therefore of searching for "Eastern" equivalents of Western classics, we were looking for what each of the several Asian traditions themselves honored as an essential part of their own heritage.

Seemingly the least problematical way of doing this was to identify the scriptures or classics already well known within the distinct ethicoreligious traditions of Islam, Hinduism, Buddhism, Confucianism, Daoism, and so on. Similarly one could find recognized classics of the literary and intellectual traditions, though these might or might not run parallel to the religious traditions. This method, proceeding inductively from the testimony of Asians themselves rather than deductively from some Western definition of a classic norm or form, has produced what might appear to be an odd assortment of genres. Great poetry exists in each of the major traditions, though it varies considerably in form. Epics that bear comparison to the *Odyssey*, *Iliad*, and *Aeneid* can be found in Iran and India, but there is nothing like them in China and Japan. The same is true in reverse of the haiku or Nō drama, classic forms in Japan but found nowhere else. Histories as monumental in their own way as Herodotus and Thucydides have been produced in the Islamic world by Ibn Khaldūn and in China by Ssu-ma Ch'ien but by no one in traditional India or Japan. Perhaps the greatest diversity, however, is exhibited among the religious scriptures, some of which can barely be regarded as "texts" in any ordinary sense of the term (for instance, although the Platform Sūtra of the Sixth Chan Patriarch is presented in one sense as authoritative scripture, in another sense it points to an abjuration of all scripture). For the purposes of our reading program, however, if there were to be any real dialogue with the multiform East, all this variety has had to be taken in and, more than that, welcomed as a healthy challenge to Western conventions of discursive and literary form.

Other problems of selection arise from the choice of four major traditions to represent the "East." The four we have identified—the Islamic world, India, China, and Japan—betray a lack of geographic and cultural congruence among themselves. The Islamic world, which covers almost half of Asia and North Africa as well, includes Iran, with its own language, civilization, and indigenous religious traditions (Zoroastrianism and Manichaeism). Our "coverage" of India (to be dealt with in a separate volume, along with the Middle East) includes Buddhism as well as Brahmanism and Hinduism, and in China and Japan, Buddhism as well as Confucianism and Daoism. Thus religion cuts across cultures even as it may also provide the underlying continuity in a given culture. For the most part, however, it is in literature that each tradition best reveals its distinguishing features and basic continuity. Hence each has had to be represented by enough classic examples to show both the unity and diversity of the traditions and to demonstrate how the great religions have assumed a different coloration in each historical and cultural setting, while also revealing the distinctive aesthetic and intellectual qualities of the tradition.

If, for instance, the case for Islam and our understanding of the Qur'ān depend heavily on how one views the distinctive claims made for it as prophecy and for Muhammad as the "seal of the prophets," the significance of that claim cannot be judged from a reading of the Qur'ān alone. We must also see how the matter is later dealt with by Al-Ghazālī in relation to Greek philosophy and Sufi mysticism or by Ibn Khaldūn in relation to the patterns of human history. The contrasting claim of Hinduism that it transcends any such particular revelation and can accommodate all other religions may be difficult to evaluate except in some relation to Islam or to the Mahāyāna Buddhist philosophy that Śankara is variously said to have refuted and assimilated into the Vedānta.

These religions or teachings, as represented by the texts we read, may not always have acknowledged each other openly, but if we know or even suspect that there was indeed an unspoken encounter among them, some reconnaissance of the alternative positions is requisite to an understanding of any one of them. By this I mean, to be more specific, that one cannot enter into any serious encounter with the early Buddhist sūtras unless one has read the Upanishads, nor can one later come to grips with Śankara if one knows nothing of the major Mahāyāna texts. Likewise, in China, while it is obviously unthinkable that one would take up such major Confucian thinkers as Mencius and Xunzi without first having read the *Analects* of Confucius, it would be no less an error to do so without reference to Laozi and Zhuangzi.

In China, though the inception of the Confucian tradition is most directly accessible through the *Analects*, if one stopped there and went no further into any of the later Confucian thinkers, one would get only an archaic, fossilized view of Confucianism. Only by going on to the Neo-Confucians Zhu Xi and Wang Yang-ming can one begin to appreciate how the classic teachings underwent further development in response to the challenge of Buddhism and Daoism. In the West, it would be like reading the Old Testament without the New, or the latter without St. Augustine, St. Thomas, or Dante. Yet it can equally well be argued that the encounter among the so-called Three Teachings in China is even more vividly brought to life in such great Chinese novels as the *Journey to the West* and the *Dream of the Red Chamber* (or, in C. T. Hsia's rendering, *A Dream of Red Mansions*). Thus reading classic fiction can give access to the dialogue in China on levels not reachable through the classical and neoclassical philosophers.

The same—and more—can be said for Japanese literature as a revelation of Buddhism's encounter with the native tradition. Often that tradition is identified with Shinto, but as there were no written texts or scriptures antedating the introduction of the Chinese script, the best one can do is look to the earliest literature in Japanese—such works as the *Manyōshū*, the *Tale of Genji*, and the *Pillow Book*, to name only a few of the finest examples—if one wishes to get, in the absence of open doctrinal debate, a more intimate glimpse of what was going on in the Japanese mind and heart behind the outward show of polite professions. This indeed is where the real struggle has taken place among the deep-seated aesthetic preferences and emotional inclinations of the Japanese as they strove to assimilate the more ascetic or moralistic doctrines imported from the continent. There too one may get a sense of the cultural situation into which Zen Buddhism was later introduced and judge from the outcome how much of contemporary Zen is actually Japanese or Chinese rather than Buddhist.

Thus unless other guests are invited, there will be no party for us to join—no way to renew the conversation with any of the great works or thinkers of the past without having others present who had engaged in the original dialogue. How long the list of participants may become is always a matter for local discretion, but in no case can just one or two works generate a real conversation. In the silence of Zen there may be such a thing as one hand clapping, but in the discourse we are entering into there is no book that speaks just to itself.

In this way, working through the natural, original associations among the recognized classics of the Asian traditions, one arrives, by the inductive process I referred to above, at a provisional set of the Asian classics or Great

Books of the East. Admittedly a modern creation, it is put together from materials quite authentic to one or another of the Asian traditions. The linkages so identified within and among these traditions, though often obscured or suppressed in the past by cultural isolationism and national or religious chauvinisms, are nonetheless real and meaningful. According to this understanding, "The East" is no mere fabrication, made to serve as a foil for the West. Rather it is an East that has emerged in its true reflected colors only since it came to be observed in a modern light.

Rabindranath Tagore, the charismatic cosmopolitan from Calcutta who thought of himself above all as a citizen of the world, was perhaps the first to appreciate this. In his new perception of the "East," brilliantly articulated in an essay on "The Eastern University" but only incompletely realized in his Visva Bharati University at Santiniketan, he saw the need for a multicultural curriculum in which the several Asian traditions would complement one another, highlighting each other's distinctive features in a way that no solitary exposure could do.

Regrettably, the direction of modern education, whether in India or elsewhere in Asia, has taken a different turn, emphasizing technical learning and specialized training at the expense of any kind of humanistic education, Eastern or Western. In this situation, as in our own, the humanities are taught as discrete disciplines and each national tradition is a separate subject of specialization, a field in which to practice the new humanities technologies. The usual result of this process is that nothing can be seen whole and every great work is subjected by analysis to unmitigated trivialization. In most Asian universities today, it is only the student majoring, say, in Sanskrit, Chinese, or Japanese studies who learns anything of the classics of his own tradition beyond the high-school level, and even then it will most likely be to specialize in a single text.[7]

Against this pessimistic estimate of the present situation, a more positive view may be offered that microscopic studies of this kind are the necessary building blocks for the construction tomorrow of a macroscopic, global edifice of human civilization. Yet this conclusion itself leads to the further question: if nothing less than a total worldview is envisaged, why should one be trying to establish an intermediate position through the Asian Humanities, as if to promote a regionalized view of the Asian traditions? Given the present trend toward world history or world-literature courses, it might seem perverse—and probably unavailing—to resist the piecemeal incorporation into them of Asian materials. Recognizing too the impacted state of the college curriculum and the difficulty of finding any time at all in it for Asia, can one afford to pass up whatever opportunities do present themselves for the inclusion of Asia in the core, even if on less than ideal terms? Depending on local circumstances, the answer may well be, perhaps not.

Yet even while conceding this much to present realities, I would still argue the need to make a place, at some point in the curriculum, for a course that includes the Asian classics in something of their traditional setting rather than, as above, completely out of context. My ground for so arguing is the same need to face squarely the implications of the global view already projected. To me this requires not necessarily that an equal priority be given to Asia and the West but only that there should be some parity of treatment for them in the overall program. To understand why I make this distinction between priority and parity, however, it may be well to step back a bit and look at some basic premises.

In the study of other cultures or civilizations, some degree of self-understanding is prerequisite to an understanding of others, and similarly an understanding of one's own situation or one's own past may be accepted as a precondition for understanding another's. Our experience with the Asian Humanities at Columbia shows how much deeper and more meaningful the new learning experience can be for those who have first come to an appreciation—or even just a keener awareness—of their own tradition. The same principle, I would readily concede, applies in reverse to the Asians' understanding of the West, which may be just as advantaged or handicapped, depending upon how well they have come to know their own culture. Those who have been deprived by an almost total uprooting from their own cultural traditions, as in China during the long blight of the Maoist era and especially during the Cultural Revolution, may be no less disadvantaged in understanding the West for all the hunger to learn from it that they now show. Not to come to terms with one's past or in some degree to master one's own tradition is to remain a hostage to it, even though unconsciously so, and thus not to become fully master of oneself. In such a condition, being unable to take responsibility for oneself and one's own past, one is in a poor position to become truly responsive to others'.

Another aspect of the "parity" issue is highlighted by the recent spectacular rise of China to a dominant role in world economics and politics. It is natural for departments and administrators to let such highly political developments influence their academic decisions and to want to mount courses that appeal to the interest or awareness generated by the headlines. A true core program must resist this if it promotes China at the expense of a long-term perspective that sees China's importance in the context of Asian civilizations as a whole. Only in a global perspective can true parity and indeed true depth be recognized.

All this may verge on rhetorical overkill, but to me such considerations are bound to enter into what I have referred to above as "parity of treatment." If one can appreciate what it would mean for the Great Books of the Western World to be represented only by Plato's *Republic* or the Book of Job—a meaningless question for anyone who had not read considerably more of the Great Books than that—one can begin to appreciate why a reading of the *Analects* alone might not do sufficient justice to the Confucian tradition; why the *Dhammapada* by itself would be inadequate to represent Buddhism; and why one would face an impossible dilemma if one had to choose between the *Dream of the Red Chamber* and the *Tale of Genji*, Śakuntalā or the Nō drama, the *Rāmāyana* or Du Fu, as candidates for infiltration into a humanities sequence or world-literature course otherwise based on the Western tradition. If the selectivity that is always a prime factor in the design of core curricula or general-education programs should be taken to rule out more than token representation for the East, and if to include the *Analects* (or, as some generous souls even proposed twenty years ago, Mao Zedong) would mean dropping Aristotle, Thomas Aquinas, Dante, John Locke, or Immanuel Kant from the list, one must wonder whether the result would do justice to either East or West.

Even while putting the question this way, I do not rule out the possibility of accepting such unpalatable choices, if only to serve the educational purpose of getting an East-West dialogue started. It all depends on knowing where you want to go and how, by what stages and means, you hope to get there. For this it is important to recognize that the risks of distortion or misrepresentation are great. If one knows how painfully abbreviated is even the usual one- or two-year sequence in the Western humanities, or how deficient the student's familiarity often is with the great works of his own tradition, one will not rush to a solution that only compounds the difficulty.

Whatever is to be done, it seems to me, should be governed by two considerations. The first is that the reading and understanding of a text should work, as much as possible, from the inside out rather than from the outside in. Granted that we are indeed outsiders looking in, we must make the effort to put ourselves in the position or situation of the author and his audience. This means that no reading of an Eastern text should be undertaken that is so removed from its original context as to be discussable only in direct juxtaposition to something Western. Such a reading leads almost inevitably to one-sided comparisons and does not serve genuine dialogue. Party to this new dialogue must be enough of the original discourse (writings presenting alternative or contrasting views) so that the issues can be defined in their own terms and not simply in opposition to, or agreement with, the West. If a world-literature course or humanities program can include enough works of the original tradition to meet this test, the risks run may be worth taking.

Since the inclusion of more than a few such works will put a strain on any reading program that is part of an already crowded core curriculum, a second set of considerations will likely come into play: how can we conceive of a total learning process that makes the best use of scarce resources (deployment of instructional staff, provision of texts and teaching materials) and, above all, of the student's time to provide a properly balanced and truly global program?

Most persons who face this question will be teachers and administrators in colleges and universities, but I do not mean to limit the discussion to academics. The need for global education is widely felt and cannot be met simply within the framework of the college curriculum. Granted that the undergraduate years are where the process should start, it is neither reasonable nor realistic to suppose that an adequate liberal education can be compressed simply within the typical four-year college program. I have long believed that there is a need for core curricula even in graduate schools, and this for more reasons than just to provide remedial instruction in matters neglected by many colleges (including the Asian humanities and much else that is antecedent to civilization). But this is not the place to argue the point, and whatever might be undertaken in graduate schools would still not do the whole job.

Having come to this point, it may be in order for me to suggest what are the classics I would consider essential to a basic reading program—a list that could be defined as what might be appropriate for an introductory, one-year course. A more generous selection is found in what follows, which gives the teacher or discussion leader more to choose from in meeting the needs of particular groups or to draw upon for somewhat more leisurely reading and a less pressured learning situation. In this light, what I propose here is not necessarily ideal, nor on the other hand does it represent the bare minimum, but rather something more like a Mean. As an introduction to the major Asian traditions, one could hope that it would not misrepresent them but rather provide enough pleasure in the reading and enough stimulus for discussion that most participants would emerge from the experience with an appetite for more and the wherewithal to pursue its satisfaction.

Here then is my list, with a brief comment on each work for the benefit of those to whom the title alone might be meaningless:

The Islamic Tradition

The Qur'ān: a book of revelation that, because of the unique claims made for it, almost defies reading as a "great book" but is nonetheless indispensable to all reading in the later tradition.

The *Assemblies* of Al Harīrī (1054–1122): a major work of classical Arabic literature that illustrates in an engaging way some of the tensions between piety and civilization and the desert and the city in Islamic culture.

The *Deliverance from Error* of Al-Ghazālī (1058–1111): a very personal statement, by perhaps the greatest of the Islamic theologians, concerning the relation of mystical experience to theology and the rational sciences.

The poems of Rūmī (1207–1273): chosen as the most representative of the Sufi poets.

The *Conference of the Birds*, by 'Aṭṭār (c. 1141–1220): a symposium on the stages of religious experience in the contemplative ascent to union with God.

The *Prolegomena* [*to World History*] of Ibn Khaldūn (1332–1406): often called the world's first "social scientist" (a subject of useful discussion in itself), Ibn Khaldūn's encyclopedic discourse on the historical factors in the rise and fall of civilizations is already a classic among modern world historians.

Options not selected above but obvious candidates for inclusion in a more ample listing: The seven Odes of pre-Islamic poetry, the *Thousand and One Nights*, other Arab philosophers including Averroes and Ibn Arabi, other Sufi poets such as Hāfiz, etc.

The Indian Tradition

Hymns from the *Rig Veda*: bedrock of the Hindu tradition.

The *Upanishads*: classic discourses that laid the foundation for Hindu religious and philosophical speculation.

The *Bhagavad Gītā*: the major work of religious and philosophical synthesis and the basic scripture of Hindu devotionalism.

The *Rāmāyana* of Vālmīki (c. 200 B.C.E.): the earlier of the two great Indian epics and the best known in Indian art and legendry. Exemplifies the fundamental values and tensions in the classical Indian tradition.

Texts of Theravāda Buddhism: No one text represents a complete statement of Buddhism, but the Dhammapada, Mahāsatipaṭṭhana Sutta, Milindapañha, and Mahāparinibbana Suttānta come closest perhaps to "basic discourses."

Scriptures of Indian Mahāyāna Buddhism: Again, no one work suffices, but the Prajñapāramita texts (especially the Heart Sūtra) and the works of Nāgārjuna and Śāntideva represent basic statements.

The *Śakuntalā*: the major work of Kālidāsa (c. 400 C.E.), the greatest Indian dramatist and arguably the greatest in Asia.

The Vedānta Sūtra, with the commentary of Śankarācārya (c. 780–820): generally regarded as the leading Indian philosopher, representing the dominant nondualistic school of the Vedānta.

The *Gītagovinda* of Jayadeva (c. twelfth century C.E.): a great religious poem in Sanskrit and major work of medieval devotionalism.

Rabindranath Tagore and Mohandas Gandhi: two contrasting views of the Indian tradition in its encounter with the West. These are the only modern writers on our list, but Tagore's poems and plays and Gandhi's so-called *Autobiography*, though admittedly not "classics," have been perennial favorites for the way they juxtapose aspects of Indian tradition in response to the challenges of the West.

Major options not availed of above: the epic Mahābhārata; the Yoga sūtras of Patañjali; Kautilya's *Artha Śāstra*, a guide to politics; the *Little Clay Cart* of King Śudraka (c. 400 C.E.), a most entertaining domestic drama; the famous collection of fables in the *Pañcatantra*; Bhartrihari's verses on worldly life, passion, and renunciation; Rāmānuja, a rival to Śankara in religious philosophy, etc., as described in the *Guide* (n. 7.)

The Chinese Tradition

The *Analects of Confucius* (551–479 B.C.E.): the best single source for the ideas of Confucius.

Mozi or Mo Di: a sharp critic of Confucianism in the fifth century B.C.E. and a major alternative voice in politics and religion.

Laozi: a basic text of Daoism that has become a world classic because of its radical challenge to the underlying assumptions of both traditional and modern civilizations.

Zhuangzi: delightful speculative ramblings and philosophical parodies by a Daoist writer of the late fourth and early third centuries B.C.E.

Mencius (*Mengzi*) (372–289 B.C.E.): a thinker second in importance only to Confucius in that school, who addressed a broad range of practical and philosophical problems.

Xunzi (third century B.C.E.): the third great statement of the Confucian teaching, with special attention to the basis of learning and rites.

Han Feizi (third century B.C.E.): the fullest theoretical statement and synthesis of the ancient Legalist school, a major influence on the Chinese political tradition.

Records of the Historian, by Sima Qian (c. 145–90 B.C.E.): a monumental history of early China, notable for its combination of chronicles, topical treatises, and biographical accounts.

The *Lotus Sūtra*: by far the most important religious scripture of Chinese Mahāyāna Buddhism, influential throughout East Asia.

Vimalakīrti Sūtra: a systematic theoretical work dealing with the more philosophical issues in Mahāyāna teaching.

The *Platform Sūtra*: an original Chinese work and early statement of Ch'an (Zen) thought, which assumed the status of both classic and scripture because of its unique claim to religious enlightenment.

Tang poetry: selections from the great poets of the Tang dynasty, generally viewed as the classic age of Chinese verse and admired by the Japanese and Koreans as well.

Zhu Xi (1130–1200): a leading exponent and synthesizer of Neo-Confucianism, which became the dominant teaching in later centuries and spread throughout East Asia.

Wang Yang-ming (1472–1529): the principal Neo-Confucian thinker of the Ming period, who modified Zhu Xi's philosophy most particularly in respect to the nature and importance of learning (especially the role of moral intuition versus cognitive learning).

Waiting for the Dawn (*Mingyi daifanglu*), by Huang Zongxi (1610–1695): a concise critique of the Chinese dynastic system by a major seventeenth-century thinker who synthesized Neo-Confucian political thought with legalist-type statecraft and the encyclopedic scholarship of the Song and Ming. Considered a classic by modern Chinese reformers of the late nineteenth and early twentieth centuries.

Journey to the West, attributed to Wu Cheng-en (c. 1506–1581): a fantastic fictional account of the historic pilgrimage to India of the Buddhist monk Xuan-zang and an allegory of Mahāyāna Buddhist syncretism.

The Dream of Red Mansions (or *The Dream of the Red Chamber*), by Cao Xüeqin (d. 1763): an eighteenth-century realistic-allegorical novel about the decline of a great family and its young heir's involvement in the world of passion and depravity.

Other options within the Chinese tradition are such Buddhist texts as *The Awakening of Faith*, the *Śurangama Sūtra*, and major novels including the *Water Margin* (*Shui hu*) (*All Men Are Brothers*), *Golden Lotus* (*Jinpingmei*), and the *Scholars* (*Rulin waishi*).

The Japanese Tradition

Here it is worthy of special note that women are prominent as authors of the earlier classic works and as dominant figures in many of the later works of drama and fiction.

Manyōshū: the earliest anthology of Japanese poetry (eighth century C.E. and before).

The Tale of Genji, by Murasaki Shikibu (978–1015?): the world's first great novel, about court life in Heian-period Japan and the loves of Prince Genji.

The Pillow Book of Sei Shōnagon (late tenth–early eleventh century C.E.): observations on life, religion, aesthetic sensibility, and taste in Heian Japan.

"An Account of My Hut," by Kamo no Chōmei (1153–1236): a kind of Japanese Thoreau, meditating on the vicissitudes of the world, the beauties of nature, and the satisfactions of the simple life—but at the farthest remove from Thoreau's civil disobedience.

Essays in Idleness, by Yoshida no Kenkō (1283–1350): observations on life, society, nature, and art by a worldly monk and classic literary stylist, in journal form.

Tales of the Heike: an epic account of the rise and fall of the Taira warrior class in medieval Japan.

Nō plays: the classic drama, distinctive to Japan but now much admired in the West as well. Preferably to be seen and heard as well as read.

The novels of Ihara Saikaku (1642–1693): fictional writings in a poetic style, expressive of the new culture of the townspeople in seventeenth-century Japan.

The poetry of Matsuo Bashō (1644–1694): poetry and prose by the master of the *haiku* and one of the greatest of all Japanese poets.

The plays of Chikamatsu (1653–1725): works written for the puppet theater by Japan's leading dramatist, focusing on conflicts between love and duty.

Alternative selections: Religious writings of the eminent Japanese monks Kūkai, Dōgen, and Hakuin, while important in the history of Japanese religion, were difficult even for the Japanese to understand and, though respected, did not have a wide readership. The more widely read literary and dramatic works were probably also more expressive of the actual religious sentiments of the Japanese, as well as of their literary preferences. These might include, in addition to the above, the major poetry anthologies *Kokinshū* and *Shinkokinshū* and the eighteenth-century drama *Chūshingura*.

The foregoing lists give, I hope, a fair representation of the different preferences and shared values among the great traditions of Asia. They include works that have withstood the tests of time not only in their own traditions but in at least sixty years of reading and discussion with American students of all ages. The optional or alternative readings have been tried from time to time and have their own strong advocates. It should be pointed out that not everything on the list is assigned in its entirety. This is especially true of the long epics and novels. We make concessions to what works in practice and accept compromises for the sake of getting the best overall mix.

The availability of adequate translations has also been a factor in our decisions, especially in the early days of the program, but it has become less of a problem as more good translations have been produced in recent years of a kind suited to our need, that is, in a form accessible to students. If earlier it was said that one test of a great book is how well it survives translation, now the test might well be restated as the classics' ability not only to survive one translation but also to attract, withstand, and outlast several others.

Today, with more than one translation available of a given work, the layman naturally wants the scholar's recommendation as to which is best. Not only laymen but even some scholars still have a touching faith in the idea that there is one "authoritative" or "definitive" translation of a work. In truth, it is possible for scholars of equal technical competence to produce translations of almost equal merit, each bringing out different meanings and nuances of the original. Burton Watson and A. C. Graham have each written excellent translations of the *Zhuangzi*; neither, I suspect, would claim his own was perfect, but Watson's may appeal more to those whose interests and tastes are literary and Graham's to the more philosophical. Interpretations like Thomas Merton's of the *Zhuangzi* also have their place but should be understood for what they are and not regarded as translations. It is also possible for nonspecialists such as Ezra Pound, Witter Bynner, or Lin Yutang sometimes to capture the meaning of certain passages in Chinese works and render them in vivid English that is less literal than the sinologue would like but more meaningful or moving to the reader.

Our practice is to recommend at least one preferred translation (if only for the sake of having a common basis for discussion) but to urge students, wherever possible, to read more than one rendering and arrive at their own sense of where the common denominator among them may lie. In this process of triangulation—getting a bearing or fix on a text from several translators' different angles of vision—the reader has his own proper judgmental part to play, bringing his or her own learning and experience to bear on the assessment of what the original might mean. If so used, translations need not stand in the way of the reader having some active, personal encounter with the text, which the great thinkers and teachers have so often called for.

Further to assist the reader in knowing what to look for in these books, I have asked colleagues knowledgeable in the several traditions to write brief essays on what they perceive to be the most essential values in the works they know well or most enjoy. Among these guest essayists are several distinguished scholars who have themselves contributed substantially to making the classics available in translation. In responding to this opportunity they have, in several cases, chosen to write about works somewhat less well known in the West than those already highly acclaimed.

In a few cases, we have included here more than one essay on a given work, to show that different readings are possible. The same, of course, could be done for any or all of the classics on our list, but to do so would have resulted in an impossibly large volume, drawing attention away from the classic texts themselves.

In conclusion, I should like to make one further point concerning the importance of reading the "Asian classics." The basic criterion for recognizing them as classics has been that they were first so admired in their own tradition. In quite a few cases, this admiration spread to other countries, and these works came to be regarded as either scriptures or great books outside their own homeland. Further, after substantial contact was made by the West with Asia in the sixteenth and seventeenth centuries, many of these works came to be translated and admired in the West as well. Some of the exotic appeal of the unknown and "mysterious" East may still attach to them, but for at least two centuries they have been essential reading for many of the best minds in the West—philosophers, historians, poets, playwrights, and indeed major writers in almost every field of thought and scholarship. Thus one whose education does not include a reading of the Asian classics today is a stranger not only to Asia but to much of the best that has been thought and written in the modern West. Many of these works and their authors have already entered the mainstream of the conversation that is going on in the West today. As that conversation is broadened to include a fairer representation of the Asian traditions, bringing out the implicit dialogue within and among them, it could indeed become a Great Conversation for all the world.

Notes

I wish to express my indebtedness to Jacques Barzun and the late Lionel Trilling for background information contained in the introductory portions of this essay, based on earlier conversations with them.

1. Listed in the flyleaf of the 1987 issue of *The Great Ideas Today*, in which portions of this essay originally appeared.
2. The Islamic tradition is no less a great tradition in much of Asia for also sharing this common ground with major religious traditions of the West. Since in

practice the major works of the Islamic tradition are rarely included among the "great books" of the West, it is appropriate to recognize them here.

3. See Richard Payne, ed., *Classics of Western Spirituality*, 60 vols. (New York: Paulist Press, 1978–); and Ewart Cousins, gen. ed., *World Spirituality: An Encyclopedic History of the Religious Quest*, 25 vols. (New York: Crossroads, 1985–).

4. Gilbert Murray, *Liberality and Civilization* (London: Allen and Unwin, 1938), 46–47.

5. Ibid., 30–31.

6. J. Bartlett Brebner et al., *Classics of the Western World* (Chicago: American Library Association, 1934), 11–12.

7. See the proceedings for the conferences on *Classics for an Emerging World* (2008) and *Asia in the Core Curriculum* (1999), ed. W. T. de Bary (New York: The Heyman Center for the Humanities, Columbia University).

2

Asia in the Core Curriculum

Wm. Theodore de Bary

In the debate that erupted during the spring of 1988 over changes in the Stanford core course on Western Civilization and later at Harvard over its general-education program, the political heat generated, and the attendant confusion of issues as these were aired in the media, did little to advance the cause of education. The cast of characters in this much publicized controversy had the so-called fundamentalists, William Bennett, Allan Bloom, and others who claimed to speak for traditional values and the Great Books, ranged against those who would sneak third-world politics, feminism, and cultural relativism into the sanctuary of Western learning. Among those who backed Stanford's innovations were some who insisted that the whole idea of a privileged canon was a latter-day imposture of Ivy League WASPS, making icons of "dead white boys" so as to protect the sacred turf of the Western (or, as some would put it, the East Coast) academic establishment. For liberationists, the need to include feminist issues, "ethnic cultures," and minority studies in the core curriculum would justify, if it came to that, even the dropping of Homer, Aristotle, Dante, Shakespeare, Darwin, Mill, and Freud from the list of required readings.

Few would deny that there are real issues at stake here. This is not much ado about nothing, blown up out of all proportion by political partisans of the right and left. Many of the views expressed are seriously held by persons in a position to affect the course of American education. Nevertheless, between the confrontational politics of some and the unyielding defensiveness of others, there seems to have been little disposition to engage in any fundamental reexamination of educational needs or exploration of new curricular possibilities. Equally valid goals have been needlessly set at cross-purposes, and the scoring of polemical points has substituted for what one might have hoped would become a "great debate" on the most basic issues.

One need not imagine it possible to isolate such a debate from all politics or ideology nor suppose that education itself can be entirely free of indoctrination. Better instead that the premises and purposes of an educational program be made explicit and that faculties openly take responsibility for the values that their curriculum is meant to serve. Better still, however, if faculties, in meeting this challenge, accept the needs of students themselves as the prime consideration, rather than the promotion of some political or social program or the pursuit of the faculties' own special interest—as well as their most natural instinct—to replicate their own academic species.

The Nature of the Core Curriculum

Most experienced college teachers, or scholars who have given real thought to problems of a core curriculum as distinct from the training of students in particular disciplines, would not, I think, deny the need for education to transmit essential civilizational values and to do so, at least to some degree, in a manner that would show their bearing on problems of compelling contemporary concern. A college education should equip students not only with the specific skills needed to make their way in the world but also with some understanding of themselves and how they can make a meaningful contribution to the increasingly complex society in which they live.

The hope of achieving this in any reasonable measure today—of providing some combination of competent instruction in specific disciplines and mature guidance in their preparation for life—must proceed from a recognition that for most students, whether in specialized training or liberal education, the best that they can realistically hope to accomplish in college is to make a good start at what will become a lifetime work. For this the core curriculum must be well defined at the start, properly structured as it develops, and open ended in facing the future.

In most colleges today, dominated as they are by practitioners of specialized disciplines and by departmental structures, there is consciousness enough of the need for systematic, sequential training in such disciplines and for the setting of priorities by those competent to judge what will contribute to a sustained, cumulative learning experience. Yet when it comes to liberal education, there is little awareness that a like need exists—for a definite structure and orderly progression toward intellectual maturity. Too often, general education is thought of simply as a brief moment of intellectual adventure before the hard business of specialization takes over. Important as is this lively sense of exploration, its pursuit should be nurtured, sustained, and cultivated rather than allowed to drift aimlessly or become diffused through random exposure to a variety of unrelated, undirected learning experiences. Nor should its free exercise be thought of simply as part of a "broadening" process, after which one settles down to concentrate on a major. A distinction is in order between free electives, which serve the student's independent growth or career ambitions, and requirements legitimately imposed to serve the shared needs of the community. For this deliberate infringement on the student's freedom the institution itself must take responsibility and be prepared to offer some justification.

For the student simply to be exposed to new ideas and experiences, valuable though these might be in themselves, is not enough. Nor can such exposure be justified purely for its shock value, as if the outcome were a matter of indifference and the experience one had could just as well lead anywhere or nowhere. Such indiscriminate openness may well be disorienting to the student if the teacher thinks that his job goes no further than to disabuse the student of his previously held convictions, leaving him with the kind of "open mind," empty of any convictions, that Allan Bloom sees as effectively closed to any genuine value commitment.

Indeed, there would be in this no basis for a valid claim on the student's time in the form of a required course. Nor, without any sense of relatedness to what has gone before or coherence with what comes after, can such a learning experience qualify as part of a core curriculum—much less as education, which always involves some "leading" on the part of the teacher and, with that, like it or not, some leadership and decision-making responsibility. In many places, exposure to something other than one's major is sought through a "distribution requirement," an arrangement that appeals to the student's desire for freedom of choice, while at the same time it suits the disposition of most faculty to share with students a taste of their own discipline, so long as such teaching does not require the scholar to step very far outside his or her own field. Keeping essentially within departmental limits, such instruction is likely to be highly controlled, as it must be for the introduction of any discipline, and academically quite "respectable." Nevertheless, it leaves important educational needs unmet.

Many of life's problems, and society's too, fit poorly into disciplinary grooves. Often students feel at a loss, having no sense of how to relate what they call "academics" to the pressing contemporary problems of which they cannot be unaware. Under such a regime, students' intellects tend to develop in a value-free, sanitized, laboratory environment, largely detached from normal human sympathies. Their moral sentiments and aesthetic sensibilities undergo no comparable process of refinement, nor are their judgmental faculties adequately exercised in regard to value questions. Left in this condition of immaturity, students' consciences are easily played upon, or preyed upon, by others with strong ideological opinions or fundamentalist convictions, only too ready with simple answers to urgent questions of the day.

The usual academic response to questions of laymen about contemporary issues is that the matter—whatever it is—is more complicated than the layman supposes. The realities of a problematic situation, so the familiar line goes, do not lend themselves to simple yes or no answers, black/white solutions. No doubt this is true and not simply an academic cop-out, as it often appears to be, yet its effect is to leave the questioner more impressed with the superior knowledge of the expert than confident of his or her own ability to grapple with the issues.

Even much of general education today falls victim to the respect for genuine academic competence. Competent scholars often disqualify themselves from teaching core-education courses, supposedly as a matter of intellectual responsibility and honesty. Or, if they cannot extricate themselves entirely from this duty, they ask to be allowed some leeway, in required courses, to teach at least something from their own particular field of specialization. Yet, in the absence of any comparable concession to students' personal predilections, once such allowance is made for the instructor, students understandably sense an asymmetry in what is demanded of both parties. The suspicion arises that there is some arbitrariness in the fixing or relaxing of criteria for the "core," and from this students begin to feel that their own preferences, even though not informed by the same academic competence, should be entitled to like consideration. Before long, as further concessions are made, the common core ceases to be either common or core.

"General education," a term that gained currency from the much publicized *Harvard Red Book* "General Education in a Free Society" (1945), expressed a need to offset the trend toward the increasing departmentalization of learning. "General" in this case meant the opposite of specialization and at its best could be taken to represent a balanced undergraduate program.

Yet, whatever the balance achieved, the vagueness of the term "general" lent itself to a wide latitude of interpretation, ranging from a more or less well-defined distribution requirement to a virtual guarantee of the student's right to freedom of choice. There was, at the center, no core, if by this one meant that students should be exposed to a common body of problems, materials, and shared discourse. Whether for such reasons or not, what developed at Harvard, later to be ratified by the Rosovsky Report of 1977, was a kind of smorgasbord of specially tempting departmental delicacies offered to a general audience by star lecturers who could be counted on to impress and captivate the minds of undergraduates, even if the program did not generate a common body of thoughtful discourse among either faculty or students of the college as a whole.

At Columbia, where the basic elements of a core curriculum had been put together in the 1920s and 1930s, the term "general education" did not come into use until much later, with Daniel Bell's report on *The Reforming of General Education* (1967). Before that, at least in the late 1940s and 1950s, "core curriculum" was the term most frequently used. Initially, the program itself was identified with a required Contemporary Civilization course that quite openly and directly addressed contemporary problems and made no pretence at conveying the essence of Western civilization or defining traditional values. Yet it did present these contemporary problems in historical perspective, as products of a long evolution in Western society and as central problems of human society, problems that had occupied the best minds of the West for centuries. Institutional history and source readings from major Western thinkers provided much of the content, while discussion in small classes, involving direct student engagement with the material (especially the source readings), provided the indispensable complement, as a flexible instructional method, to the prescribed content of the common core.

Alongside of CC developed John Erskine's Honors course, which had a different provenance: in important respects it sought to preserve the benefits of old-fashioned classical learning after the abandonment of the language requirements in Latin and Greek, based now on the reading and discussion of classic works *in translation*. As an Honors course, this could perhaps be thought "elitist," and insofar as it sought to perpetuate the liberal values of a classical education, in the manner of eighteenth- and nineteenth-century gentlemen in England, Europe, and (in Columbia's case) the remnants of the old Hudson Valley aristocracy, one could indeed think of it as perpetuating an elite tradition.

But demographic changes, the influx of large immigrant populations into New York, and Columbia's early accessibility to bright young Jews, Italians, Irish, and blacks meant that its student body by this time had become quite diverse and "democratic" compared to other Ivy League institutions. And when the Honors colloquium was transformed in 1937 into a Humanities course required of all freshmen, it had already become part of a larger movement, at first centered in New York and later spreading to Chicago, with a distinct populist flavor. Its early teachers did their work not only in Columbia classrooms but in "people's institutes," Cooper Union, adult-education centers, union halls, and in the best New York high schools, where highly talented, upwardly mobile children of immigrant and refugee families demonstrated their scholarly promise. Mortimer Adler was no WASP, and when he took the message of what he called "The Great Books" to Chicago, and thence throughout the country, his strong commitment was to democratic education, to the reform of American education at large, on all levels. Ironically, had he been less of a populist and popularizer Adler might have spared himself the condescending criticisms of a real elitist, Allan Bloom, who would later deprecate Adler's efforts as bordering on vulgarization and hucksterism.

It is ironic that Adler's practical, enterprising spirit in the packaging and sale of the Hundred Great Books, with the Syntopican as guide and the Hundred Great Ideas as the agenda for discussion, together constituting his populist program of education, should have given such defined form to the Great Books program that it assumed the monumental proportions of a fixed canon. At Columbia meanwhile, in what had begun as an experimental program, the works referred to as "classics" or "important books" (rarely as "Great Books") have won their places on the Humanities reading list and rewon them year after year not by being elevated and safely enshrined out of the reach of any tampering but by proving themselves in a dialogue perennially challenging to students and teachers alike.

Confirmation of the inherent appeal and impressiveness of the works themselves comes not only from generations of students and alumni—inveterate defenders of the Humanities course—but from the larger place that these texts have won even in the older Contemporary Civilization course. Though CC is more historically and topically oriented, experience over the years has shown that texts representing great minds and major historical figures are better suited to issue-oriented discussion than are the secondary studies and historical essays originally prepared for CC. It would seem that personal confrontation with issues and alternative ways of viewing them is more effectively induced by the individual's encounter with great thinkers. Projecting oneself into past encounters of ideas, weighing possible courses of action, and considering the historical consequences, the student mentally exercises a certain freedom of choice, practices taking responsibility for his own judgments in dialogue with others, and develops his own independence of mind. Indeed, so effective and prevalent has this practice become in CC, and so central the discussion of major texts, that those responsible for the direction of the course, while not wishing to dampen students' enthusiasm for the "great books," feel some need now to redress the balance, to direct more concerted attention to historical background, lest the discussion became elevated to an almost timeless realm.

It is true enough to say that the "canon" of classics or great books, as known in the United States today, is the creation of a particular age and educational movement, with quite precise origins, even though its character as the product of a given class or ethnic group is not easily defined, inasmuch as the era in question was one of rapid social change. No less true, however, is the fact that the creators of this modern curriculum, as educated, cultured men, were dedicated to perpetuating a long-standing tradition of classical learning formed by others quite different from themselves in race, class, and religion.

Moreover, it is a tradition that has stood the test of time—both time past and time present—consisting of works marked by the circumstances of their original creation but also surpassing them. What has survived is not the product of a unilinear development, identifiable with any given establishment or even any one tradition. The so-called Western tradition, at its inception, drew heavily on "Oriental" sources in the Near and Middle East. Much of Greek philosophy came into the hands of the medieval West through the good offices of Muslim Arabs, who recognized the importance and responded to the challenge of Greek thought at a time when it had been eclipsed in Europe during the so-called Dark Ages. Long before there were any WASPs in the world, Aristotle stood as a formidable presence in the minds of the great Islamic philosophers, al-Ghazālī and Ibn Khaldūn, as much later he would again in the eyes of modern East Asians. Plato, Aristotle, St. Augustine, Dante, Shakespeare, and Dostoyevsky, when made available to educated Japanese and Chinese, quickly established themselves as classic thinkers and writers of universal stature.

In this way, the "core" at Columbia has come to be defined through practical experience more than by an abstract definition or ideological design.

Yet, after more than seventy years of experience with these two courses, CC and Humanities, and with successive changes in their conduct, it can still be said that the basic aim of the core remains to satisfy the two interrelated needs cited earlier: first, for students to gain an understanding of Western civilization and its values in their historical development (though not necessarily seen as exclusive to the West), and second, drawing on this understanding, to confront the problems of contemporary society. More particularly, CC has sought to address contemporary problems in historical perspective and in the light of what leading thinkers in the West have said about the central problems of human society. The Humanities courses provide students with an opportunity personally to encounter certain great works of literature, thought, art, and music that can speak to the human condition and enrich the inner life of the individual. Clearly there is, and should be, some overlap between the two.

Each of these courses has changed over the years, but together they have retained the following characteristics in common as core courses:

1. They provide students and faculty, regardless of their particular academic and professional interests, with an opportunity to study and reflect upon the major ideas, values, and institutions of Western civilization that have shaped contemporary society.

2. The core courses are text and problem oriented, emphasizing the exploration of alternative views and approaches to major topics rather than initiation into specific disciplines.

3. A common body of required texts and source readings is used to encourage the individual's confrontation with challenging questions and ideas as well as to facilitate discussion of key issues with one's fellows.

4. Through such common readings and the exchange of ideas, the core courses promote a shared, nontechnical discourse that, in an age of inescapable specialization, bridges the disciplines and sustains the ability of educated persons to communicate with one another.

5. If group discussion depends for its focus on a common set of readings, the works themselves offer an uncommon combination of accessibility to readers (readily making sense to them) as well as a capacity to perplex and provoke. In this respect, the true greatness of "great books" lies not in their perfection as final statements but in their pivotal quality, their ability to focus on key issues and expose the mind to crucial alternatives. Far from settling things, they are unsettling, always open to reinterpretation. They invite and reward rereading.

6. A condition of successful group discussion in core courses is the limitation of class size. Typically at Columbia this has meant groups of twenty to thirty students, allowing for close classroom contact—long considered one of the most distinctive features of a Columbia College education. Yet such a pattern does not exclude the presentation also of special lectures by scholars of high competency as an adjunct to and enhancement of the regular class discussions. This has been done successfully in the past without compromising the basic enterprise.

7. In the Humanities courses, the inclusion of classics in the syllabus and their reinstatement year after year has come about through election and re-election by the staff, ratification by students, and later confirmation by alumni, who testify that the encounter with such challenging works has remained the most memorable and meaningful part of their college experience.

8. A "canon" so established in practice serves not so much to enshrine a hundred books as to help students to develop their own standards of evaluation. The canon (if such it be) and the questioning of it go together. There must be questioning, and there must be something of value that has stood the test of time worth questioning.

9. As the core curriculum addresses age-old human problems and finds perennial wisdom or enduring beauty in monuments of the past, it recognizes too that active repossession of the past involves constant reevaluation in the light of new knowledge and present needs. Thus the sustaining of the core requires some built-in mechanism for review and reformulation.

10. "Core," then, refers not just to content or canon but to process and method—to a well-tested body of challenging material, cultivated habits of reflective, critical discourse, and procedures for reexamination and redefinition. A viable core will neither be slave to the past nor captive to the preoccupations, pressures, or fashions of the moment. It will serve rather to advance the intellectual growth and self-awareness of the student, cultivate his powers of thought and expression, and prepare him to take a responsible part in society.

It often does this, too, for the instructors.

Extending the Core

Although CC and Humanities have, for ninety years now, represented the core of the Core, in keeping with the original premise that these were to be foundation courses, others answering to the same concerns and methods of discourse were to follow. A prime example is the "Colloquium," an upper-level seminar traditionally conducted by two instructors that has taken up additional major works of the Western tradition beyond the limited number that could be handled in the required Humanities course. At its inception, one needed no special rationale for the Colloquium; it was simply a continuation of the enormously successful Honors course initiated by John Erskine. But since the number of important works to be considered was far greater than one could include in Humanities A without strain or superficiality of treatment, and since no one imagined that the Humanities reading list represented a fixed or closed canon, it was natural for some students to want to continue the process through the Colloquium, on an optional and selective basis, into the junior and senior years.

Most important here is the sense of the core as a sustained process—starting from an adequate foundation experience, in which one is exposed to challenging ideas and develops certain habits of critical discourse, and then, through expanding horizons of intellect, imagination, and aesthetic sensibility, moving on to fresh encounters with other works, old or new. From this naturally emerged the concept and practice of the "Extended Core": a further outreach from the required core to a limited number of defined options, each of them organic outgrowths of what had gone before in terms of central concerns and discussion methods.

In this educational context and climate was born the Oriental Humanities, featuring the "Asian classics," as a natural extension of the earlier Honors, Humanities, and Colloquium programs. The manner in which this happened is described in chapter 1, but a salient fact, and a point worth sharpening here, is that the thought of including Asia in the core curriculum arose in the 1930s, well before World War II, the postwar boom in Asian studies, or the rise of third-world politics in the sixties. Efforts to remedy this lack, not just by the adding of so-called language and area studies (which were already offered at Columbia in the form of Chinese, Japanese, Indic, and Arabic studies) but by the organization of courses meeting the same criteria as CC and Humanities, were delayed by the distractions of World War II rather than hastened by America's increasing involvement in the Pacific area. But under the postwar leadership of Dean Harry Carman, courses were established first in an Oriental Colloquium, then in Oriental Humanities, and finally in Oriental Civilizations. There followed an intensive development of teaching materials, source readings, translations of major texts, study guides, syllabi, etc. Though this effort continues even now, already by the late 1960s it was possible to say that the materials on Asia for use in general education were fully equivalent to those used in the parent core courses. It could no longer be argued, as some did justifiably at midcentury, that, though the need to bring Asia into the core was clear, materials were simply not available to do the job properly. Suitable translations, texts, and guides have since been developed for use at almost any level of education. These materials are not only widely used in the United States and Canada but have been reprinted, translated, and even pirated for use in Asia as well.

These facts belie certain claims made by protagonists on both sides in recent debates. Certainly, there is no warrant here for thinking that the inclusion of Asia in the core curriculum has to be seen as a betrayal of the West, a surrender of academic integrity, or a capitulation to the political pressures of disaffected minorities—or indeed, as anything but a natural follow-through on the intentions of those who originally saw the need for a core curriculum and also foresaw that it would be incomplete if it did not make room for other major world traditions. The real issue here is not whether to include Asia but whether it is wise or necessary to do this at the substantial expense of the West in the core curriculum.

What may well provoke suspicion or arouse alarm among conservatives is the more radical claim that today East and West should be treated on a par, with no privileged status reserved for traditional values or Western civilization. This latter claim gains some plausibility and undoubted momentum from current trends toward the globalization of economic, technical, and cultural life. In the space age, with almost instant communication around the world, everyone lives in everyone else's backyard. Hence, anything that resists the inevitable breaking down of cultural barriers seems pointless and, in the longer run, fruitless. It is anachronistic—so this line goes—to try to preserve, much less erect, fences that would protect any cultural sanctuary or privileged curricular position for the Western tradition.

To Allan Bloom, this view might well seem the final surrender of the open mind to cultural relativism. I would suggest, however, that there is a sound educational middle way to be found here that is not simply a wishy-washy compromise between hard-line right and left. I would, on the one hand, take seriously the question raised by John Van Doren as to whether the Asian classics, for all their importance on a global scale, are "necessary" in the same sense that the "Great Books" of the West are necessary to students in the West. That "necessity," he says, derives from the fact that such works "already inhabit the minds of students when they come to college" and that "they have to be duly recognized if these minds are to develop properly—that is, with adequate command of their mental furniture." He says further:

> I do not mean, of course, that the students have literally read such works before they come to college. I mean that the works exist within them in the sense that the kind of language they speak, the terms they use, and the ideas they have about themselves and the world around them are derived from such writings. Of course the language is not spoken very well, nor are the terms used with much precision, nor are the ideas sufficiently understood. That is why it is necessary for students to undertake this reading in their college years, and preferably, I should think, at the beginning of their course of study. They have to discover what it is that they think they know, and perhaps how little they really know it, before they can move on to other things.[1]

This strikes me as a serious claim, and I would agree with it in the sense that what Van Doren says is equally true of students the world around. One's own cultural tradition should have priority in undergraduate education anywhere. The globalization of culture may well produce what people like to think of as a "global village," but that it will be global in character as the outcome of irresistible forces seems far more likely than that it will produce anything resembling a village. There are grounds for doubt whether our future habitation will retain any real local color, distinctive culture, or sense of intimate association. Indeed, one wonders whether it can be assumed that anything at all will survive of local culture or indigenous tradition in the face of the homogenization of all culture that attends the process of "globalization." May not universities everywhere be doomed, if not to an imposed conformity, then at least to a uniformity as anonymous, dull, and graceless as the shopping malls proliferating around the globe? These are questions that must disturb anyone contemplating the future of our universities.

If globalization of a mindless sort is not to occur, if anything of intellectual diversity and cultural pluralism is to survive in colleges and universities, they must tend the roots of their own cultures and nurture whatever there still is of distinctive excellence in their own traditions. Which is to say, in the matter of core curricula, giving some priority to the study of, and understanding in some depth, those ideas, institutions, or cultural traditions that make each of us—in East or West—what we are and can be at our best.

At the same time, no matter how well our translators do their work, studying another culture is going to be much like learning another language. There are always linguistic or cultural barriers to be overcome. This means that the further removed from our own another culture is—and this applies also to classical civilization as compared to modern—the greater the effort that will be needed to penetrate the barrier and enter deeply into that culture. In other words, the stranger the culture the less accessible it will be and the greater the risks of misunderstanding and superficiality.

In the early stages of education, this factor of accessibility and commensurate difficulty of penetration must be taken into account. In chapter 1, I argue the point in relation to proposals for bringing all major traditions together in a single classics, "Great Books," or World Civilization course. Here everything depends, as always, on how it is done, on what comparative terms are employed, and on how much time is given to it. In the present context, certainly, a crucial question would be whether adequate justice can be done to the distinctive features of each tradition—especially their inner complexity and rich diversities—in a one-year survey. One can have something like "globality" in the academic equivalent of a one-stop shopping mall but nothing like the intimate personal experience of life in a village or the sense of identification with a community for which one takes some personal responsibility.

Even after forty years' experience in dealing with the problem, for me the most essential considerations have never been better stated than they were in 1943, by one of the founding fathers of the movement, Mark Van Doren, in his *Liberal Education*:

Imagination always has work to do, whether in single minds or in the general will. It is the guardian angel of desire and decision, accounting for more right action, and for more wrong action, than anybody computes. Without it, for instance, the West can come to no conclusions about the East which war and fate are rapidly making a necessary object of its knowledge. Statistics and surveys of the East will not produce what an image can produce: an image of difference, so that no gross offenses are committed against the human fact of strangeness, and an image of similarity, even of identity, so that nothing homely is forgotten.[2]

Notes

1. John Van Doren, "Are the Great Books of the East Necessary?" in *Approaches to the Asian Classics*, ed. Wm. Theodore de Bary and Irene Bloom (New York: Columbia University Press, 1990), 361.
2. Mark Van Doren, *Liberal Education* (New York: Holt, 1943), 127.

3

Why We Read the *Analects* of Confucius

Wm. Theodore de Bary

ALTHOUGH THIS ESSAY will speak mostly to why and how I read the *Analects* of Confucius, the reason I entitle it "Why *We* Read the *Analects*" is not that I claim to speak for everyone but only that my personal reading follows from what others have thought and said about it. Ever since Confucius's disciples recorded his sayings, teachings, and examples in the fifth century C.E., later generations have been inspired to pass it on, to share it with others who have read, reflected on it, and discussed it together. Thus the *Analects* are still read because they have survived this scrutiny and reexamination over the centuries, which is why we read it today—not because it became part of a fixed canon (though in some places it did) or was required reading imposed by one generation upon the next.

I have read and discussed the *Analects* with students in my Asian Humanities class for sixty years, and their response to it is much the same, whether they are majoring in the natural or social sciences or in the humanities. So, for practical purposes, when I speak of "Why We Read the *Analects*," it means "how I and my students have read the *Analects* together," and especially how one's first impressions are formed by the early chapters. Indeed, it is no different for other audiences of any age or at any level, including adult education. If this is what is meant by "general" education, then the *Analects* speak to the generality of human beings—to their common, perennial, "core" concerns more than to the farthest outreaches of abstract thought.

This is why I avoid speaking of what I do as "teaching" the *Analects*. No doubt a teacher can help students with their reading and reflection upon the text, but basically students are rediscovering it and learning it for themselves. The book teaches itself, as most genuine "classics" do. Whatever may be done by a teacher is only an enhancement of the reader's own personal encounter in recognizing that the text speaks directly to him or herself.

For me, the latest confirmation of this fact comes from the valedictory address of a Columbia College graduate in 2008 who chose to sum up his four years' learning experience by drawing on the model of the *Analects* and some of its key sayings.[1] Understandably, our valedictorian drew first on the opening lines, which read: "The Master said: To study and at times to practice what one has learned, is that not a pleasure? To have friends coming from afar, is that not a joy? To be unembittered even if one is not recognized, is that not to be a truly noble person?" If one wishes to know more of what our valedictorian made of these lines, one can refer to the *Proceedings* just cited. In what follows, despite my disclaimer of any originality or unique expertise, I shall offer my own thoughts on these lines and other key passages that mark the *Analects* as classic.

Taken together, these opening lines tell us much about the nature and context of the *Analects*. The first lines could be addressed to and understood by any literate human being, but the last line points more specifically to "the noble person" (*junzi*). Here *junzi* refers to the traditional leadership elite, an aristocratic class born to a privileged status of would-be rulers. But Confucius emphasizes the learning process for what it takes to be worthy of a leadership role or become an exemplary person; in other words, what it means to command respect as a person, whether or not one finds oneself in a position to lead or rule. Thus he reconceives the traditional concept of *junzi* from that of "nobleman" to one that emphasizes "the noble *man* (or person)" as one whose personal character, not status, establishes him as a model to be followed—a true leader in any social role whatever, even if not successful politically.

(In the context of the times, one understands that *junzi* refers most directly to male heirs of the aristocracy, but the second half of the compound, *zi*, is literally "child" and not gender specific. Thus later Japanese empresses could appropriate to themselves the expression *tianzi*, normally understood in China as "Son of Heaven" but for them clearly open to their own hereditary claim to be a "child of Heaven" regardless of gender. Still later in China, *jun* could be a suffix applied to women as well.)

The same multifaceted expression *zi* also appears as the very first word in the *Analects*: "The Master said (*zi yue*)." As "Master," *zi* could be applied to other authority figures like *Laozi* and *Zhuangzi*, and here it clearly refers to a teacher, but the language that follows marks Confucius as distinct from any teacher who is simply dictating or preaching to his students or disciples.

Note the rhetorical cast of all three of the statements above: they are not outright assertions, much less forceful dictates. They invite and expect an implicit response from the hearer as if one's own experience would immediately confirm the truth of what Confucius is saying—he is only telling them in a sense what they already know, without invoking any higher authority. This is not the thunderous voice of the prophet, nor is it a pronouncement from the pulpit or podium. Old Testament prophets spoke first of all to God, and then they delivered God's word to His people. Confucius speaks directly to us and asks us to recognize Heaven within and around us.

His appeal to ordinary human experience is also the ground on which he talks of studying or learning. What he says may be addressed to the individual, calling on one personally to achieve fulfillment as a truly noble person, but his hearers are learning from others as well as from their own experience and practice, and their "others" here include teachers, examples from the past, as well as "friends coming from afar" with whom one can share one's experience—it is learning that can be gained from (being open to) both the past and others able to confirm and expand on one's own knowledge.

But if I have distinguished Confucius's voice from that of the Old Testament prophet, this does not mean that there is no common ground between them. Both speak to an ideal standard by which to measure and judge the conduct of kings and rulers and, by implication, anyone else who bears a responsibility for others—which means just about all of us. In Confucius's case, however, the approach is most characteristically on the means of self-cultivation by which one can develop the virtues of the Noble Person, understood as a fulfillment of the human ideal. And most characteristic of Confucianism too is the way that the *Analects* explain this as an organic growth following the pattern of ordinary human life.

Accordingly, in the passage immediately following that quoted above, the *Analects* speak of that process as grounded in the life of the family, wherein, initially by acquiring habits of respectful conduct toward others—first of all toward parents and then to one's siblings—one engenders traits essential to human life, whether one's own—in the self—or in others. Thus the second passage concludes: "The noble person concerns himself with the root, when the root is established, the Way is born. Being filial and fraternal—is this not the root of humaneness?" (1:2).

Again the rhetorical mode—appealing to anyone's first experience of life conveys the sense that the living process is interactive and interpersonal. But here the process is identified as one by which "the Way" is born, takes life. And in the context of the preceding passages, this is also understood to be the Way that a truly noble person follows.

At the same time, this Way is centered in humaneness as the prime virtue of the Noble Person, a virtue that links the self-fulfillment of the exemplary person to the fulfillment of others. But fulfillment is the product of a sequential process for anyone and everyone. Filiality is the seed from which, with due cultivation, the growth process can be fulfilled in the flowering of humaneness or true humanity. In this respect, filiality may be considered the genetic virtue of Confucianism—important in its priority—but its full fruit or flower is humaneness (consummate virtue).

There is a widespread impression that filiality is the most characteristic virtue of Confucianism, and this notion is not just a modern misconception or misreading by foreign observers. The early critic of the Confucian school, Mozi, seized on this family virtue as almost an obsession of the Confucians he knew. And the early Legalists also took issue with the Confucians on this point, seeing a family ethic rooted in filiality as prejudicial to public-mindedness on a wider scale (as indeed Mozi had). Moreover, the powerful hold of filiality on Confucian culture was demonstrated by the resistance that it showed to Buddhism upon the latter's introduction to China.

But before we pursue this issue further, we do well to note another early reference to filiality in the *Analects*. When a disciple, Mang Wu Bo, is quoted as asking Confucius about filiality or filial piety (*xiao*), the terse answer given is somewhat perplexing in its obliqueness: "Parents' only concern should be lest their children be sick" (2:6). Traditional commentators have tended to interpret this as implying primarily an obligation on the child to take proper care of itself—attending to one's own person in bodily and moral health. No doubt this was a distinct and enduring feature of Confucian teaching and practice, and its strong sense of the person as a bodily self is what offered resistance to Buddhist questioning of the reality of any substantial self. But one should not ignore the underlying assumption here that the filial child is responding to the loving concern of his parents. Filiality is a reflection of parental love. It partakes of the basic Confucian principle of reciprocity, in the light of which filiality is to be seen not as an absolute value requiring blind obedience to parents but as a relative one to the extent that it is qualified and conditioned by a parental love that is taken for granted in the passage just quoted—one of the many natural assumptions underlying Confucian discourse.

Another later anecdote in the *Analects* underscores the same point. Confucius's disciple Zai Wo asked him about the customary three years' mourning for one's parents, expressing the thought that one year's mourning should be enough. Confucius asks him: "If you were to eat good food and wear fine clothing, would you feel at ease?" Zai Wo responds: "I would feel at ease." "If you would feel at ease, then do it. But the noble person throughout the mourning period derives no pleasure from the food that he eats, no joy from the music that he hears, and no comfort from his dwelling. But you would feel at ease and so you should do it." After Wo leaves, the Master adds: "How inhuman Yü [Zai Wo] is! Only when a child is three years old does it leave its parents' arms. The three years' mourning is the universal custom everywhere under Heaven. And Yü, was he not the darling of his father and mother for three years?"

In this case, Confucius shows a basic respect for the essentially voluntary character of ethical behavior while also upholding the standards of reciprocity that should ordinarily apply. The standard, however, presumes that natural feeling should underlie and prompt one's actions. It would do no good to make a pretense of virtue. Thus natural feelings of reciprocity engendered in the normal process of life, from birth and infancy to maturity, are the root of humaneness, as in the earlier example.

The primacy of natural sentiments born in the bosom of the family is underscored by another episode, in which the Duke of She tells Confucius: "In our part of the country there is one upright Gong. His father stole a sheep and the son bore witness against him." Confucius says: "In our part of the country, the upright are different from that. A father is shielded by his son, and a son is shielded by his father. Uprightness lies in this" (13:18). In other words, the intimacy of the family is privileged over the claims of the state, for the state cannot stand if trust within the family—the root of public trust—is undermined.

Soon after this, the primacy of sentiment or feeling over rational discourse was reaffirmed for Confucians in the *Mencius*, where Mencius defined the goodness of human nature as moral awareness (literally, "good knowing" or natural knowledge, *liang zhih*), and further when he defined the basic relationship or bond between parent and child not in terms of filiality but as one of "intimate affection" or mutual love to be cultivated (of course) in the light of reason (the sense of right and wrong, *yi*).

But since from the outset of the *Analects*, as in all the literate discourse that its readers are engaged in, there is the possibility that verbalization and rationalization might intrude on one's ordinary conduct, it is important that what one learns and says be guided and informed by both one's own feelings and one's consciousness of right and wrong (*yi*). Thus the *Analects'* early exposition of the Way of Humaneness includes the following: "A young man is to be filial within his family and respectful outside it. He is to be earnest and faithful, overflowing with love for all living beings and intimate with those who are humane. If after such practice he has strength to spare, he may use it in the study of literate culture (*wen*)" (1:6). Although the importance of study and learning had already been asserted in the opening lines—and Confucian scholarship became widely known among East Asian teachings as the most rational—here the priority of moral cultivation over literate discourse (*wen*), essential though the latter was to civilized life, is established early on in the *Analects*.

We saw in the opening lines how the process of learning started first by interaction with others but ended with the Noble Person able to stand, so to speak, on his own. He knew where he stood regardless of the approval or disapproval of others. This is not the same as a radical individuality asserting its complete autonomy but is rather a self in a state of personal balance or poise. The same conception then informs our understanding of other Confucian values connected with the Noble Person as a model of humaneness. In chapter 1:4, one of Confucius's closest disciples is quoted approvingly as follows: "Everyday I examine myself on three things: In planning on behalf of others, have I failed to be loyal? When dealing with friends have I failed to be trustworthy? In receiving what has been transmitted, have I failed to practice it?"

Among each of these cases there is a connection or continuity that involves more than an obedient adherence to or following of others. "Loyalty" (as *zhong* is usually translated) is represented by the graph for "center" underlain by the graph for "mind-and-heart"; it bespeaks a centered mind and heart, one in a state of balance within the self but also balanced with others. It means being true to oneself as well as to others (not just following or obeying the latter). This then connects up with the other two values cited. "Trustworthiness" is our rendering here for *xin*, sometimes also translated as "good faith," both of which express the idea that one's actions and conduct are consistent with one's stated professions, being true to one's word. (Ezra

Pound, as a poet and amateur translator playing around with the *Analects*, notes that the character for *xin* [trust] included the graph for man or person at the left and the graph for "word" or "saying" beside it on the right, which suggested to him the felicitous rendering of it as "man standing by his word.")

This same notion is implicit in Confucian "loyalty," being true at once to one's self and others, and it connects up with the faithful practice of one's professions in service to others. Another notable passage in the *Analects* speaks of the "man of service" (*shi*), here roughly equivalent to the "noble person," in the following terms: "The man of service cannot but be stout-hearted and enduring; for his burden is heavy and his way is long. To be truly humane is the burden he bears; is it not heavy? Only in death does his practice of the Way come to an end; is that not long?" (8:7).

Here the burden of humaneness is heavy because service to others that is also true to oneself can be exacting and demanding of one's own inner resources. Whether in a position of leadership or sharing in the responsibilities of government, to be truly reliable and trustworthy meant to be fully honest with oneself and unflinchingly forthright in advising others. Often, it would involve courageous honesty in counseling rulers who might resent hearing the truth, especially about themselves.

In the Confucian tradition of civil service, especially in ministerial roles, this courageous honesty was the hallmark of true loyalty on the part of those who were "stout-hearted and enduring" even to the point of martyrdom, when the true scholar-official's Way ended in death at the hands of a despotic ruler. But being true to one's word and professions had an importance beyond the individual in Confucius's whole scheme of things. A prime vocation for the man of service was the business of human governance, and the *Analects* has much to say about this. Here a few examples may suffice: When a disciple asked Confucius about government, the latter replied tersely, "Sufficient food, sufficient military strength, and the confidence (trust) of the people [are the three requisites]." When asked further "if unavoidably one had to dispense with any of these three, which of them would you forego?" the Master replied: "Let go of the military strength." The disciple next asked: If one had, unavoidably, to dispense with one of the remaining two, which should go first? The Master said: "Do without the food, for from of old there has always been death, but without such confidence (trust) a people cannot stand" (12:7).

Mutual trust, among the people and their leaders, is thus the most essential ingredient of any human society—a principle that underlies another response of Confucius to the question of what is essential to government: "Should you try to lead them by means of regulations or keep order among them through laws and punishments, the people will evade these and lack any sense of shame. Lead them [on the other hand] by personal virtue (*de*) and keep order among them through rites (*li*), then the people, having a sense of shame, will correct themselves" (2:3).

Here Confucius's depreciation of laws and punishment fits with his eschewal of coercive force ("military strength") except as a possible backup from the passage just cited before. For him, voluntarism is the basic predicate of any human society, as it had been traditionally in households cooperatively engaged in family-managed agriculture. One can rely better on a person's or people's sense of self-respect (the corollary of "the sense of shame" referred to here) to motivate people's cooperation with their leaders, just as the latter's personal virtue should exhibit exemplary self-respect combined with respect for others.

Note, however, that personal virtue and respect alone are not enough; the rites are especially involved and indispensable. This is because rites and proper customs establish practical norms of conduct that are themselves voluntaristic, cooperative, educational—and not coercive. They are the means by which the self, in the normal process of life, engages with others. They give form to things, forms and norms naturally conducive to the harmonious development of human relations or political action.

This is the basis for the "harmony" that others have seen as the keynote of Confucianism, regardless of whether they always understood its voluntarism or reciprocity in the same terms. When in seventh-century Japan Prince Shōtoku tried to incorporate Confucianism in his nation's first formal constitution, the first word that he used was "Harmony," followed by his exhortation on behalf of a consensual society. Much later, after the Communists in China recoiled from the vicious class struggle of the Cultural Revolution, they turned back, at least in name, to Confucian harmony as an essential Chinese value to undergird "Chinese Socialism."

Much more is said in the *Analects* about the rites (or ritual decorum) in daily life as they relate to personal and social health. But I am limiting myself in this essay only to a few key themes that one encounters in a first reading that give us initial bearings on what follows in the text.

In the remainder of this essay, I wish to focus on something no less important to one's reading of the *Analects* than the key teachings: the character of Confucius and his sense of personal vocation and mission. This image of him in the pages of the *Analects* comes through as almost more compelling and memorable than his teachings and aphorisms, to such an extent that, despite his own disclaimers of his disciples' attributions of sagehood to him, among latter-day Confucians the picture of him as he appeared in the *Analects* became the very model of the Sage (though none could hardly boast of emulating the modesty of the Sage).

The first thing to note is his becoming modesty and lack of pretension to great personal authority, which are already implicit in the conversational mode of the opening lines. He did not claim to be proclaiming any new order or teaching. "I am a transmitter, not a creator," he said (7:1). Whether he was actually creative in the process of transmitting, that is, in his interpretation and exposition of ancient ideals, is another question, but posterity has generally judged him so. One must also allow for the possibility that "in transmitting" what he had received from past tradition he was being more than just conservative. The posture of "upholding past ideals" could also appear as a critique of existing institutions that fail to measure up. Thus one episode in Confucius's teaching career portrays him, in the course of his travels, sending a disciple to ask directions from a farmer who, when he learns that the disciple's master is Confucius, recognizes the latter as a would-be counselor to rulers, going from state to state looking for one who would take his advice.

The farmer has a skeptical view of this mission; he regards the world as so unruly that the best one can do is tend to his own field. "Instead of following a scholar who distances himself from one ruler after another, it would be better to follow one who withdraws from the whole world of men" (18.6). When the disciple reports this to Confucius, the Master sighs: "One cannot herd with the beasts or flock with the birds. If I am not to go along in the company of other human beings, with whom should I associate? If the Way prevailed in the world, I would not be trying to change things" (18.6). Mere "transmitter" though he was, Confucius did see his mission as trying to change things. Received tradition itself contained the seeds of reform, but it was Confucius who saw the need to rectify the evils that would not just resolve themselves.

Confucius was known in his time as a scholar persistent in his call to be of public service, but he was equally known for his diffidence in serving any ruler whose actions were inconsistent with his own principles. On another occasion someone asked Confucius: "Why does the master not take part in government?" The master said: "What do the *Documents* [The Classic of History] say about being filial? Be filial. Just being filial and being friendly with one's brothers contributes to governance. Why should one have to take office to do this?" (2:21).

Again Confucius's answer is somewhat terse and a little oblique, but it takes us back to where we started in the *Analects*: filiality as the value underlying all social and civic virtue. Public service is not performed only by those in office; anyone who practices and promotes such civic virtues is rendering a public service. And indeed the practice of such values is the precondition for anyone who might qualify for office. Elsewhere Confucius says: "One should not be anxious about having an official position but about having the wherewithal to hold office. One should not be anxious about not being recognized [for office] but about not being worthy of such recognition" (4:14).

Again we are taken back to the starting point of our reading: the Noble Person who can stand on his own even if he is not recognized. The course that he has followed (and we in following the *Analects* thus far) is summed up in Confucius's own brief summation of his life experience: "At fifteen I set my heart on learning. At thirty I was established in its pursuit. By forty I had no great doubts [about what I was doing]. At fifty I heard what Heaven commanded of me. At sixty I could heed it. At seventy I could follow my heart's desire without transgressing" (2:4).

In the light of our previous discussion, we may be able to fill in the spaces in this spare outline of his personal history. That it starts with learning we already know. That it takes time to learn from the past and others' experience we can readily understand. Confucius's growing from adolescence to increasing security at thirty and maturity at forty—these are familiar stages in the life process. What may be somewhat unexpected is that only at fifty did he "hear" what Heaven expected of him. The language used here for "Heaven's command" is itself not unfamiliar, but earlier it had referred to what is usually translated as the "Mandate of Heaven" (*tian ming*), a claim made by rulers or their spokesmen to justify their taking power and exercising authority, ostensibly in the name of Heaven. For Confucius, that claim could only be considered legitimate if in fact the ruler or his dynasty ruled virtuously on behalf of the people. And it is this sense of responsibility attaching to the claim of legitimacy or public trust that is key to Confucius's understanding of Heaven's command or charge.

Confucius himself was in no position to rule. At some point, nevertheless, he must have felt that he had some capacity and obligation to make use of what he had learned on behalf of the public good. (Whether or not this occurred exactly at fifty in this schematic sequence is not the point.) More significant is that Confucius takes this charge upon himself personally; it is not just a political concept applying to dynastic rulers but a commission that Heaven was entrusting directly to himself. We are already aware from other references to Heaven in the *Analects* that Confucius felt some personal relation to it—a kind of religious relationship between Heaven theistically conceived (a divine creator) and its creation. Heaven spoke directly and personally to him and he had a filial obligation to listen.

Confucianism may not be thought of as a "religion" in the usual sense, but Confucius bespoke a reverential attitude toward Heaven, and the deep respect in which he held all life was a reflection of this. In response to questions put to him by disciples about the Noble Person, he said: "He cultivates himself with reverence" (14:45), and even more to the point here: "Without knowing (or understanding) what Heaven has ordained (*tian ming*), i.e., its charge or command, one has no way to become a Noble Person" (20:3). Indeed, the attitude and virtue of reverence remained a key element in later Confucianism. It was not a purely secular ethic, as some have supposed it to be.

But if Heaven charged Confucius personally with a responsibility for public service, we know already how conflicted he was about taking office, and we can understand the difficulty that he might face in trying to carry out that charge. This is perhaps why it took him time (here, another ten years) actually to "heed" what we he had heard earlier, that is, to find a way to resolve his conscience in this regard. My own supposition is that his resolution of the matter was in keeping with the response that he gave to those who had questioned him about his refusal to take office: both in the given circumstances and in the larger scheme of things, taking office was not the only way to fulfill one's obligation to be of service to Heaven and humankind. Teaching was also a public service when it contributed to the individual's and people's education on behalf of the public trust.

Finally, when we are told that at seventy Confucius had satisfied his heart's desire, we are reminded that at fifteen he had "set his heart on learning," and so, in carrying out Heaven's charge to him, the outcome—his satisfaction as a scholar and teacher in lieu of an official career—fulfilled not only that early aspiration but also any political ambitions he might have had. This was not accomplished without a struggle of the kind that one who had to bear the burden of humaneness to the end might endure. But that end was, after all, marked by some measure of satisfaction and fulfillment.

To be sure, this was not exactly a supreme epiphany or sudden moment of enlightenment but rather a threshold of accumulated learning and experience. Nor does it, on the other hand, result from the sort of profound confrontation with evil and suffering that we see, say, in St. Augustine or Dostoyevsky. Including Confucius in such a range of perspectives, one can see his as a relatively optimistic or even idealistic view of life. But it is reassuring for those who have followed him in the *Analects* to believe that this good man could live out a life worthy of a truly Noble Man—the goal he set out for himself at the start.

The foregoing is just one among several ways of explaining why or how we read the *Analects*. There are others. However important it is to read the text directly and personally, the one we read always bears the imprint of the tradition that has passed it on. And if we want to know how others have received and understood it, showing a decent respect for the opinions of readers and writers before us in other places and times, we might go on to consider how it was understood by those who had a major impact on other civilized peoples.

This would be especially true of those East Asian peoples whose education was structured in the form given by the pervasive Neo-Confucian movement from the eleventh to the nineteenth centuries. Over the course of this long premodern period, the *Analects* was read as one of the so-called Four Books, a special packaging of the Confucian classics mainly attributed to the great Neo-Confucian philosopher Zhu Xi (1130–1200). In that form, the *Analects* was not the first thing one read. It came after the text of the *Great Learning*, a chapter from the *Record of Rites* (*Liji*) attributed to Confucius's disciple Zengzi, which was provided with a special preface and commentary by Zhu Xi that he thought propedeutic to any reading of the other classics included in the Four Books. Thus how one read the *Analects* itself was conditioned by Zhu's own way of introducing us to "How to Read a Book." The book is still a classic, but now it is the product of a subsequent tradition, and this is not exactly the same as "reading it in the original." Zhu Xi was now presenting it in a form adapted to his own age, in which "new age" Confucians, that is, Neo-Confucians, responded to the challenge of Mahāyāna Buddhism by providing a metaphysical explanation to accompany the text. The basic message remained the same, as Zhu Xi summed it up in his preface: "Self-cultivation for the Governance of Humankind" (*xiuji zhiren*), a memorable slogan in later literature. Now, however, it was elaborated upon in terms of a new cosmology and a more sophisticated philosophy of human nature (*dao xue* and *xingli xue*). (Incidentally, this is how the *Analects* was reported on by the American art critic Ernest Fenollosa, who read it in a Japanese edition of the Four Books and handed it on to people like Ezra Pound. But this is what we all do—read it on the recommendation of someone else in a form more or less adapted to the latest scene.)

However, it did not take long for even this Neo-Confucian version of the traditional classic to be called into question by textual critics of the seventeenth through nineteenth centuries, who pointed out differences between these supposed "classic" or traditional Four Books and the versions that had been "classic" before. This led inevitably to efforts by modern critics to rediscover or reconstruct "the original *Analects*." If we want to incorporate any of these new versions into our own core curriculum, however, which are we to choose? No working curriculum that tries to provide a humanities component for undergraduate education (or even alongside graduate training) can get into all of the complexities that this historical development entails. If we read what some modern scholar reconstructs as "The Original Analects," it is not what traditional education in East Asia would have recognized nor what would have entered into the intellectual and moral formation of generations of East Asians. It would simply be another academic discovery.

There is no perfect solution to this educational dilemma, but if we are willing to think of working solutions rather than final ones, we can try to provide a repertoire of approaches by which one can adapt these resources to different educational situations and different levels of learning. The important thing is that the first reading be a personal encounter with a classic text (however "classic" may be interpreted) and that it be understood as only a first reading, one to be followed up as best one can by more or other readings.

Note

1. *Proceedings of the Conference on Classics for an Emerging World, Columbia University, January 19–20, 2008* (New York: University Committee on Asia and the Middle East, 2008).

4

MENCIUS

Irene Bloom

T HE *MENCIUS* HAS had a long career as a classic in China and in East Asia as a whole. Dating from perhaps the third century B.C.E.—about a century after Mencius himself lived—it has been studied, memorized, absorbed, quoted, reflected upon, and argued about in China over the course of some twenty-three centuries. With a possible interlude during the period of the Cultural Revolution in the late 1960s and early 1970s, the text of the *Mencius* has continued its career, and despite official hostility toward Confucianism earlier, it is being studied in Communist China today. It has also exerted great influence throughout the recorded history of Korea, Japan, and Vietnam. There is probably no text more influential in terms of the way that all of the Confucianized people of East Asia have come to think about human nature and what it means to be human.

In its traditional Chinese context, the *Mencius* was unambiguously one of the "great books." For many centuries it was counted as one of the Thirteen Classics. These thirteen—a very varied groups of texts that evolved between, roughly, the eleventh century B.C.E. and the second century C.E.— were regarded as cultural expressions of timeless value. One might note, however, that, while we use the English term "classic," deriving from the Latin *classicus*, to translate the Chinese word *jing*, their connotations are quite different. Unlike the Latin *classicus*, referring to the classes of the Roman people and, by implication, to a production of the first or highest class, the Chinese word *jing* has no association with social class. The Chinese character is composed of two elements: on the left is the radical denoting "silk," which is an artifact, a production of human civilization; on the right is a representation of an underground stream, a phenomenon of nature. "Classics," for the Chinese, have something of that character: they are human products, but they also incorporate something of the natural, as if a classic involved a particularly apt human response to the realities of a larger nature in which human beings participate. Such an idea—the confluence of the human and the natural—is above all manifest in the *Classic of Change* (or the *Book of Changes*) and discernible in a different way in the *Mencius*. But whereas the *Book of Changes* has an oracular tone, Mencius's view of what it means to be human and how human nature figures into nature as a whole is communicated in a distinctly personal voice.

Mencius was among the first followers of Confucius to elaborate the original Confucian vision both in the area of political philosophy and in the philosophy of mind and human nature. Thus to understand what Mencius was about, we need some perspective on the seminal role of Confucius. Confucius had been active in the late sixth and early fifth centuries B.C.E. The reigning Zhou dynasty was in an advanced state of decline. Power had devolved into the hands of a number of feudal rulers who engaged in elaborate power plays and were constantly at war, heedless of its human consequences. The mission of Confucius, if one can summarize briefly something that in cultural terms was enormously involved, was (1) to transfer attention from a supernatural world largely beyond human control to the human world and to the value and efficacy of an ethical attitude, (2) to promote a livelier and more egalitarian conception of humanity, (3) to advocate humane government based on respect for a common humanity, and (4) to stress a reliance on ritual or ceremony as an alternative to harsh and arbitrary laws. Confucius had been a peripatetic, traveling from state to state, seeking a hearing that might lead to official employment. While he made no influential converts among the hardened rulers of that violent age, he did attract an unprecedented following as a teacher. By the time of Mencius, who lived in the late fourth and early third centuries B.C.E., Confucius had also acquired the reputation of a sage.

Mencius's career was similar. During the Warring States Period (463–222 B.C.E.), when warfare had become even more prevalent and the fate of the Zhou dynasty even more problematical, he traveled from state to state, talking with rulers and pleading the practicality of humaneness. By then the political situation had deteriorated. Mencius's response to it was determined yet subtle: a reaffirmation of a profound Confucian confidence in the efficacy of morality but also, at the same time, a resignation to the possibility that he himself might not figure into, or even witness, the restoration of a moral order.

A number of recent writers have urged attending especially to the beginnings and ends of texts. As John Drury observes in his essay on Luke in the *Literary Guide to the Bible*: "It is when books begin and end that their relation to the world is most problematic. In mid-reading we are in the book's world, but starting and finishing we are in transition between world and book. At these exits and entrances the artificiality of texts is troublesome."[1] Though the text of the *Mencius* was not written by Mencius himself but compiled after his life on the basis of his teachings, the beginning and ending of the text are indeed troublesome.

The tone of the entire text is set in the opening exchange (1A:1). Mencius, braving a journey of some hundreds of miles, has come to visit King Hui of Liang and is greeted by the king:

> "Venerable sir," said the King. "You have come all this distance, thinking nothing of a thousand *li*. You must surely have some way of profiting my kingdom?"
>
> "Your Majesty," answered Mencius. "What is the point of mentioning the word 'profit'? All that matters is that there should be humaneness and rightness. If your Majesty says, 'How can I profit my state?' and the Counselors say, 'How can I profit my family?' and the Gentlemen and Commoners say, 'How can I profit my person?' then those above and those below will be trying to profit at the expense of one another and the state will be imperiled. When regicide is committed in a state of ten thousand chariots, it is certain to be by a vassal with a thousand chariots, and when it is committed in a state of a thousand chariots, it is certain to be by a vassal with a hundred chariots. A share of a thousand in ten thousand or a hundred in a thousand is by no means insignificant, yet if profit is put before rightness, there is no satisfaction short of total usurpation. No humane man ever abandons his parents, and no righteous man ever puts his prince last. Perhaps you will now endorse what I have said, 'All that matters is that there should be humaneness and rightness. What is the point of mentioning the word "profit"?'"

The language Mencius uses here is, by Chinese standards, very strong. He confronts this king with a stunning boldness and a sublime confidence.

The king is extremely polite, addressing Mencius as "venerable sir" and leading with a question that conveys a respectful assurance of his attention. Mencius lashes out at him with a stinging rebuke, not only for the question, which to us seems utterly innocent, but for his whole moral stance. He even has the temerity to imply that rulers who put profit ahead of humaneness court regicide. As readers—and this is obviously as true of Chinese readers as of Western readers—we are at this point still in the transition between world and book, and the message we are given in the beginning is that moral commitment is not only of the utmost seriousness but of the most certain efficacy. More than that, a lack of commitment to humaneness must have awful consequences. We shall return to this opening conversation shortly.

For the moment, however, let us skip to the close of the book (7B:38), so that we have both the beginning and the end clearly in mind. At the end we find the venerable Mencius revealing some doubt about his own role as a vehicle for the transmission of the moral Way. He must feel intimations of mortality; though near his life's close, the efficacy of his teachings is far from clear to him. Warfare continues. He seems to brood over the possibility that the transmission he believed had passed over the course of centuries, from the ancient sage kings to the founder of the Shang dynasty, and from him down to the founders of the Zhou dynasty, and from the early Zhou rulers down to Confucius, might be broken if there were no one in his own time capable of carrying on the mission of the sage. At the very end, the last thing we hear before the voice fades is: "From Confucius to the present day there have intervened something over a hundred years. We are so little removed from the time of the sage and so close to the place where he dwelled. Is there then no one? Then indeed there is no one" (7B:38).

The mode of expression of classical Chinese is spare and economical. The text does not specify the nature of the absence, yet we feel that, while Mencius longs to be assured of his own capacity for sagehood, he is resigned to the possibility that he may not figure into the tradition as the sages of the past had done. At the same time, the unpromising nature of the historical situation makes the depth of his aspiration and his devotion to Confucius as an exemplar of sagehood that much more unambiguous. And so there is an interplay of doubt and confidence, neither cancelling out the other. In exiting from the text and returning to the world, the reader must be affected by the subtle blend of high moral idealism and thoroughgoing realism. This seems to become part of the Confucian fiber and may be seen later on as quintessentially Confucian.

In midreading, while we are still very much in the book's world, Mencius also presents us with a philosophy of human nature, stating it in terms memorable to Chinese readers and to Western readers alike. I will say more about this view of human nature in what follows. What is relevant to our appreciation of the place of Mencius in the Chinese tradition is that this view of human nature—which confirms both our fundamental similarity to one another and our potential for goodness—is rather like a spring that is in turn the source for a stream that runs through the entire Chinese philosophical tradition. With the later development of Neo-Confucianism from the tenth century on, it becomes the mainstream. It even permeates the most distinctive forms of Chinese Buddhism, including Chan (Zen), filtering through to the rest of East Asia not only through Confucian channels but through Buddhist channels as well.

In addition to reflecting on human nature in a mode that some might call idealistic, Mencius in midbook is also highly realistic and practical in his awareness that human beings have certain basic needs for food, clothing, shelter, and education—and that these must be met if our very existence as human beings is to be possible. Without these essentials, human life is susceptible to appalling degradation. What he says about the responsibility of the state in meeting basic needs prefigures ongoing Confucian concerns for the material well-being of the people and may figure as significantly as Marxism does in contemporary Chinese "materialism" and the focus on what we in the West call economic and social rights.

Mencius, like Confucius, was concerned both with fundamental human questions, such as the nature of human nature and the functioning of consciousness, and with the matter of government. Nor did he see these issues as in any way separate or distinct. Modern readers are bound to be struck by how continuous the world of Mencius appears to have been, the private and public spheres being experienced as entirely interfused. Apparently the concerns that those grounded in Western thought might see subsumed under the categories of "moral philosophy" and "political philosophy" or pertaining to "private" and "public" spheres were so continuous for Mencius that he saw no need to argue for or even to explain their relation. It probably would not have occurred to him to propose that the components of individual personality might serve as an analogy for the constituents of the state, as did Plato in the *Republic*. (The very fact of Socrates' proposing this analogy in the great dialogue "on justice" indicates that he is juxtaposing two realities that are ordinarily regarded as distinct in order to challenge

Glaucon et al. to discover the relation between the two.) Mencius hardly speaks about individuals apart from society: we see no attempt to consider what human beings might be like prior to society, or apart from it, or even, as with Aristotle in his *Politics*, what human beings might be like in different kinds of polities.

There are at least two factors that might explain why, for Mencius, the private and public worlds are continuous rather than analogous. The first has to do with the Confucian view of the family. Mencius seems to take as a given that the patriarchal family and the monarchical state are constant features of social life. It is not simply that one is the model for the other. The family is the source for the profound sense of relatedness and mutual regard on which civilization as a whole is predicated. The sentiments originally nurtured within the family are the same that guide all of the transactions of human life. The private life of the family is based on an affirmation of human interrelatedness, and such an affirmation is thought to be natural in the public sphere as well. Readers of the *Republic* may be struck with the fact that Plato and Mencius have such different views of the family. For Plato, family is a narrow and constricted environment that contrasts with the public world of the *polis*; in Mencius's view, it is the source and matrix for humane attitudes that are to be extended outward in widening circles of concern.

Another factor involved in Mencius's view of the continuity of private and public life is his conviction that human nature is universal and that human beings are essentially alike. The belief that human beings are fundamentally similar and mutually responsive tends to link the private and the public spheres: people are expected to have, on the one hand, the same fundamental needs and wants and, on the other, the same potential for recognizing themselves in others. As Mencius argues in interviews with several rulers, the humaneness of rulers involves the recognition of a shared humanity; the reciprocal of this is that the subjects of a humane ruler can be counted on to recognize and support him as such. The problem of ethical and political life is to encourage individuals and rulers alike to fulfill the potential of their natures by playing their allotted roles as well as possible. This always involves affirming their interrelatedness.

Not only the connection between private and public spheres but also the connection between the lofty idealism and the intense realism of Mencius may be discovered in his commitment to *ren*, variously translated as goodness, benevolence, or humaneness. *Ren* is the term that expresses the notion of interrelatedness in its moral dimension. The Chinese character for *ren* is made up of a radical element denoting a person or the human on the left and, on the right, the number two, a multiplier, suggesting a person together with others or interaction among human beings.

The term was one that Mencius had inherited from Confucius. But when Confucius spoke about *ren*, he would always leave its significance open for further reflection, as though he preferred his hearers to ponder it rather than presume that they could fully grasp it. The term eludes definition, and Confucius seemed intent on our appreciating this. Mencius builds on the vision of human relatedness found in the *Analects*, and says much more about *ren*, making it almost possible to grasp, though certainly not to exhaust, its meaning. It emerges that *ren* involves moral responsiveness, being able to put oneself in the position of the other, being able to recognize oneself in the other. Rather than personal attributes or qualities that we possess as individuals, it involves the quality of the interactions to which we are party. We may glimpse a kind of "golden rule" here, but it becomes clear that it is a matter of empathy more than precept.

In a sense, the *Mencius* is a more public text than the *Analects*. Mencius may have been as complex and multifaceted a personality as the Confucius that we encounter in the *Analects*, but we do not observe him, as we do Confucius, in intimate and personal exchanges with his disciples, nor do we discover him in moments of informality or striking personal candor. Mencius usually appears to us, as in the opening chapters of the work, in direct exchanges with rulers of the contending feudal states of the time or at occasions, apparently rather formal in character, when he is engaged in encounters with memorable antagonists over major philosophical questions. His discussions of *ren* come up first in the context of his conversations with rulers of several of the feudal states of the late Zhou period. In these conversations, Mencius tries to convey to them what constitutes humane government, how the ruler may recognize in himself the impulse to humaneness, and why a humane government is bound to be effective.

To return now to the conversation between Mencius and the aged and besieged King Hui of Liang with which the text opens: recall that the king has suggested hopefully that Mencius, who has just arrived in Liang, must have journeyed there prepared with strategies for profiting the state. Mencius dismisses this question as inappropriate, contending with the utmost conviction that "profit," as a motive, must prove divisive and destructive. Once the ruler begins to think in terms of "profit," everyone in the state, from the ministers to the common people, will do the same. When every-one thinks in terms of profit, the common good will have been forgotten, and there can be no greater loss than this. The conclusion is that "all that matters is that there should be humaneness and rightness. What is the point of mentioning the word 'profit'?"

We may note that, in advancing such an argument, Mencius articulated a view with as much moral resonance as any in Confucian teaching. Echo-ing and reechoing in virtually all later Confucian discourse is the idea that what ultimately matters in human interaction is the motivation of the ac-tors and their capacity for mutual respect and regard based on recognition of a common humanity. This common humanity is understood to be vari-ously expressed by individuals performing distinct roles and confronting the different circumstances of life according to the complementary principle of *yi* or rightness, a complex idea of what is right in particular situations cou-pled with a sense of the judgment required to ensure appropriate behavior.

The depth of Mencius's interest in human motivation and commitment to the ethical complementarity of *ren* and *yi* becomes clear when his central concerns are set against the most compelling alternative views of the time. One of these was Legalism. Though Mencius lived before the time of Han Fei, who produced the classic distillation of Legalist thought in the late third century B.C.E., the hard-bitten approach to the problems of govern-ment that came to be labeled "the school of laws" had already been current for several centuries. Mencius, when conversing with various rulers of the time, does not allude to Legalist philosophy per se, but it is clear that he is arguing, at least indirectly, against the kind of tough-minded *Realpolitik* that appealed to many who were dedicated to advancing the interests of their states in an age of bitter contention and brutal warfare. The Legalists, in their pragmatism, their exaltation of military might, their reliance on the coercive force of laws and punishments, their contempt for culture, and their almost exclusive concern with the advantage or "profit" of rulers, show little concern for the capacity for moral responsiveness that, for Mencius, is the very essence of being human.

Many of Mencius's pronouncements about humaneness and rightness are targeted at rulers who seem both skeptical of what he has to say and steeped in an alternative, and much less generous, set of values. It is no doubt a measure of his absolute confidence in the rightness and cogency of his own moral standpoint that he is direct to the point of acerbity in making his case with several rulers against the squandering of life and resources in warfare and belligerence. Nor has he any compunction about informing King Xuan of Qi, who may well have had some sensitivity on this score, that there is no moral principle that precludes the ousting of a ruler who "mutilates humaneness and cripples rightness." Mencius insists that, historically, it was extreme corruption that led to the overthrow of the last ruler of the Xia dynasty by the Shang founder and, in turn, of the last ruler of the Shang by the Zhou founders. These acts, having been morally justified, were not regicide but merely the "punishment" of rulers who had done violence against others and against their own humanity (1B:8). This judgment, often understood as representing a defense by Mencius of a "right of revolution," was no doubt intended to apply to only the most extreme circumstances. However, given the high moral standards proposed by Mencius for any ruler, it is hardly surprising that many throughout the centuries have been made decidedly uneasy by it.

Philosophically speaking, Mencius identifies his primary antagonists as the adherents of the schools of Yang Zhu and Mo Zi (3B:9). Yang Zhu, sometimes characterized as an individualist, evidently defended the individual's withdrawal from public life or from official service in the interests of self-preservation. As Mencius understood him, Yang saw the individual as appropriately self-regarding, a view that Confucians would consistently condemn as morally vacant. Mozi, often described as a utilitarian, espoused a morality predicated on the idea that a purely rational calculation of personal advantage should prompt everyone to adopt the imperative of universal love, or love without discrimination. Such love, which was to be extended to everyone equally, and correspondingly to be received from everyone equally, without regard to the primacy of familial bonds, put morality at a remove from the familial context that Confucians believed was its natural source and matrix.

For Mencius, Yang Zhu's view involved the denial of one's ruler, and Mozi's, the denial of one's parents. Because his own morality was based on a conception of the subtlety and richness of the human moral sense, which is rooted in the deepest dimensions of biological and psychic life and its ramifications in the whole of human experience, both of these represented a denial of what he took to be truly human:

If the way of Yang and the way of Mo are not stopped and the Way of Confucius is not made manifest, the people will be deluded by perverse views and humaneness and rightness will be blocked. When humaneness and rightness are blocked, then we lead animals to devour humans, and humans to devour one another. I am alarmed about this and am determined to defend the way of the former sages by opposing Yang and Mo.

Profit, whether it is understood to entail the advantage of an individual, a ruler, or the state as a whole, is rejected by Mencius as an appropriate motive for action. But that profit is rejected as a motive does not mean that any concession is made in regard to the potential efficacy of humane government. It is clear from conversations that Mencius has with King Hui, his successor King Xiang, King Xuan of Qi, and others that he is convinced that it is the complementarity of humaneness and rightness that finally "works." Any narrower calculation of what might be advantageous to a ruler or even to a state as a whole is bound ultimately to be self-defeating, because such a calculation fails to encourage mutual regard and fellow feeling, impulses that lead in the direction of *ren* and are conducive to that most enduringly important of all political phenomena, human unity.

Ren, for Mencius, involves more than a disposition of the mind and heart. It is that, but it also necessarily carries over into action and, in the case of a ruler, into policy. Mencius's awareness that people share basic needs for food, clothing, shelter, and education is reflected in an active interest in the ruler's policies in the areas of landholding, taxation, famine relief, the establishment of schools, hunting, arboriculture, and sericulture (1A:3, 2A:5, 3A:3). In the measures he advocates, Mencius seems considerably more specific than the Mohists in projecting what must be done by a ruler in order to provide for these needs on a long-term basis. And whereas the Mohists are concerned almost as much as the Legalists with the mobilization and control of the people in order to stave off disorder, always underlying Mencius's philosophy of government is a concern with motivation and with moral authority. Such authority depends above all on the ruler's ability to empathize with his people and to exercise "the transforming influence of morality" (2A:3).

The ability to exercise a "transforming influence" is the mark of a sage. What makes it possible for a sage to perform such a function is that human beings are highly responsive to one another, and they are responsive because they are both alike by nature and aware of this likeness. They differ, according to Mencius, primarily owing to the environment in which they are nurtured. In one of the many passages in the *Mencius* that employ agricultural analogies of plants and growing things (6A:7), the human condition is likened to that of seeds that grow more or less well depending on the richness of the soil, the regularity of the rain and dew, and the amount of human effort invested in cultivation. "Now things of the same kind are all alike. Why should we have doubts when it comes to man? The sage and I are of the same kind." Not only are human beings similar by nature, but they are also capable of growing to the kind of perfection exemplified by the sages Yao and Shun of antiquity.

When we survey the history of Confucian thought, Mencius was unquestionably the single most influential contributor to a view of human nature that ultimately became dominant not only in China but in the rest of Confucianized East Asia as well, and not only in the thought of an intellectual and social elite but in the value system of an entire culture. It is a view quite different from that of the Biblical religions, which share a conception of human beings as inherently flawed and having to struggle to reverse the distance between themselves and God, a defect that entered the Western definition of humanness almost at the beginning of human history. Mencius, for his part, does not delve into the creation of the universe and of man. By the time he begins his reflections, both are understood to be in place, human history to be well underway, and the patterns of human behavior and relationship already set. Mencius begins with the here and now and with the actual lives of his contemporaries, all of whom, he finds, have within themselves the potential for goodness.

The evidence he adduces, in perhaps the most celebrated passage in the work (2A:6), rests on a single powerful example. "All men," he says, "have a mind (or heart) which cannot bear to see the sufferings of others."

> I say that all men have a mind which cannot bear to see the sufferings of others, knowing that any of our contemporaries, seeing a child about to fall into a well, will without exception experience a feeling of alarm and distress. They will feel so, not so as to gain the favor of the child's parents, nor so as to seek the praise of their neighbors and friends, nor from dislike of the reputation of having been unmoved by such a thing.

Mencius does not need to tell us what the person who sees the child teetering on the edge of a well will do. We ourselves fill this in out of our own humanity. We recognize that all human beings can be counted on, insofar as they retain their humanity, to act on the spontaneous impulse to save the child by pulling it from danger.

According to Mencius, the human mind or heart that cannot bear to see the sufferings of others is, in a positive sense, compassion. "Whoever is devoid of the mind of compassion is not human," he says. Then he extends the argument considerably by adding: "Whoever is devoid of the mind of shame is not human, whoever is devoid of the mind of courtesy and modesty is not human, and whoever is devoid of the mind of right and wrong is not human." These four—compassion, shame, courtesy and modesty, and the sense of right and wrong—he calls the "four beginnings" or the "four seeds" of virtue. These he believes are present in every human being.

As promptings of the mind or heart, as sentiments, these inclinations are not confirmed or complete at any given point in a person's life. Developing them is a matter of experience, effort, and cultivation, but they are always there as a potential. The sense of compassion Mencius recognizes as the beginning of humaneness; the sense of shame, the beginning of rightness; the sense of modesty, the beginning of propriety; and the sense of right and wrong, the beginning of wisdom. These promptings are present in every person, without exception. As Mencius puts it:

> Human beings have these four beginnings just as they have their four limbs. When one who has these four beginnings, says of himself that he cannot develop them, he acts as a thief to himself, and one who says of his prince that he cannot develop them, acts as a thief to his prince. We have these four beginnings within us, and if we know how to develop and complete them, it will be like a fire starting to burn or a spring beginning to come through. By bringing them to completion, we are able to protect all within the four seas. In failing to bring them to completion, we have not even the wherewithal to serve our parents.

One may cultivate the "four beginnings" in oneself, or one may not. If one does not, one injures oneself and one's intimates quite as much as others. By even expressing skepticism about the moral capacity of another, one injures that person—one literally steals from him something that is his and that is precious.

Some may notice that when Mencius speaks of the "beginnings" of virtue—compassion, for example—he is referring to affective or emotional responses. He believes "thinking" or "reflection" to be distinctively human, but nowhere does he speak of a distinct faculty of reason, nor does he separate "thinking" from the emotions, desires, and appetites. In fact, the terms "mind" and "heart" are not distinguished in Chinese. There is just one word—*xin*. There is also no mind-body dualism here, suggesting that Mencius stands at the beginning of a philosophical tradition that was to be quite different from the one that evolved in the West from Plato to Spinoza. Nor does Mencius make any mention of a soul, which, of course, again separates him from Plato, for whom the essential person is, finally, the soul.

As we get further into it, we realize that Mencius's conception of the human is different from that found in the Biblical or Platonic traditions. Mencius does not analyze human beings in terms of distinct components: body, mind, soul. The human moral capacity derives, in this view, not from some still, small voice within us that guides us toward the right and away from the wrong but from a kind of energy that is built up within ourselves over the course of our entire experience and education. When he speaks about his personal strengths, he understands them to be an insight into language, in other words, a capacity for communication; and skill in cultivating his "flood-like *qi*" (or, as one translator aptly put it, his "overwhelming energy"). This energy belongs to every living thing. In humans, it is, as he says,

> in the highest degree, vast and unyielding. Nourish it with integrity and place no obstacle in its path and it will fill the space between Heaven and Earth. It is *ch'i* [*qi*] which unites rightness and the Way. Deprive it of these and it will collapse. It is born of accumulated rightness and cannot be appropriated by anyone through a sporadic show of rightness. Whenever one acts in a way that falls below the standard in one's heart, it will collapse.   (2A:2)

Mencius is arguing in this case against his principal antagonist, Gaozi, who maintains (6A:4) that whereas humaneness is internal, rightness is external, something assimilated through learning or conditioning but not inherently in us as part of our nature. Mencius for his part sees that rightness—doing what is right in given circumstances—is related to our psychophysical energy, to our feelings of vitality and well-being, and to our positive sense of identity as persons. Doing right, and doing so consistently, not sporadically, bears on our stamina and affects the energy with which we lead our lives. It is associated with a sense of human dignity, which prompts us to do certain things and to refrain from doing others. It suggests certain priorities that on grounds of simple self-interest might be unintelligible. This qi, or psychophysical energy, which Mencius would have us carefully and actively cultivate, is powerful yet fragile, dependent on and sensitive to the quality and rightness of our moral lives.

Later Chinese philosophy owes an enormous debt to Mencius. No small part of this debt is for enlarging and clarifying the very sense of what it means to be human—a sense that is quite definite and particular yet also consciously open and rich with possibilities. "Humaneness is what it means to be human," he says. "When these two are conjoined, the result is 'the Way'" (7B:16). "Humaneness is the mind of man, and rightness his road" (6A:11). However the concepts of humaneness and rightness were interpreted and reinterpreted following Mencius, they would always imply the primary value of the dignity of persons and, particularly, the connectedness among them and the directedness in their moral lives. It is as if the work of Confucius—which involved drawing attention to the natural equality of human beings, their fundamental relatedness, and their ability to control their own lives through learning and effort—was confirmed by Mencius.

It was also furthered by him through his remarkable psychological insight and his secure sense for the scope of the human enterprise. There is in Mencius a deepened confidence concerning the place of human beings in the universe. Near the end of the text that bears his name he speaks about the relation of human beings to nature or to the universe as a whole: "One who gives full realization to his mind (or heart) understands his own nature, and by knowing his own nature, knows Heaven. Preserving one's mind and nourishing one's nature is the way to serve Heaven" (7A:1).

Here the word that has been translated as "Heaven" may also be understood as Nature or the natural process as a whole. Following on his affirmation of the connectedness among persons past and present, such an affirmation of the connectedness between human beings and the universe is rich with possibilities. Is this a kind of mysticism, we wonder? Idealism? Possibly even realism? The categories themselves begin to seem arbitrary, perhaps a little hollow. What is clear is that Mencius's conception of the human is essentially biological and his conception of Nature, a biosphere in which everything is mutually interreactive. His affirmation of the connectedness among persons and between human beings and the universe as a whole has had a long and fruitful career in East Asia. It may have much to say to the modern West as well.

Note

1. Robert Alter and Frank Kermode, eds., *A Literary Guide to the Bible* (Cambridge: Belknap Press of Harvard University Press, 1987), 422.

5

Laozi

Franciscus Verellen

T HE *LAOZI* IS a short collection of aphorisms that probably took shape in the fourth century B.C.E. The oldest extant version of the *Laozi* was discovered in 1993, inscribed on a bundle of bamboo slips, in a late fourth-century B.C.E. tomb in Guodian, Hubei. Two silk manuscripts discovered in 1973 in a tomb in Mawangdui near Changsha, Hunan, date from the beginning of the second century B.C.E. The oldest extant commentaries on the *Laozi* are found in the book of Hanfeizi (d. 233 B.C.E.). The commentary by Wang Bi (226–249 C.E.), some five centuries after the *Hanfeizi*, is the earliest to which both a date and an author may be confidently assigned. By the end of the Tang, in a preface dated 901 C.E., a scholiastic editor of the official commentary promulgated by Emperor Xuanzong (r. 712–756) listed no fewer than sixty-one commentators preceding him. Today, the number of commentaries is said to exceed two hundred.

For all its brevity and mystery, the *Laozi* indeed constitutes one of the most challenging, intriguing, and influential sets of propositions put forward in the history of both Chinese philosophy and religion. Over the last century, several probing translations and many popular renditions have secured for it a permanent place in the literature of the West as well. One reason for this abiding interest and the perennial supply of reinterpretations is suggested in the *Laozi* itself: "My words are very easy to understand and very easy to practice. In the whole world nobody is able to understand them and nobody is able to practice them" (chap. 70).

Interpretations are indeed apt to differ between any two individuals, let alone readers widely separated by intellectual background and historical period. The quotations from the *Laozi* in this brief introduction reflect my own interpretations while also drawing on translations of the relevant passages by Wing-tsit Chan, J. J. L. Duyvendak, Max Kaltenmark, Bernhard Karlgren, D. C. Lau, and Arthur Waley.

The Laozi Legend in Antiquity

Despite the remarkable discovery of the ancient manuscripts at Guodian and Mawangdui, the history of Laozi teaching prior to the compilation of the work bearing his name remains difficult to ascertain. Already by former Han times (206 B.C.E.–8 C.E.), the most circumstantial biographical account of the sage consisted of a composite legend incorporating episodes from the lives of several distinct figures. These early traditions about Laozi's career and reluctant bequest of his teaching to the world serve at any rate as indications of the views held by an early school of followers concerning their founder and the transmission of his teaching during the Warring States period (475–221 B.C.E.).

The main elements of the ancient legend are as follows: the real name of Laozi, to whom several early texts also refer as Lao Dan, was Li Er or Li Dan. He was a native of Huxian in the state of Chu, not far from modern Boxian (Anhui), and the site has been officially revered as Laozi's birthplace since Han times. He is said to have served as curator of archives under the Eastern Zhou (770–256) in Luoyang.

An alleged visit by Confucius (551–479), and Laozi's lofty rebuke of his interlocutor, afforded an opportunity for polemics between the rival schools. A later polemic, Laozi's "conversion of the [Western] barbarians," suggested that Buddhism was nothing but a return of Laozi's teachings in India and aimed to challenge the independent status of Buddhism in China. Eventually, Laozi departed from the court of the declining Zhou to journey to Kunlun, the mythical sacred mountain of the Western regions. On the point of leaving the Middle Kingdoms, however, Laozi was detained by the guardian of the Hangu Pass, a hundred miles west of Luoyang. This discerning officer, named Yin Xi, persuaded the sage to impart his teaching, which he then committed to writing. The result, the *Book of Five Thousand* [Characters] (*Wu-qien wen*), as the *Laozi* also came to be known, was thus procured and transmitted by Yin Xi.

The Way and Virtue

The third traditional title for the work is *Daodejing*, or "Classic of Dao and De." The two silk manuscripts from Mawangdui mentioned above confirm the division of the ancient text into two sections, though arranged in the reverse order—"De" followed by "Dao." One of the two manuscripts actually features those terms as headings.

Bibliographic considerations aside, the concepts "Way" (*dao*) and "Virtue" (*de*), the latter in the sense of "inherent power" or "operative influence," are indeed central to the philosophy of the *Laozi*. A direct relationship between the two is often implied by translating the pair as "the Way and its Virtue (or power)." The opening lines of the *Laozi* read: "The Way that can be defined is not the unchanging Way. The name that can be named is not the unchanging name. Nameless, [the Way] is at the origin of Heaven and Earth. Having a name, it is the mother of all things" (chap. 1).

The ineffable eternal Dao, which existed before the universe, also has a particular, manifest aspect that is inherent in all things constituting the phenomenal world. As such, it is endowed with qualities. Hence it is capable of being conceptualized, and it is subject to change: "There was something formless but complete which existed prior to Heaven and Earth. Soundless and indistinct, it stands alone, unchanging; it pervades all, unfailing. It can be regarded as the mother of all things. We do not know its name but style it 'Dao.' If I were compelled to name it, I would say 'Da' (the Great)" (chap. 25).

Because the eternal Dao is devoid of the qualities of phenomenal existence, termed *yu* (literally "to have"), the *Laozi* attributes to it the quality of nothingness, *wu* (literally "not to have"). Nothingness, in contrast to "non-being," harbors the potential of every thing: "The Dao is empty, yet it can be used without ever being filled. How deep it is: the ancestor of all things!" (chap. 4).

The terms "valley," "mother," and "womb" stand in the *Laozi* for the receptivity and potential productivity of emptiness (*xu*), as do also various hollow implements: "The space between Heaven and Earth is like a bellows or a flute: though empty, it is inexhaustible. In operation, it produces ever more" (chap. 5). "Thirty spokes make a wheel, yet the use of the cart depends on that which does not contain anything [i.e., the hub]. We shape clay to make a vessel, yet the use of the vessel depends on that which does not contain anything" (chap. 11).

If, as we have said, the Dao in its aspect of nothingness harbors the potential of all things, then Virtue, De, is the aspect of Dao that lends specific potency to each particular thing or being. In man, De is, for example, the skill necessary to perform a specific task. "Skillful action leaves no trace, skillful speech is unblemished, a skilled reckoner uses no tallies, a well-closed [door] needs neither bolts nor bars yet cannot be opened, a well-tied knot needs neither rope nor twine yet cannot be loosened" (chap. 27).

It is also the moral influence that causes one to hold sway over fellow men. The true possessor of De is unaware of Virtue and never strives to use it to advantage: "Superior Virtue does not [pretend to] Virtue; thereby Virtue is possessed. Inferior Virtue does not disregard Virtue; thereby Virtue is not possessed. Superior Virtue does not act, but has no reason to act. Inferior Virtue acts, but has its [ulterior] reasons for acting" (chap. 38).

In the examples of De as skill quoted above from chapter 27, the practitioner refrains from imposing himself or any extraneous means on his work. In fact, his ability to recognize the operative principle inherent in a thing or situation allows him to utilize its natural, spontaneous (*ziran*) efficacy, unhampered by his interference. This is the mode of efficacious action of the Dao itself, which the *Laozi* literally calls "absence of [purposive] action" (*wu-wei*) and which might usefully be rendered as "nonintervention": "The Dao never acts, yet nothing is left undone. If lords and princes adhered to this [principle], all things would evolve spontaneously" (chap. 37).

Before examining some topical aspects of Laozi's application of *wu-wei* to political theory, we shall consider for a moment another approach to his philosophy of Dao, De, and *wu-wei* that suggests a rather different dimension to the work.

Laozi as Mystic

In the last phrase of the opening section of the *Laozi*, in its present arrangement, the chapter's cryptic pronouncements concerning the eternal Dao and the different existential modes decidedly adopt the language of mystical contemplation: "Together, [*wu* and *yu*] are called mysterious (*xuan*), the mystery of mysteries, the gate to all wonders" (chap. 1).

The notion of the ineffable eternal Dao ("The Way that can be defined is not the unchanging Way," etc.) itself evokes the familiar theme in mystical literature of the unchanging and undifferentiated first principle in which everything coexists simultaneously, as One: "I find only an undifferentiated

Unity. . . . Indiscernible, it cannot be named" (chap. 14). From the One proceed all of creation, and the One proceeds from the Dao: "Dao produced the One. The One produced the two. Two produced the three. And three produced the ten thousand things" (chap. 42).

For many mystics, the postulate of unity, the idea that everything is ultimately one, has given rise to the expectation of *gnosis*, the possibility of an esoteric knowledge of spiritual mysteries, if not of union with the Absolute. The *Laozi* is a case in point:

> Attain complete emptiness and hold fast to quiescence. All things arise together. I thereby witness their return. Creatures flourish profusely, but each returns to its root. To return to one's root means quiescence, quiescence is the return to one's destiny, the return to one's destiny is called the Eternal. To know the Eternal is called illumination. Not to know the Eternal is to act in vain and invite misfortune.   (chap. 16)

Laozi's law of the return to the origin appears to be universal. There is no conclusive evidence that the work reflects the cult of immortality that was to flourish under the Han. It does, however, emphasize the ideal of longevity attainable through a regime of spiritual and physical discipline, in particular quiescence and yoga-like techniques of breath control (chap. 10).

Paradoxical discourse, a feature of prophetic and mystical writings in many traditions, is another way in which the *Laozi* draws the reader into a mystical mode of enquiry and apprehension: strong is weak and vice versa; female, soft, and passive prevail over male, hard, and active; water, the most pliant of elements, endures; single drops in time penetrate the hardest rock; the dark valley is where the waters gather; the low and submissive are exalted, the proud and exalted brought low; the infant and the "uncarved block" are symbols of the power to become; the obscure "spirit of the valley" is the mystical matrix of the creative and productive forces of the Dao.

In this context, *wu-wei* becomes mystical quiescence: not absolute stillness but nonresistance to the Way, as water runs its course, passively but inexorably, in compliance with the law of gravity and the lay of the land.

Classical Daoism

The term "Daoist" (*daojia*) originated as a category of ancient books in the imperial library of the Former Han dynasty. In the catalogue *Qilüe* (6 B.C.E), it designated the branch of philosophical learning that included the *Laozi*. Han sources also mention the doctrine of Huang-Lao (named after the mythical Yellow Emperor Huangdi and Laozi), which enjoyed considerable influence up to the reign of Emperor Wudi (140–87 B.C.E). The textual traditions associated with the terms *daojia* and Huang-Lao constitute the classical corpus of Taoist literature.

Though it is an open question to what extent Han bibliographical classifications reflected historical movements as well as sets of texts, it is useful to consider the teaching of the *Laozi* against the background of some of the rival schools of political philosophy that flourished during the Warring States period.

Philosophical debate in the mid-third century B.C.E. was characterized by intense competition for the implementation of theories of statecraft addressing such topics as military tactics, economic policy, and law and administration. In 221 B.C.E., both the practical and the theoretical aspects of this contention came to a head with the foundation of the Qin empire, the first to unite all of China under one rule.

The strategy of the successful state of Qin was based on policies proposed by the Legalists (*fajia*), a school that advocated the administration of a rigorous system of penal law to control every aspect of society and the state. While the nature and extent of the interaction between Daoist and Legalist thought remain to be fully explored, the major tenet of Legalism was plainly in conflict with the *Laozi*'s policy of government by nonintervention: "The more laws and ordinances are promulgated, the more thieves and robbers there will be" (chap. 57).

Half of the occurrences of the term *wu-wei* in the *Laozi* refer explicitly to laissez-faire governmental policies. Many additional passages convey the same advice. The famous line "governing a large kingdom is like cooking small fish" (that is, don't overdo it) from chapter 60 was appropriately adduced by a recent U.S. president advocating "small government."

In a passage that parallels the examples of skillful work cited above from chapter 27, the *Lao Tzu* requires a successful leader to refrain from coercion: "A skillful commander does not seem martial, a skillful warrior does not display anger, a skillful victor does not contend, a skillful user of men humbles himself. This is called the Virtue of not contending" (chap. 68).

The *Laozi* regretfully admits the necessity of certain military operations (chap. 69). Despite its visions of a utopian society living in peace, harmony, self-sufficiency, and simple contentment (chap. 47), its political attitudes are on the whole pragmatic, and its mystical insights, rather than denying worldly reality, claim a "truer" grasp of the sources and exercise of power.

Although Legalism briefly won the day in 221 B.C.E., the only ancient indigenous school of thought with which Daoism was to contend beyond the Han period was Confucianism. It would appear that the compilers of the *Laozi* were already taking issue with some of the positions of Confucianism, for example, in rejecting the importance that Confucians attached to humaneness (*ren*) and morality and to learning and education: "When the great Way fell into disuse, humaneness and sense of duty (*i*) arose. When intellect and cleverness appeared, great falsehood came into being. When the six relations of kinship were in disharmony, filial piety and parental love came into being. When the state fell into anarchy, loyal subjects came into being" (chap. 18).

Consistent with the above and in striking contrast to Confucian thinking is the *Laozi*'s insistence on the indifference of both the cosmic powers and the sage (*shengren*) to human affairs: "Heaven and Earth are not humane. They treat the ten thousand creatures as [sacrificial] straw dogs. Sages are not humane. They treat the people as straw dogs" (chap. 5).

In a similar vein, the *Laozi* seemed to condemn the Confucian ideals of government through moral influence, by means of education (chap. 65), and through the performance of rites (chap. 38). Perhaps on a more fundamental level, however, the *Laozi* raised the question of the comparative values of the active and the contemplative roles of the sage (*sheng*) in human society, an issue eventually incorporated and reexamined over the centuries within the Confucian tradition itself.

Laozi in Medieval Thought and Religion

Favored by the Huang-Lao tradition and by association with messianic movements devoted to the fall of the Later Han dynasty (25–220 C.E.), the Laozi legend took a dramatic turn in the second century with the apotheosis of the founder as a cosmic deity titled Most High Lord Lao (Taishang laojun). By the end of the century, the *Laozi* had accordingly attained the status of a revealed scripture and was the object of fervent recitations by followers of Heavenly Master Daoism in western China.

The third century saw the celebrated syncretic revival of Daoist and Confucian philosophy under the Xuanxue school led by Wang Bi. The name of this movement, Study of Mysteries, was inspired by the passage in chapter 1 of the *Laozi* quoted above ("Together, [*wu* and *yu*] are called mysterious . . . "). Wang Bi's principal contribution consisted in a refinement of Laozi's theory of the existential modes *wu* and *yu*, coupled with the complementary concepts of "substantiality" (*ti*) and "functionality" (*yong*).

Following its encounter with Confucian thought in *xuanxue*, Daoist philosophy entered in the fourth century into an ongoing intellectual exchange with Mahāyāna Buddhism, on the subject of existential and ontological issues (on which Chinese Buddhists brought a rich Indian legacy to bear) and in the area of mystical gnosis and meditation techniques. The resulting interpenetration of Buddhist and Daoist ideas in the latter domain was to become instrumental to the development of Chan (Zen) Buddhism under the Tang (618–907).

The ruling Li clan of the Tang dynasty declared Laozi their ancestor. Emperor Xuanzong, promulgator of the official commentary mentioned above, canonized the *Laozi* as the most important scripture recognized by the state, to be revered throughout the empire. Under the Tang, the *Laozi* also became a civil-service examination text.

In medieval China, and to the present day, the *Laozi* continued to be regarded as the fundamental religious scripture of Daoism. The ancient category of *daojia* philosophers had since Han times assumed the new meaning of "Daoist clergy." In the fifth century, the religious tradition based on the early Heavenly Master movement in Sichuan, and incorporating subsequent scriptural and liturgical developments, codified its teaching into a structured Daoist Canon with a division consecrated to the *Laozi*.

By Tang times, a uniform ordination system had evolved that linked the initiation into each grade of the hierarchy to the transmission of a set body of sacred texts, including the *Daodejing*. The transmission of the *Laozi* thus became institutionalized as part of an esoteric instruction passed on from Daoist master to disciple.

6

ZHUANGZI

Paul Contino

I ONCE TOOK a memorable class called "Liberation" with a teacher who was something of a Daoist sage. He could lecture to a class of sixty-five students and be attuned to each person in the hall. At times he would be passionately elucidating an abstract concept and would notice confusion—some scrunched-up faces, a few furrowed brows. And he'd respond: "Don't fret about the words; just get the music."[1] In other words, pay attention, but stay loose; don't get tight with "muscular effort."[2] Simone Weil contrasts such tightness with the "negative effort" entailed in attention: "Attention consists of suspending our thought, leaving it detached, empty, and ready to be penetrated by the object. . . . Above all our thought should be empty, waiting, not seeking anything, but ready to receive in its naked truth the object that is to penetrate it."

I think of Weil's essay on attentiveness whenever I teach Zhuangzi. I was reminded of my teacher when rereading the final words of Burton Watson's edition[3] of the work: "Words exist because of meaning; once you've gotten the meaning, you can forget the words. Where can I find a man who has forgotten words so I can have a word with him?" (140). Words do matter for Zhuangzi—after all, he employs them—but the "music" matters more. Further, these final lines reprise Zhuangzi's recurring note of paradoxical humor. Students laugh at passages like this and others in the text: they enjoy Zhuangzi the joker. But then they run the risk of not taking him seriously. If, however, they make an earnest effort to understand him, his persistent disruption of conventional wisdom may irritate them. Students can resist by asking questions and challenging his claims. "People suppose that words are different from the peeps of baby birds, but is there any difference, or isn't there?" (34); if words are dispensable, why attend to Zhuangzi's? "Those who discriminate fail to see" (39); if the scholarly task of making precise distinctions is folly, why pursue academic study? When Zhuangzi's wife dies, he is found "sitting with his legs sprawled out, pounding on a tub and singing" (113): how can he so cavalierly dispense with ritual (*li*), which is intrinsic to the Confucian conception of humanity? Why does he refer to a human being as "a thing [among other things]" (84)? If wisdom is to "leave the confusion and muddle as it is" (42), if the path to happiness lies in non-doing, why invest in studious effort, especially with a text as baffling as Zhuangzi's? "The paths of right and wrong are hopelessly snarled and jumbled" (41); if Zhuangzi refuses to distinguish between them, isn't he a moral relativist? Since Zhuangzi counsels indifference toward "likes or dislikes" (72), isn't he advocating apathy?

Even for scholars of ancient Chinese philosophy, these remain legitimate, perennial questions.[4] But Zhuangzi offers a way of pursuing them that relaxes the furrowed brow and invites a deep "breathing with [one's] heels" (74). Indeed, he offers a way of life applicable to students grown cramped and anxious in their studies—especially when midterms and finals loom closer. "Relax," counsels Zhuangzi—open yourself to the unexpected and inexorable mutations of reality. If you do, you may experience liberation (to hearken back to the college course I mentioned). Zhuangzi uses humor to humble his readers, to bring them down to earth, the "humus." He baffles them with the aim of activating their "negative capability," the state described by John Keats in an 1817 letter to his brother: "when man is capable of being in uncertainties, mysteries, doubts, without any irritable reaching after fact & reason."[5] Living in the fourth century B.C.E., in the thick of China's hazardous Warring States period, Zhuangzi witnessed the irritable reaching after fact and reason among court scholars and advisors—and saw that it could cost them their lives. He saw people striving simply to be acknowledged, applauded, and rewarded. But "seekers of fame and gain" are destroyed (52). At the very least, the egocentric desire to impress and possess and to insistently assert one's limited perspective blinds one to larger reality. Further, the insistent assertion of will, especially in reaction to situations in which the will meets its limits, only shrivels it and depletes the life force (*qi*). As Zhuangzi writes: "If you use what is limited to pursue what has no limit, you will be in danger" (46); "do not hobble your will or you will be departing from the Way!" (103).

One of the most memorable books we read in the "Liberation" class was Leslie Farber's *Ways of the Will*, the themes of which cohere with Zhuangzi's.[6] As a therapist, Farber sought to free people of the anxiety wrought by willfulness. He observes the numerous states that we may desire but cannot will, situations with which we can only be in a receptive, open relationship. Farber distinguishes between "two realms of the will": one "moves us toward a particular objective. . . . This could be said to be a utilitarian will, in that we do this to get that" (78), and is roughly equivalent to *yu-wei* action, a term familiar to the philosophers of Zhuangzi's day, meaning "deliberate, analytic, and goal-oriented thought and action."[7] The other realm "moves in a direction rather than toward a particular object" (77) and is related to the Daoist emphasis upon *wu-wei*, "unpremeditated, nondeliberative, noncalculating, nonpurposive action (or, more accurately, behavior)."[8] Farber offers helpful examples to illustrate the two realms of the will:

> I can will knowledge, but not wisdom; going to bed, but not sleeping; eating but not hunger; meekness, but not humility; scrupulosity, but not virtue; self-assertion or bravado, but not courage; lust, but not love; commiseration, but not sympathy; congratulations, but not admiration; religiosity, but not faith; reading, but not understanding. I would emphasize that the consequence of willing what cannot be willed is that we fall into the distress we call anxiety.[9]

Like Farber, Zhuangzi seeks to free us from the life-depleting anxiety wrought by an overwrought insistence upon *you-wei* action. Zhuangzi offers an alternative to *yu-wei*, a path of open willingness as opposed to rigid willfulness, and the promise that we might—like the sages—harmonize our will with the Dao, the Way. Yet the Way—represented by the Yin/Yang image—is protean, flowing, contrary, often confusing; "'this' and 'that' give birth to each other" constantly (35). Thus, receptive immersion within the Dao necessitates uncertainty if one is to make peace with the chaos. But through a contemplative "fasting of the mind" (54) and the paradoxical practice of *wu-wei*, one can recover the freedom found in forgetting oneself and the negative capability of being receptively alive in the Dao.

To sense that such an experience might occur in one's own life is to take Zhuangzi seriously. And through attentive reading, discussion, and writing, students *do* come to take Zhuangzi seriously. They sense the ways in which his counsel can move them more toward an excellence of effort, in even their most ordinary activities, than they thought possible. In essays and discussion, students can apply Zhuangzi's wisdom to their activities of writing, acting, musical performance, athletic contest, friendship, and love. In this way, among the many classic works, Western and Eastern, that I have been privileged to teach, *Zhuangzi* stands out as one of the most potentially transformative.

"There is a beginning. There is a not yet beginning to be a beginning. There is a not yet beginning to be a not yet beginning to be a beginning" (38). Nevertheless, I will begin with Zhuangzi's beginning, section 1, "Free and Easy Wandering," in which he describes the huge fish Kun, who "becomes a bird whose name is Peng" (23–26). Hearing this, the cicada, little dove, and little quail laugh in derisive disbelief, providing Zhuangzi's first examples of "little understanding [which] cannot come up to great understanding." These three find their human counterpart in an emblematic court official "who has wisdom to fill one office effectively, good conduct enough to impress one community, virtue enough to please one ruler, or talent enough to be called into service in one state, [and] has the same kind of self-pride as these little creatures." From the start, Zhuangzi links "little understanding" not simply (or, perhaps, at all) to the exercise of "good conduct" and "virtue" but, rather, to the quest to "please" and "impress" and to be marked by "self-pride" and "vain show" (34) in acting virtuously. Song Rung-zi also laughs with derision—but his criticism of this petty man reflects his great understanding, as Zhuangzi relates: "The whole world could praise Song Rung-zi and it wouldn't make him exert himself; the whole world could condemn him and it wouldn't make him mope." He is Zhuangzi's first example of the sage, one who "doesn't fret and worry," who "has no self," "has no merit," and "has no fame."

These opening pages, taken as they are from the first of the seven "inner chapters" traditionally ascribed to the hand of Zhuangzi himself, can be usefully read alongside the story of the frog in the caved-in well, from one of the "outer chapters" included by Watson: section 17, "Autumn Floods" (107–109). Here we meet the proud logician Gong-sun Long, who brags about his achievements to the Daoist Prince Mou of Wei. One need only count the number of times that Gong-sun Long uses the word "I" to see how ego ridden and driven by the praise of others he is:

When I was young I studied the Way of the former kings, and when I grew older I came to understand the conduct of benevolence and righteousness. I reconciled difference and sameness, distinguished hardness and whiteness, and proved that not so was so, that the unacceptable was acceptable. I confounded the wisdom of the hundred schools and demolished the arguments of a host of speakers. I believed that I had attained the highest degree of accomplishment. But now I have heard the words of Zhuangzi and I am bewildered by their strangeness. I don't know whether my arguments are not as good as his, or whether I am no match for him in understanding. I find now that I can't even open my beak. May I ask what you advise?

One might see humility in Gong-sun's admission of bafflement and in his seeking of Prince Mou's counsel. But he will use this advice to become Zhuangzi's "match" and, once again, assertively open his "beak." His opening words emphasize the way that he employs his knowledge to "confound" and "demolish" others. Thus Prince Mou's sigh and his laughter when he thinks of Gong-sun's similarity to "the frog in the caved-in well." The frog relishes his diminutive dwelling because he believes that "none of [his fellow creatures] can match [him]." Like Gong-sun, the frog's language is "I"-ridden. His solipsism keeps him from seeing the reality that transcends him; he insists that he can "command" and "monopolize" all he sees. But confronted by the great turtle of the Eastern Sea, the frog soon finds himself "dumfounded with surprise, crestfallen, and completely at a loss." The great turtle never says "I." He simply describes the "greatness," depth, and constancy of the Eastern Sea, in which he abides. The turtle, like Zhuangzi, dwells "in utter freedom" and "dissolves himself in the four directions and drowns himself in the unfathomable." In contrast, Gong-sun seeks "victory" and has "come niggling along [to] try to spy [Zhuangzi] out or fix some name to him," to assert power through linguistic labeling. Prince Mou warns that he had better leave immediately, that his egocentric attempt to will the unwillable will cripple him:

"You'd better be on your way! Or perhaps you've never heard about the young boy of Shou-ling who went to learn the Han-tan Walk. He hadn't mastered what the Han-tan people had to teach him when he forgot his old way of walking, so that he had to crawl all the way back home. Now if you don't get on your way, you're likely to forget what you knew before and be out of a job!" Gong-sun Lung's mouth fell open and wouldn't stay closed. His tongue stuck to the roof of his mouth and wouldn't come down. In the end he broke into a run and fled.

The joke is on Gong-sun, especially as he reveals that his biggest fear is to lose his job. Employment is the source of his *amour propre* (Rousseau's term for self-love bound by social anxieties), to which Gong-sun clings through victory in intellectual combat.

Holding a job is not high among Zhuangzi's priorities. He sees it as almost inevitably leading to the kind of psychic entrapment exemplified by Gong-sun. Nevertheless, Zhuangzi does not simply advise that one quit work, withdraw from society, and take up a solitary existence in the forest (although he himself refuses to "wear himself out over the affairs of the world" [27] and would rather "drag his tail in the mud" [109]). He positively depicts characters who *are* employed but who go about their work in such a manner that they are not distracted by the desire for approval or fame. Through the practice of *wu-wei* action—a way of doing that is "not doing anything," that "let[s] things be" (39)—these characters accomplish work that the blunt assertion of *yu-wei* cannot achieve. Zhuangzi's first example is Cook Ding, whose task of butchering an ox teaches "The Secret of Caring for Life" (section 3, 46–47). Observing the cook, Lord Wen-hui is astounded by his "skill." But, in a typical reversal of hierarchy, Cook Ding corrects his Lord:

> What I care about is the Way, which goes beyond skill. When I first began cutting up oxen, all I could see was the ox itself. After three years I no longer saw the whole ox. And now—I go at it by spirit and don't look with my eyes. Perception and understanding have come to a stop and spirit moves where it wants. I go along with the natural makeup, strike in the big hollows, guide the knife through the big openings, and follow things as they are. So I never touch the smallest ligament or tendon, much less a main joint.

In nineteen years, Ding has never needed to change his knife. But he is no magician. He simply takes care to go along with the Way. Even now he must be careful to keep his ego out of the way:

> However, whenever I come to a complicated place, I size up the difficulties, tell myself to watch out and be careful, keep my eyes on what

I'm doing, work very slowly, and move the knife with the greatest
subtlety, until—flop!—the whole thing comes apart like a clod of earth
crumbling to the ground. I stand there holding the knife and look all
around me, completely satisfied and reluctant to move on, and then I
wipe off the knife and put it away.

I agree with Burton Watson's interpretation that "the extreme care and
caution which the cook uses when he comes to a difficult place is also part
of Zhuangzi's 'secret of caring for life.' " (47, n. 4). In this sense, *wu-wei* holds
a place for *you-wei*. (And vice versa: recall Mencius's story of the farmer from
Sung who impatiently pulls up his rice plants in order to make them grow.
Here, Mencius's Confucian emphasis upon *you-wei* makes room for *wu-wei*—
an understanding of *you-wei* purposive action that must always be guided
by practical wisdom [*zhih*] and thus remain receptive to the real).[10] Furthermore, Cook Ding is careful not to rest complacently in his moment of
achievement. He may be tempted to reify the moment as a tableau for the
sight of others (notice the way he looks around), but, without fuss, he resists
it, cleans his knife, and moves on.

His counterpart is Woodworker Qing, a figure that appears in one of the
outer chapters, "Mastering Life" (section 19, 126–127). This brief story is
well worth recording in full:

Woodworker Qing carved a piece of wood and made a bell stand, and
when it was finished, everyone who saw it marveled, for it seemed to
be the work of gods or spirits. When the marquis of Lu saw it, he
asked, "What art is it you have?"

Qing replied, "I am only a craftsman—how could I have any art?
There is one thing, however. When I am going to make a bell stand, I
never let it wear out my energy. I always fast in order to still my mind.
When I have fasted for three days, I no longer have any thought of
congratulations or rewards, of titles or stipends. When I have fasted
for five days, I no longer have any thought of praise or blame, of skill
or clumsiness. And when I have fasted for seven days, I am so still that
I forget I have four limbs and a form and body. By that time, the ruler
and his court no longer exist for me. My skill is concentrated and all
outside distractions fade away. After that I go into the mountain forest and examine the nature of the trees. If I find one of superlative
form, and I can see a bell stand there, I put my hand to the job of carv-

ing; if not, I let it go. This way I am simply matching up 'Heaven' with 'Heaven.' That's probably the reason that people wonder if the results were not made by spirits."

This story exemplifies the themes that run throughout Zhuangzi's work. It enriches the reader's understanding of three crucial dimensions of the spiritual life—an area that our students, no matter what their religious backgrounds, yearn to explore:[11] the need for the virtue of humility; the way humility opens up a place for receptivity; and the way in which such receptivity can foster a spirit of *wu-wei*—or, to move toward interreligious dialogue, a spirit of prayerful receptivity to the will of God—in any activity in which a person engages.[12]

First notice the parabolic structure of the story. As John Dominick Crossan and others have observed, parables overturn our expectations.[13] Here the Marquis of Lu's expectations are overturned: given the wonder of the woodcarver Qing's artistry, he must have some secret or be employing some kind of magic! Qing teaches the prince humility: "I am only a craftsman." Ch'ing is humble enough to admit that he does practice a process of preparation: he avoids distractions, he fasts, and, in the process, he learns to forget the distractions that feed the anxious quest for "congratulations or rewards, titles or stipends." He even forgets to think about the prince and his court: "The ruler and his court no longer exist for me."

No longer anxious about the way that he and his work will be received by others, Qing is able to be receptive to the reality of his task, his work of crafting the bell stand. He can now perceive the particularity of the tree that is just right, and he remains calm enough to abandon the whole project if that tree does not appear.

Finally, he acts not as a subject acting upon an inert and reified object, not as an "I" willfully imposing his will upon an inanimate "it,"[14] like the emperors boring holes in Hun Tun and, in the process, killing him (95). He is, rather, open to the particular reality of *this* tree—its *haecceitas*, "thisness," to employ Duns Scotus's Latin term. Thus he can perceive its "superlative form." His action thus entails a receptive responding, a doing that is also non-doing.[15]

The three steps exemplified by the woodworker Qing—humility, receptivity, and action marked by *wu-wei*—offer an invaluable way for our students to not only understand Zhuangzi's path of Daoism but to see the way that another religious tradition might deepen an understanding of their own. For example, if the words from Psalm 40, "Here I am Lord, I come to do your will," are crucial to the Jewish and Christian traditions, the simple workman Qing has much to teach our students (and their teachers) as we face the many demands in our work and strive to sustain spiritual lives in the process.[16] In addition, Zhuangzi is pointing to the possibility of finding in our work that which Mikhail Csikszentmihalyi calls "flow":

> The best moments usually occur when a person's body of mind is stretched to its limits in a voluntary effort to accomplish something difficult and worthwhile. . . . Optimal experiences add up to a sense of mastery—or perhaps better, a sense of *participation* in determining the content of life—that comes as close to what is usually meant by happiness as anything else we can conceivably imagine.[17]

Notice his emphasis upon *participation*, which suggests a willing coopera- tion with the way of things as opposed to an assertion of the subjective will.

Qing makes very clear that he must "fast" before he can set out upon his work, and the attentive reader of Zhuangzi will recall the way that the wise Confucius—another delightful and generous Zhuangzian surprise!— counsels his disciple Yen Hui to engage in a meditative "fasting of the mind" before counseling the ruler of Wei:

> "May I ask what the fasting of the mind is?"
>
> Confucius said, "Make your will one! Don't listen with your ears, listen with your mind. No, don't listen with your mind, but listen with your spirit. Listening stops with the ears, the mind stops with recog- nition, but spirit is empty and waits on all things. The Way gathers in emptiness alone. Emptiness is the fasting of the mind."
>
> Yen Hui said, "Before I heard this, I was certain that I was Hui. But now that I have heard it, there is no more Hui. Can this be called emptiness?"
>
> "That's all there is to it," said Confucius. "Now I will tell you. You may go and play in his bird cage, but never be moved by fame. If he listens, then sing; if not keep still. . . . But if you do not keep still—that is what is called racing around."   (54)

Confucius—and Zhuangzi behind him—have no illusions about politi- cal life: most who serve in the court race around in egocentric quests, depleting their energy and truncating their lives. But if Yen Hui can sustain self-forgetfulness, if he can see court life as the "bird cage" that it truly is within the larger scheme of the Dao, and if he can keep still and offer counsel in the spirit of *wu-wei*, then he will succeed in the work he feels called to do and flourish.[18]

If readers can rest in "mysteries, uncertainties, and doubts," Zhuangzi can orient them in the direction of Great Understanding, which is "broad and unhurried" (32). For "words are not just wind" (34), and those of Great Understanding speak words that are "clear and limpid" (32). These contrast with those of "little understanding," "cramped and busy," who employ words that are "shrill and quarrelsome," who "cling to their position as if they had sworn before the gods, sure that they are holding on to victory," and who "dwindle day by day" (32). Zhuangzi can enliven the dwindling spirit. He doesn't reject language, but he recognizes its boundaries, which those engaged in the "Supreme Swindle" willfully ignore by labeling reality from a limited perspective (43). He is less an antirealist than a "perspectival realist," advising that we become aware of our situatedness before insisting that we are absolutely right.[19] He is not so much a deconstructionist as he is respectful of the ineffable, aware that "name is only the guest of reality" (26). He is not a moral relativist; rather, he accepts the "fate" of filial piety and the "duty" (*yi*) of obeying one's ruler as the "two great decrees" (56). But he sees a more virtuous path in "leav[ing] off . . . teaching men virtue," (63) "know[ing] what you can't do anything about, and . . . be[ing] content with it as you would with fate" (66).[20] While resisting the rigidities of propriety, he doesn't so much reject ritual as revise it: the "true man of old" "regarded rites as the wings" (75), but if attunement to the Way dictates singing in the presence of a friend's corpse, he lets it be (82–83). Above all, while suspicious of the active life of employment, he recognizes the way that the spontaneity of *wu-wei* can be brought into the practice of work "in the world of men." Even a king can be enlightened if he lets go of the desire for "promotion or praise" (91–92). Read attentively, Zhuangzi orients the will toward the Way. His words can engage his reader's negative capability and her or his capacity to flourish.

Notes

1. This teacher's name is Edward Weisband. The class was taught in the fall of 1976 at Binghamton University. Weisband currently holds the Edward S. Diggs

Endowed Chair Professorship in the Department of Political Science at Virginia Tech University.

2. Simone Weil, "Reflections on the Right Use of School Studies with a View to the Love of God," in *Waiting for God*, trans. Emma Craufurd (New York: Harper and Row, 1973), 110–112.

3. *Chuang Tzu: Basic Writings*, trans. Burton Watson (New York: Columbia University Press, 1996. All of my quotations are from this edition, although I employ the common, currently-used Pinyin Romanization of the philosopher's name. References to specific page numbers appear in parentheses in the text.

4. Especially helpful commentators on the perennial questions that Zhuangzi raises include Benjamin I. Schwartz, *The World of Thought in Ancient China* (Cambridge: Harvard University Press, 1985), which I cite in this essay; as well as A. C. Graham, *Disputers of the Tao: Philosophical Argument in Ancient China* (La Salle, Ill.: Open Court Press, 1989); Robert E. Allinson, *Chuang-Tzu: An Analysis of the Inner Chapters* (Albany, N.Y.: SUNY Press, 1989); Joel J. Kupperman, *Classic Asian Philosophy: A Guide to the Essential Texts* (Oxford: Oxford University Press, 2001); and Philip J. Ivanhoe's "Zhuangzi on Scepticism, Skill and the Ineffable Dao," *Journal of the American Academy of Religion* 61, no. 4 (Winter 1993): 639–654. I am also grateful to Janet Lynn Kerr, my former colleague at Christ College, the honors college of Valparaiso University. Before her untimely death on October 5, 1999, Janet introduced me and countless others to the riches of Chinese literature, including the work of Zhuangzi.

5. John Keats, quoted in http://www.mrbauld.com/negcap.html.

6. Leslie H. Farber, *The Ways of the Will: Selected Essays*, ed. Robert Boyers and Anne Farber (New York: Basic Books, 2000). I cite here the essay "Thinking About Will."

7. Schwartz, *The World of Thought in Ancient China*, 190.

8. Ibid., 188.

9. Farber, *The Ways of the Will*, 79.

10. See Mencius 2A2. For another example of Confucian *wu-wei*, see the famous passage from the *Analects* in which Confucius describes his development (in a way similar to Cook Ting's): "The Master said, At fifteen I set my heart upon learning. At thirty, I had planted my feet firm upon the ground. At forty, I no longer suffered from perplexities. At fifty, I knew what were the biddings of Heaven. At sixty, I heard them with docile ear. At seventy, I could follow the dictates of my own heart; for what I desired no longer overstepped the boundaries of right" (2.4).

11. See Alexander W. Astin, Helen S. Astin, and Jennifer A. Lindholm, *Cultivating the Spirit: How College Can Enhance Students' Inner Lives* (San Francisco: Jossey-Bass, 2010), which is based upon a major study of college students by the Higher Education Research Institute at UCLA. See also the essays in *The American University in a Postsecular Age*, ed. Douglas Jacobsen and Rhonda Hustedt Jacobsen (Oxford: Oxford University Press, 2008).

12. My reading of the Woodworker Qing story is influenced by the reading of Parker Palmer in *The Active Life: A Spirituality of Work, Creativity, and Caring* (San Francisco: Jossey-Bass, 1999). In my discussion here, I have drawn on my discussion of Woodworker Qing in "Zhuangzi as an Exemplary Classic," in *Classics for an Emerging World: Proceedings of a Conference on Liberal Education and the Core Curriculum, January 19–20, 2008*, ed. Wm. Theodore de Bary, Shang Wei, and Rachel E. Chung (New York: Columbia University Committee on Asia and the Middle East, 2008).

13. See John Dominic Crossan, *The Dark Interval: Towards a Theology of Story.* (Niles, Ill.: Argus, 1975).

14. In *I and Tao: Martin Buber's Encounter with Chuang Tzu* (Albany, N.Y.: SUNY Press, 1996), Jonathan Herman explores the way in which "the Taoist work [of Zhuangzi] represented not only a transitional stage between Buber's very early Hasidic studies and the first edition of *I and Thou*, but also the onset of his ongoing involvement with Chinese philosophy and religion" (xi).

15. The concept of *wu-wei* bears a kinship to the concept of *Gellassenheit*, Meister Eckhart's word to describe one's properly open relationship to God: "detachment [*Gellassenheit*] is receptive to nothing at all except God." *The Essential Sermons, Commentaries, Treatises, and Defense*, trans. Edmund Colledge and Bernard McGinn (New York: Paulist Press, 1981).

16. The interreligious dialogue of Thomas Merton is exemplary here. In 1965, Merton published *The Way of Chuang Tzu* (New York: New Directions, 1965), a selection of parables from Zhuangzi, based upon various translations. In his "Note to the Reader," Merton denies that he will be pulling "Christian rabbits out of a Taoist hat" but makes clear that Zhuangzi's thought has enriched his own, much as Augustine's was enriched by that of Plotinus and Aquinas's by Aristotle and Averroes—"(both of them certainly a long way further from Christianity than Zhuangzi ever was!)" (10–11). Merton was a longtime friend of the Zen Buddhist D. T. Suzuki and called Thich Nhat Hanh his "brother." Appropriately, in 1996, almost fifty Buddhist and Christian monks and nuns, including the Dalai Lama, met in Abbey of Gethsemane, Merton's home until his death in Thailand

in 1968, to discuss commonalities and differences between Buddhism and Christianity.

17. Mihaly Csikszentmihalyi, *Flow: The Psychology of Optimal Experience* (New York: Harper Perennial, 1991), 3–4.

18. In Confucius' Taoist counsel to Yen Hui, I hear resonances with three classics from the Western tradition. "Make your will one": Søren Kierkegaard famously titled one of his later works *Purity of Heart Is to Will One Thing.* "Go and play in his bird cage": William Shakespeare's Lear articulates his late-found insight into court life when, on their way to prison, he promises Cordelia, "We two alone will sing like birds i' th' cage" (5.2.9). And, finally, "keep still." Long before the technological distractions we now face daily, Blaise Pascal wrote: "I have often said that the sole cause of man's unhappiness is that he does not know how to stay quietly in his own room." *Pensées*, trans. A. J. Krailsheimer (New York: Penguin, 1995), no. 136.

19. Here I disagree with Joel J. Kupperman (cited in note 4, above), who writes that Zhuangzi's work "is permeated with metaphysical anti-realism" (114). In suggesting Zhuangzi's "perspectival realism," I am employing a term coined by Susan M. Felch to distinguish the linguistic views of Mikhail Bakhtin from those of Jacques Derrida. Felch writes that perspectival realism "retains a correspondence view of truth—that is the world is a certain way regardless of our thinking about it—but it substitutes a realist epistemology (that the world is the object of our awareness) for a representational epistemology (that appearances and concepts are the objects of our awareness). It also gives up the modernist goal of exhaustive knowledge (that to have truth we must map out the isomorphic relationships of our perceptions to reality) for the promise of genuine knowledge (that our various perceptions do give us access to a real world). . . . Language, then, is seen not as an end in itself but as one of the media, or means, by which we respond to and act in the world." See her essay "Words and Things: The Hope of Perspectival Realism," in *Faithful Imagination in the Academy: Explorations in Religious Belief and Scholarship*, ed. Janet M. Curry and Ronald A. Wells (Lexington, 2008), 26.

20. Here I recall an adage attributed to St. Francis of Assisi: "Preach the gospel always. If necessary, use words."

7

Xunzi

Wm. Theodore de Bary

F EW READERS OF Xunzi will fail to recognize the importance of the
issues addressed therein or the salience of Xunzi's arguments. He has
been considered one of the classic Masters for almost two millennia, and
even though he was not chosen by the great Neo-Confucian philosopher
Zhu Xi for inclusion in Zhu's highly selective Four Books, which later became canonical, Zhu's own curriculum included him as one of the Masters,
along with Laozi, Zhuangzi, and Han Feizi. As such, Xunzi is a classic deserving of any educated person's attention.[1]

It is also a measure of Xunzi's classic status that he has so often in the
past been paired with his predecessor Mencius, and for an understandable reason: he took issue with Mencius on a central issue of Confucian
discourse—the goodness of human nature. That readers have also tended
to oversimplify and overread this difference is understandable in view of
the ease with which human memory reduces things to simple binaries of opposition. We shall deal with this issue later, but for the present let us just be
on guard against the tendency to read this difference into everything Xunzi
says.

The fact of the matter is that the view of human nature as evil only appears quite late in the standard text, and there is no reason to assume that
it is a fundamental theoretical postulate that necessarily underlies and explains everything else in Xunzi. Indeed, one can read the major, earlier parts
of Xunzi without seeing any direct reference to "human nature is evil." Thus

it is better to read this very late chapter in the light of what goes before it rather than vice versa.

When we do this, we can see that the title of this twenty-third chapter, "Xing-e," ("Human (Inborn) Nature, Evil") can be understood just as well as "Human Nature as Evil" (or Awful) or "The Evil in Human Nature" rather than as affirming an original corruption or the total depravity of human nature. Even the opening lines of this chapter should warn us against taking this as a radical, all-pervasive stain on human nature:

> Human nature is evil: its goodness derives from conscious activity. Now it is human nature to be born with a fondness for profit. Indulging this leads to contention and strife, and the sense of modesty and yielding is lost. One is born with feelings of envy and hate, and, by indulging these, one is led into banditry and theft, so that the sense of being true and trustworthy disappears. One is born with the desires of the ears and eyes and with a fondness for beautiful sights and sounds, and, by indulging these, one is led to licentiousness and chaos, so that the sense of ritual decorum and right reason is lost. Hence, following human nature and indulging human emotions will inevitably lead to contention and strife, causing one to rebel against one's proper duty, reduce principles to chaos, and revert to violence. Therefore one must be transformed by the example of a teacher and guided by the way of ritual and rightness before one will attain modesty and yielding, accord with refinement and ritual, and return to order. From this perspective it is apparent that human nature is evil and that its goodness is the result of conscious activity.
>
> (SCT, 1:179)

In a passage following this, Xunzi explains that by "human nature" he means nature in the raw. "Now it is human nature that as soon as a person is born he departs from his original substance and from his natural disposition, so that he must inevitably lose and destroy them. Seen in this way, it is apparent that human nature is evil" (SCT, 1:179–180).

Here the word for original substance is *pu*, but *pu* is an expression found in the *Laozi* for undifferentiated or raw, unmarked substance. The graph for Mencius's *xing*, on the other hand, includes the radical for heart and mind and connotes an inner, inborn consciousness. Given the fundamental difference in Xunzi's assumptions with regard to "human nature," the question naturally arises how "being true and trustworthy" and capable of "ritual decorum and right reason" could become lost if they were not somehow intrinsic to one's nature to begin with. Xunzi addresses this question in the following:

> A questioner asks: If human nature is evil, then where do ritual and rightness come from? I reply: ritual and rightness are always created by the conscious activity of the sages; essentially they are not created by human nature. Thus a potter molds clay and makes a vessel, but the vessel is created by the conscious activity of the potter and is not created by his human nature. In the same way a carpenter carves a piece of wood and makes a utensil, but the utensil is created through the conscious activity of the carpenter and is not created by his human nature. A sage gathers his thoughts and reflections, engages in conscious activity, and thus creates ritual and rightness and produces models and regulations. Hence ritual, rightness, models, and limits are created by the conscious activity of the sage and not by his human nature. (SCT, 1:181)

The plausibility of this argument depends on whether one accepts the idea that such consciousnesses arise only in a social context. Xunzi's preference for couching his argument in terms of the binary "raw substance (*pu*) versus rational consciousness" rather than in terms of inborn moral consciousness suggests that more is at work here than an argument between Xunzi and Mencius. Laozi's view of raw original substance (*pu*) versus social or civil reason has entered into the received discourse. In other words, for Xunzi, good cannot be inherent in this undifferentiated substance; for the latter to survive, however, it must necessarily be self-seeking, which leads it into evil.

Xunzi goes on to explain how the moral consciousness arises from an awareness of what one lacks but needs in order to survive in society:

> When a person desires to do good he always does so because his nature is evil. A person who is shallow aspires to depth; one who is ugly aspires to beauty; one who is narrow aspires to breadth; one who is poor aspires to wealth; one who is humble aspires to esteem.

Whatever one lacks in oneself he must seek outside. Therefore if a person is rich, he will not aspire to wealth, and if he is esteemed, he will not long for power. What a person possesses in himself he need not seek outside. One can see from this that the reason human beings desire to do good is that their nature is evil.

Now human nature is definitely devoid of ritual and rightness. Therefore, they compel themselves to study and to seek to possess them. The nature knows nothing of ritual and rightness, and therefore one reflects and ponders and seeks to understand them. Thus the nature is inborn, that is all; and human beings neither possess ritual and rightness, nor do they understand them.   (SCT, 1:181–182)

Xunzi's argument is good as it goes, but it presumes that one's moral awareness is wholly induced from outside, and it does not explain the susceptibility of human beings to such external influences or why the distinctive human response, civilized life, is not found in other conscious creatures.

There is much more that could be said about Xunzi's argument with Mencius, but to go further than this would only be to compound the overemphasis on this issue as compared to the much more significant features of Xunzi's thoughts. Suffice it to say here that Xunzi recognizes in his chapter 23 what is most importantly assumed in the rest of his writings: that humans have both a capacity for and a need for learning. Whether this capacity is part of his inborn nature is a matter of definitions.

If we start with Xunzi's chapter 1, instead of chapter 23, we will recognize why Xunzi, for all his apparent differences with Mencius, is a Confucian from the start in all key respects: he understands the importance of self-cultivation, the need for sustained and systematic learning in the arts of civilized life, the crucial role of ritual as a vital element in the learning process and in the ordering of society, and, in the end as in the beginning, the prime value of the cultivated human person as the keystone of human flourishing. All this is implicit in the early chapters.

At the outset of his first chapter, Xunzi likens human nature to wood in its natural state, which can be bent by the craftsman to serve human purposes.

Wood as straight as a plumb line may be bent into a wheel that is as round as if it were drawn with a compass, and, even after the wood has dried, it will not straighten out again because this is the way it has been bent. Thus wood marked by the plumb line will become straight, and metal that is put to a whetstone will become sharp. The noble person who studies widely and examines himself each day will become clear in his knowing and faultless in his conduct.

(*SCT*, 1:161)

But achieving this result depends mostly on the assiduous effort of the individual:

> Therefore if you do not climb a high mountain, you will not know the height of Heaven; if you do not look down into a deep valley, you will not know the depth of the earth; and if you do not hear the words handed down from the ancient kings, you will not know the greatness of learning and inquiry. . . . Once I spent an entire day in thought (introspection), but it was not as good as a moment of study. Once I stood on tiptoe to gaze into the distance, but it was not as good as climbing to a high place to get a broad view. Climbing to a high place and waving will not make your arm any longer, but you can be seen from farther away. Shouting down the wind will give your voice no added urgency, but you can be heard more distinctly. By borrowing a horse and carriage you will not improve your feet, but you can cover a thousand *li*. By borrowing a boat and paddles you will not improve your ability in water, but you can cross rivers and seas. The noble person is by birth no different from others, but he is good at borrowing from external things. (*SCT*, 1:161–162)

To accomplish this, one must have seen models set by the sage-kings and standards established in social rituals, but the process must start with determined effort by the individual, which contrasts with Laozi's strictures against any assertion of the moral will.

> Accumulate earth to make a mountain, and wind and rain will flourish there. Accumulate water to make a deep pool, and dragons will be born from it. Accumulate goodness to create virtue, and spiritual clarity will naturally be acquired; there the mind of the sage will be fully realized. Thus if you do not accumulate little steps, you will not have the means to journey a thousand *li*, and if you do not pile up small streams, you will have no way to fill a river or a sea. Though a thoroughbred like Qiji cannot cover ten paces in one leap,

the sorriest nag can do it in ten yokings. Achievement consists of never giving up.   (*SCT*, 1:162)

This sustained effort, however, is useless if it lacks a proper starting point and direction to a definite goal.

> In the west there is a tree called the *yegan*. Its trunk is no more than four inches tall, and it grows on top of high mountains, looking down into chasms a hundred fathoms deep. This is not because the tree's trunk is able to grow, but, rather, because of the place where it stands. If raspberry vines grow in the midst of hemp, they will stand up straight without being staked; if white sand is mixed with mud, it too will turn black. If the root of the orchid and the rhizome of the valerian are soaked in the water used to wash rice, the noble person will not go near them, and the commoner will not water them—not because their substance is not beautiful but because of what they have been soaked in. Therefore the noble person will choose with care the place where he will reside, and will be accompanied by scholars when he travels. In this way he avoids depravity and meanness and approaches central-ity and correctness.   (*SCT*, 1:162)

There is little here that would distinguish Xunzi from other Confucians or that would be at odds particularly with Mencius. On the other hand, there is much that stands in opposition to the basic teachings of Laozi later found in the *Daodejing*. Although Laozi is not the direct target of attack here, texts and concepts attributed to or associated with him were already in circulation well before Xunzi's time, and it is not difficult to see how Xunzi's dim view of the original nature is at odds with Laozi's "naturalness" and spontaneity (*ziran*). Likewise, Xunzi's corollary, the need for human art and culture (*wen*) or artifice (*wei*) is directly opposed to the Daoist coun-tercultural preference for "no deliberate or purposive action" (*wu-wei*) that would interfere with the natural spontaneity of *zi ran*. Thus the basic argu-ment is more with Laozi than with Mencius, who would line up with Xunzi on these issues.

Further to the same point is Xunzi's insistence on the need for value judgments as a premise for all action and effort. We have already seen this in Xunzi in the need to choose a proper starting point for one's efforts, but it is most striking in the following passage: "If there is no dark and dogged will there will be no shining accomplishment; if there is no dull and determined effort there will be no brilliant achievement. He who tries to travel two roads at once will get nowhere" (*SCT*, 1:162).

After starting in the right place and choosing the right direction in which to go, the next choice to be made by those who need and want to learn is to have the proper aim in learning. It may surprise those who see the good of society as always, for Xunzi, dominating the individual, to find him quoting Confucius: "In antiquity learning was carried on for the sake of one's self; today learning is carried on for the sake of others. The learning of the noble person is for the sake of beautifying himself; the learning of the lesser man is offering bird and beast [to win attention from others]" (*SCT*, 1:163).

Nevertheless, even if one aims to learn for one's own sake and not for others, one still needs to learn from others what is in one's own best interest, and for this one will need a teacher:

> In learning nothing works so well as to be near a person of learning. The *Rites* and the "Music" provide models but no explanations. The *Odes* and the *Documents* are devoted to antiquity and lack immediacy. The *Spring and Autumn Annals* is laconic and not readily acceptable. But following alongside a person of learning and repeating the explanations of the Noble Person bring one honor everywhere and allow one comprehensive knowledge of the world. Therefore it is said that "In learning nothing works so well as to be near a person of learning."
>
> (*SCT*, 1:163)

Here both teachers and classics are closely linked, but the need to learn from seasoned experience is the key. Classics offer the wisdom of past ages, but the accumulation of knowledge, especially through book learning, will not avail unless an experienced teacher is there to help one make wise choices among the array of received texts and traditions.

> In the course of learning there is nothing more expedient than to devote yourself to a person of learning, and next to this is to pay homage to the rites. If you can neither devote yourself to a person of learning, and next to this pay homage to the rites, how will you do anything more than learn randomly or passively follow the *Odes* and the *Documents*? In this case you will never to the end of your days escape from being merely a vulgar pedant. (*SCT*, 1:163)

The centrality of the classics in the curriculum is based on their survival through the ages, but the process of survival is not unaccompanied by problems of authenticity and disparate interpretation, so one needs help from an experienced teacher in learning how to sort things out. Venerable texts and respectful questions go together, and schools are indispensable to learning. Xunzi is thus a major advocate of both scholarship and education.

Finally, Xunzi concludes this first chapter on learning by drawing a conclusion that sets the tone for the rest of the work.

> The noble person knows that what is not complete or what is not pure is unworthy to be called beautiful. Therefore he recites and reiterates so as to integrate it, reflects and ponders so as to comprehend it, determines his associations so that he may dwell in it, and eliminates what is harmful in order to preserve and nourish it. He causes his eyes to be devoid of any desire to see what is not right, and his mind to be devoid of any desire to think what is not right. Having arrived at this he takes utmost pleasure in it.   (SCT, 1:164)

In the above, Xunzi is talking about the self as a whole person and sees its fulfillment as something beautiful in itself—not a self socialized to fit in with or become a tool of society, much less one that is self-satisfied in terms of social success. At this point his desires are not so much indulged as truly satisfied, and "his mind will benefit more from it than in the possession of the world." It has achieved something truly beautiful.

> Therefore he cannot be subverted by power or profit, swayed by the masses and multitudes, or unsettled by the whole world. He follows this in life; he follows it in death—this is what is called holding firm to virtue. He who holds firm to virtue is able to order himself; being able to order himself, he can then respond to others. He who is able to order himself and respond to others is called the complete man. Heaven manifests itself in its brightness; earth manifests itself in its breadth; the noble person values his completeness.   (SCT, 1:164)

The word "complete" here has the sense of "brought to completeness," fulfilled or perfected by "learning for oneself," and not dependent on acceptance by others. It is an organic process whereby the individual's self-fulfillment is both the starting point and the end of the process. Here again Xunzi's concluding argument is not with Mencius, who largely shares his ideal of the noble person as one who is able to order himself and then respond to others, but lies rather in how he appropriates for himself the key values in Laozi, for whom the Way was above all a constant Way that when followed led to inner peace. The constancy of Xunzi's noble person lies in following the Way of right desires in both life and death to achieve an inner peace, holding firm to an inner power (*de*) that is understood as true moral virtue, full of right desires (not "empty" of them).

For us as readers, this should be the actual starting point for understanding Xunzi, better than the idea that "human nature is evil." And next, as Xunzi further explains, ritual is vital to the process, and the question naturally arises as to how ritual accords with personal self-fulfillment.

> Ritual is the means by which one's person is rectified; the teacher is the means by which ritual is rectified. Without ritual, how can you rectify yourself? Without a teacher, how can you know which ritual is correct? By behaving according to ritual, your emotions will find peace in ritual. By speaking as your teacher speaks, your understanding becomes like that of your teacher. When your emotions find peace in ritual and your understanding is like that of your teacher, then you have become a sage. Therefore to reject ritual is to be without a guide, and to renounce one's teacher is to be without a teacher. Not to approve of a teacher and a guide, preferring to do everything your own way, is like relying on a blind man trying to distinguish colors or a deaf man, tones. There is no way to put aside chaos and confusion. Therefore learning means looking to ritual as your guide. The teacher takes his own person as the standard of proper conduct and values that in himself which is at peace.
>
> (*SCT*, 1:166)

Some modern readers, prepared to believe that ritual is an imposition on the individual as a means of socialization or as an instrument of authoritarian repression, especially if this goes along with Xunzi's view that "human nature is evil," will find his chapter on ritual decorum most revealing. It gives the lie to any idea that for Xunzi the desires are intrinsically evil in themselves.

What is the origin of rites? I reply, human beings are born with desires, and when they do not achieve their desires, they cannot but seek
the means to do so. If their seeking knows no limit or degree, they
cannot but contend with one another. With contention comes chaos,
and with chaos comes exhaustion. The ancient kings hated chaos and
therefore established rites and rightness in order to limit it, to nurture
people's desires, and to give them a means of satisfaction. They saw to
it that desires did not exhaust material things and that material things
did not fall short of desires. Thus both desires and things were supported and satisfied. This was the origin of rites.   (*SCT*, 1:174–175)

Here the purpose of the rites is not to suppress desires but to "nurture"
them and give them a means of satisfaction. However, satisfaction is not
satiation. Both the rites and sense of rightness provide means by which reasonable satisfaction is kept within limits to avoid overindulgence and ener-
vation of the desires. Balance is the key, and it is the key both for the nurturing of the desires and for the ordering of society. Rites do not just keep the
individual in line. In fact, desires are actually to be sustained as a vital life
energy. But sustaining desire and sustaining the socioeconomic order go
together.

How society may be ordered so as to sustain human life and desire is a
subject that Xunzi deals with in other important chapters of the text. But
before we go on to these, let us take one last look at the main theme of the
chapter on rites, which deals with more than just the sustaining or restrain-
ing of desires.

The supreme value here, as in the conclusion of chapter 1, is not social
order or economic regulation, but beauty: "It is always true that rites, when
they serve the living, are an adornment to joy and when they serve the dead,
an adornment to grief. In sacrifices they are an adornment to reverence,
and in military affairs, an adornment to authority. This was the same for
the rites of the hundred kings; it is what unites antiquity and the present. The
source for this we do not know" (*SCT*, 1:177).

Two things stand out here. First is the prime value of the rites as adorn-
ing or ornamenting life. Second is the acknowledgment by the rationalist
Xunzi that the rites partake of the ultimate mystery of life. They are religious in their origin, as the graph for *li* (rites) clearly associates it with
prayer and sacrificial offerings from time immemorial. This, however, lies
beyond the range of human knowledge. What one can understand is how

the rites and music serve to fulfill individual human desires, refining and elevating them.

> Sacrificial rites give expression to the feelings of remembrance and longing for the dead. There inevitably come times when one is overwhelmed by emotions of grief and loss, and a loyal minister or a filial son finds that, even while others are given to the enjoyment of congenial company, these sorrowful emotions arrive. If when they come to him, and he is greatly moved, he nonetheless represses them, his feelings of remembrance and longing will be thwarted and unfulfilled, and his ritual practice will be deficient and incomplete. Therefore the ancient kings established certain forms so that the duty of honoring those who deserve honor and demonstrating affection for those who deserve affection might be fulfilled. Therefore I say that the sacrificial rites give expression to the feelings of remembrance and longing. They are the perfection of loyalty, good faith, love and reverence, and the flourishing of ritual deportment and refined demeanor.
>
> (SCT, 1:177)

Note in midpassage here that Xunzi specifically rejects the idea that one's deepest feelings can be dealt with by trying to repress them, for either individual or social purposes. They must find satisfaction in elegant form.

The rites are obviously social institutions, but their justification is no less the fulfillment of personal desires than of ensuring social stability. This takes us back to the early chapters on learning and self-cultivation as the prime foci of the work.

Of the remaining chapters of the text, most of them relate directly or indirectly to governance. Those most indicative of Xunzi's approach are

Contra Twelve Masters
On Confucius
The Teachings of the Confucians
The Regulations of the King
Enriching the State
Of Kings and Lords
The Way of Ministers
Recruiting Scholar-Officials
Military Issues

Correct Terminology
Nobility

The terms used in the titles are fairly typical of Confucian discourse and in themselves suggest that Xunzi is working out of a received tradition. But numerous alternative teachings had appeared by his time, and, as we have seen in the indirect reference to Daoist thinkers above, Xunzi is speaking to a large and varied audience, the most influential of whom, beside the Daoists, are the school of Mozi and the Legalists.

Mozi and his followers were known for their populist moralism, which was accompanied by humanitarian activism, a "follow-the-leader" authoritarianism, a strict puritanical frugality, the rejection of offensive warfare, and a deprecation of Confucian elitism and high culture (especially ritual and the arts) and of what was alleged to be a Confucian fatalism implicit in the concept of Heaven's destiny or mandate (*tian-ming*). In our discussion of human governance according to Xunzi, it will not be difficult to see how often he challenges Mohist pieties, puritanism, and anti-intellectualism.

Besides the Mohist and Daoist views, those of the so-called Legalist school represented the greatest challenge to Xunzi. "Legalism" is an expression that has come to be applied to a growing movement in the statecraft of the late Zhou. "Legalism" focuses on one aspect of this development insofar as it stresses the need for uniform laws and heavy punishments. But penal law was only one feature of this broad movement, spoken of as the Fajia ("School of Law"), which dealt as much, if not more, with administrative and civil law—the systematic organization of power and resources (both material and human).

Indeed, *fa* has such a wide range of meanings that no one English word suffices: it includes both theoretical and practical methods of many kinds that could serve to strengthen the state. In fact, so flexible and adaptable was *fa* that it could be used later to render the basic but equally broad Buddhist concept of *dharma* (law, truth, teaching).

For all its wide uses, *fa* was also contested ground for Xunzi. To him it meant a prime model, and much of what follows here has to do with what that model, ultimate norm, or ideal should be. In that respect, he is taking up the challenge of the Legalists and contesting their most fundamental concept: the impersonality and impartiality of the law.

In the late Zhou period, as the enfeoffment system was weakening and the strengthening of the state was overcoming particularistic loyalties, both the Mohists and Legalists offered strategies to organize power and resources in ways that would benefit the "people" materially—providing for their most material needs or physical security, as the most common denominator among human beings. Both approaches would do this through strong leadership based on a more systematic organization of power.

Xunzi thought to achieve some of the same systematic organization, but through means less impersonal, dealing with the people less as a mass and more in recognition of their greater complexity and diversity. One key to this was to have a proper human model—one that could serve at once as a personal model for the ruler and as a model for the individual in realizing his full humanity. Both of these objectives could be satisfied by upholding the ideal of the truly noble person (*junzi*), exemplified at the top by the sage-king and at successive lower levels by a leadership ideal adapted to the particular needs at each level for personal and reciprocal working relationships.

The sage-king was of course a traditional ideal of the Confucians, but Xunzi updated it somewhat by choosing as his prime sages the founding fathers of the Zhou: King Wen and the Duke of Zhou. This brought the focus more within the reach of recorded history, as Xunzi's exemplars were less like Mozi's great hero, the Great Yü, whose mythic exploits were just barely imaginable. Xunzi's treatment also differed from the typical Legalist deprecation of the traditional sages, who were dismissed as icons of a past no longer relevant to the contemporary situation. According to Xunzi, the founding fathers of the Zhou had bequeathed to posterity institutions (primarily rites) that could serve as workable norms. Although Xunzi often referred in general to the "Hundred Kings" as sages, for practical purposes it was the constitutional order of King Wen and the Duke of Zhou that emphasized workable, historically verifiable norms.

Thus far, Xunzi's conception of the *fa* as model or norm, though differing from the Mohists and Legalists (to say nothing of the Daoists) does not depart from Confucian usage in essential respects. Most Confucians looked to King Wen and the Duke of Zhou as models, and their exemplary actions (*xian fa*) were regarded as constitutional precedents (hence the same term is applied to modern constitutions). Even Mencius noted how important institutional or programmatic models were to sage rule.

After stressing the need for the ruler to develop his own inner sensitivity and employ empathetic virtue as a bond with the people at large, he insisted that subjective virtue and good intentions were not enough; proper models were also needed:

> Though one may have a human heart and a reputation for humaneness, one from whom the people receive no benefits will not serve as a model (*fa*) for later generations because he does not practice the Way of the Former Kings. Therefore it is said "Goodness alone does not suffice for the conduct of government. Laws (*fa*) alone do not implement themselves.... No one has ever erred by following the laws (*fa*) of the former kings."   (Mencius 4A1; *SCT*, 1:136–137)

The models that Mencius refers to, such as the land and tax systems, evoke vivid, concrete images such as the well fields, which memorably illustrate key principles of equality and community cooperation for the common good. Xunzi does not neglect such things, but he sums them up succinctly:

> On the model of a king: He fixes the several rates of taxation, regulates affairs, and utilizes the myriad things in order to nourish the myriad people. From the product of the fields, the tax rate is one part in ten. At the barriers and in the marketplaces, goods are inspected, but no tax is imposed. The mountains and forests, marshes and weirs, are closed or opened according to the season, but taxes are not levied. Land is inspected for its quality, and taxes are differentially assessed. The distance over which goods must be transported is taken into account in fixing tribute payments. The circulation of resources and grain is unimpeded, allowing them to be offered and exchanged so that "all within the four seas are like one family."   (*SCT*, 1:169)

Xunzi's larger vision is of a much more comprehensive and complex structure, but if one wants to sum it up in one model, it is in the figure of the Noble Person.

This may not be surprising if one remembers that it is also the guiding theme of Xunzi's first chapter, which discusses learning how to become a complete human being who is also capable of true leadership because he is able to make the necessary value distinctions. What is added to the micro-scopic personification of the Noble Person is the holistic conception that places this human ideal at the center of a cosmic order. Again, Xunzi sums this up in his chapter on the "Regulations of a King":

> Heaven and Earth are the beginning of life; rites and rightness are the beginning of order; and the noble person is the beginning of rites and rightness. Enacting them, practicing them, accumulating them, and loving them more than anything else—this is the beginning of the noble person. Therefore Heaven and Earth produce the noble person, and the noble person forms a triad with Heaven and Earth; he is the agent of the myriad things, father and mother of the people.
>
> (SCT, 1:169)

Here the Noble Person is the ideal king, the Son of Heaven, who plays a crucial role in realizing the creative powers of Heaven and Earth. A later chapter expands on this idea and explains more precisely the human role in this process:

> To bring to completion without acting, to obtain without seeking—this is called the working of Heaven. Thus, although one is profound, he does not contemplate it; although great, he adds nothing to its abil-ity; although clever, he does not attempt to search it out. Hence it is said that he does not contend with Heaven for its work; Heaven has its seasons; Earth has its resources; man has his government. For this reason it is said that they may form a triad. If one abandons that which allows him to form a triad, yet longs for the triad, he is deluded.
>
> (SCT, 1:171)

Elsewhere, Xunzi dwells on the constancy and self-sufficiency of Heaven and Earth. It is left to humankind to observe this order and adapt it to its own needs for ordered governance, without trying to complete or contend with them by supernatural means, instead reproducing that order and regu-larity in those affairs of men within human control.

Inherent in this triadic order is the principle of the differentiation of function (each has its own sphere), and the sage-king's task is to extend that function to human governance through the defining of distinct roles.

However, in contrast to the Mohists and Legalists, for whom functionality is understood primarily in utilitarian, material terms, Xunzi sees it in social relations as defined by the rites. Differentiation is the natural order of things, and the rites deal with all things respectfully, according to their proper natures—respectfully and, of course, beautifully, as Heaven and Earth naturally do, but also elegantly, as the sage-king, the Noble Person, and the Son of Heaven should do.

Much of Xunzi's *Regulations of the King* and other chapters dealing with human governance are devoted not to the economic, political, and legal systems (*fa*) that occupy Mozi and the Legalists but to establishing a hierarchy of value distinctions congruent with a viable social structure—a social system that is personalized and a political system based on merit and ability, not birth or inheritance. Class distinctions count, but they must defer to moral worth and life-sustaining values, balancing personal respect with service of the common good.

Xunzi is by no means oblivious to the need for practical statecraft. In fact, he gives special credit to statesmen like the Duke of Zhou who provided executive leadership to the founding of the Zhou, and he devotes much attention to the choice of prime ministers, who set the tone for all administrative services.

Through it all, and supporting it all, there must be a hierarchy of values, a structured order that provides the constancy, reliability, security, and order that should be man's distinctive contribution to the harmonious, complementary functioning of Heaven, Earth, and Humankind.

At the central axis of this universe would be Xunzi's Noble Person, serving in the role of sage-king, Son of Heaven, kingpin, or what-have-you at every level of the hierarchy. But if Xunzi were right about the evil in human nature, the Noble Person, the Beautiful Person, the Elegant Person would not have much company. Anyone can do it, Xunzi says, but few actually make it. The Noble Man as sage-king will be there at the top, pretty much alone in his solitary, unmatched splendor.

Translations

Basic Writings of Hsun tzu. Trans. Burton Watson. New York: Columbia University Press, 1963.

Wm. Theodore de Bary and Irene Bloom, eds., *Sources of Chinese Tradition*, 2nd ed., 159–189. New York: Columbia University Press, 2000.

Xunzi: A Translation and Study of the Complete Works. Trans. John Knoblock. 3 vols. Stanford, Calif.: Stanford University Press, 1988.

Note

1. Wm. Theodore de Bary and Irene Bloom, eds., *Sources of Chinese Tradition*, 2nd ed. (New York: Columbia University Press, 2000), 1:140. Hereafter abbreviated in the text as *SCT*.

8

THE LOTUS SŪTRA

Wing-tsit Chan

NO ONE CAN understand the Far East without some knowledge of the teachings of the *Lotus Sūtra*, because it is the most important scripture of Mahāyāna Buddhism, which cuts across the entire Far East. In a narrow sense, it is a scripture of the Tian-tai School in China and Tendai in Japan and is the chief sūtra of the Nichiren School in Japan. But in a broad sense, it is the most basic sūtra for all Mahāyāna, shared by practically all the different schools. It was the first to preach revolutionary Mahāyāna doctrines and is still the most comprehensive statement of them, and most important of all, it has been the source of inspiration for Buddhist practice in the Far East for the last 1,500 years. If out of several hundred Mahāyāna sūtras one were to choose only one as the most representative and most meaningful, most students would select the *Lotus*. No wonder that when Chang Rong, an ardent advocate of the harmony of Confucianism, Buddhism, and Daoism, died in 497 C.E., he held in his left hand a copy of the *Classic of Filial Piety* and the *Daodejing* and in his right hand the *Lotus*.

Ever since its appearance in China in the third century, and especially after the fifth, the study of the *Lotus* has been pursued most vigorously and extensively. According to the *Biographies of Eminent Monks (Gao-seng juan)*, of twenty-one monks famous for reciting sūtras, sixteen recited the *Lotus*. More lectures have been given, more research conducted into its subject matter and terminology, and more commentaries written on it than on any other Buddhist scripture.

This scripture is written in the form of a drama, but it is a drama only in the loosest sense of the word, as it takes place on the greatest scale ever conceived by man. Its stage comprises many Buddha-worlds. Its timeframe is eternity. And its actors are the Lord Buddha Śākyamuni and innumerable other beings. The scene opens with Śākyamuni sitting in a trance. Gathered before him are twelve thousand arhats, six thousand nuns headed by his mother and including his wife, eight thousand bodhisattvas, sixty thousand gods, Brahma with his twelve thousand dragon kings, and hundreds of thousands of heavenly beings, demons, and other beings. As the members of the congregation fold their hands in homage to him, a ray of light issues forth from his forehead, which illuminates the eighteen thousand Buddha-worlds in the East, in each of which a Buddha is preaching. The entire universe is shaking; flowers rain all over and perfume fills all space. It is announced that the Lord is now going to give a discourse (chap. 1).

Coming out of his trance, the Buddha begins to speak. He says that only Buddhas have perfect knowledge and are qualified to preach and that they are now preaching to all beings. At this, the proud arhats, the saints of Hīnayāna or Small Vehicle Buddhism (or rather Theravāda Buddhism), who consider themselves already perfectly enlightened, leave in silent protest. Śākyamuni does not teach the Three Vehicles—those of the Śrāvakas who attain their salvation by hearing the Buddha's teaching, the Pratyeka-buddhas who attain to their personal enlightenment by their own exertions, and the bodhisattvas who postpone their own departure from the world for the sake of helping all beings to be saved. Instead he teaches only the One Vehicle. He has taught the other vehicles merely as an expedient or convenient means for those who were not yet ready for the highest truth, the One Vehicle. In this vehicle, Nirvāṇa is not the extinction of existence, but the extinction of illusions and ignorance. Everyone will be saved. Anyone who practices charity; is patient; observes discipline; is diligent in spiritual cultivation; makes offerings to the Buddha; builds a stupa with gold, silver, crystal, amber, sandalwood, clay, or, in the case of a child at play, sand; who carves a Buddha figure in copper, pewter, or lacquered cloth or paints a Buddha figure with a brush or even a fingernail; makes music; recites a verse; offers a sound or a flower to the Buddha; or merely raises his head, folds his hands, or utters a simple word of admiration, *namo*, will attain salvation (chap. 2).

The disciple Śāriputra is now filled with joy and in ecstasy. He realizes that he is really a son of the Buddha, produced from the Buddha Law or

Dharma and born out of the Buddha's mouth. He is assured by the Lord that he will be the Flower-light Buddha in the Buddha-world whose ground is crystal with eight broad walks lined with golden ropes and where a jeweled flower will spring up wherever the feet of his disciples tread. Anyone with devotion and faith will become a Buddha. He applies expedient and convenient means to save them all in accordance with the requirements of the circumstances, just as a father whose house is on fire but whose sons still think of play, offers them a goat cart, a deer cart, and an ox cart to lure them out. Thus saved, they are given only the ox cart, the best of all carts; that is, not the Three Vehicles but the One Vehicle (chap. 3). Śāriputra is also compared to the wandering son who comes to work for hire without realizing who his employer is and who receives from his loving father not only wages but all his wealth (chap. 4).

Speaking to Mahākāśyapa and other disciples, the Lord tells the parable of rain. It falls on all plants, though they are ignorant of the fact that because their natures differ they respond to the rain in different ways. Only the Buddha knows the true character and reality of existence. He will care for all beings and enable them to become Buddhas, provided they have faith, however simple (chap. 5).

Śākyamuni then foretells many future Buddhas. So-and-so will become Buddha Radiance, in the Buddha-world of Brilliant Virtue, whose period will last for thirty-two kalpas, or billions of years, and will be called Great Splendor. So-and-so will become the Buddha of Sandalwood Fragrance in the Buddha-world called Happy Feeling, whose period, called Perfect Joy, will be 104 kalpas. And so on (chap. 6).

Interrupting his predictions, he tells of an Ancient Buddha who, he remembers, had a life of 5,400,000 myriads of ten million cycles. After attaining enlightenment, he recited the *Lotus* for eight thousand cycles. His sixteen sons have all become Buddhas and continue to recite the sūtra. His last son, Śākyamuni, is the one repeating it now (chap. 7). Then he continues to foretell the future of all disciples, monks, and the multitude: they will all be Buddhas and live in Buddha-worlds where there will be no evil ways or women (chap. 8). The surest way to become a Buddha is to revere the *Lotus Sūtra*, whether by obeying its teachings, studying it, expounding it, copying it, distributing it, or offering it in temples. Reciting even one verse will lead to salvation. On the other hand, a single word of blasphemy is a great sin (chaps. 9–10).

Now a great seven-jeweled stupa arises from the ground and is suspended in midair. As a voice emanates from within, Śākyamuni tells the congregation that inside is the total body of the Buddha, Prabhūtaratna, who has vowed to appear wherever the *Lotus Sūtra* is first proclaimed. As Śākyamuni issues a light from his forehead, illuminating all of the Buddha-worlds, Buddhas as innumerable as the grains of sand in the Ganges arrive before the shrine, which Śākyamuni opens with his finger. There the Ancient Buddha sits on a lion throne, in meditation. He has come, he says, as he has vowed, to hear the gospel. He invites Śākyamuni to sit beside him in the shrine (chap. 11). Following this, all present vow to proclaim the *Lotus*. A girl who wants to do the same has to change her sex in order to do so (chaps. 12–13).

Now Śākyamuni turns to Mañjuśrī and other bodhisattvas and explains to them how to preach the *Lotus*. The preaching, he says, is to be done in four ways: with right actions and intimacy; with a serene, pure, honest, brave, and joyful heart; with uprightness and no depravity; and with great compassion (chap. 14). Some offer to continue to preach the *Lotus* after Śākyamuni departs, but he assures them that it is unnecessary, for the earth will always bring forth an infinite number of bodhisattvas to do the work. Asked how he could have taught so many followers in only forty years of teaching, he replies that in fact he has been teaching throughout eternity (chap. 15). For the Buddha is really eternal. His true character knows neither being nor nonbeing, neither life nor death. Before restoring the stupa to its place, the two Buddhas, Śākyamuni and Prabhūtaratna, continue to preach for one hundred thousand years.

As the eternal preaching goes on, all the believers receive immense rewards, such as happiness (chap. 17), freedom from ailments, being born among gods, fulfillment of all their wishes (chap. 18), and special powers such as the ability to hear the sound of the universe (chap. 19). The bodhisattvas are always ready to help the believers and bestow these blessings, and thus it is very important that bodhisattvas be revered (chap. 20). At this point, the Buddha reveals the miraculous power (chap. 21). Amazed and awed, all beings now approach the shrine (chap. 22). Touching the foreheads of an infinite number of bodhisattvas, the Ancient Buddha urges them to spread the gospel. All depart rejoicing (chap. 22), and the drama ends.

The remaining chapters explain that the *Lotus* can heal the sick (chap. 23) and tell the story of Buddha Wonder Sound, who manifests himself to preach the sūtra and to save people by transforming himself, if necessary, into a woman (chap. 24), and about bodhisattva Avalokiteśvara (Guan-yin in Chinese and Kannon in Japanese), who will save people from fire, water, prison, and punishment, whether or not they are guilty, possess evil desires, or suffer from ignorance and delusions, and who will bestow children, both boys and girls, upon all (chap. 25). Other chapters describe certain spells (chap. 26), relate the conversion of King Wonderful Splendor (chap. 27), and describe bodhisattva Universal Virtue's offer to protect the *Lotus* (chap. 28).

This drama is as fascinating as it is fantastic. It is full of light, color, sound, fragrance, and action. It has a great deal of suspense and anticipation. It contains verses and fables. And it is a beautiful blending of fact and imagination. As a literary piece it is too repetitious, for what is said in prose is virtually all repeated in verse form. It lacks unity and balance. The climax comes too early, with the stupa's appearance in chapter 11. Buddhist scholars have tried their best to argue that the first fourteen chapters deal with manifestations of the "realm of traces" while the last fourteen deal with reality or "the realm of origin,"[1] or that the first half deals with salvation of the world or, figuratively speaking, the lotus flower, while the second half deals with the nature and personality of the Buddha, or the lotus seed. This, however, makes the sūtra more systematic and more philosophical than it really is. The *Lotus* is neither a theological treatise nor a philosophical essay. There is only a very brief passage in chapter 14 expressing the idea of the Void: that dharmas are neither born nor annihilated, neither begin nor end, neither rise nor fall. Rather, it is a dramatic presentation of fresh and revolutionary ideas offered as a message to enable religious practice and enrich religious experience. As such it is personal, dynamic, warm, and inspiring. It is a message of faith, hope, and love.

These novel and appealing religious ideas are not presented in abstract terms but in concrete images and living symbols. More than any other scripture, the *Lotus* has been the source of motifs of Buddhist art. Its figures dominate such famous caves as Dun-huang and Yün-gang. For several hundred years, the twin figures of the two Buddhas in the shrine were the most popular subjects in Buddhist painting and sculpture.[2]

Of all the symbols, the lotus flower is the central one, and it has penetrated both Buddhist and non-Buddhist Far Eastern culture. It has been and remains the symbol for Buddhism in general. In a popular sense, it stands for purity, as it rises from mud but remains clean, and it is in this sense that most Chinese and Japanese understand it, especially women, who take it to symbolize their feminine purity. The Neo-Confucian philosopher, Zhou Dunyi (1017–1073), in his famous essay on the lotus, saw in it nobility of character. But in its original meaning, the symbol has a far more philosophical import. It means the source of life and the power to continue to give life.[3]

When the *Lotus Sūtra* says that wherever the Buddha's disciples tread, flowers will grow, it means that Buddhas will be born out of the lotus. Thus the springing up of a lotus means the beginning of a new life. When Chinese poets secularized the Buddhist symbol and described women's small feet as lotuses, saying that with every step a lotus would spring up, they were thinking only of feminine beauty and did not realize that unwittingly they had hit upon the central idea of the lotus symbol, namely, that it is life giving. This is the idea underlying all Mahāyāna concepts.

What are these concepts as expressed in the *Lotus Sūtra*? First and foremost is the new concept of the Buddha. He is no longer just an ascetic who preached for forty years in India. Instead he is an eternal being, omniscient, omnipotent, and omnipresent. He is neither one Buddha nor many, and therefore Western terms such as monotheism are meaningless for Buddhism. He is the father of all Buddhas. He is both the hero of the drama and its organizer and proprietor. He both acts in the drama and leads all the dramatic personnel, including the most humble, who in time too will have a role to play. In short, he is a living Buddha whose voice of teaching continues for all time and is heard everywhere. The truth preached by him and all the Buddha-sons is living truth, continuously unfolding itself and continuously enlightening people, just as lotuses are continuously springing up. This concept of the Supreme Being makes Mahāyāna radically different from Hīnayāna Buddhism, which insists that the Buddha was simply a man in history. It also satisfies a dire need in the Far East not met by Confucian humanism or Daoist naturalism.

Equally revolutionary and important is the doctrine of universal salvation. Instead of having each arhat work out his own salvation, as in Hīnayāna, the new message promises that all will be saved by bodhisattvas. No misfortune, ignorance, or even sin will condemn a being to eternal suffering. This is the Great Vehicle, salvation for all.

This Great Vehicle (or Great Career) is the career of the bodhisattva, who voluntarily postpones Buddhahood to help save all beings. An infinite number of bodhisattvas endure all sufferings in order to save others. The whole personality and career of the bodhisattva can be characterized by one word: compassion. They inspire, console, protect, and lead all beings to ultimate Buddhahood. They have taken vows and dedicated themselves to this end, and they will not become Buddhas until all become so. What a magnificent concept! These Buddhas and bodhisattvas are willing to undertake tremendous efforts, travel anywhere, and use any means necessary to bring about salvation. Like the father saving his sons from the burning house, they are highly resourceful. This is not only a benevolent concept but also a very liberal one: the very narrow path of rigid discipline to salvation in the Hīnayāna has now been broadened; none will be prevented from entering Buddha Land.

This doctrine of convenient means has sometimes been misinterpreted in the West in terms of the end justifying any means. Like any other religion, Buddhism has not been free from abuse. But the four ways required for teaching the *Lotus* already mentioned should leave no doubt about the moral and spiritual prerequisites for any action. In reality, the various convenient means are but different phases of the same thing. It is the One Vehicle. The other Vehicles are but expedients to meet the requirements of those who have not seen the highest truth but understand only the common truth. People with an either/or point of view will find this Buddhist doctrine of twofold truth difficult to understand. But there is nothing contradictory in viewing the lotus on the common level as flower, leaves, and stem and on the higher level as the lotus itself, that is, as the seed. Similarly, viewed as common truth, the Buddha is Śākyamuni, a historical being, a Buddha of the "realm of traces," but viewed on a higher level, he is Tathāgata, the eternal being, or Buddha of the "realm of origin." These two levels are not contradictory but harmonious.

The ever-readiness of bodhisattvas to save beings by all means does not suggest that people should be passive. On their part, they must show devotion and faith. Faith, even as expressed in so simple a form as reciting the name of the Buddha, will lead to salvation. This is another aspect of Mahāyāna Buddhism that satisfied a great need in the Far East, where Confucian and Daoist rationalism left little room for such tender feelings as faith and devotion in religion. Whether or not the element of devotion was derived from Hinduism, it gives the great multitude hope for salvation through simple means.

This hope for salvation is beautifully and affectionately personified in the most popular bodhisattva, Guanyin. The embodiment of mercy and compassion, he endures much suffering and assumes the forms of both a Buddha and of animals, and journeys everywhere and anywhere to save all beings. He can have four, eight, eighteen, or a thousand hands, all of which he uses to save beings, in all possible ways under all possible circumstances. In Japan, Kannon retains his transcendental character as a Future Buddha. In China, however, he is presented in feminine form, perhaps to satisfy the Chinese love of sensuous beauty; perhaps to represent more appropriately the quality of compassion, especially as a protector of women and bestower of children; or perhaps to give Buddhism a loving Mother, much like the Virgin Mary of Christianity. At any rate, Guanyin has been for centuries an inexhaustible source of comfort and inspiration for the Chinese. The twenty-fifth chapter of the *Lotus Sūtra* is especially devoted to him and has been singled out as a separate sūtra. It has been studied, recited, copied, distributed, and offered in temples as expressions of devotion and faith by millions and millions of followers, century after century.

These basic Mahāyāna ideas—the eternal Buddha, universal salvation, the bodhisattva doctrine, the teaching of convenient means, the gospel of the One Vehicle, the message of salvation by faith and devotion, and the compassion of Guanyin—are all here presented in a single sūtra for the first time in Buddhism. It would be claiming too much for the *Lotus* to say that it contains all the important Mahāyāna doctrines. Those on the Void, Two-fold Truth, Instantaneous Transformation, Meditation, among others, are not treated here. But as a single document, it contains more important ideas than any other Buddhist scripture.

All this is contained in a book of twenty-eight chapters totaling about 69,000 Chinese characters. This, of course, refers to the Chinese translation *Miao-fa lien-hua jing*[4] made by Kumārajīva (344–413). This is the version used and revered by the Chinese and Japanese and the one rendered, with some abridgment, into English by W. E. Soothill, entitled *The Lotus of the Wonderful Law, or the Lotus Gospel.*[5] We have no idea who the author or authors of the sūtra were, when it was written, or in what language. It must be older than 255 C.E., because the first Chinese translation, a partial one, was done by an unknown missionary in China in 255 or 256.[6] Of the three extant Chinese translations—by Dharmaraksha (Zhu Fa-hu), called *Zheng fa-hua jing*, in 286; by Kumārajīva in 406; and jointly by Jñānagupta and Dharmagupta, called *Tian-pin miao-fa lien-hua jing*, in 601—Kumārajīva's has been accepted over the last fifteen centuries as the most authoritative. His original translation contained only twenty-seven chapters. The famous Chinese monk Fa-xian (d. 497), in quest of the twenty-eighth chapter, started for India in 475. He found in Khotan the chapter on Devadatta, a traitorous cousin of the Buddha. He returned and requested that Fa-i translate it. This chapter has since been added to the Kumārajīva version.

Kumārajīva's version has surpassed others partly because it is the translation of the oldest text. Most probably the original came from Khotan. Jñānagupta said that it agreed with a manuscript in the Kuchean language, which he had seen. Since Mahāyāna Buddhism developed in northern

India or even further north in Central Asia, its early sūtras were in local dialects of these areas and only later put into Sanskrit. Kumārajīva's version also agrees with the Tibetan version, and Tibetan translations are generally taken from the oldest texts. Takakusu believes Kumārajīva's original to be the oldest because, among other things, it quotes from Nāgārjuna (c. 100–200).[7] On the basis of textual criticism, scholars believe that the original contained twenty-one chapters, dated about 250 C.E., and was later expanded to twenty-eight.[8]

The more important reason for the supremacy of the Kumārajīva version is Kumārajīva himself. He opened up new studies in Buddhism in China, inaugurated a new era in translation, and trained as his pupils some of the most prominent Buddhist scholars, including the so-called Ten Philosophers of the Kumārajīva School, in Chinese history. Half Indian and half Kuchean, Kumārajīva became a monk at seven. He had such a great reputation in the Western regions that a Chinese king sent a general to bring him to China. After the general had kept him in northwestern China for seventeen years, another Chinese king dispatched an army to bring him to the capital in 401. There he enjoyed the highest honors and had the highest title of National Teacher conferred on him. Over a thousand monks attended his daily lectures. When he translated the *Lotus*, no fewer than two thousand scholars from all parts of China gathered around him. His scholarship and Chinese literary ability matched the best of the age. All in all, he inaugurated a new epoch in Chinese Buddhism, and the *Lotus* is one of the monuments of that achievement.

Since the translation agrees with the Tibetan, its accuracy cannot be questioned. However, Kumārajīva did take liberties. For example, he translated *tathāgataśarīra* (literally, "bone of the Tathāgata") as *ru-lai quan-shen*, "Total Body of the Buddha" (chaps. 11 and 19).[9] Evidently, he preferred to preserve the spirit of the work rather than translate literally. No wonder the lively Mahāyāna spirit prevails throughout the whole book.

How should we read this text today? We should not look for arguments or information in it. Since it was written and has been used for religious practice and experience, it is to be appreciated with goodwill and understanding. It does not matter whether you read it in its entirety or in part, whether this or that section first, whether in great seriousness or with a carefree spirit. You should approach it as you would approach a lotus flower. Look at its color now and then, and occasionally take in its fragrance. If you are in the proper spirit, a new lotus may even spring up for you.

Notes

The Lotus Sūtra remains a basic scripture for several Japanese Buddhist sects today, who are active in translating and disseminating it worldwide. The standard scholarly translation into English of Kumārajīva's Chinese version is by Leon Hurwitz, published by Columbia University Press in 1976, under the title *The Scripture of the Lotus Blossom of the Fine Dharma*. A partial English translation by W. E. Soothill, *The Lotus of the Wonderful Law* (Oxford: Clarendon Press, 1931), omits many repetitious passages, but generally preserves the inspirational qualities of Kumārajīva's version. The translation of H. Kern, *The Saddharma Puṇḍarīka or the Lotus of the True Law* (Oxford: Clarendon Press, 1984), is complete, but it is from a Sanskrit manuscript dated 1039, much later than the Kumārajīva text.

1. Junjirō Takakusu, *The Essentials of Buddhist Philosophy*, ed. Charles Moore and Wing-tsit Chan (Honolulu: University Press of Hawaii, 1947), 182.
2. J. Leroy Davidson, *The Lotus Sutra in Chinese Art* (New Haven, Conn.: Yale University Press, 1954), 24ff.
3. A. K. Coomaraswamy, *Elements of Buddhist Iconography* (Cambridge, Mass.: Harvard University Press, 1935), 18.
4. Sanskrit title: *Saddharma-puṇḍarīka Sūtra*. For a good study of the sutra, see Edward J. Thomas, *The History of Buddhistic Thought* (London: Kegan Paul, 1933), chap. 14.
5. *The Lotus of the Wonderful Law, or the Lotus Gospel*, trans. W. E. Soothill (Oxford: Clarendon Press, 1930).
6. Another translation, now lost, was done in 335 by Chih Tao-ken.
7. Takakusu, *Essentials of Buddhist Philosophy*, 178.
8. Ibid., 177; H. Kern, *The Saddharmapuṇḍarīka or the Lotus of the True Law*, vol. 21 of *Sacred Books of the East* (Oxford: Clarendon Press, 1884), xxii.
9. Fuse Kōgaku, "Hokkekyō no seishin to yakkai no mondai [The Spirit of the Lotus and Problems of Its Translation and Interpretation]," *Journal of Indian and Buddhist Studies* 5, no. 1 (January 1957): 73–82.

9

THE TEACHING OF VIMALAKĪRTI

Robert A. F. Thurman

THE TEACHING OF *Vimalakīrti* has been one of the most popular of Asian classics for about two thousand years. It was originally written in Sanskrit, based on accounts preserved in colloquial Indic languages, probably in the first century B.C.E. It nevertheless presents itself as recording events and conversations that took place in the time of Śākyamuni Buddha, over four hundred years earlier. It was first translated into Chinese in 170 C.E.; into Korean, Uighur, and Tibetan in the seventh through ninth centuries; and eventually into Mongolian and Manchu, as well as twice more into Chinese. In modern times, it has been translated into over ten languages, including most European languages, and at least five times into English.[1]

The *Vimalakīrti* is one of a class of texts called *Ārya Mahāyāna Sūtra*, "Holy Scripture of the Universal Vehicle" of Buddhism. These texts form the "Bibles" of Mahāyāna Buddhists, the Buddhists who flourished in first-millennium C.E. India and in Central and East Asia. These scriptures include hundreds of major texts and thousands of minor ones, with thousands more reportedly lost over the millennia. They began to emerge in India during the first century B.C.E. They purported to proclaim a new gospel of the Buddha, adding to the monastic Buddhist concern for individual liberation from suffering a teaching of universal love and compassion for all beings. They claimed that this explicitly messianic teaching had been taught by the same Śākyamuni Buddha but had been kept esoteric for four hundred years, waiting for Indian civilization to develop the need for such a socially progressive doctrine. For, despite the fact that many monastic Buddhists did not (and still do not) consider these Mahāyāna Scriptures to be authentic teachings of the Buddha, these texts sparked a messianic movement that reached out from the monastic strongholds that the Buddha's earlier teaching had established all over India to inspire lay men and women with the "bodhisattva ideal." This ideal was that each person should assume responsibility for the salvation of all others, not accepting personal liberation in Nirvāṇa until becoming a perfect Buddha, defined as an enlightened savior with the actual ability to save all beings.

Whatever the provenance of the text, the *Vimalakīrti* attained its importance and popularity as much for its readability as for its sanctity. It opens with the Buddha and his company living in the pleasure grove of Āmrapālī, a famous *femme fatale* of the great merchant city of Vaiśālī. It is a slightly unconventional situation. This elegant lady had won a race to invite the Buddha and company as her guests, beating the delegation of the fathers of the city. The dignified society of the city had taken some offense and thus were temporarily refraining from visiting the Buddha. As the scene opens, however, a group of five hundred noble youths, the cream of the city's younger generation, does come from the city to the grove to visit the Buddha and request his teaching.

They bring five hundred jeweled parasols as offerings, and the Buddha at once performs a miracle, forging them into a jeweled dome over the audience. In its bright surfaces, all behold reflected all parts of the universe, like a magical planetarium. After their awe has abated and they have sung his praises, they ask the Buddha not "How do we attain enlightenment?" or "What is the true nature of reality?" but "How does the bodhisattva perfect the Buddha land?" Or, in more modern terms: "How does the messianic idealist make a perfect world for the benefit of all beings?" The Buddha answers with an elaborate description of the perfections of a Buddha-land and how they evolved from the perfections of the bodhisattva who becomes a Buddha.

At the end of this discourse, the wise and saintly monk Śāriputra, one of the Buddha's closest "apostles," becomes doubtful about this notion of a "perfect world," thinking that it contradicts the "holy truth of suffering" and that the world he sees around him is far from perfect. The Buddha reads his mind, chides him for his lack of faith and insight, plants his toe on the ground, and miraculously grants the entire audience a second vision, a vision of the universe as a place of utter perfection, with each being exalted in his or her own highest fulfillment and enjoyment. He then lifts his toe and withdraws the vision. These dramatic events at the opening of the text set up the core tension of the *Vimalakīrti*, which is perhaps the central problematic of the Universal Vehicle itself. If Buddhahood is the perfection of the world as well as of the self, the saving of all beings as well as the freeing of the individual, then why did not the turbulent history of the planet come to an end with the Buddhahood of Śākyamuni? Why did not the struggle of evolution terminate with the Buddhahood of the first bodhisattva? Or, if this world is perfect to enlightened eyes, why does this perfection appear to the so highly evolved human beings as a faulty mess, an endless, seemingly futile struggle filled with needless suffering?

Once this problem has been posed, the scene shifts to downtown Vaiśālī, and the wealthy householder Vimalakīrti is introduced as the very embodiment of a Buddha's liberative arts. He is respected by all the citizens from highest to lowest and is a jack of all trades, a deeply religious man, and an accomplished philosopher known for his inspiring brilliance and matchless eloquence. Indeed, as we soon come to see, he is thought by some to be a little too eloquent. As the plot moves forward, Vimalakīrti becomes sick and uses the occasion to lecture the citizens of Vaiśālī about the inadequacy of the ordinary body and the unlivability of the unenlightened life, contrasting his miserable state with the blissful perfect health of an enlightened Buddha, who enjoys a body made of diamond. He also complains that, now that he has become ill, the monks of Buddha's company do not come to call on him, to cheer him and raise his spirits.

The scene then changes back to the Buddha in his grove, where, on cue, the Buddha asks his major disciples, monks, and lay supporters if they would not be so kind as to go to town to pay a sick call on the good Vimalakīrti. To his surprise, no one wants to go. Each of the major apostles among the saintly and learned monks tells a story about the last time he met with Vimalakīrti, in which Vimalakīrti challenged the narrowness of some central idea precious to that saint, refuting such partiality and powerfully opening up a whole new vista, but in the process overwhelming his poor visitor and leaving him speechless. Each of the major lay supporters has a similar tale to tell. All are united in their aversion to another encounter with the whirlwind of Vimalakīrti's adamant eloquence. Fortunately, the bodhisattva Mañjuśrī, known as the "crown prince of wisdom," finally volunteers to go, both to save the community the embarrassment of failing to pay a call on one of their most respected members during his time of sickness and to enjoy a chat with the householder sage.

As soon as Mañjuśrī decides to go, the entire community decides to follow along, as the conversation between Vimalakīrti and Mañjuśrī promises to be richly entertaining. The scene again shifts to the house of Vimalakīrti, where the central episodes of the drama occur. First, the two sages engage in cryptic dialogues, during which the profound side of the Mahāyāna is clearly expounded, involving the teachings of subjective and objective selflessness and absolute emptiness. For example:

Mañjuśrī: "Householder, why is your house empty? Why have you no servants?" Vimalakīrti: "Mañjuśrī, all buddha-lands are also empty." M: "What makes them empty?" V: "They are empty because of emptiness." M: "What is empty about emptiness?" V: "Constructions are empty, because of emptiness." M: "Can emptiness be conceptually constructed?" V: "Even that concept is itself empty, and emptiness cannot construct emptiness." M: "Householder, where should emptiness be sought?" V: "Mañjuśrī, emptiness should be sought among the sixty-two false convictions." M: "Where should the sixty-two convictions be sought?" V: "They should be sought in the liberation of the Tathāgatas." M: "Where should the liberation of the Tathāgatas be sought?" V: "It should be sought in the prime mental activity of all beings."

(*HTV*, 43–44)

Vimalakīrti here turns an ordinary question into a probe into the ultimate nature of things, declaring it to be total emptiness of all intrinsic reality. Mañjuśrī presses him on this, looking for traces of a nihilistic reification of emptiness into a real nothingness. Vimalakīrti holds his ground and reaffirms the emptiness of emptiness, which logically necessitates the reality of the world of relativity, which contains both delusions and enlightenment. Enlightenment itself is not something far away from ordinary life but something perhaps so close to the heart of every being that it tends to go unnoticed. This nondualism, based on a critique of the monastic Buddhist reification of Nirvāṇa as a realm of freedom apart from *saṃsāric* life, is the hallmark of the Mahāyāna movement, underlying its ultimate concern for universal compassion.

These dialogues were highly cherished by those Daoist intellectuals devoted to "enlightening conversation" during Buddhism's early years in

China, since they used wit and earnest conversation to open up the deep experience of reality. They served as the earliest model for the type of master-disciple exchanges eventually recorded in the *kōan,* or "public cases," of the Chan (Zen) tradition. But they were a little much for Śāriputra, who found himself quite at a loss, with no place to stand or chair to sit on in the realm of ultimate groundlessness.

Once emptiness is opened up for the audience, Vimalakīrti begins to play with the dimensions of relativity as well. He obtains giant lion thrones from another universe and seats everyone upon one, making each feel as tall as a mountain. He then teaches the "inconceivable liberation of the bodhisattvas," a teaching of the miraculous reality, which describes how anything is possible for the compassionate activity of the bodhisattva. He declares that to understand that teaching, one must understand the mystery of how a bodhisattva in the inconceivable liberation can place the axial mountain, Sumeru, into a mustard seed, without shrinking the mountain or rupturing the seed. Based on emptiness, he presents the mutual interpenetration and mutual nonobstruction of all things.

He and Mañjuśrī then discuss the problems of the paradoxical mutual indispensability of wisdom and compassion, insight and liberative art. Overjoyed by the inspiring teachings, the goddess of wisdom, Prajñāpāramitā herself, becomes manifest to bless the audience with flowers. After some deep conversations, she ends up teasing Śāriputra, the typical "male chauvinist" of those times, teaching him about the lack of the intrinsic reality of maleness and femaleness in the most charming and graphic way imaginable.

Vimalakīrti and Mañjuśrī then turn to the problem of good and evil, as Vimalakīrti expounds the code of bodhisattva deeds called "the reconciliation of dichotomies." The high point of events in the mansion is reached after Vimalakīrti has asked twenty-five of the advanced bodhisattvas present to give their views of the truth of nonduality, the highest expression of ultimate Truth. Each teaches deeply and subtly, though Mañjuśrī expresses some dissatisfaction with their teachings before offering his own ideas. Then they all ask Vimalakīrti for his idea, but he maintains a thunderous silence. Vimalakīrti's silence is perhaps the most famous silence in all Buddhist literature. It is the equivalent of the "Great Statement" of ultimate Truth in the Upanishads, "That Thou Art!" But perhaps Vimalakīrti felt that all his audience were so much *That* that he needed absolutely not to say so! This silence had a special impact coming from him, of course, as he usually spoke so inexhaustibly.

After this "lion's roar" of great silence, Vimalakīrti sends out to another universe for lunch, bringing a few grains of rice from the Buddha Sugandhakūta of the Perfume Universe, which he multiplies to feed the great crowd that has magically fit into his empty house. Along with the food comes a group of perfume bodhisattvas from that universe, who are curious to see the "Barely Tolerable" (*Sahā*) universe of Buddha Śākyamuni and the amazing bodhisattva Vimalakīrti, who had beamed an emanation out across the galaxies to bring back lunch! They are shocked to see how unheavenly our universe is compared to theirs, and they and Vimalakīrti have an extended dialogue, during which he presents the "answer" to the problem posed in the beginning of the text. He persuades the perfume bodhisattvas that Śākyamuni's "Tolerable" universe is ideal for bodhisattvas, indeed better than a heavenly perfume world, precisely because there is so much struggle and hardship in it. This difficulty of life is just what is needed for the development of compassion. Wisdom can certainly be cultivated by deep contemplation under a perfume tree, perhaps more conveniently than in our busy world. But without struggle, without nearness to suffering and without relationships with earthly beings, it is impossible to develop great compassion. And it is only compassion that creates eventually the Body of Buddhahood, just as wisdom creates the Mind. This section presents one of the clearest rationalizations of suffering in any Mahāyāna text; it is a veritable Buddhist "theodicy."

The scene changes again for the final act of the drama, as Vimalakīrti demonstrates his inconceivable level of liberation yet again. He miniaturizes the entire assembly, picks it up in his hand, and places it gently down outside of town in the grove of Āmrapālī, in the presence of the Buddha. There is a reunion between the monk Buddha and the layman Buddha, as Vimalakīrti at this point is now described. Vimalakīrti stands directly before the (monk) Buddha and gives a penetrating discourse about how only one who does not see any Buddha can actually see the Buddha, as the Buddha is not this body of form, not sensation, not ideation, and so forth. The Buddha accepts that he is not there as well as there and praises his householder colleague.

It is eventually revealed that Vimalakīrti is an Emanation Body of the Akṣobhya Buddha of the Buddha-land known as Abhirati (Intense Delight). Vimalakīrti performs a last miracle, bringing the entire Abhirati world in miniature form on the palm of his hand into this world to show it to all present. Abhirati is described as a paradise, but a paradise much more like our world, much more earthly than the heavenly Buddha-lands of perfume and jewel-lotus palaces. The main difference between Abhirati and our world is that the stairways from its earth to its heavens are always visible, and gods and humans mingle equally, all gravitating around the august presence of Akṣobhya Buddha. This is the culminating dramatic symbol of the text: Vimalakīrti's holding out of a hope for the future of this planet of ours in the Sahā universe.

The *Vimalakīrti* seems to have been designed as a kind of anthology of the major themes of all Mahāyāna scriptures. The wisdom teachings of especially chapters 5 and 9 are as if drawn from the *Transcendent Wisdom* (*Prajñāpāramitā*) scriptures. The miraculous glimpses of various "pure" Buddha-lands are cameos of the *Pure Land of Bliss* (*Sukhāvatī*) scriptures. The third and fourth chapters of dialogues between Vimalakīrti and various monks and laymen could have been drawn from any of the early *Jewel Heap* (*Ratnakūṭa*) scriptures, which are full of the controversies between those clinging to the strict dualism of the old monastic Buddhism and those inspired with the messianic nonduality of the Mahāyāna. The second chapter on "liberative art" or "technique" as well as the chapters proving to the perfume bodhisattvas the greater perfection of this seemingly imperfect Buddha-land of Śākyamuni echo the central message of the *White Lotus of Holy Truth* (*Saddharma Puṇḍarīkā*) scriptures. The sixth chapter on "Inconceivable Liberation" explicitly refers to the *Avataṃsaka* (*Garland*) scriptures, presenting the teaching of the chapter as a drop of that ocean, and the first miracle of the jeweled canopy resonates with the famous "Jewel Net of Indra" analogy for the mutually interpenetrative nature of all things, which is a central vision of the *Garland*. And finally, the ritual and magical nature of the mansion of Vimalakīrti, the enthronement of all members of the audience, the consecration of all by the goddess of wisdom, the teachings of the "Family of the Tathāgatas" and the reconciliation of dichotomies, and finally the magical, spiritual feast that cannot be digested until the participant achieves a higher stage of enlightenment—all these elements unquestionably convey an atmosphere of esoteric Buddhism, the apocalyptic vehicle later codified in the Buddhist Tantras.

The *Vimalakīrti* can be read in a single sitting. Its drama, visions, and humor can carry a reader past some of the difficult passages. But it can also be repeatedly browsed in, as its mysterious dialogues and paradoxes can stimulate contemplative thinking. For those new to Buddhist literature or more generally the wisdom literature of India, it can serve as an excellent introduction. And for those who have read widely, studied deeply, and taken time to contemplate, it endures as a quintessential summary.

Note

1. Chapter numbering and references in this chapter are to Robert Thurman, *The Holy Teaching of Vimalakīrti* (University Park: Pennsylvania State University Press, 1976). For a full translation from the Tibetan version, see this text.

The *Platform Sūtra* of the Sixth Patriarch

Philip Yampolsky

T HE PLATFORM SŪTRA is one of the most celebrated works in the vast literature of Chan (Zen) Buddhism, representing the "autobiography" and the recorded sayings of the Sixth Patriarch, Huineng, the Chinese master from whom all later Chan derives. Compilation was assigned to a monk by the name of Fa-hai, identified in the work itself as a resident monk in charge of Huineng's temple. The work has gone through numerous recensions, ranging from the primitive and error-filled manuscript found in the Tun-huang caves to the greatly enlarged Yuan-dynasty versions of some five centuries later. Huineng is honored as the illiterate firewood gatherer who, by his innate understanding of the principles of Buddhism, became heir to the Chan teachings and in turn handed them down to all future generations.

The *Platform Sūtra*, particularly the expanded Yuan-dynasty version, has been reprinted numerous times over the centuries, and it remains one of the most popular of Chan works. Until modern times, one can count almost a hundred different printings in China, Korea, and Japan, many of them ordered by pious believers seeking merit for the virtue of widening the distribution of the text. The work has had enormous popularity, particularly as a text for laymen to read and monks to admire. Surprisingly, the work, although often praised, has been the subject of very few commentaries and seems not to have been widely used as a source for the study of Chan or for the subject of lectures by Chan masters.

The *Platform Sūtra* is distinctly a Chan work; it champions a Chan teacher and emphasizes a particular meditative tradition. Yet at the same time it is characteristically Buddhist, very much in the tradition of other works of the time. Elements common to all Buddhism, such as liturgy, refuges, repentances, vows, acceptance of the precepts, and various standardized formulae, are very much in evidence in the *Platform Sūtra*. The work shares much with other schools of Tang Buddhism; its concerns are very much the concerns of all Buddhism. The four vows, intoned today by virtually all Buddhist groups, are here in a form almost identical with contemporary usage, and we may assume that they, along with the refuges and repentances, were in the repertoire of all schools of Buddhism. The giving of the precepts and their acceptance by both monks and laymen were widely practiced throughout the history of Buddhism in China. The appeal of the work and its immense popularity over the centuries stem perhaps from the combination of standard Buddhist concepts shared by Chan and all forms of Mahāyāna Buddhism with many of the encounter stories so characteristic of later Chan literature.

The Formless Precepts are an important element of the *Platform Sūtra*. It has been suggested that one of the particular functions of this text was to assist in giving these precepts. If this suggestion is correct, it would help solve one of the more puzzling features of the work, its title. The term *sūtra* is used exclusively for works said to have been spoken by the Buddha. Only in this one peculiar instance is the term applied to the sayings of a patriarch. There are, however, several works relating to the precepts that bear in their title the term "platform precept book" (*jieh-tan tu jing*), and it is quite likely that the term for *Platform Sūtra* (*tan-ching*) derives from the contraction of these two words.

While the *Platform Sūtra* holds an honored position as an early Chan text that champions the teachings of a revered founder, it differs considerably from the various genres of Chan writings that follow it. The *Platform Sūtra* is obviously composed of various layers: an autobiographical section, the basic sermons attributed to Huineng, and a number of miscellaneous independent pieces: verses, stories, the genealogy of the school, and admonitions and exhortations to students of Chan. The autobiography seems designed to emphasize the humble origins of the Sixth Patriarch, his illiteracy, and the availability of the teaching to laymen. Although we are told that Huineng cannot read, and later Chan makes much of the claim that it is a silent transmission from master to disciple without recourse to words and letters, it is obvious from the frequent quotations from canonical works that the person who delivered the sermons was fully conversant with scriptural literature. We can, however, gain little knowledge of how Chan was taught, what methods were used, or what was expected of the student. Obviously, sermons aimed at both monks and laymen played an important part in Chan teaching. Recorded by a disciple, they may well serve as predecessors to the later "Recorded Sayings" (*yü-lu*) genre of Chan literature. Individual monks appear to have come virtually at will to question the master, probably in public assemblies, although private meetings were held as well. There is no evidence as yet of the kōan interview between master and disciple, in which the student gave his solution to the brief story, or kōan, on which he was meditating at the time. The question-and-answer encounter between Huineng and Shen-hui contained in the *Platform Sūtra* is representative of the type of story that was later adopted for use in kōan meditation. In the early days of Chan, there was no organized monastic community; the elaborate regulations and rules developed later. Monks came and went at will. Those for whom the Master's teaching was attractive might stay and eventually become disciples and heirs; others might wander off in search of teachers more suitable to their temperaments. We may assume that intensive meditations were practiced, although nowhere are the techniques described nor the role of the teacher specified.

But if we examine the biography of Huineng and the work that is attributed to his name from the unclouded vantage of historical plausibility, we are at once confronted with a series of problems. Although there is little doubt that a monk by the name of Huineng existed and that the dates assigned to him, 638–713, are in all probability correct, there is little else that we really know about him. His autobiography, as contained in the *Platform Sūtra*, and all later biographies are fabrications of later generations. The standard history of early Chan, the "official" history that has been handed down over the centuries, is replete with unfounded simplifications; the forgotten history, revealed in the documents discovered at Dunhuang, is a combination of fact and deliberate fabrication; the actual history that can be reconstructed from the above two, despite lacunae and areas of uncertainty, is the story of the struggle of various Chan factions to establish themselves during the eighth century and of the eventual emergence of a group that had little connection with the Chan of the *Platform Sūtra* but that nevertheless traced its origins to the Sixth Patriarch, Huineng.

The work known as the *Platform Sūtra* has a curious and in many ways an obscure history. A cursory examination of the earliest version we have, the Dunhuang manuscript, which bears an elaborate title that reads in part: "Southern School Sudden Doctrine, Supreme Mahāyāna Great Perfection of Wisdom: The Platform Sūtra preached by the Sixth Patriarch Huineng at the Dafan Temple . . . " indicates that it itself is a copy of an earlier, no longer extant, version. Evidence, both external and internal, indicates that an original text dating to around 780 must have existed and that the present Dunhuang manuscript is written in a calligraphic style that would place it around 820. The great popularity that the work has enjoyed in China is attested to by the large number of versions that have appeared over the centuries. In the Song dynasty, there were several editions, some preserved in Japan and others now lost, that were fairly faithful to the early Tun-huang text; they correct errors, improve on the literary style, and eliminate certain sections that are no longer pertinent. By the Yuan dynasty, some ten different versions can be accounted for. The two different Yuan texts, of 1290 and 1291, are largely expanded works, twice the size of the Dunhuang edition. While they treat to a large extent the same teachings that are expounded in the earlier versions, the biographical sections are greatly enlarged, and a wealth of new stories of Huineng's encounters with other monks is provided.

To understand the significance of the *Platform Sūtra*, one must examine briefly the background from which it emerged. Our knowledge of this background derives largely from the documents discovered at Dunhuang, of which the *Platform Sūtra* is but one. Numerous works relating to Chan Buddhism in the seventh and eighth centuries were discovered in the caves at Dunhuang, and they form the primary source of our knowledge of Chan history. Chan was, of course, only one of several forms of Buddhism, some esoteric, some scholarly, some popular, that flourished during the Tang dynasty. In the early eighth century, Chan was in the process of attempting to establish itself, and several competing groups were striving for recognition. The most prominent among them was a group descended from the Fifth Patriarch, Hung-jen, which based its teaching on the *Laṅkāvatāra Sūtra* and which devised genealogical histories of its own tradition to strengthen its claim for legitimacy. This group traced its origins to the semilegendary Bodhidharma, the first patriarch in China, who had brought the teachings from India and who had handed down, through successive patriarchs, the teachings of the *Laṅkāvatāra Sūtra*.

This group and its heirs came to be known as the Northern Chan, although it did not initially refer to itself as such. Most prominent among this group was a famous monk, Shen-xiu (606?–706), later to be maligned in the *Platform Sūtra*, who was greatly honored by the Tang court and treated with the utmost pomp and respect. For the first decades of the eighth century, Shen-xiu and his descendants dominated the Chan of the capital cities.

In 732, however, an obscure monk by the name of Shen-hui (684–758; his dates have recently been revised, based on the discovery on the mainland of his stele) mounted a platform at his temple in Hua-tai, northeast of Loyang, and launched a virulent attack on Pu-ji (561–739), the heir of Shen-xiu, before a large audience. In speeches and in written texts Shen-hui, who had studied briefly with Huineng, denounced what he called Northern Chan and extolled the Southern School of Huineng. Huineng was the legitimate Sixth Patriarch, he maintained; Shen-xiu never pretended to that station, but now his heir claims to be the Seventh Patriarch. Shen-hui went on to assign to the leaders of Northern Chan a variety of crimes: Pu-ji is accused of sending an emissary to remove the head from Huineng's mummified body and of having sent a disciple to efface the inscription on Huineng's stele and to substitute one that stated that Shen-xiu was the Sixth Patriarch. Shen-hui wrote in detail the biography of Huineng, either inventing details or repeating legends current at the time. He never quotes from the *Platform Sūtra*, although there are numerous instances where his writings and those of the *Sūtra* are identical. Shen-hui did not limit his invective to accusations of the misrepresentation of the lineage; he attacked Northern Chan for the quality and content of its teaching. The most radical claim was that it was not the *Lańkāvatāra Sūtra* that had been handed down from Bodhidharma but rather the *Diamond Sūtra*. This was a complete fabrication on Shen-hui's part, yet it has been accepted by all later biographers of Huineng. Perhaps the most damaging accusation was that Northern Chan adopted a gradual, step-by-step method of attaining enlightenment, whereas Huineng's Southern School called for a sudden method for awakening to the self-nature. Whether this attack was justified is quite debatable—the Northern School in all probability advocated a more sophisticated process—but it was effective. By the year 780, Shen-hui had won the battle; Huineng was accepted by all schools of Chan as the legitimate Sixth Patriarch. Shen-hui himself and the line that descended from him did not share in the success. He was never recognized as a legitimate heir to the teachings, and his descendants failed to prosper. He virtually disappeared from the pages of traditional Chan history; it was not until the documents at Dunhuang were discovered that his real role was made clear.

Up to now it has been assumed by modern scholars that Shen-hui or one of his followers was the actual compiler of the *Platform Sūtra*. Recent research by the distinguished Japanese scholar Yanagida Seizan has shown rather persuasively that the *Platform Sūtra* was compiled by a certain Fa-hai, who was a member of the Ox-head School of Chan, a group that has been little studied but that flourished contemporaneously with the Southern and Northern schools. The Ox-head School, as did all the Chan schools of the time, traced its origins to the early teachers of Chan, but its major development as a school appears to have been during the last decades of the eighth century. The Ox-head School in all probability developed along independent lines, perhaps in reaction to the Northern and Southern schools. Four distinct lineages can be identified, each based on the teachings of specific masters, some of whom gained substantial recognition and for whom biographical materials remain. Less available, however, are texts that describe the content of the Ox-head teaching. It appears to have rejected the so-called gradual practices of Northern Chan and to have advocated a negation that did away with stated aims, techniques of meditation, and moralistic standards. The Ox-head School, together with groups that flourished in Szequan, may well have served to transcend the sectarian distinctions of North and South and to have established a connection with the groups that were moving toward a new developing Chan.

There is no room here for a detailed discussion, but biographical information indicates that Fa-hai was a highly literate monk who was concerned with the precepts, familiar with poetry, and active around the year 780, when the *Platform Sūtra* appears to have been written. By this time, most if not all schools of Chan had come to accept Huineng without reservation as the Sixth Patriarch. Internal evidence from the *Platform Sūtra*, combined with known facts, give much credence to Professor Yanagida's view that the Ox-head monk Fa-hai was the actual compiler of the *Platform Sūtra*. Making use of stories and legends current at the time, Fa-hai wrote a biography of Huineng, championed the Southern School of sudden enlightenment, and condemned the gradual approach associated with Northern Chan. However, Fa-hai avoided the invective and violent accusations that accompanied Shen-hui's attack. That the *Platform Sūtra* makes little mention of Shen-hui and includes the lineage of twenty-eight Indian patriarchs accepted in both Northern Chan and the Ox-head School but quite different from the lineage espoused in Shen-hui's works lends credence to the attribution. If one discounts the error-filled version that represents the Dunhuang text as nothing more than a copy by a less-than-literate monk, the identification of the work as a product of Fa-hai and the Ox-head School appears quite appropriate.

If we examine the texts of the sermons, we find that the major concepts are drawn from scriptural works. Although the autobiographical section places great emphasis on the *Diamond Sūtra*, the concepts described derive more from the *Nirvāṇa Sūtra* and the *Awakening of Faith*. Huineng, in his sermon, is quoted as saying that the teachings derive from the sages of the past and are not his original concepts. Stress is placed on the identity of meditation and wisdom; to conceive that one precedes the other implies dualism. Wisdom is inherent; it is the original nature with which we all are endowed, and the realization of this is akin to enlightenment. Emphasized is the concept of no-thought. Thoughts are spoken of as progressing endlessly from past to present to future, and attachment to a single thought leads to attachment to a succession of thoughts; however, by cutting off this attachment one may achieve no-thought, which in itself is a state of enlightenment. The Perfection of Wisdom is given prominence in the *Platform Sūtra*; indeed, the term is contained in the original title of the work. The standard Chan doctrine of "seeing into one's own nature" is constantly invoked. One must not seek on the outside but always look within one's own mind and obtain awakening for one's self. Failing this, a good teacher may be sought as a guide, but in the end it is only you yourself who must perform the practice.

All these are concepts that are associated with Chan, yet they are found in other schools of Mahāyāna Buddhism as well. The *Platform Sūtra*, then, is not characterized by contributions that can be regarded as uniquely representative of Chan Buddhism. Yet historically the work is of great importance. That an unlettered "barbarian" from the south was able to attain the highest position in Chan emphasized the availability of the teaching to all. The work marks a shift in emphasis in Chinese Buddhism, a move from an abstract Nirvāṇa to an individual enlightenment available to anyone who seeks to realize through meditation the Buddha nature inherent within him. The content of Buddhism does not change; Chan is always Mahāyāna Buddhism, but the method of teaching assumes a different cast, with a greater emphasis placed on meditation. The decline of the Tang court, domestic upheavals, and persecutions of Buddhism all contributed to the emergence of Chan as the dominant form of Buddhism in the early ninth century. Although we find no direct link between the Tang of the *Platform Sūtra* and that of the Hongzhou School that gained prominence at this time and from which all later Chan derives, the position of Huineng had become such that the founding fathers of this new form of Chan all traced their ancestry to him. Huineng always remains the Sixth Patriarch, the dominant figure in the early history of Chan Buddhism.

Note

Two translations of the early Dunhuang version are available: Wing-tsit Chan, *The Platform Scripture* (New York: St. John's University Press, 1963); and Philip Yampolsky, *The Platform Sutra of the Sixth Patriarch* (New York: Columbia University Press, 1967). Translations of the enlarged Yuan version have been made by Wong Mou-lam, *The Sutra of Wei-lang (Hui-neng)* (London: Luzae, 1953); and Lu Kuan-yu (Charles Luk), in *Ch'an and Zen Teachings*, vol. 3 (London: Rider, 1963).

The *Platform Sūtra* as a Chinese Classic

Wm. Theodore de Bary

IMPLICIT IN OUR title above is a distinction between a "Sūtra" and a "Classic," which would not ordinarily be made, given the use of the same Chinese term *jing* for both Chinese and Buddhist works viewed as canonical. To some extent, the *Platform Sūtra* is being naturalized as Chinese, in ways that are already pointed to by the formal title for the work, which reads as follows:

> *Southern School Sudden Doctrine, Supreme Mahāyāna Great Perfection of Wisdom: The Platform Sūtra preached by the Sixth Patriarch Huineng at the Da-fan Temple in Shao-zhou, one roll, recorded by the spreader of the Dharma, the disciple Fahai, who at the same time received the Precepts of Formlessness*

Here the preaching of the simple monk Huineng is formally identified as a canonical Buddhist sūtra, a designation that would normally be reserved for scripture claiming to be the original word of the Buddha Śākyamuni himself (or at least claiming his sanction), and here also the *Platform Sūtra* is represented as the culmination of Buddhist tradition in the form of "The Supreme Mahāyāna Great Perfection of Wisdom." This invocation of the highest metaphysical philosophy of the Mahāyāna tradition, with all its sacred aura, is followed by a reference to something much more everyday and prosaic: a sermon preached by an ordinary Chinese monk, which is described in the opening passage of the text.

> The Master Huineng ascended the high seat at the lecture hall of Da-fan Temple, expounded the Dharma of the Great Perfection of Wisdom, and transmitted the precepts of formlessness. At that time over ten thousand monks, nuns, and lay followers sat before him. The prefect of Shao-zhou, Wei Qù, some thirty officials from various departments and some thirty Confucian scholars all begged the Master to preach on the Dharma of the Great Perfection of Wisdom. The prefect then had the monk-disciple Fa-hai record his words so that they might become known to later generations and be of benefit to students of the Way, in order that they might receive the pivot of the teaching and transmit it among themselves, taking these words as their authority.

The simple matter-of-factness of the Chinese text might pass unnoticed were it not in such contrast to the lofty invocation of the Highest Perfect Wisdom (*prajñā paramita*), with its high-flown metaphysics, most often propounded in a supernatural setting. Here the local scene, the specificity of time and place, the official audience, and the attention to the historical record are redolent not only of the more quotidian Chinese approach to life but even more of the distinct historical consciousness of the Chinese, in contrast to the timelessness and transcendence that permeates the typical Mahāyāna sūtra. This account of things is more reminiscent of the Chinese classics, especially the Confucian *Classic of History* (*Classic of Documents*) or *Chronicle of Tsuo*, and invites a more down-to-earth, factual approach to the subject.

What explains this sharp juxtaposing (or perhaps conflating?) of seemingly disparate worlds—the hierarchical and the egalitarian, the sacred and even mystical with the secular and practical? Both possibilities are inherent in the Chinese term for canonical texts, *jing*, which can apply to both traditional religious scripture, for example, the Daoist *Daodejing*, or to "classic" as it might apply to a wide range of human experience embodied in history, literature, and ritual decorum. How do they fit together here?

The answer is not easily found by recourse to some singular authorial identity or the defining circumstances of its creation, both of which have been subject to much critical scrutiny and controversy in the case of the *Platform Sūtra*. We have to rely first of all on what sense we make of the plain text itself, but this is rendered difficult by the extremely heterogeneous nature of the contents. It is quite episodic and uneven, without any logical thread running from one passage to another, and by its nature it resists systematic philosophical argument. In fact, as a genre it fits into a distinctive narrative tradition in Chinese Buddhism that features the miraculous power of the *Diamond Sūtra* in the lives of ordinary Chinese. Though not the first of the genre, it became classic for reasons we shall consider here.

There is, first of all, the autobiographical account of Huineng, which is itself selective enough to highlight certain pointed messages. Then there are texts identified as formal sermons or special literary genres and still others that address, more or less at random, issues raised in the religious controversies of the time, some of which might be labeled partisan or polemical. The following summary is no substitute for a reading of the text itself, but it may point out certain tendencies that give a degree of coherence to an otherwise rather disjointed narrative.

The opening passage, as we have seen, presents Huineng as a very ordinary human being, unless one considers that he is more disadvantaged than most other humans in being poor, orphaned, and illiterate. There would hardly be a greater contrast to this—the picture of the lowliest of human beings speaking authoritatively as a Buddha—than the original picture of the Buddha Śākyamuni as a prince, with all the prestige of the Aryan aristocratic class and speaking also as if for the traditional religious elite, the Brahmin priestly class.

In the later Mahāyāna development, which features lay Buddhism distancing itself from an alleged elitist Hīnayāna, this lay ideal is identified with Vimalakīrti, who is portrayed as a rich man with many accomplishments that serve his role as a teacher to all. Yet the literature surrounding the high ideal of Vimalakīrti was spoken of as a teaching of equality, partly because it reached out to all, and it is this egalitarian strain that is brought to its radical conclusion in the more egalitarian climate of Chinese society, which, compared to the hereditary caste system of India, was virtually classless. Thus Huineng appears as the lowest common denominator in Chinese populism—"Everyman" stripped down to the minimum. In this too the *Platform Sūtra* qualifies as typically Chinese.

Nevertheless, in the ordinary course of making a hard living, Huineng accidentally hears someone recite the *Diamond Sūtra* and immediately experiences a kind of enlightenment. At this point, his uneducated intelligence is exposed to a text symbolic of the Highest Perfect Wisdom (that is, Mahāyāna tradition in its perfected form as literate discourse). Just what kind of understanding this involves on the part of the illiterate Huineng is left unexplained (and remains so to the end), but it is enough to incline him to take advantage of the opportunity that comes his way to visit the so-called Fifth Patriarch. The text takes for granted both his and our awareness of some such patriarchy, but the crucial nature of such an encounter is assumed as a simple given in this case (for reasons that I hope will emerge more clearly as we go along).

At their initial meeting, Huineng is put to the test. The Fifth Patriarch questions his status as a candidate for instruction, since Huineng is from Lingnan, a frontier area only half civilized. Huineng responds that culture and civilization are irrelevant to the attainment of enlightenment; the universality of the Buddha nature (as affirmed by the Mahāyāna) is subject to no limitations of geography or local culture. "There is no north or south in the Buddha nature." Thereupon the sūtra says: "The Master wished to continue his discussion with me, but seeing other people nearby he said no more. Then he sent me to work with the assembly . . . and then to the threshing room, where I spent over eight months treading the pestle."[1]

This tells us that the Fifth Patriarch is guarding the strict privacy of individual instruction; the matter does not lend itself to further explication, and even for others to overhear it could be prejudicial to the outcome. Instead, the disciple would be better off submitting to the discipline of routine work.

The next episode finds the Fifth Patriarch asking his disciples to look into themselves, grasp the original nature of their *prajñā* intuition, "and then compose a poem expressing it for him." Without going into all the details, the upshot of this, simply put, is that the head monk Shen-xiu and Huineng each compose a poem for the Fifth Patriarch (centering on the inexpressibility of the Buddha nature), the latter chooses Huineng's as better expressing the "original nature of *prajñā* intuition," and on that basis he is prepared to designate Huineng as successor to the Patriarchy. But "being afraid lest the assembly knows this," the Fifth Patriarch dismisses the assembly and waits until midnight to call Huineng for a personal interview. As Huineng recounts it:

> At midnight the Fifth Patriarch called me into the hall and expounded
> the Diamond Sūtra to me. Hearing it once, I was immediately

awakened, and that night I received the Dharma. None of the others
knew anything about it. Then he transmitted to me the Dharma of
Sudden Enlightenment and the robe, saying: "I make you the Sixth
Patriarch. The robe is the proof and is to be handed down from generation to generation. My Dharma must be transmitted from mind to
mind. You must make people awaken to themselves."

The Fifth Patriarch told me: "From ancient times the transmission
of the Dharma has been as tenuous as a dangling thread. If you stay
here there are people who will harm you. You must leave at once."

(133)

The extreme secrecy with which the patriarchal succession is conveyed
to Huineng is only too evident. "For three years do not spread the teaching or else calamity will befall the Dharma" (133). The reason for this soon
becomes apparent. After he leaves, "unknown to me several hundred
men were following behind me wishing to kill me and steal my robe and
Dharma" (134).

Huineng survives this brutal attempt to steal the emblems of transmission, so manifestly incompatible with its inherent spiritual nature, but as
the story is told we become aware that behind this is a contest of authority.
This sūtra itself is meant to discredit other claimants to patriarchal succession. Somehow the issue has to be dealt with, but it strains the need for
secrecy. One has to deal with it in some overt manner.

But there was one monk with the family name of Chen, whose personal name was Huiming. Formerly he had been a general of the
third rank and he was by nature and conduct coarse and violent.
Reaching the top of the mountain, he caught up with me and threatened me. I handed over the dharma-robe, but he was not willing to
take it.

[He said]: "I have come this long distance just to seek the Dharma,
I have no need for the robe." Then, on top of the mountain, I transmitted the Dharma to Huiming, who when he heard it, was at once
enlightened.   (134)

Here the transmission of the Dharma is spoken of first in terms of the outward symbol of the robe—its seeming importance but actual dispensability—
which takes place without any reference to the content of the teaching. This

absence/avoidance of any substantial content remains a characteristic of the sūtra throughout.

The rhetoric of transmission is consistently couched in the qualified language of nondualism, for instance in such terms as the unity of meditation and wisdom:

> Good friends, my teaching of the Dharma takes meditation (*ding*) and wisdom (*hui*) as its basis. Never under any circumstances say mistakenly that meditation and wisdom are different; they are a unity, not two things. Meditation itself is the substance of wisdom; wisdom itself is the function of meditation. At the very moment when there is meditation, then wisdom exists in meditation. Good friends, this means that meditation and wisdom are alike. Students, be careful not to say that meditation gives rise to wisdom, or that wisdom gives rise to meditation, or that meditation and wisdom are different from each other.
>
> (135)

The same unity is expressed in terms of the "*samādhi* of oneness," which is explained in terms of "nonattachment":

> The *samādhi* of oneness is straightforward mind (direct intuition) at all times, walking, staying, sitting, and lying. The *Qing-ming jing* says "Straightforward mind is the place of practice; straightforward mind is the Pure Land." Do not with a dishonest mind speak of the straightforwardness of the dharma. If while speaking of the *samādhi* of oneness, you fail to practice straightforward mind, you will not be disciples of the Buddha. Only practicing straightforward mind, and in all things having no attachments whatsoever, is called the *samādhi* of oneness.
>
> (136)

Another way of expressing the same directness of intuition is "no-thought": "To be unstained in all environments is so-called 'no-thought.' If on the basis of your own thoughts you separate from environment, then, in regard to things, thoughts are not produced. If you stop thinking of the myriad things, and cast aside all thoughts, as soon as one instant of thought is cut off, you will be reborn in another realm" (138).

"No-thought" is also directly connected to "sitting in meditation": "Now that we know that this is so, what is it in this teaching that we call 'sitting in meditation' (*zuo-chan*)? In this teaching 'sitting' means without any obstruction anywhere, outwardly and under all circumstances, not to activate thoughts. 'Meditation' is internally to see the original nature and not become confused" (140).

If this perfection of wisdom so steadfastly abjures any defined content, what is it that the Bodhisattva can convey to other beings in order to assist their salvation? Huineng, in a preacherly vein, says:

> Good friends, when I say "I vow to save all sentient beings everywhere," it is not that I will save you, but that sentient beings, each with their own natures, must save themselves. What is meant by "saving yourselves with your own natures"? Despite heterodox views, passions, ignorance, and delusions, in your own physical bodies you have in yourselves the attributes of inherent enlightenment, so that with correct views you can be saved.
>
> "I vow to achieve the unsurpassed Buddha way" is always to act humbly, to practice reverence for all things, to separate oneself from erroneous attachments, and to awaken to the wisdom of *prajñā*. When delusions are cast aside you are self-enlightened, you achieve the Buddha Way. (143–144)

In other passages, this ultimate wisdom of "no-thought," "nonabiding," and "oneness of *samādhi*" is explained in the language of long-standing Buddhist tradition as embodied in the Three Treasures (the Buddha, the Dharma, and the Religious Orders) as well as the Three-fold Body of the Buddha (*Trikāya*). This concludes with:

> The Master said: Good friends, take refuge in enlightenment [the Buddha], the most honored among two-legged beings; take refuge in the truth [the Dharma], the most noble [doctrine which sets people] free from desires; take refuge in purity [the Sangha], the most honored among sentient beings. From now on you will call enlightenment your master and will not rely on other teachings which are deluded and heretical. Always prove it clearly yourselves with the Three Treasures of your own natures. (145)

Should a person of the Mahayana hear the Diamond Sūtra, his mind will open and he will gain awakening. Therefore we can say that in the original nature itself the wisdom of *prajñā* exists, and that by using this wisdom yourself and illuminating with it, there is no need to depend on written words.   (149)

From the foregoing passages, a pattern emerges that reaffirms the inexpressibility of true enlightenment, yet it compromises this by arguing that Chan is the only true fulfillment of the Mahāyāna, to the exclusion and denigration of other teachings. Despite the essential "wordlessness" of Chan, it must still find words to assert and defend itself in the face of competing alternatives.

Quite apart from these obvious attempts to equate Chan with the hallmarks of traditional Buddhism, nothing could be more traditional than Chan/Zen itself (which is cognate with the Sanskrit *dhyāna* and our "trance"), the meditative concentration that was the culmination of the original "Noble Eightfold Path" of the Theravada. But by this time in the development of the Mahāyāna, meditation itself had been subjected to enough interpretation and adaptation so that the *Platform Sūtra* had to take these alternative views and practices into account. In other words, among the assorted and often disconnected passages in the *Platform Sūtra* there are some in which the authorial voice differs depending on whether what is being portrayed is Huineng engaging in direct personal instruction of a kind that might approximate "mind-to-mind" transmission of an essentially private nature or other explanatory teachings that engage more with the contemporary discourse that takes place in the public domain and cannot simply be ignored.

Among these current issues are the claims made by other schools or sects, among which a major competitor of Chan in the Tang and after was the Pure Land School, of whose claims the *Platform Sūtra* devotes considerable attention in refuting. This is something it can do only by meeting it on its own terms, in, as it were, the going rhetoric of the public forum.

Another way that the *Platform Sūtra* attempts to establish its credentials in a public way is by claiming a pedigree going back to the Buddha Śākyamuni, that is, by constructing a patriarchal lineage with the Chan teaching passing from "mind to mind" but embodied now in at least putative historical succession. Here we have another concession to prevailing Chinese tradition inasmuch as the status and legitimacy of both political and religious groups in the Tang were established through claims to high ancestry. The compiling or inventing of genealogies was the name of the game in the seventh and eighth centuries. Indeed, the Tang dynasty itself as a ruling house was provided with a pedigree going back to Laozi, and likewise patriarchal succession was common among indigenous religious movements.

Even the title of the *Platform Sūtra* betrays this conception and practice in calling itself the *Platform Sūtra of the Sixth Patriarch*. What is translated here as "patriarch" (*zu*) has the sense of paternal ancestor and was common to all Chinese families and clans claiming descent from a common ancestor. Thus even Chan, though insisting on "transmission of mind to mind," that is, direct intuition, found it opportune to establish itself in a conventional Chinese manner so as to survive in the world of public discourse.

In the *Platform Sūtra* there is abundant evidence that the open contest for recognition was going on within the Chan sect itself (and even within the school claiming descent from Hongren, the Fifth Patriarch). The sūtra makes no secret of this. It often refers to the crass ambitions, venality, and jealousies among Huineng's fellow monks, from which the Fifth Patriarch tries to protect Huineng in episode after episode. Though such enviousness and covetousness is in no way considered acceptable, it is still taken for granted as a fact of life, as something to be dealt with, on the one hand by reaffirming the essential privacy of the spiritual transmission and on the other by identifying Huineng as the authentic heir to Hongren within the realm of public discourse.

> The Fifth Patriarch realized that I had a splendid understanding of the cardinal meaning. Being afraid lest the assembly know this, he said to them: "This is still not complete understanding." At midnight the Fifth Patriarch called me into the hall and expounded the Diamond Sutra to me. Hearing it but once, I was immediately awakened, and that night I received the Dharma. None of the others knew anything about it. Then he transmitted to me the dharma of Sudden Enlightenment and the robe, saying: "I make you the Sixth Patriarch. The robe is the proof and is to be handed down from generation to generation. My Dharma must be transmitted from mind to mind. You must make people awaken to themselves."

Note that Huineng's legitimacy derives from Hongren's perception of his superior insight, not from any demonstration of superior moral character or heroic virtue. The transmission is still secret, but now at least the guardians of the secret have a story. They have broken the self-imposed silence of

Chan/Zen and put forth a lineage by which to establish a claim to legitimacy and authority in the public sphere.

In the text itself, the patriarchal lineage is given prominence in a detailed recounting of the transmission from the original Buddha through thirty-nine predecessors down to Huineng. This appears as the penultimate teaching from Huineng. At the point of his departure from this world, he is begged by his disciples to impart to them his last testament (in a manner mimicking the last words of the Buddha in the Lotus and Nirvana sūtras). After listing the names of all thirty-nine patriarchs, with a detailed specificity meant to lend a sense of exactitude to it as veritable history (echoing at the end the facticity of the opening scene), Huineng is quoted as saying: "From today on transmit the teaching among yourselves but be sure you have the same sanction and do not let the essentials of the teaching become lost" (179). From this one can see how essential the lineage has become as sanction for the essential teaching, which would otherwise be lost without an anchor in the turbulent seas of sectarian divisions.

None of that transmission or tradition would have survived except in the institutional context of the monastery, which is simply assumed as the natural setting for the *Platform Sūtra*. Huineng is living in the company of others identified as monks living together under the aegis and direction of the master. Whether it was an entirely self-sufficient community or not, an essential component of monastic life was manual labor and other tasks necessary to the survival of a religious community. The Chan/Zen tradition often emphasized the indispensability of this practical work. Huineng himself is described as spending most of his time in such humble tasks. Nevertheless, meditation is clearly the main occupation of the monk, and much of the *Platform Sūtra* is devoted to directions for proper meditation. Thus monastic rules became a major form of Chan/Zen instruction, and disciplinary rules proved to be an essential part of Chan/Zen literature. Strict discipline was among the elements in Chan that impressed Japanese visitors such as Eisai and Dōgen and became a main feature of Chan transmission to Japan.

In the Mahāyāna critique of the so-called Hīnayāna or "lesser vehicle," the limitations of monastic isolation from the larger lay community had been a key issue, but in a form of Buddhism centered so much on meditation, it is not surprising that Chan/Zen would find the monastic setting essential for providing both the support and isolation that solitary meditation requires.

As such, the monastic community blended, on a small scale, the privacy of meditation and the regulated communal life of the monks; in other words, it required Chan/Zen to create a kind of well-defined and limited public sphere of its own. Although only glimpses of this are found in the *Platform Sūtra*, Chan/Zen sustained itself through this form of institutional organization and regulation. This is another way in which the condition of survival of even such a secret transmission and private religious experience had to come to terms with some kind of public life and develop its own rhetoric for communicating this.

In the Song period, the codification of monastic rules was increasingly a focus of Chan life, as in the "Pure Rules for Chan Cloisters" (*Chan Yuan qinggui*), and given the prime attention to these rules one can understand how this defining and codification facilitated the adoption of Chan/Zen in medieval Japan, where it served as a counterpart to the samurai code. It gave pilgrims like Eisai and Dōgen, pioneers in the importation and spread of Zen, a definite handle on a subject otherwise heavily dependent on implicit understandings.

Finally, one of the most important of such formulations in the Song was the *gongan* (*kōan*), which does not appear in the *Platform Sūtra* but is a significant extension of tendencies already seen in this classic text. The term *gongan* is literally a "public case" or "public thesis." It represents another formula resorted to in Chan to bridge the gap between the indeterminacy of private experience and the need for some formula by which it might be conveyed to others and thus survive in the larger public world. The *gongan* poses a conundrum that defies a rational solution but compels the practitioner to go beyond logic, rationalization, and paradox to some deeper insight. The fact that it is called a "public case" indicates that the *gongan* is trying to reconcile private and public in a way necessary to transmission of the teaching. Not surprisingly, some Chan teachers in the Song, upholding the radical indeterminacy of Chan enlightenment, condemned this modest concession to public rhetoric as a travesty of true Chan.

Apart from such radical fundamentalists, however, Chan as a whole survived by making concessions to human society and culture that may be summarized as:

1. The attempt to claim fidelity to the hallmarks of the main doctrinal expressions of the Mahāyāna and in the process openly contest the claims of other schools or sects.

2. Claiming a patriarchal succession or lineage over time as tangible evidence of its authority, openly asserted against rival claimants.
3. The institutionalization of the teaching in monasteries with their own defined rules.
4. The use of the public case or gambit as a key formula for instruction, recorded and complied in a publishable form that could travel as a rhetorical device for hinting at the essence of Chan/Zen.

Given these adaptations of Chan to the sustaining of its life in public, a question remains as to whether, in the course of this involvement with the public sphere, these concessions to public life prepared Chan to deal with public affairs in a way that addresses the problems and value issues of human society itself. The *Platform Sūtra* is not unmindful of this question and gives its own answer at the conclusion of Huineng's parting message to his disciples:

> After I am gone, do not weep worldly tears, nor accept condolences, money, and silks from people, nor wear mourning garments. If you did so it would not accord with the sacred Dharma, nor would you be true disciples of mine. Be the same as you would if I were here, and sit all together in meditation. If you are only peacefully calm and quiet, without motion, without stillness, without birth, without destruction, without coming, without going, without judgments of right and wrong, without staying and without going—this then is the Great Way. (181)

This final statement, reminiscent of the *Sūtra of the Humane King* and its nondualist conception of the ruler, leaves one wondering how one could deal with issues of public affairs and governance without some consideration of right and wrong. Such a value-free stance was undoubtedly what later the Neo-Confucian Fan Zhongyan (989–1052) had in mind when he proposed an alternative conception of the Confucian ideal as "The Noble Man first concerns himself with the concerns of the world and only then finds his own contentment in it." Peace of mind for him, if not for Huineng, came from acting on and satisfying his own moral conscience first.

Nevertheless, the spiritual ideal of Huineng, as found par excellence in the *Platform Sūtra*, challenged the Neo-Confucians to match Chan praxis with its own "quiet sitting." Thus something of Chan survived by transmigrating and being reborn through a more substantial adaptation to Chinese tradition.

Note

1. Philip Yampolsky, *The Platform Sutra of the Sixth Patriarch* (New York: Columbia University Press, 1967), 128. Subsequent references to this source appear in the text.

11

TANG POETRY

A RETURN TO BASICS

Burton Watson

T HE HISTORY OF Chinese poetry begins around 600 B.C.E., with the compilation of an anthology, the *Shijing* or *Classic of Odes*, which contains poems that probably date back several centuries earlier. It continues with barely a break down to the present day. Naturally, such an extended period of development saw the evolution of a number of different poetic forms and styles and countless ebbs and flows in the tide of artistic inspiration.

It has generally been agreed by Chinese critics—and non-Chinese students of the language have found no reason to disagree—that the highest peak in literary achievement in this long process of growth was reached during the Tang dynasty, which ruled China from 618 to 907 C.E., particularly the middle years of this period. This was the age of Li Bo, Du Fu, Bo Juyi, and numerous other figures renowned in Chinese literary history, when the art of poetry reached levels of expressive force and achieved a universality of statement it was seldom to rival again. I would like here to try to convey some idea of the nature of this poetry and discuss its appeal for English readers of today. Rather than attempting generalities, I will center the discussion around specific examples of Tang poetry, touching upon the qualities that can be effectively brought across in translation and those that must inevitably be lost.

Unlike the peoples of Europe and India, the Chinese did not develop a tradition of epic poetry. Though they had their internecine wars and campaigns against foreign invaders—Ezra Pound's "Song of the Bowmen of

Shu" is a translation of an early work from the *Classic of Odes* dealing with one such campaign—they seldom made feats of arms a theme of poetry. An overwhelmingly agricultural people, they have preferred in their poetry to focus mainly upon the scenes and events of everyday life, which accounts for the generally low-key and ungrandiose tone of so much of Chinese poetry. It is also one reason why many of their works, even those written centuries ago, sound strikingly modern in translation.

The first work to be quoted is by the government official and poet Bo Zhuyi (772–846). Bo was one of the most prolific of the major Tang poets, and his works are particularly well preserved, in part because he took the trouble to compile and edit them himself and deposit copies in the libraries of several important Buddhist temples. The poem was written in 835 and is addressed to Bo's friend Liu Yüxi (772–842), a fellow poet and bureaucrat who was the same age as Bo. The Chinese frequently exchanged poems with friends, often replying to one another's poems as one would reply to a letter, the practice constituting both an expression of friendship and an opportunity to exercise literary abilities and invite critical comment. When responding to a friend's poem, one customarily employed the same poetic form and sometimes the same rhymes or rhyme words as the original poem, in order to add an element of challenge to the game.

> On Old Age, to Send to Mengde (Liu Yüxi)*
>
> The two of us both in old age now,
> I ask myself what it means to be old.
> Eyes bleary, evenings you're the first to bed;
> hair a bother, mornings you leave it uncombed.
> Sometimes you go out, a stick to prop you;
> sometimes, gate shut, you stay indoors the whole day.
> Neglecting to look into the newly polished mirror,
> no longer reading books if the characters are very small,
> your thoughts dwelling more and more on old friends,
> your activities far removed from those of the young,
> only idle chatter rouses your interest . . .
> When we meet, we still have lots of that, don't we!

The subject of the poem is so universal an experience and the presentation so straightforward that comment seems almost superfluous. The poet, sixty-three at the time, begins by speaking directly to his friend Liu but then quickly falls into a kind of private reverie on the subject of old age and the changes that it brings. In the very last line, he abruptly shakes himself out of his musings and addresses his friend once more. Unlike many traditional Chinese poems, this one employs no erudite allusions to earlier literature, though, as may readily be seen in the translation, it makes considerable use of verbal parallelism, a device common in both Chinese prose and poetry. The poem is in *shi* form, essentially the same form used in the *Shijing* or *Book of Odes*. It employs a line five characters or syllables in length, and it is in the relatively free "old-style" form, which means that there is no limit on the number of lines. A single rhyme is employed throughout, the rhymes occurring at the end of the even-numbered lines.

Bo Zhuyi is particularly remembered for his relaxed, warmly personal works. He himself, however, placed a much higher value on his poems of social criticism. Confucius had emphasized the didactic function of poetry, citing the poems of the *Book of Odes* as examples, and Confucian-minded officials in later centuries often employed poetic forms to voice criticisms of the government or expose the ills of society. Bo Zhuyi in his youthful years as an official enthusiastically carried on this tradition, writing a number of outspoken works that he hoped would bring about changes in government policy. The following is a famous example.

The poem is entitled "Light Furs, Fat Horses," an allusion to a passage in the Confucian *Analects* (6.3) in which Confucius censures luxurious living among public officials. It was written in 810, when the poet held advisory posts in the capital and while the region south of the Yangzi River was plagued by drought. The poet had previously asked that the government take steps to aid the drought victims, but his pleas went unheeded. The poem depicts a banquet at a military encampment in or near the capital. It is in the same form as the poem previously quoted.

Light Furs, Fat Horses

A show of arrogant spirit fills the road;
a glitter of saddles and horses lights up the dust.
I ask who these people are—
trusted servants of the ruler, I'm told.
The vermilion sashes are all high-ranking courtiers;
the purple ribbons are probably generals.

Proudly they repair to the regimental feast,
their galloping horses passing like clouds.
Tankards and wine cups brim with nine kinds of spirits;
from water and land, an array of eight delicacies.
For fruit they break open Dongting oranges,
for fish salad, carve up scaly bounty from Tianzhih.
Stuffed with food, they rest content in heart;
livened by wine, their mood grows merrier than ever.
This year there's a drought south of the Yangtze.
In Chu-zhou, people are eating people.

Tang poetry—or at least all that has come down to us—is almost entirely the product of a single group in society, the literati or scholar-bureaucrats, men who had received a firm grounding in the classical texts and had chosen to enter government service, often after passing the civil-service examinations. For these men, the writing of poetry was no mere hobby or diversion but an integral part of their lives as gentlemen and public servants, a means of airing their opinions, fulfilling their responsibilities to society, and furthering their spiritual cultivation.

The greatness of Tang poetry probably derives first of all from the tone of moral seriousness that pervades so much of it. There were other periods in Chinese literary history when poetry was mainly a pleasant pastime for members of the court or aristocracy, a vehicle for displaying verbal ingenuity or embroidering upon the patterns of the past. The Tang poets, though certainly not incapable of frivolous verse, generally had far more serious purposes in mind when they employed the medium, as we have seen in the example just quoted. They returned poetry to what they believed to be its original function: the addressing of important social and ethical issues.

At the same time, as evidenced in the first poem quoted above, they were not afraid to be frankly personal in their writing. Though this personal note was shunned during some periods, the best of the Tang poets, such as Du Fu or Bo Zhuyi, did not hesitate to record the experiences and emotional crises of their daily lives in their works, employing poetry much as the diary or autobiography forms are used in other cultures. To do so was for them a kind of literary and spiritual discipline.

The poet-official Wang Wei (699?–761), much of whose poetry describes the scenes of his daily life, purchased a country estate at a place called Wang

River in the mountains south of Chang-an, the Tang capital. The estate had formerly belonged to another well-known poet-official, Song Zhiwen (d. 712?). In the following poem, the first in a famous series describing scenic spots on the estate, the poet muses on the passing of time, as graphically exemplified in the dying willows planted by the former owner, along with his own feelings of pity for Song Zhiwen and the pity that owners of the estate in years to come might feel for him. This ability of the Tang poets, often within the span of a scant four lines, to open huge vistas in time or space is one of the qualities that endows their poetry with its characteristic air of grandeur and mythic proportions.

Meng-cheng Hollow

A new home at the mouth of Meng-cheng;
old trees—last of a stand of dying willows:
years to come, who will be its owner,
vainly pitying the one who had it before?

The Tang poets in their subject matter did not confine themselves to the autobiographical, however. Following a very old practice in Chinese poetry, they frequently adopted a persona from the folk-song tradition in order to enlarge the breadth and social significance of their material, speaking, for example, through the voice of a peasant pressed into military service, a neglected wife, or a soldier on frontier duty. Here is such a work by Li Bo (701–762), a poet particularly famed for his lyric gift and his works in the folk-song form. It is entitled "Zi-yeh Song," Zi-yeh being the name of a courtesan of earlier times who was noted for her brief and poignant songs. The poem is set in autumn, the time when women traditionally fulled (that is, scoured and thickened) cloth to make clothes to send to the soldiers at the border, and pictures a woman in the capital city of Chang-an dreaming of her husband at Jade Pass in Gansu, far to the west.

Zi-yeh Song

Chang-an—one slip of moon;
in ten thousand houses, the sound of fulling mallets.
Autumn winds keep on blowing,

all things make me think of Jade Pass!
When will they put down the barbarians
and my good man come home from his far campaign?

Before leaving the poem, we may note that, according to some commentators, the first line should be interpreted to read, "Chang-an—one swath of moonlight." The question, in effect, is whether one chooses to imagine the women working under the thin crescent of a new moon or under a full moon that floods the ground with light. Famous as these poems are and as often as they have been commented upon, the nature of the classical Chinese language is such that differences of interpretation of this kind continue to exist.

The poems quoted so far have all dealt with the world of human affairs, but Tang poets did not neglect the natural scene around them, either. In very early times, nature was looked on as rather fearful, the abode of fierce beasts or malevolent spirits. But from around the fifth century on, Chinese painters and poets began to show a much greater appreciation of the beauties of the natural world, particularly the mist-filled mountain and river landscapes of southern China. The period was one of foreign invasion and political turmoil, and these mountain landscapes came to be seen as places of peace and safety where one might escape from the perils of official life and perhaps even acquire the secrets of longevity.

This interest in natural beauty continued to be an important theme in Tang poetry, and it was often bound up with religious overtones linking it to Buddhism or Daoism. The following poem, from a group of some three hundred poems attributed to a recluse known as Hanshan or the Master of Cold Mountain, is an example. Hanshan was said to have lived at a place called Cold Mountain (Hanshan) in the Tiantai mountains of Zhejiang province, the site of many Buddhist and Daoist temples. It is uncertain when he lived, though the late eighth and early ninth centuries has been suggested as the most likely possibility. The poem is untitled.

I climb the road to Cold Mountain,
the road to Cold Mountain that never ends.
The valleys are long and strewn with stones,
the streams broad and banked with thick grass.
Moss is slippery, though no rain has fallen;
pines sigh but it isn't the wind.

Who can break from the snares of the world
and sit with me among the white clouds?

On the literal level, the poem is a description of the scenery along the kind of mountain trail that I myself have climbed in the Tian-tai range, with its rocky streambeds and pine-clad slopes. At the same time, the imagery of the ascent suggests a process of spiritual cultivation and the attainment of higher realms of understanding, while the white clouds of the last line—clouds that the Chinese believed were literally breathed forth by the mountain itself—are a frequently recurring symbol in Chinese literature for purity and detachment.

The next poem to be quoted, by the ninth-century writer Gao Pien, also deals with the natural scene. But this is nature carefully cultivated and seen in close conjunction with human habitation. As the title "Mountain Pavilion, Summer Day" tells us, the scene is a pleasant country retreat in the hush of a long, hot summer's day. We are shown the masses of shade trees surrounding the house, the reflections of the building and terrace as they appear upside down in the pond that fronts them, and the trellis of roses whose fragrance is so strong in the courtyard. Beyond the courtyard, a curtain strung with crystal beads stirs gently in the cool breeze, but just who is napping behind the curtains we are not told. The poem is an example of the kind of mood piece at which the Tang poets excelled, deft sketches made up of a few artfully chosen details that serve to rouse the reader's curiosity and invite him to fill out the remainder of the scene from his own imagination.

Mountain Pavilion, Summer Day*

Thick shade of green trees, long summer day,
lodge and terrace casting their images upside down in the pond.
Crystal-beaded curtains stir, a faint breeze rising;
one trellis of roses, the courtyard full of its scent.

This poem, along with the Wang Wei poem quoted earlier, is written in a form known as *jueju*, or "cut-off lines." The form is limited to four lines in length and usually employs a line of five or seven characters. Chinese is a tonal language, and the *jueju* form, in addition to employing end rhyme, obeys elaborate rules governing the tonal pattern of the words. We do not know just how the four tones of Tang-period Chinese were pronounced, and even if we did, the effect of such tonal patterns could not be reproduced in a nontonal language such as English. But it is well to keep in mind that, though translations of Tang poetry may give an impression of relative freedom, the originals are often in highly controlled forms. That the Tang poets not only complied with the exacting prosodic restrictions placed upon them but even succeeded in dancing in their chains is one of the wonders of their poetry.

One writer who seems to have welcomed the challenges presented by such demanding forms and who produced in them works of great power and originality was Du Fu (712–770), often referred to as China's greatest poet. He is particularly noted for the keen observations of nature recorded in his works as well as for his tone of passionate sincerity and concern for the welfare of the nation. The following poem, entitled simply *Jue jü*, was written in his late years, when conditions of unrest in the country forced him to live the life of a wanderer in the upper reaches of the Yangzi River, hoping always for an opportunity to return to his home in the northeast.

The poem begins with two lines in strict parallel form recording thoughtfully noted observations on the river scene: that the river gulls appear whiter than ever when seen against the intense blue of the river and that the buds of spring blossoms—probably peach-tree buds—seem like so many flames about to burst into color. In the second couplet, however, the tense objectivity of the opening lines suddenly gives way to a rush of feeling as the poet realizes that yet another spring has come and is about to depart while he is still far from his homeland.

Jue jü*

River cobalt-blue, birds whiter against it;
mountains green, blossoms about to flame:
as I watch, this spring too passes—
what day will I ever go home?

The last poem in my selection, like the first one, is addressed to a friend and deals with the theme of friendship and separation. It was the custom of Chinese gentlemen to write poems of commemoration when they gathered for a banquet, outing, or other social occasion, and this was particularly true when the purpose of the gathering was to see one of their number off on a journey. Official assignments kept the scholar-bureaucrats moving constantly about the empire, and there are numerous works by Tang poets bidding farewell to a friend or thanking friends for such a sendoff. This poem is by Li Bo and is addressed to his friend Meng Hao-ran (689–740), who was sailing east down the Yangzi to Yangzhou (Guang-ling) in Jiangsu. The farewell party was held at a place called Yellow Crane Tower, overlooking the river at Wuchang in Hupei. All this information is carefully recorded in the heading of the poem, since the Chinese tend to feel that the circumstances that led to the writing of a poem are an important part of its meaning.

> At Yellow Crane Tower Taking Leave of Meng Haoran as He
>   Sets off for Guangling
>
> My old friend takes leave of the west at Yellow Crane Tower, in
>   misty third-month blossoms goes downstream to Yangzhou.
> The far-off shape of his lone sail disappears in the blue-green
>   void,
> and all I see is the long river flowing to the edge of the sky.

Like Wang Wei's poem quoted above on the successive owners of his country estate, this one opens up vistas, here spatial ones that show us the sweeping mountain ranges and river systems of continental China. And unspoken but underlying it is the aching contrast between these vast, long-enduring features of the landscape and the frailty of human existence, as symbolized by the lone sail of Meng's boat fading from view on the horizon.

Tang poetry, to sum up, stands out in the long history of Chinese poetic development because, eschewing the superficiality of an earlier age and the tendency toward bland impersonality and mannered manipulation of stock themes and images, it restored to Chinese poetry the lost note of personal concern. The Tang poets were not afraid to employ poetry to record their deepest and most intimate feelings, crying out for the alleviation of social ills, noting with wry candor the waning of their physical powers, longing for absent friends, or dreaming of the last journey home. And because they dealt with the basic impulses of the human being, their works easily survive the transition into another language and milieu. Tang poetry, as one who reads it will readily perceive, is not just the product of a particularly golden age in China's literary history but a part of the universal human heritage.

Note

Poems marked with an asterisk were translated especially for this article and are published here for the first time. Other poems are taken from my *Columbia Book of Chinese Poetry* (New York: Columbia University Press, 1984).

JOURNEY TO THE WEST

C. T. Hsia

A S A W O R K of comic fantasy, *Journey to the West* (*Xi yu* ji) is readily accessible to the Western imagination, as witness the popularity of Arthur Waley's abridged version, *Monkey*, with the general public and especially with the college audience. But Waley has chosen to present only a few of the forty-odd adventures in the latter half of the book; translated in their entirety, many of the episodes may seem tiresome to the Western reader as repetitious in character. Even so, he will find it a civilized and humane book and one, moreover, that meets his expectation of what a novel of comic adventure should be. Though, like *Three Kingdoms* (*San guo*) and *Water Margin* (*Shui hu*), the *Journey* is crowded with characters and episodes, its design of a journey makes it inevitable that the pilgrims are the objects of continual attention while the assorted gods, monsters, and human characters they meet on the road claim only secondary interest. And its author, Wu Cheng-en, though he also builds upon an earlier, simpler version of the story, proves his originality precisely in his subordination of story as such to the larger considerations of theme and character and in his firm comic portrayal of the main pilgrims—Tripitaka, Monkey, and Pigsy. The last two, especially, are fully as memorable as another pair of complementary characters famed in world literature: Don Quixote and Sancho Panza. As a satiric fantasy grounded in realistic observation and philosophical wisdom, the *Journey* does suggest *Don Quixote*—two works of comparable importance in the respective developments of Chinese and European fiction.

Ever since Hu Shi published his pioneer study of the novel in 1923, the authorship of the hundred-chapter *Journey* has by general scholarly agreement been assigned to Wu Cheng-en (c. 1506–1582), a native of Shan-yang xian, Huai-an fu (in present-day northern Jiangsu), who enjoyed a reputation among his friends for wit and literary talent. None of the premodern editions of *Journey*, however, bear his name as author or compiler, and Glen Dudbridge has recently questioned the slim documentary basis for this attribution. It is highly unlikely, however, that anyone will come up with a stronger candidate, and all circumstantial evidence seems to indicate that Wu Cheng-en possessed the necessary leisure, incentive, and talent for the composition of this novel. If we agree with the general opinion that the *Journey* is the work of an individual author who adapted his sources in the Shakespearean fashion of exuberant invention, then the hundred-chapter novel as we now have it poses few perplexing problems as to its text and derivation.

The novel has its historical basis in the epic pilgrimage of Xuanzang to India. Also known by his honorific title Tripitaka or Tang San-zang, this saintly monk of great intellectual ability is a major figure in Chinese Buddhism. He traveled abroad for seventeen years (629–645) and brought back from India 657 Buddhist texts. Upon his return, he devoted the remainder of his life to translating these scriptures and establishing the abstruse Mere Ideation school of Chinese Buddhism. His school was never that popular, but even during his lifetime his travels became a matter of public interest.

As his legend grew with his fame, Xuanzang became, like the Liangshan heroes, a popular subject for storytellers. There is extant a brief promptbook of seventeen chapters (the first chapter is missing) dating from the Southern Song period entitled *Da-Tang San-zang qü-jing shi-hua* ("The tale, interspersed with verses, of the quest of scriptures by Tripitaka of the great Tang dynasty"). In it we can already see that Monkey has emerged as Xuanzang's chief guardian on the road and that the adventures they encounter are fantastic in character, involving gods, demons, and bizarre kingdoms.

The evolution of the Tripitaka legend properly culminates in Wu Cheng-en's massive creation. What must be apparent to every reader of the *Journey* is that the Tripitaka of the novel, who often appears as a deliberate caricature of a saintly monk, could not have borne any resemblance to his historical counterpart. Though Xuanzang's initial difficulties in the desert had provided clues for the storytellers, few details of his subsequent journey could have interested them. Soon after crossing the desert, the historical Xuanzang meets with the king of Turfan, who sends him off with a splendid retinue, letters of recommendation to rulers of other countries, and an abundant supply of gold, silver, and silk. It is true that the handsomely equipped traveler once meets with robbers and is on another occasion about to be sacrificed by pirates when a miraculous storm saves him, but during the years spent at the various courts in India in the company of kings, holy men, and leading scholars, Xuanzang appears primarily as a man of piety, courage, and tact, and one, moreover, endowed with great intellectual curiosity and deeply versed in scholastic Indian logic. We find no trace of this revered foreign intellectual in the popular literary representations of Tripitaka.

The Tripitaka of the novel is based on at least three different persons. First of all, he is the saintly monk of popular legend, a mythical hero suggestive of Moses and Oedipus. Son of a *zhuang-yuan* (one who has earned the highest honors at the palace examination) and a prime minister's daughter, soon after his birth he is abandoned by his mother out of fear that someone is going to kill him. He drifts on a river until he is picked up by a Buddhist abbot, who rears him. At eighteen, he is ordained as a priest and goes in search of his lost parents. After he has found them both, his filial piety and evident holiness attract so much attention at court that he is soon entrusted by Emperor Taizong with a mission to India to procure Mahāyāna Buddhist scriptures. Modeled upon many earlier legends of Buddhist saints, the youthful Tripitaka is strictly a product of the popular imagination.

This second aspect of Tripitaka as a potential Buddha is central to the plot of the novel. After all, the monsters and demons are not interested in a monk from China, however saintly he may be, but in a magic host whose flesh can confer upon them everlasting life. But insofar as Tripitaka is aware of himself as an object of supreme temptation, he becomes in the novel a person forever apprehensive of his danger. His initial image as a pious monk endowed with wisdom and determination notwithstanding, Wu Cheng-en therefore presents Tripitaka primarily in his third aspect, as an ordinary mortal undertaking a hazardous journey and easily upset by the smallest inconvenience. Peevish and humorless, he is a bad leader partial to the most indolent of his group and shows little true faith in his role as a strict Pharisee, ostentatiously attempting to keep to his vegetarian diet and avoid compromising female company. Certainly he suggests nothing of the courage of his historic namesake nor of the fortitude of Christian saints willing to undergo temptation in order to reach the higher stages of sanctification. He neither withstands nor yields to the cannibalistic and sexual assaults of the demons and monsters; he is merely helpless. Whereas in such Western allegories as

Everyman and *The Pilgrim's Progress* the hero goes through a carefully charted journey to enable him to accept death or enter heaven at the end, Tripitaka shows no sign of spiritual improvement during his adventures. If anything, he gets even more peevish and ill-tempered as his journey progresses. Even while he is being ferried to the Further Shore of Salvation to face Buddha himself and receive the scriptures, he is angry at Monkey, who has pushed him into the bottomless boat and gotten him soaked. "Sitting miserably here, he wrung out his clothes, shook out his shoes, and grumbled at Monkey for having got him into this scrape."[1]

As a comic figure in his own right, Tripitaka is indeed Everyman, as critics have often remarked, but the religious implications of that designation can be understood only by reference to the kind of idealistic Buddhist philosophy that the novel exemplifies. If Tripitaka shows no spiritual progress on his journey, it is because in the light of that philosophy he is the embodiment of fearful self-consciousness forever enslaved by phenomena and therefore forever incapable of reaching that peace of mind which alone can rout the terror of the senses. Early on his journey, after he has taken Monkey and Pigsy as disciples but before his meeting with Sandy, he is instructed to seek out the Zen master Crow Nest (Wu-chao) and to receive from him the *Heart Sūtra*, which is duly recorded in the novel in the historical Xuanzang's own standard translation. Tripitaka appears so transported by the truth of that sūtra that he immediately composes a poem to indicate his new state of spiritual illumination. What has so far escaped the notice of modern critics is that, like his monster-disciples, the sūtra is itself a spiritual companion appointed for Tripitaka's protection on his perilous journey. And in the scheme of the Buddhist allegory, it is a far more important guide than any of his disciples, since a Tripitaka in true possession of its teaching would have no need for their service and would realize the illusory character of his calamities.

Because of its brevity, the *Heart Sūtra* is the central wisdom (*prajñāpāramitā*) text of Mahāyāna Buddhism. Historically, it was a text dear to Xuanzang, "for when he was crossing the desert in 629," Waley informs us, "the recitation of it had routed the desert-goblins that attacked him far more effectively than appeals to the Bodhisattva Avalokiteśvara [Guan-yin]." In the primitive Song version of the story, accordingly, we find that the receiving of this sūtra constitutes the crowning success of Tripitaka's quest. He has already been to the kingdom of Tian-zhu (the traditional Chinese name for India), where he received 5,048 scrolls of Buddhist scriptures; though none of these are identified by name, it is pointedly mentioned that the *Heart Sūtra* is still missing. Now on his return journey, he stops by the Fragrant Grove Market (or Fragrant Grove Temple) of the Pan-lu Kingdom, and a god informs him in a dream that he is going to receive the *Heart Sūtra* the next day. And, the next day, a Buddha who looks like a fifteen-year-old monk descends upon a cloud and hands him the sūtra, saying, "I transmit to you this Heart Sūtra. When you return to court, you must protect it and cherish it. Its power reaches to heaven and hell. It is compact with the mysterious forces of yin and yang, and therefore do not lightly transmit it to anybody. It will be extremely difficult for the less fortunate multitudes to receive it."

By the time the storytellers' version was recorded in the Yuan period, we may presume that, in view of its climactic importance in the primitive version, the episode of the transmission of the *Heart Sūtra* must have been transposed to a much earlier section of the narrative, so that the meaning of that sūtra could be further expounded by the pilgrims on their journey. And we may further maintain that, in adapting this source, Wu Cheng-en has done nothing less than make his whole novel a philosophical commentary on the sūtra. George Steiner has brilliantly observed that the major characters in Tolstoy and Dostoevsky, when confronted with personal problems of crucial moral importance, often recite and discuss passages from the New Testament, which in turn keynote and illuminate the meaning of the novels in which these characters appear. In *Journey*, the *Heart Sūtra* is a subject of repeated discussion between Tripitaka and Monkey and serves the same novelistic function.

Though Tripitaka seems to have gained immediate illumination upon receiving the sūtra and recites it constantly afterward, its transcendent teaching that "form is emptiness and the very emptiness is form" is so beyond his mortal understanding that every calamity that befalls him demonstrates anew his actual incomprehension. During pauses between adventures, therefore, it is Monkey, with his far superior spiritual understanding, that repeatedly asks his master to heed the sūtra. Thus, in chapter 43, he makes another attempt:

Reverend master, you have forgotten the verse, "No eye, ear, nose, tongue, body, mind." Of all of us who have forsaken the world, our eyes should not see color, our ears should not hear sound, our nose should not smell, our tongue should not taste, our body should not feel cold and heat, and our mind should not harbor vain illusions: this is known as "routing the six thieves." Now your mind is constantly occupied with the task of seeking the scriptures, you are afraid of the monsters and unwilling to give up your body, you beg for food and move your tongue, you are fond of sweet smells and titillate your nose, you listen to sounds and excite your ear, you see things around you and strain your pupils. Since you have welcomed these six thieves on your own invitation, how can you hope to see Buddha in the Western Paradise?"

Tripitaka is often aware of Monkey's superior understanding. In chapter 93, when Pigsy and Sandy laugh at Monkey's pretensions as a Zen master because he has again reminded their master to heed the *Heart Sūtra*, Tripitaka upbraids the two less discerning disciples, "Sandy and Pigsy, don't talk so foolishly. What Monkey comprehends is the wordless language. This is true comprehension." Measured against the standard of nonattachment upheld by Monkey, therefore, Tripitaka's every manifestation of fear and credulity, of fanatical obsession with correct conduct and peevish concern over his creaturely comforts is as much part of a deliberate comedy as the obviously gross behavior of Pigsy.

But Tripitaka is not only enslaved by his senses. His humanitarian pity—the most endearing trait about him—is itself a form of enslavement. Upon joining Tripitaka, Monkey's first act is to slay the six thieves—Eye, Ear, Nose, Tongue, Mind, Body—an allegorical event indicative of his superior detachment in comparison with the other pilgrims. But Tripitaka is horrified because, among his other frailties, he is still obsessed with love and compassion for phenomenal beings. This episode causes the first temporary rift between master and disciple, and Monkey is later twice punished with dismissal, following his seemingly merciless killing of first a demon in a pathetic human disguise and then a number of brigands. From the viewpoint of popular Buddhism, Tripitaka has on all occasions followed the command not to kill, but because the novel inculcates the kind of Buddhist wisdom that excludes even the finest human sentiments as a guide to salvation, he is seen as a victim of perpetual delusion and can never make the same kind of spiritual progress as the hero of a Christian allegory. The novel, however, ultimately demonstrates the paradoxical character of this wisdom in that its nominal hero is granted Buddhahood at the end precisely because he has done nothing to earn it. To consciously strive for Buddhahood would again have placed him under bondage.

Monkey (*Sun Wu-kong*, or Sun Aware of Vacuity), who repeatedly warns Tripitaka of his spiritual blindness, is, of course, the real hero of the book. He has already assumed the role of Tripitaka's protector on the road in the Song *shih-hua*, and many of his deeds familiar to the reader of the hundred-chapter novel must have appeared in the Yuan version, in however sketchy a fashion. But it is Wu Cheng-en who has enlarged upon these deeds and consistently defined his hero's character in terms of his spiritual detachment, his prankish humor, his restless energy, and his passionate devotion to his master.

Especially during the Tang, merchants from Central Asia carried on an active trade in China, and they brought with them stories of their own regions, which stimulated the Chinese literati to compose tales of a romantic and supernatural cast known as *quan-ji*. The *Rāmāyana* may or may not have contributed to the character Sun Wu-kong, but there is no doubt that his many tricks and feats along with other supernatural motives in the novel are ultimately traceable to the influence of Indian as well as Persian and Arab literature. Monkey, for example, is an adept at magical transformations. In his celebrated battle with the celestial general Erh-lang Shen in chapter 6, the two combatants pursue each other through a series of disguises. I quote a small excerpt:

> Monkey, trembling in every limb, hastily turned his cudgel into an embroidery needle, and hiding it about his person, changed himself into a fish, and slipped into the stream. Rushing down to the bank, Erh-lang could see nothing of him. "This simian," he said, "has certainly changed himself into a fish and hidden under the water. I must change myself too if I am to catch him. So he changed himself into a cormorant and skimmed hither and thither over the stream. Monkey, looking up out of the water, suddenly saw a bird hovering above. It was like a blue kite, but its plumage was not blue. It was like a heron, but had no tuft on its head. It was like a crane, but its feet were not red. "I'll be bound that's Erh-lang looking for me . . . " He released a few bubbles and swam swiftly away. "That fish letting bubbles," said Erh-lang to himself, "is like a carp, but its tail is not red; it is like a tench, but there are no patterns on its scales. It is like a black-fish, but there are no stars

on its head; it is like a bream, but there are no bristles on its gills. Why did it make off like that when it saw me? I'll be bound it's Monkey, who has changed himself into a fish." And swooping down, he opened his beak and snapped at him. Monkey whisked out of the water, and changed himself into a freckled bustard, standing all alone on the bank.[2]

Though we find even in pre-Tang literature legendary or fictitious characters who are able to transform themselves into bestial shapes, the possessors of such powers could not assume any shape at will and certainly could not put on a performance of magical virtuosity like that of Monkey and Erh-lang. Their resemblance in this respect to the combatants from *The Arabian Nights* does not mean that the makers of the Monkey legend were specifically indebted to that book, but it certainly indicates their general awareness of the popular literature of the Middle and Near East.

In chapter 1, as the leader of the monkeys on the Flower and Fruit Mountain, he enjoys an idyllic existence of pure bliss. Provided with an infinite supply of food and unmolested by hunters or predators, the monkey colony behind the Water Curtain Cave is far more carefree than the Peach Fountain colony celebrated by T'ao Ch'ien. Yet Monkey is not content:

"Your Majesty is very hard to please," said the monkeys, laughing. "Every day we have happy meetings on fairy mountains, in blessed spots, in ancient caves, on holy islands. We are not subject to the Unicorn or Phoenix, nor to the restraints of any human king. Such freedom is an immeasurable blessing. What can it be that causes you this sad misgiving?" "It is true," said the Monkey King, "that to-day I am not answerable to the law of any human king, nor need I fear the menace of any beast or bird. But the time will come when I shall grow old and weak. Yama, King of Death, is secretly waiting to destroy me. Is there no way by which, instead of being born again on earth, I might live forever among the people of the sky?"[3]

His ambition, then, is to seek immortality, to perpetuate his enjoyment of life beyond the control of Yama. He presently undertakes a long voyage across the oceans to seek a master able to teach him how to conquer death. Allegorically, it is a quest for spiritual understanding, but in the larger mythical framework of the novel it is also a quest for magical power. Even for the most exalted celestials, their badges of power are invariably instruments of life-sustaining and death-causing magic. Laozi (Tai-shang Lao-jün), the supreme deity in the Daoist pantheon, cherishes as his chief possession the Crucible of the Eight Trigrams, by means of which he manufactures longevity pills and melts down intransigent enemies. And Subodhi, the Zen patriarch whom Monkey has chosen to serve, also respects his desire to prolong life and learn magical arts. Monkey is eventually dismissed because he has become vain of his attainments before the other disciples, but the inherent desirability of these arts is not held in question.

Monkey was hatched from a stone egg, under the influence of the sun and moon. Like many other Chinese novels, *Journey* begins at the beginning, with the creation myth. In this regard, Monkey's discontent with a pastoral mode of life and his ambition to seek power and knowledge can be seen as signs of a conscious striving upward—from inanimate stone to animal shape with human intelligence to the highest spiritual attainment possible. Until this striving is deflected into the Buddhist path of obedient service, following his humiliating defeat in the palm of Buddha, Monkey is but the smartest of all the monsters, who share with him this unquenchable desire for evolution.

Even in his rebellious phase, he differs from the other monsters and from Ravana and the Satan of *Paradise Lost* in his ability to view himself in a humorous light and remain detached from whatever business he is engaged in. He is never too solemn, even when fighting an entire battalion of heavenly troops. Without his sense of humor, Monkey would become a tragic hero or share the fate of the other monsters. With it, however, he can turn from rebel to Buddha's obedient servant without forfeiting our sympathy. This sense of humor, however coarsely and at times cruelly expressed at the expense of his companions and enemies, implies his ultimate transcendence of all human desires, to which Pigsy remains prey and from which Tripitaka barely detaches himself through his vigilant self-control. But to the end he retains the comic image of a mischievous monkey whose very zeal and mockery become an expression of gay detachment.

If Monkey is always the spirit of mischief when he is in command of a situation, there are occasions, nevertheless, when he impresses us with his passionate sorrow and anger. If humanitarian pity remains an endearing trait of Tripitaka, then, with all his superior understanding and mocking detachment, Monkey is also the antithesis of Buddhist emptiness in his passionate attachment to the cause of the journey and to his master.

Moreover, Tripitaka is so selfish that once, after Monkey has dispatched two brigands, Tripitaka prays for their peace and explicitly dissociates himself from the supposed crime:

> He is Sun,
> And I am Chen –
> Our surnames differ.
> To redress your wrong,
> Seek your murderer –
> Pray do not incriminate me,
> A monk on his way to get the scriptures.[4]

In chapter 27, after Monkey has finally killed a demon who has thrice assumed human shape to deceive the pilgrims, the enraged Tripitaka gives him a note of dismissal, saying, "Monkey-head, take this as proof that I no longer want you as my disciple. If I ever see you again, may I be instantly condemned to the Avici Hell!" Monkey, who has killed the demon to protect his master, takes this extremely hard.

It is this passionate devotion to his home, to Tripitaka and his cause, that sets Monkey apart from the rest of the pilgrims. Above and beyond his mythic and comic roles, he shows himself as an endearing person subject to misunderstanding and jealousy and given to frequent outbursts of genuine emotion. He, too, belies his superior attainment in Buddhist wisdom with his incorrigible humanity.

In the preceding section, I have sketched Tripitaka and Monkey against their historical-literary backgrounds and, in doing so, have indicated the intricate connections between the diverse modes of myth, allegory, and comedy to be observed in the novel. In view of this complexity of structure, it is understandable that critics have tended to emphasize one mode at the expense of the others. Traditional commentators, more attuned to the mystical teaching of the book, have one and all stressed its allegory. Starting with Hu Shi, modern critics have repudiated the allegorical interpretation and stressed its wealth of comedy and satire. "Freed from all kinds of allegorical interpretations by Buddhist, Daoist, and Confucianist commentators," declares Hu Shi in his foreword to Waley's translation, "*Monkey* is simply a book of good humor, profound nonsense, good-natured satire and delightful entertainment." (The phrase "profound nonsense," however, concedes the necessity for philosophical or allegorical interpretation.) Communist critics have further elaborated on the political aspects of the comedy, paying special attention to the revolutionary implications of its satire on traditional bureaucracy. They have cited instances in Ming history of gross official injustice and of the pampered arrogance of Daoist priests at court, a class repeatedly ridiculed in the novel, as sources of Wu Cheng-en's satiric inspiration.

The Communist approach, however, presupposes a political novelist deliberately scoring the evils of his time. But, under the autocratic rule of the Ming, it is very unlikely that Wu would have dared to make political remarks or concoct political fables in the Swiftian manner even if he had felt the urge to do so. A repeated failure at the examinations (he finally earned a senior licentiateship in 1544 and many years later served briefly in a minor official capacity), he could have become an embittered satirist of political intent, but, judging by his novel as well as his poetry and prose, he was rather a man of genial humor and not at all obsessed with his lack of worldly success or with the degeneracy of the Ming court at his time. He records in his novel, to be sure, many shrewd observations on Chinese bureaucracy, but they strike us as the quintessence of folk wisdom rather than as pointed satire of contemporary events. As a matter of fact, he regularly quotes proverbs for comic effect and makes fun of all traditional butts of satire. If Daoist priests are derided in some of the most hilarious episodes, Buddhists fared little better, since Tripitaka himself is seen as the constant source of ridicule. Yet in his didactic moments the novelist is not above adopting the traditional gesture of showing equal reverence for the three teachings: Confucianism, Buddhism, and Daoism.

In extolling the novel as satire, however, modern critics have paid inadequate attention to its mythical strength. They have, of course, praised its author's mythological imagination, but they see it at work mainly in his elaboration of the many fantastic episodes presumably already present in the Yuan version. Yet, as a critical concept in the study of literature, "myth" actually refers to the representation of any reality suggestive of the archetypal situations of primordial humanity. *Ulysses* is structured on myth though it deals with the Dublin of the early twentieth century. In like fashion, the mythical significance of *Journey* lies not so much in its use of Indic, Buddhist, and Daoist mythologies as in its rendition of archetypal characters and events. With *Journey*, even a reader of Waley's abridgment will be struck by the resemblance of its major episodes to classic embodiments of mythical reality in Western and Indic literature. The story of the

Crow-Cock Kingdom, for instance, has the makings of a Hamlet myth: a foully murdered king, a crafty confidant who usurps his throne and his conjugal bed, and an estranged prince enjoined with the task of revenge. In the story of the Cart-Slow Kingdom, the Buddhist inhabitants suffer the same fate as the Israelites in their Egyptian captivity, and Monkey and Pigsy vanquish the king's three Daoist counselors in the same magical fashion as Moses and Aaron triumphed over Pharaoh's priests. As for the monster that rules over the River That Leads to Heaven, his demand for an annual sacrifice of live children makes him kin to such familiar figures of Western and Chinese mythology as the Minotaur and Ho-po.

But in the last three episodes instanced and numerous other episodes of this type left out of Waley's version, their possibly coincidental resemblance to earlier myths is a less impressive proof of their mythical status than their striking suggestion of the fertility cults of primitive man. Thus the monster at the River That Leads to Heaven has to be propitiated because failure to observe the annual sacrifice will bring agricultural ruin to the area under his control. Similarly, the three Daoists enjoy the complete trust of their king because, as rain makers of proved competence, they guarantee the fertility of his country. And, upon entering the Crow-Cock Kingdom, the future usurper breaks a long siege of drought and thereby earns the gratitude and love of the king. In this respect, the wizard is even more suggestive of Oedipus than of Claudius, in that his clearly manifested mana entitles him to the slaying of the powerless king and the possession of his wife. Yet, on the other hand, the story of the Crow-Cock Kingdom only goes through the motions of primitive ritual and tragic murder. Though the king is pushed into the well, he reposes down there quite unharmed and is eventually revived. The usurper is a castrated lion, so that, with all the lewdness implicit in his violation of the queen and the harem, the ladies actually complain of his neglect. And, quite unlike Hamlet, the prince is filial to his mother rather than obsessed with her supposed perfidy; with the aid of the pilgrims, he restores the old order without bloodshed. And after his spree on earth, the lion is reclaimed by his owner, the bodhisattva Manjusri. With this episode as with numerous other episodes, myth is ultimately placed in a larger comic framework: a primordial reality is represented so that its unreality may be the more effectively exposed.

With his sense of the ridiculous anchored in the Buddhist doctrine of emptiness, therefore, the author mocks all the monsters just as he mocks all the pilgrims and celestials in the book. Not only is everything infinitely amusing to his observant eye, but in the ultimate religious sense everything that exists is but maya with which we are infatuated. Even Monkey, the most serious character and the one nearest to approaching an understanding of emptiness, is not spared this affectionate ridicule. To readers conditioned to accept the reality of literary fiction, this attempt at constant negation can be at times very unsettling. Writing from the Christian viewpoint, which accords reality to every soul be it suffering eternal damnation in hell or rejoicing in eternal bliss in paradise, Dante created a massive comedy of substantial reality designed to elicit our strongest emotional responses. Wu Cheng-en, on the other hand, provides in episode after comic episode the illusion of mythical reality, but he then inevitably exposes the falsehood of that reality in furtherance of his Buddhist comedy. Every time he kills off a fascinating monster or arbitrarily returns him to heaven, we are justified in feeling that he is mocking our emotional attachment to that monster. Like Tripitaka himself, we are too much creatures of the senses and of humanitarian sympathy to be able to adjust adequately to the Buddhist reality of emptiness.

Wu Cheng-en's supreme comic creation is Pigsy, who symbolizes the gross sensual life in the absence of religious striving and mythical ambition. He is doubly comic, because as a reluctant pilgrim he has no calling whatever for the monastic life and because for all his monstrous size and strength he entertains no ambition beyond a huge meal and a good sleep with a woman in his arms. He is the average sensual man writ large. He deteriorates on the road, turning into an envious, mendacious, and cowardly glutton obsessed with the life of sensual ease, precisely because his journey lacks incentives for worldly success and domestic contentment. The son-in-law in the Kao family, he is a selfish and hard-working individualist, no different from any conscientious family man who works all day and comes home in the evening to attend to his family and beautify his home. Though lecherous, he is perfectly happy if he has the nightly consolation of sleeping with his wife. By ordinary standards, therefore, he is something of a model husband. His father-in-law may object to his hideous features, but he cannot complain that he does not work extremely hard on the farm. Even his huge appetite is a direct consequence of his hard labor.

In other scenes, the author brings out the sinister aspect of Pigsy's selfishness and the unbelievable childishness of the easily despondent Tripitaka. Both are self-centered: Pigsy cares only for his own welfare, and Tripitaka thinks only of his personal danger. Both therefore are often seen in league against Monkey. If, with his superior understanding, Monkey exposes Tripitaka's obsession with fear, with his zest for a life of disinterested action he puts to shame Pigsy's sensuality, sloth, and envy. The allegorical meaning of these contrasts is quite obvious, but on a more literal level, in their frequent altercations these three are simply travelers on an arduous journey who sooner or later must get on each other's nerves. In this realistic perspective, Tripitaka's role is that of the unobservant, easily flattered father, while Monkey and Pigsy are rival brothers, in the fashion of Tom Jones and Blifil.

With all its wild conceits about food, *Journey* bears some important resemblance to *Gargantua and Pantagruel*. Rabelais and Wu Cheng-en, moreover, were almost exact contemporaries, and both bequeathed to their respective national cultures two comic masterpieces unsurpassed for their sheer animal exuberance. In their grosser passages, both works can shock the more fastidious modern taste in their disregard of humanitarian feelings. Just as Gargantua, Pantagruel, and Friar John show the greatest contempt for their enemies and slaughter them for a joke, so does Monkey. And Pigsy, when he shakes off his usual indolence to share his fellow pilgrim's prankish sense of humor, displays the liveliest spirit in teasing and punishing their defenseless enemies.

But, despite their comparable senses of humor, the two authors differ in their attitudes toward appetite. For all his comic exuberance, Wu Cheng-en is not a Renaissance humanist; in point of moral sensibility, he is far more Chaucerian than Rabelaisian, in that he finds man's insatiable appetite ultimately laughable and as a negative confirmation of his absurdity. Pigsy, his major symbol of appetite, has no spiritual and intellectual pretensions whatever. In addition, the author can good-humoredly indulge his character's appetite for food since, in Chinese eyes, gluttony calls for far less moral disapprobation than lechery and is typically a matter for comic attention.

In *Allegory and Courtesy in Spenser*, one of the few fruitful ventures into comparative studies of Chinese and Western literature and manners, H. C. Chang has admirably stated that whereas Western allegory as represented by *The Faerie Queene* personifies abstract mental and moral states, Chinese allegory, which is expressive of a more practical ethical impulse, primarily illustrates the fact of temptation. The temptation of Pigsy is therefore far more suggestive of a latter-day Western allegory like Tolstoy's story "How Much Land Does a Man Need?" in its impulse toward concrete fictional realization. Given the simpler conventions of Chinese storytelling, it is as gripping a study of lust as the latter is a study of greed. It is certainly far more psychologically subtle than anything in *The Water Margin* or *The Romance of the Three Kingdoms.*

The characterization of Pigsy in this self-contained allegory, one may further note, is of a piece with his characterization in the rest of the novel. The Pigsy that wants to marry and stay on the widow's estate is the same person who reluctantly bids farewell to the Gao family. As always, he is an object of ridicule to the others, but he himself is serious throughout. He is very much on his best behavior in his negotiations with the widow, even though time and again his impatience betrays his desperation. He is apologetic about his appearance but brags about his usefulness on the farm. His sexual hunger is given astonishing reality when, faced with the daughters' refusal, he begs the widow to marry him. But this sexual hunger is inseparable from his hunger for purposive activity. Like any other spiritually ungifted average sensual person, Pigsy sees challenge in the ownership and management of a large estate but no challenge at all in a wearisome pilgrimage. In *The Faerie Queene*, the voluptuous nymphs in the Bower of Bliss appear primarily in the aspect of naked sensuality, and the men who succumb to their lures immediately lose their self-respect and turn bestial in their obliviousness to all duties and responsibilities. With Pigsy, the sight of beautiful women in possession of a fabulous estate only fully arouses his domestic instinct. (In his subsequent temptation by the spider spirits, who are mere sirens without property, Pigsy behaves far more impudently, because he is not serious about them.) If he is starved of sex on his journey, he is at the same time stultified by his lack of opportunity to prove his usefulness as a householder. In Pigsy, with all his unflattering physical and moral features, Wu Cheng-en has drawn the portrait of every common man who finds fulfillment in his pursuit of respectable, mundane goals.

Notes

1. Wu Cheng-en, *Monkey: Folk Novel of China*, trans. Arthur Waley (New York: Evergreen Books, 1994), 281–282. This passage occurs in chapter 98.
2. Cf. Chang T'ien-i, "*Hsi-yu-chi* cha-chi" (Notes on *Hss-yu-chi*), *Hsi-yu-chi yen-chiu lun-wen chi*. It originally appeared in *Jen-min Wen-hsüeh* (February 1954)
3. Wu Cheng-en, *Monkey*, 14 (*Xi yu ji*, chap. 1).
4. *Xi yu ji*, chap. 56, p. 649.

13

A DREAM OF RED MANSIONS

C. T. Hsia

A DREAM OF *Red Mansions* (*Honglou meng*) is the greatest novel in the Chinese literary tradition. As an eighteenth-century work, it draws fully upon that tradition and can indeed be regarded as its crowning achievement. As that tradition is early distinguished by its poetry and philosophy, we expectedly find in *Dream* numerous poems in a variety of meters, including an elegy in the style of *Chuzi* (*Songs of the South*, an ancient anthology), along with philosophic conversations that echo the sages of antiquity (Laozi, Zhuangzi, Mencius) and utilize the subtle language of Zen Buddhism. As a late-traditional man of letters, its principal author is further aware of the encyclopedic scope of Chinese learning and the heritage of earlier fiction and drama. He has made obvious use of the Ming domestic novel *Jinping mei* and the romantic masterpieces of Yuan-Ming drama such as *The Romance of the Western Chamber* (*Xi-xiang ji*) and *The Peony Pavilion* (*Mu-dan ting*). But his novel is greater than these not only for its fuller representation of Chinese culture and thought but for its incomparably richer delineation of character in psychological terms. That latter achievement must be solely credited to the genius of its principal author.

That author is Cao Xüeqin (1715?–1763), an ethnic Chinese from a family that had served the Manchu emperors of the Qing dynasty for generations. Though mere bondservants to the throne in status, Cao's great-grandfather, grandfather, and father or uncle all held the highly lucrative post of commissioner of imperial textile mills, first briefly in Soochow and then in

Nanking. The grandfather Cao Yin played host to the Kangxi emperor during his four southern excursions from Peking. The Yungzheng emperor, who succeeded Kangxi in 1723, was far less friendly to the Cao house. In 1728 he dismissed Cao Fu, most probably Xüeqin's father, from his post as textile commissioner of Nanking and confiscated much of his property. Then thirteen or fourteen years old, Xüeqin moved with his parents to Peking, in much reduced circumstances. It is believed that the Cao clan temporarily regained favor after the Qianlong emperor ascended the throne in 1736. But by 1744, when Xüeqin started composing his novel, he had moved to the western suburbs of Peking, again living in poverty: the Cao family must have suffered another disaster, from which it never recovered. The novelist lost a young son a few months before his death in February 1763 and was survived by a second wife, of whom we know nothing further.

By all indications, Cao Xüeqin should have had ample time to complete *Dream* to his own satisfaction, but it would seem that at the time of his death this novel of autobiographical inspiration—about a great family in decline and its young heir—was not yet in publishable shape, even though manuscripts of the first eighty chapters, known by title as *The Story of the Stone*, had been in circulation for some time. Scholars now believe that Cao must have completed at least one draft of the whole novel but went on revising it, partly to please the commentators among his kinsmen, most prominently a cousin known by his studio name of Red Inkstone (Zhihyan chai) and partly to remove any grounds for suspicion that his work was critical of the government in devoting space to the tribulations of a family justly deserving of imperial punishment. If Cao had indeed completed the last portion of the novel but did not allow it to circulate, it could have been due to fear of a literary inquisition.

A corrected second edition of the 120-chapter *Dream of Red Mansions* came out in 1792, only a few months after the first edition of 1791. The new edition contains, in addition to the original preface by Cheng Weiyüan, a new preface by Gao Ê and a joint foreword by the two. Earlier scholars arbitrarily took Cheng to be a bookseller who had acquired manuscripts of the later chapters and had asked the scholar Gao Ê to put them into shape and edit the work as a whole. Some would even regard Gao Ê as a forger. Now we know that Cheng Wei-yüan was a staffmember of the gigantic imperial project to assemble a "Complete Library in Four Branches of Learning and Literature" (*Ssu-k'u ch'üan-shu*). Ho-shen, a Manchu minister enjoying the complete trust of the Qianlong emperor, was made a director general of the project, and according to a new theory advanced by Zhou Ru-chang, a leading authority on the novel, it was Ho-shen himself who had ordered Cheng and Gao to prepare a politically harmless version for the perusal of the emperor. This theory should be taken seriously, inasmuch as Cheng and Gao could not have dreamed of putting out a movable-type edition of a massive novel without the backing of a powerful minister like Ho-shen and without the printing facilities of the imperial court.

Whatever its faults, the Cheng-Gao edition has remained the standard text for Chinese readers for two hundred years. Scholars, of course, will continue to regret that Cao Xüeqin did not live long enough to complete or oversee the publication of his own novel and belittle or give grudging praise to Gao Ê's contributions as an editor and continuator of the first eighty chapters. But if the last forty chapters are not what they should be, the first eighty are also by no means a coherent narrative of seamless unity. In addition to minor inconsistencies in the storyline, Cao's inveterate habit for revision would seem to be responsible for more serious instances of narrative ineptitude as well. One plausible theory (endorsed by David Hawkes) proposes that even before starting on his great project, Cao Xüeqin had acquired or himself written a manuscript called *A Mirror for the Romantic* (*Feng-yüe bao-chian*), about unhappy youths and maidens belatedly awakened to the illusory nature of love. He was apparently very fond of this manuscript and inserted some of its cautionary tales into his novel. He did so, of course, at the cost of upsetting its temporal scheme, since the autobiographical hero and his female cousins lead quite unhurried lives, while the trials of the deluded Jia Rui in chapter 12 and of the hapless Yu sisters in chapters 64 through 67 consume weeks in a matter of pages. Try as he might, Cao could not have got himself out of this narrative impasse if he was determined to save these somewhat extraneous tales.

The story of the novel's composition and publication thus remains a very complicated affair, one demanding further research by specialists. The novel itself, however, should pose few difficulties for the Western reader, unless he is intimidated right away by its sheer size. But the undaunted reader will be amply rewarded and will cherish the experience of having spent days and weeks with many memorable characters in a Chinese setting. *A Dream of Red Mansions* is about the aristocratic Jia clan, which, like the Cao family, has enjoyed imperial favor for generations. Its two main branches dwell in adjoining compounds, styled Ningguofu and Rongguofu, in the capital. The nominal head of the Ningguofu compound is a selfish student of Daoist alchemy who eventually dies its victim; his son Jia Zhen and grandson Chia Yong are both sensualists. Grandmother Jia, also known as the Lady Dowager in the Yang translation, presides over the Rongguofu compound. She has two sons, Jia She and Jia Zheng. Jia Lien, Jia She's pleasure-seeking son, is married to an extremely capable woman, Wang Xi-feng (Phoenix). Despite her early triumphs in managing the household finances and driving her love rivals to suicide, this handsome and vivacious lady eventually languishes in ill health and dies. Her nefarious dealings are in large part responsible for the raiding of the Jia compounds by imperial guards and the confiscation of their property.

The dowager's other son, Jia Zheng, is the only conscientious Confucian member of the family in active government service. A lonely man of narrow vision but undeniable rectitude, he has lost a promising son before the novel opens. Naturally, he expects his younger son by his legitimate wife, Lady Wang, to study hard and prepare for the civil-service examinations. But Baoyü, early spoiled by his grandmother, mother, and other female relatives, detests conventional learning and prefers the company of his female cousins and the maidservants. Since late childhood, he has had as a playmate a cousin of delicate beauty beloved by the dowager, Lin Dai-yü (Black Jade). Some years later, another beautiful cousin, Xüe Bao-chai (Precious Clasp), also moves into the Rungguofu compound. In spite of Baoyü's repeated assurances of his love, Black Jade regards Precious Clasp as her rival and feels very insecure. As she progressively ruins her health by wallowing in self-pity, Precious Clasp replaces her as the family's preferred candidate for Baoyü's wife. But the marriage when it does take place brings no joy to Bao-chai, since by that time Baoyü has turned into an idiot. And brokenhearted and unable to forgive, Black Jade dies on their wedding night.

Baoyü eventually recovers and obtains the degree of *juren*. But instead of returning home after taking the examination, he renounces the world and becomes a monk. The desolate Precious Clasp takes comfort in her pregnancy. A faithful maid, Xi-ren (called Aroma in Hawkes and Minford) is eventually happily married to an actor friend of Baoyü's. Another maid, Qing-wen (Skybright in Hawkes and Minford), to whom Baoyü was also much attached, had died of calumny and sickness long before his marriage.

Chinese novels before *Dream* are mostly about characters in history and legend. Though a type of short novel about talented and good-looking young lovers had become popular before his time, Cao Xüeqin quite properly dismisses these stereotyped romances in his novel for their palpable unreality.

But his use of what we may call diurnal realism, the technique of advancing the novel with seemingly inconsequential accounts of day-to-day events and of lingering over days of family significance, clearly shows his indebtedness to the aforementioned *Jin ping mei*, the only one of the four major Ming novels devoted to tracing the fortunes of a discordant large family. (The other three, all available in English translation, are: *Romance of the Three Kingdoms* [*San-guo-zhih-yan-i*], *Outlaws of the Marsh* [*Shui-hu zhuan*], and *Journey to the West* [*Xi yu ji*].) But whereas *Jin ping mei* is notorious for its graphic descriptions of Xi-men Qing's sexual life with his concubines and paramours, *Dream* is never pornographic, despite its larger cast of male sensualists. The novel maintains instead a note of high culture by focusing attention on the hero and on several gifted young ladies whose poetic parties and conversations with him invariably touch upon intellectual and aesthetic matters. The life story of Jia Baoyü, especially, is tested against all the major ideals of Chinese culture.

At the very beginning of the first chapter, Cao places his hero in a creation myth that mocks his Faustian desire for experience, knowledge, and pleasure. When the goddess Nü-gua is repairing the Dome of Heaven, she rejects as unfit for use a huge boulder of considerable intelligence, which consequently bemoans its fate and develops a longing for the pleasures of the mundane world. It can now shrink itself into the size of a stone and, with the help of a Buddhist monk and a Daoist priest, it is eventually born with a piece of jade in his mouth as our hero (Baoyü means "precious jade"). As a supramundane allegory, then, *Dream* is the transcription of a record as inscribed on the Stone itself after it has returned to its original site in the Green Fable Mountains. The Stone found human life wanting, its pleasures and pains all illusory, and its detailed record—our novel—is by allegorical design a massive substantiation of that truth. Throughout the novel, the celestial agents of that allegory, the mangy Buddhist and lame Daoist, while watching over the spiritual welfare of Baoyü, periodically mock or enlighten other deluded earthlings as well.

Jia Baoyü is next characterized in chapter 2 by two knowledgeable outsiders as an unconventional individualist of the romantic tradition firmly opposed to the Confucian ideal of morality and service, as represented by his father. To illustrate his propensity for love, our hero, while taking a nap in the bedchamber of Qin Ko-qing (Jia Jong's wife) in chapter 5, is transported to the Land of Illusion, which is presided over by the fairy Disenchantment. After warning him of the dangers of the kind of crazy love prized by the romantics, she introduces her own sister to him for the purpose of sexual initiation, so that he may see through the vanity of passion and return to the path of Confucian service. The fairy Ke-qing, who combines in her person the charms of both Black Jade and Precious Clasp, of course enraptures Baoyü, but he soon wakes up screaming after being chased by demons and wild beasts.

When lecturing Baoyü, the fairy Disenchantment does allow a distinction between lust (*yin*) and love (*qing*), and as someone truly committed to *qing* (also meaning "feeling"), our hero is in no danger of being confused with several of his kinsmen who are often driven by lust to trample upon human feelings. But Baoyü is so free of the taint of lust that the dream allegory confuses matters by presenting him as someone desperate for salvation after only a brief interlude of sexual bliss. Contrary to popular belief among Chinese readers, Baoyü is not a great lover, nor does he function principally as a lover in the novel. It is true that remembrance of the sweeter portion of the dream leads him to make love to the maid Aroma the same evening. For all we know, they may continue to share sexual intimacy thereafter, but his enjoyment of her body, explicitly referred to only once and rarely emphasized again, alters not a whit his high regard for her as a person and a friend. Baoyü is actually more drawn to his other maid, Skybright, because of her entrancing beauty and fiery temperament, but she dies complaining of being a virgin, untouched by her young master.

Baoyü is every girl's true friend. Once the Daguanyüan, a spacious garden built in honor of his elder sister, an imperial concubine, becomes the residential quarters of Baoyü and his female cousins, he sees them and their maids all the time and gives daily proof of his unfeigned friendship and solicitude for their welfare. He admires each and every one of these girls as an embodiment of celestial beauty and understanding but worries about the time when they will leave the garden to get married. He knows only too well that with marriage their celestial essence will be obscured and that, if they survive their unhappiness, they will become as mean spirited as the older women in the Jia mansions.

As the sole young master in the Daguanyüan, Baoyü therefore does his best to keep the young ladies and maids amused and to lull their awareness of the misery of approaching adulthood. But for all their lively parties and conversations, the young ladies have to leave one by one, by marriage, death, or abduction (in the case of the resident nun Miao-yu). It is these tragedies that reduce our helpless hero to a state of idiocy and prepare him for his eventual acceptance of his fate as an insensible Stone heedless of suffering humanity. In that allegorical dream, the fairy Disenchantment warns him only of his romantic propensity. But though he is grievously hurt when his elders rob him of his intended bride and marry him to Precious Clasp, ordinarily he is much more occupied by the tragic fate of Black Jade and of all the other girls deprived of life or happiness. In accordance with the author's allegoric scheme, we should perhaps feel happy that he has finally gained wisdom and leaves this world of suffering for the life of a monk. But we cannot help feeling that his spiritual wisdom is gained at the expense of his most endearing trait: his active love and compassion for fellow human beings. Despite his irrepressible charm and gaiety, Jia Baoyü must be regarded as the most tragic hero in all Chinese literature for ultimately choosing the path of self-liberation because his sympathy and compassion have failed him.

Baoyü has a few like-minded male friends whom he sees occasionally, but inside the Jia mansions there are no men to whom he can unburden his soul. Even if he is not partial to girls, he has only them to turn to for genuine companionship. And it is a tribute to Cao's extraordinary genius that he is able to provide Baoyü with so many sharply individualized companions to talk and joke with, to compete with as poets, and to care for and love. Among these, Black Jade naturally takes pride of place as the principal heroine, with whose fate Baoyü is most concerned. Alone of the major heroines, she is assigned a role in the supramundane allegory complementary to the hero's. She is supposed to be a plant that blossoms into a fairy after the Stone, then serving as a page at the court of Disenchantment, has daily sprinkled it with dew. The fairy has vowed to repay his kindness with tears if she may join him on earth, and judging by the occasions that Black Jade has to cry while living as an orphan among relatives, never sure of her status in the Rong-guofu nor of her marital future, she has certainly more than repaid her debt to her former benefactor.

Yet as is the case with Baoyü's allegoric dream, Cao Xüeqin almost deliberately misleads with his fairy tale about Black Jade as a grateful plant. The reality of the two cousins in love is far more complex and fascinating than any allegory can suggest. Long before Black Jade is in danger of being rejected by her elders, she seethes with discontent. Her every meeting with Baoyü ends in a misunderstanding or quarrel, and these quarrels are, for her, fraught with bitter and lacerated feelings. This is so because the two are diametrically opposed in temperament despite the similarity of their tastes.

Baoyü is a person of active sympathy capable of ultimate self-transcendence; Black Jade is a self-centered neurotic who courts self-destruction. Her attraction for Baoyü lies not merely in her fragile beauty and poetic sensibility but in her very contrariness—a jealous self-obsession so unlike his expansive gaiety that his love for her is always tinged with infinite sadness.

Black Jade, on her part, can never be sure of Baoyü's love yet maintains a fierce pride in her studied indifference to her marital prospects. One could almost say that her tragedy lies in her stubborn impracticality, in the perverse contradiction between her very natural desire to get married to the man of her choice and her fear of compromising herself in the eyes of the world by doing anything to bring about that result. In time her temper gets worse, and so does her health. Cao Xüeqin never flinches from physiological details as he traces her growing emotional sickness in terms of her bodily deterioration. Her dream scene in chapter 82, where Baoyü slashes open his chest in order to show her his heart but finds it missing, and her ghastly death scene in chapter 98 are among the most powerful in the novel. Gao Ê must be given high praise if he indeed had a substantial hand in the writing of these chapters.

Because Precious Clasp nominally gets her man, Chinese readers partial to Black Jade are less sympathetic toward her and find personal satisfaction in seeing her as a hypocritical schemer. This misreading is, of course, unwarranted. It is true that, as a sensible girl docilely accepting her place in a Confucian society, Precious Clasp may have less appeal for Baoyü and for the modern reader than Black Jade, with her neurotic sensibility and volatile temper. Yet both are strictly comparable in talent and beauty, and both are fatherless children living more or less as dependents among relatives. Though Black Jade is initially jealous, she and Precious Clasp become the best of friends after chapter 45: two helpless pawns in the hands of their elders with no control over their marital fate. If the elders prefer Precious Clasp as Baoyü's bride, at the same time they show little regard for her welfare. Though Baoyü was once a desirable match, by the time the wedding is proposed he is a very sick person with no immediate prospect for recovery. Even more than Black Jade, Precious Clasp is the victim of a cruel hoax, since there can be no doubt that the hastily arranged wedding is regarded by the elder Jia ladies as medicine for Baoyü. Madame Xüe cannot well refuse the match, but she feels profoundly sorry for her daughter. Precious Clasp herself, to whom her mother's word is law, "bowed her head and didn't say anything in reply; later on, she let her tears fall." With due allowance for all the evil perpetrated by the matriarch, Madame Wang, and Phoenix, Black Jade has finally only herself to blame for ruining her health and alienating their affections in the first place; for Precious Clasp's martyrdom, their brutal and desperate self-interest is alone responsible.

As the wife of Baoyü, Precious Clasp remains to the end a Confucian trying to dissuade him from the path of "self-liberation." She is in that respect not unlike his parents in wishing to see him enter government service and get settled as a family man. But in the end she uses the Mencian argument to counter his Daoist resolve to leave the world. Even if the world is full of evil and suffering, or especially because it is so, how can he bear to sever human ties, to leave those who need his love most? How can one remain human by denying the most instinctive promptings of his heart? Precious Clasp cannot figure this out, and Baoyü cannot answer her on the rational level of human discourse. It is only by placing human life in the cosmological scheme of craving and suffering that one can see the need to liberate oneself. It would be too cruel even for the enlightened Baoyü to tell Precious Clasp that to cling to love and compassion is to persist in delusion: in the primordial antiquity of Daoism there was no need to love or commiserate.

With the exception of a discerning few, traditional and modern commentators alike have compared Precious Clasp unfavorably with Black Jade. In earlier Communist criticism, with the important exception of one critic, Precious Clasp has even been more grossly vilified: in marked contrast to the "revolutionary martyr" Black Jade, she is made out to be a cunning and hypocritical schemer thriving under feudalism. This curiously subjective reaction, as has been earlier suggested, is partly due to an instinctive preference for sensibility over sense. Precious Clasp is a virtuous and obedient girl and, as mentioned above, since she nominally gets her man, it is understandable that her goodness should be counted against her. But when one examines all the passages adduced to prove her cunning and hypocrisy, one finds that every single one of them is based on deliberate misreading. Precious Clasp, of course, is not a rebel: she accepts the role of woman in a Confucian society and believes that it is a scholar's duty to prove his usefulness through the examinations and in the official world. In that sense, Black Jade, who shares Baoyü's scorn for the "eight-legged essay" and for officialdom, is much less "vulgar" and certainly to be preferred. But whereas Black Jade's detestation of vulgarity only hardens her egocentricism, Precious Clasp's acceptance of Confucian morality implies a deliberate suppression of her poetic sensibility. If Precious Clasp can turn to her mother for love and solace, one must remember that she lives in a house of discord dominated by her moronic and wildly irresponsible brother. With her precocity and complicated life at home, she must display the patience and humility of a saint to mold herself into the accepted pattern of virtue. A poet and encyclopedic scholar busying herself with needlework, a peacemaker and loyal friend enduring enmity at home and envy abroad, she is finally the perfect wife, but she is sacrificed at the will of the Matriarch to serve a dying idiot.

Once married to Baoyü, Precious Clasp of course does her level best to change her intolerable situation: to restore her husband to health and to the world of human sentiments. Given his strange indifference in his reawakened state, however, she is willing to forgo comfort, wealth, and rank to renounce conjugal love. What she wants (and what Pervading Fragrance also wants) from Baoyü is consideration and kindness. Her final shock is that the person whose sensitiveness to suffering has always been his most endearing trait now does not care. In reacquiring his spiritual essence, Baoyü has turned into a stone.

At this point in the narrative we are introduced to a crucial philosophical debate that presents explicitly the irreconcilable claims of compassion and personal salvation. Earlier in chapter 118, Baoyü's calm admiration for the decision of Compassion Spring and Purple Cuckoo to become nuns has already deeply tormented Precious Clasp and Pervading Fragrance, who would normally expect him to make a tearful commotion over their renunciation of the world. As Cao relates it:

> After seeing Madame Wang off, Baoyü began to study "Autumn Floods" [a chapter in *Zhuangzi*] with minute attention. Emerging from the inner chamber, Precious Clasp noticed his exultant absentmindedness; she walked toward him to see what he was reading, and then her heart became very heavy. She thought, "He persists in regarding 'escape from the world and detachment from humanity' as his only concern; this is not good." Knowing it would be impossible to dissuade him in his present rapt state, she sat down beside him, watching him intently. Finally noticing her presence, Baoyü asked, "What are you staring for?" Precious Clasp replied, "It just occurred to me that since we are man and wife you are my lifelong support, even though I agree this relationship is not necessarily built upon our selfish feelings and desires. As for glory and wealth, they are but like fleeting smoke and cloud. But I am thinking that since the time of the ancient

sages it has always been stressed that one should cultivate his 'moral character.'"

Baoyü didn't have the patience to listen to the end; he put aside his book and said with a smile, "Just now you mentioned 'moral character' and 'ancient sages,' not knowing that what the ancient sages have stressed is the importance of 'not losing the heart of a newborn baby.' What's so precious about the newborn baby except that he has no perception, no knowledge, no greed, and no envy? Once we are born, we all sink deeper and deeper in the mire of greed, hate, and passion; how can we ever escape from the net of red dust? I have just now realized that the ancient saying, 'Whether we are together or apart, what we enjoy is but a floating life,' has awakened few. As for one's moral character, who has ever reached the condition of living in the state of primordial antiquity?"

Precious Clasp answered, "Since you mentioned 'the heart of a newborn baby,' you must know that the ancient sages regard loyalty and filial piety as characteristic of the heart of the newborn baby and not escape from the world and detachment from humanity. Yao, Shun, Yü, Tang, the Duke of Zhou, and Confucius all ceaselessly set their hearts on helping the people and benefiting the world, and the so-called newborn baby's heart finally amounts to 'not being able to bear the pain or suffering about one.' Just now you spoke of being able to bear the pain of forsaking the basic human relationships—what kind of absurdity is this?" Baoyü nodded his head and smiled. "Yao and Shun did not force their way of life upon Chao Fu and Xü Yu, nor did King Wen and the Duke of Zhou force theirs upon Bo-yi and Shu-qi . . . " Not waiting for him to finish, Precious Clasp retorted, "Your words are getting more and more absurd. If the ancients were all like Chao Fu, Xü Yu, Bo-yi, and Shu-qi, how come people today still revere Yao, Shun, the Duke of Zhou, and Confucius as sages? Moreover, it's even more ridiculous to compare yourself to Bo-yi and Shu-qi. Victims of the declining fortunes of the Shang, they faced many difficulties and so they thought up some excuse for leaving the world. Now, under the present beneficent reign, our family has for generations enjoyed imperial favor, living in splendid style and luxury. Not to say that all your life your late grandmother, your father and mother have all cherished you like a precious jewel. Just think, is it right for you to maintain all that you just said?" Baoyü took all this in but made no reply; he only tilted his head and smiled.

This debate is the perennial debate in Chinese thought. Both Mencius and Laozi invoke the newborn baby as the norm of human excellence. But whereas for Laozi the baby is desireless and witless, for Mencius the baby is precious because he contains within himself all the virtues of Yao and Shun. To Mencius, love and sympathy are the basic facts of human life; so they are to Precious Clasp, and so they are to Baoyü until his "awakening." If not being able to bear the sight of pain (*bu-ren* is a Mencian phrase) is not the test of one's humanity, what is? How can one remain human by denying the most instinctive promptings of his heart? Precious Clasp cannot figure this out, and Baoyü cannot answer her on the rational level of human discourse. It is only by placing human life in the cosmological scheme of craving and suffering that one can conceive of the need to liberate oneself. It would be too cruel even for the enlightened Baoyü to tell Precious Clasp that to cling to love and compassion is to persist in delusion: in the primordial antiquity of Daoism there was no need to love or commiserate.

As a tragedy, *A Dream of Red Mansions* has the overtones of a bitter and sardonic comedy. The Buddhist-Daoist view of the world prevails with Baoyü in the end, yet the reader cannot but feel that the reality of love and suffering as depicted in the novel stirs far deeper layers of one's being than the reality of Buddhist-Daoist wisdom. This Chinese masterpiece is therefore like all the greatest novels of the world in that no philosophic or religious message one extracts therefrom can at all do justice to its unfolding panorama of wondrous but perverse humanity. For any reader who would like a panoramic view of traditional Chinese life through the portrayal of many unforgettable characters in an authentic social and cultural setting, there can be no richer and more fascinating work than Cao Xüeqin's *A Dream of Red Mansions*.

Note

The novel *Hongloumeng* is customarily known in English as *The Dream of the Red Chamber* (with or without the definite article) because earlier partial translations bear this rather enigmatic title. Today, however, its continuing use is unjustified, since we have a complete translation in three volumes by Yang

Hsien-yi and Gladys Yang (Peking: Foreign Languages Press, 1978–1980) under the apt title *A Dream of Red Mansions*. Another complete translation in five volumes by David Hawkes and John Minford is called *The Story of the Stone* (New York: Penguin Books, 1973–1986), which accurately renders the novel's alternative title *Shitouji*. However, since the work is best known in Chinese as *Hongloumeng*, *A Dream of Red Mansions* should be its preferred title in English—even though the Hawkes-Minford version is richer in style and more interesting to read.

14

Zhu Xi and the Four Books

Wm. Theodore de Bary

W HEN EDUCATED PERSONS of the premodern era in East Asia
referred to the Confucian Classics, they almost always spoke first
of the Four Books. These were based on early texts of the classic age B.C. in
China, but no one of that earlier age would have recognized what was meant
by "The Four Books," which was the label attached to these classic texts
when the great Neo-Confucian scholar Zhu Xi (1130–1200) chose them as
introductory readings for the core curriculum, which became standard for
most education in thirteenth- through nineteenth-century East Asia.

Zhu Xi's Four Books comprised the *Analects* of Confucius and the text
of Mencius, as well as the *Great Learning* (*Daxue*) and the *Mean* (*Zhongyong*).
These latter two texts had been selected out of a much larger compilation,
the classic *Record of Rites*. What was it then that led Zhu Xi to single out these
relatively brief texts, almost hidden among the wide variety of ritual material collected in the *Record of Rites*, for special attention? Even more of a
question is why Zhu set the *Great Learning* as first among the Four Books,
even ahead of the *Analects* and *Mencius*. What justified giving it such a high
priority and seeming primacy among these classics?

The answers to these questions are both historical and philosophical.
First the historical. In the development of Song Confucian thought, Zhu Xi
stood out as highly creative and original in his synthesis of his predecessors' contributions to the reformulation of the Confucian tradition. Much
new thinking entered into the process, and this is what justifies our calling

it "Neo-Confucian" and our thinking of the Four Books as "neoclassical" rather than simply as generic classics.

Indicative of this process is a quote from Zhu's predecessor, Cheng Yi, at the beginning of his own version of the *Great Learning*:

> The Great Learning (*Daxue*) is learning to become a great person. "Clearly manifesting" (*ming*) means clarifying. "Luminous virtue" (*mingde*) is what a person gets from Heaven. Open, spiritual, and unobscured, it is replete with all the principles by which one responds to the myriad things and affairs, but being hampered by the physical endowment and obstructed by human [selfish] desires, there are times when it becomes obscured. Nevertheless, the radiance of the original substance [nature] is never lost, and one who pursues learning need only keep to what emerges from it and clarify it, so as to restore it to its original condition.[1]

Two things stand out here. First is that the *Great Learning* is a surviving text of the Confucian school, and second is the extraordinary claim that it is the "key to the pursuit of learning," even ahead of the *Analects* and *Mencius*.

The survival of the text might seem an obvious enough fact, but in an age when Chan (Zen) Buddhism had dismissed textual evidence as irrelevant, calling itself "a separate teaching outside scriptures, not dependent on written texts," the Confucians had to reassert the importance of written evidence as publicly attesting to Neo-Confucian claims of an authentic transmission. This was not just a transmission from mind to mind (subjective) as in Chan (Zen) but part of a publicly attested evidential record. It is also on the basis of this evidence that Cheng Yi and Zhu Xi can make the further claim that in the *Great Learning* there was a definite process to learning, an orderly sequence. This too was defined in a public way: it was not just an indefinable private transmission from one Chan mastermind to another and then on to a line of putative successors.

Here we have another stage in a process that had started earlier in the confrontation between Mahāyāna Buddhism and Confucianism. Already in the late Tang, Han Yü had singled out the *Great Learning* as emblematic of a crucial difference between the two teachings. They were not, according to Han Yü, just different versions of essentially the same Way. Han Yü differentiated the Confucian Way from both Buddhism and Daoism, as being a Way that sustained human civilized life in a public manner—in language and texts that enabled people to communicate with each other and settle human affairs together. Neither Buddhism nor Daoism purported to do this.[2]

So conscious was Zhu of the need to base himself on a veritable record that at the close of his preface to the *Great Learning* he describes his efforts to gather up the surviving works of his predecessors as a basis for his own work. At the close of the preface he speaks of how the Cheng brothers connected up with the received Confucian tradition by "rearranging the fragmented text [of the *Great Learning*] to bring out its essential message. Although I myself am not very clever, it was my good fortune . . . to hear about this. Considering that the work still suffers some damage and loss . . . I went ahead to gather up the fragments, rearrange them, and insert my own ideas, and here and there to fill in for what was missing."[3]

For Zhu, tradition was anything but fast and fixed, and in his preface to the *Mean* he explains at great length the precariousness of the Way and the difficulty of restoring it, a process that he termed "The Reconstruction or Reconstitution of the Way" (*dao tong*). This he believed had to be retrieved by a combination of textual restoration and the insightful recognition by his Song predecessors of the relevance of the texts to the problems of their own and his own day.

In order to accomplish this, Zhu had to work with both classic texts and with the writings of Song thinkers that spoke to their contemporary relevance. One important product of this effort was his compiling of an anthology of passages in the works of the Song masters that bore not only on matters of textual exegesis but on how they spoke to current issues. This anthology he entitled *Jinsilu*, which can be translated as Wing-Tsit Chan has done, "Reflections on Things at Hand," but also as "Record of Recent Thought." "Things at Hand" refers to the original use of the term *jinsi* in the Confucian *Analects* as relating to the nearest, most immediate needs of human life. But the double meaning of *jinsi* as "Recent Thought" testifies to Zhu's belief in the important contribution of modern thinkers to the problems of Song society and thought.

Thus Zhu Xi's project was not just that of a classicist but that of a neoclassicist as well, which means that in the Four Books we have a neoclassical recovery of tradition in the same vein as other "medieval" synthesizers in other major traditions, for example, St. Thomas Aquinas in the West, al-Ghazālī in the Islamic world, and Saṅkārāchārya in the Indian. In this perspective the Four Books reminds us that "classics" are not just ancient texts or generic classics but part of an evolving rather than static tradition.

Zhu Xi's *Jinsilu*, as a reconstitution of classic tradition in a contemporary mode, reflects also his judgment of how a particular classic text, the *Great Learning*, can provide both an interpretation of the classics and a definite method for relating the classics to the educational needs of Song society, which was much more complex than the classic age and offered expanded technology—that is, printing—for meeting these needs.

In compiling his anthology, Zhu further showed how central the *Great Learning* was to his thinking. In his *Jinsilu*, he structured the quotations from earlier writings in the same sequence as in the *Great Learning*, but at the same time he cited them in the order of the Song masters, stressing that they made up a line of continuity or a teaching lineage. That is, he constructed the aforementioned Succession to the Way as analogous to the purported line of Buddhist patriarchs' "mind-to-mind" transmission.

Following is the table of contents as found in Wing-tsit Chan's translation, followed by my own comments on their significance in the *Great Learning* for education in Zhu Xi's time.

I. On the Substance of the Way

II. The Essentials of Learning

III. The Investigation of things and the pursuit of principle to the utmost

IV. Preserving one's mind and nourishing one's nature

V. Correcting mistakes, improving oneself, self-discipline and returning to propriety

VI. The Way to regulate the family

VII. On serving or not serving in the Government, advancing or withdrawing, and accepting or declining office

VIII. On the principles of governing the state and bringing peace to the world

IX. Systems and institutions

X. Methods of handling affairs

XI. The way to teach

XII. Correcting mistakes and the defects of the human mind

XIII. Sifting the heterodoxical doctrines

XIV. On the dispositions of Sages and worthies[4]

The first thing to note here is what Zhu puts first: his explanation of the overall philosophy and basic principles that should provide the context for the steps outlined in the *Great Learning*, which are summed up in sections III through VIII of the contents. Zhu starts with the Substance of the Way in order to provide an overview or a metaphysical base for his educational program: defined principles that provide a stated, public ground on which the *Great Learning* can take a stand for a substantial rationality versus Daoism and Buddhism. Sections IX through XIII deal with contemporary problems and how the principles of the *Great Learning* can be applied to issues that have arisen in the more complex and philosophically conflicted Song "modernity."

Methodologically, Zhu thought that the Substance of the Way (the philosophical ground) should come first, but he recognized that for many readers of the *Great Learning* as an introductory text the metaphysics of the Way would be hard to grasp. Therefore in his preface he suggested that they bypass this theoretical chapter and go straight to the practicalities of learning. I shall follow the same policy and bring in the philosophy only as needed to explain the core items of the *Great Learning*.

In the Neo-Confucian curriculum of premodern East Asia, the *Jinsilu* was treated as a classic accompaniment to the Four Books, but for our purposes here it is treated as supplementary reading to the Four Books; thus the discussion that follows focuses on *The Great Learning* itself and the so-called Eight Items (*Ba tiaomu*) that traditionally summed up Zhu Xi's basic approach to learning in the text as edited by him.

The Recognition of Things (*ge-wu*)

The usual rendering of *ge-wu* in English translations has been "the Investigation of Things," and this speaks to that aspect of learning that most closely approximates, and resonates with, the modern proclivity for "objective," value-free inquiry in scientific research. It is, however, a little one sided. Zhu understood *ge* more as "meeting" or "matching." In the early encounter with Buddhism, Chinese translators had tried to find Chinese equivalents for Indian Buddhist terms, a process spoken of as *ge yi*, "matching concepts." Often these were not very exact matches, as in the case of the Chinese word *fa* to render *dharma*, but at least it asserted some correspondence (here, "law") between the two, that is, convergence if not exact equivalence.

Zhu Xi thought of *ge-wu* as somewhat similar. Instead of thinking of *wu*, "things," simply as objects external to the mind, he saw the possibility of knowing or understanding "things" as dependent on a matching of subject and object through the recognition in each of a common principle. Unless there were some common principles inherent in each, there would be no true understanding; subject and object would remain separate.

At this point, we recall Zhu Xi's quotation earlier about human nature as "luminous virtue"; it is "what a person gets from Heaven. Open, spiritual and unobscured [transparent], it is replete with all the principles by which one responds to the myriad things and affairs." In other words, if the mind really "gets" something, it brings something of principle in itself (subjective) to the corresponding principle in the "object."

Principle (*li*) had already become a key concept in the Song philosophical lexicon, with a variety of applications. Suffice it to say here that for Zhu Xi all things, whether as subject or object, partake of principle. Principle inhered in things as actualized or embodied in *qi*, matter energy or material form. One could not truly grasp the nature of things unless one also understood how the particular principle or thing also related to principle in all things, whether in the knowing subject or in the universe at large. "Principle is one: its particularizations are diverse" implied that this combination was irreducible. One could not know or grasp anything apart from the principle that linked it to oneself and all things under Heaven. Thus, for instance, human nature could not be understood apart from nature in general (*tian-ren he yi*). Individuality could not be "recognized" except in the context of overall relationships, which included both objective relations and value relations.

One of the most important points made by Zhu Xi in his commentary on the *Great Learning* reflected the special pains he took to clarify this issue through a special note on "recognizing things and extending ones knowledge" (*ge-wu, zhi zhi*). Here he speaks for Cheng Yi:

> "The extension of knowing lies in the investigation of things" means that if we wish to extend our knowing, it consists in fathoming the principle of any thing or affair we come into contact with, for the intelligent [spiritual] human mind always has the capacity to know [learn], and the things of this world all have their principles, but if a principle remains unfathomed, one's knowing [learning] is not fully realized. Hence the initial teaching of the Great Learning insists that the learner, as he comes upon the things of the world, must proceed from principles already known and further fathom them until he reaches the limit. After exerting himself for a long time, he will one day experience a breakthrough to integral comprehension. Then the qual-

ities of all things, whether internal or external, refined or coarse, will be apprehended and the mind, in its whole substance and great functioning, will all be clearly manifested. This is "things [having been] recognized." This is the utmost of knowing.

Zhu's reference to a sudden "breakthrough to integral comprehension" carried with it a sense of self-realization and self-fulfillment akin to a mystical experience, and it is not surprising that some understood it as an enlightenment similar in certain respects but different in both theory and practice from Chan (Zen) Buddhism. Interpretation of this suggestive passage remained highly controversial among later Neo-Confucians. What seems clear is that Zhu Xi thought of this culmination neither as a comprehensive grasp of empirical knowledge (that is, encyclopedic learning, "knowing everything") nor as a transrational, transmoral gnosis ("knowing nothing") but rather as a thorough empathetic understanding or enlargement of the spirit that overcomes any sense of self and other, inner and outer, subjective and objective.[5]

Zhu's special point about the learning process as culminating in a holistic experience of a "sudden breakthrough to integral comprehension," with its resemblance to sudden enlightenment in Zen, should alert us to the fact that something significant is being added to the "recognition of things." If we look at what Zhu quotes in the opening passage of chapter II of the *Jinsilu*, "The Essentials of Learning," the tone is noticeably different from the plain text of the *Great Learning*:

1. Master Lien-Xi [Zhou Dunyi] said: The sage aspires to become Heaven, the worthy aspires to become a sage, and the gentleman aspires to become worthy. I-yin and Yen Yüan were great worthies. I-yin was ashamed that his ruler would not become a sage-emperor like Yao and Shun, and if a single person in the empire was not well adjusted, he felt that he himself was as disgraced as if he had been whipped in public. Yen Yüan "did not transfer his anger; he did not repeat a mistake," and "for three months there would be nothing in his mind contrary to humanity (ren)." If one desires what I-yin desired and learns what Yenzi learned, he will become a sage if he reaches the proper degree. Even if he does not, he will not miss a good reputation.

3. [Cheng Yi] Someone asked: "in the school of Confucius there were three thousand pupils. Yenzi alone was praised as loving to

learn. It is not that the three thousand scholars had not studied and mastered the Six Arts such as the Book of Odes and the Book of History. Then what was it that Yen Zi alone loved to learn?[6]

The question put to Cheng Yi here is a commonsensical one on the part of anyone who has read the original Confucian texts, which discuss the possibility of anyone becoming a sage. Anyone could aspire to become a sage-king or Son of Heaven, as in Mencius and Xunzi, although even Confucius disavowed being a sage himself (though others credited him with such authority). The sages most discussed in the classics were the Sage Kings, who were invested with a supreme governing authority. When Mencius called for a ruler to measure up to the model of the sage-kings, he insisted that rulers could not evade the issue by denying any capability for attaining sagely virtue. Now the potential for sagehood is seen as inherent in human nature, and it is this potential that Cheng Yi says inheres in all human beings, Everyman. Thus in the passage above, Yenzi, even in a lonely, impoverished state, becomes a Neo-Confucian icon of sageliness. From this, learning to be a sage becomes a common theme of the *Jinsilu*, and it establishes a different role for this "Neo-Confucian" classic as responding to the spirituality of Mahāyāna Buddhism, which emphasized the universality of the Buddha nature and the possibility for all beings to achieve Buddhahood through direct introspection. To this mystical conception of the Buddha nature, which was beyond all definition, the Song masters were advancing a spirituality that could be expressed as the end point of a definable learning process.

Turning now to the text of the *Great Learning* itself, we notice that Zhu Xi strikes certain notes at the beginning that will guide our reading of the text. First, he makes a point of providing a preface that will point people in a proper direction for understanding the original text. He starts off by asserting the universality of the Heaven-endowed nature in all human beings and the need for them to bring their actual psychophysical nature (as differentiated and individualized in material force, *qi*) into conformity with the ideal nature. To do this requires both self-cultivation according to the steps outlined in the original text of the *Great Learning* and schooling provided by the state, which the ruler is obligated to make available from the capital down to the local village. This idea proved of historic importance inasmuch as most later dynasties of the premodern era had accepted this ideal as the norm even if they failed to fulfill it. Zhu Xi's other important text, the *Ele-*

mentary Learning, dealt with early training in the home, but we shall keep our focus here on the basic process of the *Great Learning* itself.

The "original" text of the *Great Learning*, as received by the Cheng-Zhu school, spoke of the need for good government in the empire to rely on ordered states and well-regulated families and for them in turn to depend on individual cultivation, however or wherever conducted. But the bulk of the *Great Learning* is devoted to self-cultivation (five of the eight steps), and systematic institutional matters are passed over lightly.

We have already touched on the first two steps, the Recognition of Things and Extending One's Knowledge. These we have seen included both intellectual operations and moral sensibility, but the third and fourth items, Making One's Intentions Sincere and Rectification of the Mind-and-Heart, accentuate the moral aspect as both moral self-awareness and self-control. Here, however, we face a question as to how the "self" is to be understood. And for this purpose we do well to refer to Zhu's preface to the *Mean*, the importance of which is indicated by the fact that Zhu prepared such prefaces especially for the *Great Learning* and the *Mean* but not for the *Analects* and *Mencius*.

The main feature of the preface to the *Mean* was Zhu's Sixteen-Word Formula for the direction and control of the Mind-and-Heart (*xin*), couched in obscure, archaic language: "The human mind is precarious; the mind of Heaven is subtle (barely perceptible). Be discriminating, be one. Hold fast to the Mean."

Zhu explains this as follows:

> As I have maintained, the mind in its empty spirituality [pure intelligence and consciousness] is one and only one. But if we make a distinction between the human mind and the mind of the Way, it is because consciousness differs insofar as it may spring from the self-centeredness of one's individual physical form or may have its source in the correctness of one's innate nature and moral imperative. This being so, the one may be precarious and insecure, while the other may be subtle and barely perceptible. But humans all have physical form, so even the wisest do not lack this human mind; and all have the inborn nature, so even the most stupid do not lack the mind of the Way.
>
> These two [tendencies] are mixed together in the square-inch of the mind-and-heart, and if one does not know how to order them, the

precariousness becomes even more precarious, and the barely perceptible becomes even less perceptible, so that even the sense of the common good [impartiality] of heaven's principle [in the mind of the Way] is unable in the end to overcome the selfishness of human desires. "Be discriminating" means to distinguish between the two and not let them be confused. "Be one [with the mind of the Way]" means to preserve the correctness of the original mind and not become separated from it. If one applies oneself to this without any interruption, making sure that the mind of the Way is master of one's self and that the human mind always listens to its commands, then the precariousness and insecurity will yield to peace and security, and what is subtle and barely perceptible will become clearly manifest. Then, whether in action or repose, in whatever one says or does, one will not err by going too far or not far enough."[7]

The Message of the Mind (*xinfa*), also alluded to in the preface to the Great Learning, refers to the sixteen-word message coming down from the sage kings Yao and Shun concerning the human mind and the mind of the Way, human nature, and instruction featured in the first chapter of the *Mean*, which was to become the basis of Neo-Confucian mind cultivation. It focused on the conflict in a human mind precariously balanced between selfish and unselfish tendencies—the former identified with what were called "human desires" (customarily used to mean "selfish desires") and the latter with the moral imperatives of the Way, implanted in human nature, as received from Heaven. A distinction is made between Heaven's principles and human desires in the *Record of Rites*' "Record of Music" (*Yueji*), where "human desires" are identified with various excesses harmful to others, and in the subcommentary with greed and lust, in contrast to the purity of the Heaven-endowed moral nature. The contested ground between them was natural inclinations, affections, and appetites constitutive of one's individual psychophysical makeup, which could readily be made to serve the common good (*gong*) when directed by the Mind of the Way and the Principles of Heaven or else could be turned to selfish ends. The easy susceptibility to abuse of one's legitimate self-interest, one's fallibility, and one's proneness to self-deception found expression by Zhu Xi in terms of "the human mind is precarious, the mind of the Way is subtle [and difficult to perceive]." Thus careful self-examination was called for, consisting of "refined discrimination" as to what was fair and proper, even what was legitimately self-regarding (for example, the proper care of one's person), in contrast to what was ulterior and selfish, that is, prejudicial to others, to the common good and even to one's true selfhood. "Single-mindedness" meant adherence to the unity of principle in a shared humanity (*ren*); "holding to the Mean" referred to a mind properly balanced in this respect and not given to partiality.[8]

One can see how this Sixteen-Word Formula could easily be assimilated to "Making the Intentions Sincere" and "Rectifying the Mind" and how they would become catchwords for the fifth item of the *Great Learning*: self-cultivation. The institutions referred to in the sixth, seventh, and eighth items (family, state, and empire) received comparatively less attention. In the end, the final words of the preface to the *Great Learning* summed up the whole teaching as "self-cultivation (or self-discipline) for the governance of mankind." This meant the same self-cultivation for all, whether the ruler or the governed.

Although Zhu Xi did not fail to address institutional (as distinct from individual) matters elsewhere in his writings, it was this intense focus on the self that became a mark of "Neo-Confucianism" and its wide influence across East Asia. Indeed, other scholars after Zhu Xi in the Song, Ming, and Qing sought to redress this imbalance by studies in statecraft that dealt more with the institutional contexts in which individuals had to work. But for Zhu Xi it was the prime reality of the self that took precedence in an age wherein Buddhism had emptied the self of all public meaning.

However, the political and social contexts elsewhere in East Asia were different enough from China so that the pertinence of Neo-Confucianism could be more easily recognized in personal education than in institutional forms. In Japan, Korea, and Vietnam, the political and social systems were different enough so that the schooling Zhu prescribed found no exact counterpart elsewhere but rather met conservative resistance. For instance, the lack of a civil service in feudal Japan obviated what Zhu had said about the civil-examination system but not what he had to say about civil values in reeducating individual members of the warrior class.

Self-cultivation for the governance of humankind gained general acceptance wherever the Neo-Confucian philosophy of a common human nature could be shared. On this basis, then, the Four Books could everywhere become the heart of the curriculum, even in the temple schools (*terakoya*) of Japan, where the shogunate did nothing to establish a universal school system, leaving this function to local "private" schools. These schools all picked up on the Four Books as relevant to the secular needs of Tokugawa society and as a supplement to religious instruction.

Indeed, it was by this route that early Western observers in Japan (not just the Jesuits in China) recognized the fundamental importance of the Four Books to an understanding of Japanese culture in the nineteenth century, first the art historian Ernest Fenollosa and then the American poet Ezra Pound, who published his own translation of the Four Books as classics in his Square Dollar series. Although Mortimer Adler failed to catch up with this by including the Four Books in his Hundred Great Books, we would do well to consider them as world classics for the twenty-first-century core curriculum.

Notes

1. Wm. Theodore de Bary and Irene Bloom, eds., *Sources of Chinese Tradition*, 2nd ed. (New York: Columbia University Press, 2000), 725.
2. Ibid., 568–570.
3. Ibid., 724.
4. *Reflections on Things at Hand*, translated by Wing-tsit Chan (New York: Columbia University Press, 1967).
5. de Bary and Bloom, *Sources of Chinese Tradition*, 729–730.
6. *Reflections on Things at Hand*, 35.
7. de Bary and Bloom, *Sources of Chinese Tradition*, 733
8. Ibid., 731.

15

WAITING FOR THE DAWN

HUANG ZONGXI'S CRITIQUE OF THE CHINESE
DYNASTIC SYSTEM

Wm. Theodore de Bary

H UANG ZONGXI (1610–1695) was the son of a high Ming official, affiliated with the reformist Donglin party, who died in prison at the hands of court eunuchs. At the age of eighteen, after the fall of Wei Zhongxian, the chief eunuch, Huang avenged his father's death by bringing to justice or personally attacking those responsible for it. Thereafter he devoted himself to study, took part in a flurry of political agitation at Nanjing just before the fall of the Ming dynasty, and then engaged in prolonged but unsuccessful guerrilla resistance to the Manchus in southeastern China. There is evidence that he even took part in a mission to Japan, hoping to obtain aid. After finally giving up the struggle, Huang settled down to a career as an independent scholar and teacher, refusing all offers of employment from the Manchu regime.

Warfare being less total and intensive in those days, Huang was probably not forced to neglect his intellectual interests altogether during those unsettled years. Nevertheless, it is remarkable that his most productive years should have come so late in life. His first important work, *Waiting for the Dawn* (*Mingyi daifang lu*), was produced at the age of fifty-two. Thereafter, he worked on a massive anthology of Ming-dynasty prose and a broad survey of Ming thought, *Mingru xuean*, which is the first notable attempt in China at a systematic and critical intellectual history. At his death, he was compiling a similar survey for the Song and Yuan dynasties. Huang's range of interests included mathematics, calendrical science, geography, and the critical study of the classics, as well as literature and philosophy. In most of these fields, however, his approach is that of a historian, and this underlying bent is reflected in the fact that his most outstanding disciples and followers in the Manchu period also distinguished themselves in historical studies. Huang was an independent and creative scholar who questioned whether individual self-cultivation (self-discipline) was a self-sufficient means of achieving good governance. His father had been a heroic example of Confucian personal character defeated by a system that gave power to less worthy men. Hence Huang balanced the predominant Neo-Confucian emphasis on individual virtue as the key to governance by stressing the need for constitutional law and systemic reform as well.

In his synthesis, Huang drew upon several major strains of Chinese thought that readers of Chinese classics will recognize. As a successor to the Donglin school of political, social, and moral reform, he combined the basic principles of the Neo-Confucian Four Books with the statecraft thinking of the Song period, which took into account the power factors that had been so prominent in early Legalist thinking and later in the so-called New Laws of Wang An-shi.

Zhu Xi's key formula (in his preface to the *Great Learning*) had been "self-cultivation" (or self-discipline) for the governance of humankind," and the essence of his sixteen-word formula for the mind-and-heart was the balancing of legitimate self-interest with the interests of others to achieve the common good. This was an imperative incumbent on all, both leaders and the led, which meant, among other things, that everyone had to be a leader of all in self-control.

This same principle is affirmed in Huang's opening discussion of "The Prince" (*Yuan jun*), in which he recognizes the legitimacy of individual self-interest but also affirms that leadership in the ruler calls for him to subordinate his own self-interest to the interests of all. He is taking into account (but expresses in his own human terms) the classic argument over the goodness of human nature (Mencius) and human nature as evil (Xunzi). People do naturally act in their own interest, but there is nothing inherently bad or wrong in this as long as it is subordinated to the fulfillment of the shared or common good. Nor can the need for self-denying leadership be taken as a denial of the legitimacy of individual self-interest.

This balancing act had already been performed by the Neo-Confucians in their philosophy of human nature, primarily in regard to individual subjectivity versus objective needs in human society. Huang now extends this to the management of institutions as power systems. One can see this as responding to the objective economic circumstances in the Ming and early Qing: the continuing rise of the middle class and its profit-oriented mentality in the midst of many others' impoverishment. However, there is little in *Waiting for the Dawn* that could be interpreted as a program that asserts middle-class interests as opposed to those of others. Virtually all of his programmatic recommendations are governed by the standards of universality, equality, and individual merit, not class interest. Here we have Legalist system building, but not in the interest of the state. Huang's "Laws" or systems (*fa*), instead of aiming at enhancing state power at the expense of the people, are systems that control and direct state institutions to serve the people's interest generally. This is neither Legalist state building nor one class dominating another but a Confucian communitarian ideal.

In effect, "waiting for the dawn" means "waiting for the prince" to come and listen to Huang's plan for him. Here the primary function of the prince is service to the people; all exercise of his authority is to be in their interests. The same is true of Huang's discussion of the duties and functions of government ministers; instead of treating them just as officials of state, that is, bureaucrats or servants of the ruler, he calls them "ministers," in keeping with the moral responsibility invested in that term especially by Mencius. The Legalists had defined things functionally, but Huang, while taking the moral aspect as primary (rather than the practical or utilitarian), at the same time takes cognizance of the practical power factors at work by devoting a whole chapter to the need for maintaining the independence of the prime minister as a separate leadership function within the same ruling class. Both ruler and minister shared the same principled purpose, but along with functional differentiation within the system, a shaping and balancing of power was no less essential to the effective service of the common good.

Among traditional Chinese institutions, the one that comes closest to Huang's conception of consensual rule is probably the community compact or community assembly (*xiang yue*) that Zhu Xi had sought to promote and that earlier Ming reformers had hoped to "revive." But by Huang's time, this institution had been taken over by the Ming founder for his own purposes and became largely co-opted by the bureaucracy. It is not surprising that Huang would not look to it as a source of political reform but would rather see the leviathan state as so dominating the political landscape that nothing short of its wholesale transformation would suffice for fundamental reform. As Huang saw it, this it necessitated a basic reconceiving of law—not as dynastic law based on the patriarchal enactments of the founding father of the dynasty[1] but as something more like a state constitution with a separation of powers that would ensure and protect collegial rule.

In China, the dynastic state put a high value on scholarly expertise, and, paradoxically, the schools suffered for it. This is because the state's interest in education was closely linked to its recruitment of men with talents useful in government: literary skills, a knowledge of historical precedents, and competence in the rituals so important to the legitimizing of government. While government schools were maintained in the capital and the principal seats of provincial administration, their main object was to prepare those who passed the district examinations for higher degrees leading to eventual employment in the bureaucracy. Meanwhile, an overwhelming majority of the people went uneducated. Except for the select number who gained admission to official schools and the Imperial College, instruction could be obtained only from private tutors or teachers in private academies, which few could afford. Thus the state's interest in the recruiting of scholars did not have the effect of developing any general system of education. Even without such universal education or a public-school system, however, a degree of uniformity prevailed in education comparable to that achieved by modern states through centralized public-school systems. This was because virtually all instruction in China, whether public or private, was oriented toward the civil-service examinations. These were the gateway to advancement in government and, in Chinese society, official status was seen as the main road to success, influence, and often affluence. The government did not need to maintain an extensive school system with a curriculum and texts of its own choosing. Simply by prescribing what was to be called for in the examinations, it could determine what most aspiring students would find it in their interest to learn, whether in or out of state schools.

Against this background we can appreciate why Huang attaches such great importance to educational reform. He wishes to remedy the lack of general education and the prevalence of careerism in education by creating a universal public-school system with functions much broader than the mere training of officials. In classical times, he attempts to show, schools were centers of all-important community and state activities; they had a major role too, he claims, in debating public questions and advising the prince. Ideally, then, schools should serve the people in two ways: providing an education for all and acting as organs for the expression of public opinion. Likewise, the prince had two corresponding obligations: to maintain schools for the benefit of all and to give the people a voice in government through the schools. In ancient times, "the emperor did not dare to determine right and wrong himself, so he left to the schools the determination of right and wrong." But since the rise of the Q'in, "right and wrong have been determined entirely by the court. If the emperor favored such and such, everyone hastened to think it right. If he frowned upon such and such, everyone condemned it as wrong."

This argument is suggestive again of Confucian antipathy for Legalist doctrines that had been absorbed into the authoritarian dogma of subsequent dynasties. Han Feizi had said: "Whatever he [the ruler] considers good is to be regarded as good by the officials and people. Whatever he does not consider good is not to be regarded as good by the officials and the people." The Legalist statesman, Li Si, who was chiefly responsible for suppressing free speech in independent schools, memorialized the throne as follows:

> At present your Majesty possesses a unified empire and has laid down distinctions of right and wrong, consolidating for himself a single position of eminence. Yet there are those who ... teach what is not according to the laws. When they hear orders promulgated, they criticize them in the light of their own teachings. ... To cast disrepute on their ruler they regard as a thing worthy of fame; to hold different views they regard as high conduct. ... If such conditions are not prohibited, the imperial power will decline. (*SCT*, 1:209–210)

According to Huang, the prevalence of this view that the ruler determines what is right and wrong deprived the schools of one of their most important functions. They could no longer discuss public issues freely, and because the authority of the state was set against the autonomy of the academies, an unnatural separation arose between the two. Thereafter, the schools could not even fulfill the functions remaining to them of training scholars for office, because the true aims of education were lost sight of in the mad scramble for advancement and the desperate endeavor to conform. Thinking men, in their search for true education, turned more and more to the local, quasi-private academies that had become centers of Neo-Confucian thought in the Song and Ming dynasties. But the independence and heterodox views of these academies brought repeated attempts at suppression by the Ming state.

Thus the arbitrary separation of school and state ended in open conflict between them, which was detrimental to the true interests of both. Though

Huang defends the local academies, which had been so much blamed for the political troubles of the late Ming, his real purpose is not to assert the claims of independent private schools. These are a recourse only in the absence of true public education, which, according to the Confucians, it is the duty of the ruler to provide. Instead, Huang advocates a system of universal public education maintained by the state but free of all centralized control. There are to be schools from the capital down through every city and town to even the smallest hamlets, but on each level supervision is to be independent of control from above. The principal units of administration, the prefectures and districts, would be presided over by superintendents of education chosen locally, not appointed by the court. These men need never have served as officials before or have qualified for the civil service. Not only should they have complete freedom in ordinary educational matters, including the right to override the provincial education intendants in the appointment of licentiates (those who have achieved the first degree in the prefectural examinations), but their pronouncements on any matter affecting the community should be listened to respectfully by the local magistrate. Similarly, at the capital the libationer (or chancellor) of the Imperial College should lead a discussion each month on important questions, with the emperor and his ministers attending in the role of students.

This arrangement, and the political function it serves, are of paramount importance to our understanding of Huang's whole plan. His unhappiness over the "unnatural separation between school and state" and his belief that the semiprivate local academies are no substitute for an adequate system of universal education underlies much of what follows.

The rest of *Waiting for the Dawn* extends this same type of analysis to other aspects of organized society, recognizing that many of the essential functions involve a practicality that cannot be reduced simply to either moral principles or utilitarian expediency. Instead, morality needs to take into account different aspects of material reality, especially the condition of agriculture and the burdens put on it (as the prime economic base) by taxation, finances, and military conscription. The need for the decentralization and sharing of power is what leads Huang to an acceptance of "feudalism," in the form of the enfeoffment of military commanders at the frontiers. In this respect, we see the persistence of the Mencian conception of the enfeoffment system as preferable to centralized control.

Here the limits of power and the need to adjust to local circumstances set a limit on the extension of an otherwise "universal" system. In this way

Huang's principles can be thought of as universally applicable but at the same time differentiated in their application to particular circumstances.

Huang wants both to regularize and diversify the examination system, but he does not propose to base his meritocracy on an electoral process. The important function of public discussion and participation is as we have seen located in largely autonomous schools, locally based. In other words, Huang does not conceive of public opinion (*gong-lun*) as something that would be better served through an electoral process, operating in the form of party politics rather than through institutions already grounded in established practice. Consultative and consensual processes can work as long as autonomy is respected and open discussion allowed. How this kind of suasive process can be established without power struggles is not a question directly addressed by Huang, but suffice to say that formal elections are not among the options (systems) that occur to him.

Nevertheless, although Huang has made a definite advance in articulating a constitutional order with checks and balances appropriate to a mature centralized bureaucratic system (such as neither Mencius nor Xunzi knew) and has defined a kind of public sphere or civil society that might mitigate the authoritarianism and offset the concentration of power in the late imperial system, we are still left uncertain as to whether the custodians of that public sphere, as a scholarly elite, might not still become isolated from the common people, serving more their own sectional or class interests than the general welfare.

A modern observer might be more mindful of how easily ruling elites can convince themselves that they know what the people want or need better than the people do themselves, as did later the Communist elites, who, often idealistically and quite conscientiously, lent their services to a "dictatorship of the people's democracy" that made up its own mind about what was best for the people. From this heightened perspective, we can still appreciate Huang's achievement in recognizing the need for a constitutional order and a public sphere as a check on the ruler, but we remain conscious of the ambiguity that attaches to the Confucian scholar-official's ambivalent status between the ruler and the common people. With no middle class to support him, with little of a popular press, without a consensus-making infrastructure other than the schools and academies of the scholar-officials (*shi*), and without a defined electoral process for expressing the wishes of the common people, the public service of the scholar-official, even when conscientiously rendered as a Confucian Noble Man, leaves him in a precarious, dubious, and insecure position between the ruler and the common people (*min*). To what extent can the common people be considered an active constituency representing the general welfare or public interest?

To pose the question in these terms is not to suggest that a perfect solution to the problem has ever been at hand. Modern electoral processes in themselves, being subject to some pressures and manipulation, are not as such any guarantee of effective representative government, though in East Asia they have already proven superior to "people's democracies" led by a one-party dictatorship and controlled by "democratic" centralism (which, in the words of one-time People's Republic of China President Liu Shao-qi, could dispense with elections as "needless formalities"). Even in modern states, something like Huang's parliament of scholars, if carried on in autonomous schools and conducted in the open manner he suggests, could serve to offset concentrations of power in entrenched authoritarian regimes, which though unlikely to accept multiparty politics might allow a measure of latitude to scholars and scientists upon whom they depend for technical expertise. In this latter case, however, the scholars and scientists would still, somehow, have to be, as Huang insists, persons of conscience, people liberally educated to meet their public responsibilities.

Whether or not I am right in thinking that Huang's plan still has relevance to the persistent problems of contemporary China, recent scholarship in both China and Japan has confirmed his stature as a major figure in the overall development of Chinese political thought. Some writers emphasize Huang's debt to his immediate scholarly forebears. I myself see in Huang's plan the product of a significant long-term development of Neo-Confucian thought and scholarship, neither just a retread or recycling of Mencius, on the one hand, nor a work of genius sui generis on the other—a star that suddenly shot across the seventeenth-century firmament and disappeared into the night of Manchu rule. Huang and his work stand out as a singular synthesis of Confucian thought with the thinking that emerged from the Chinese experience under late imperial, Legalist-type, dynastic institutions. From the Neo-Confucian experience, Huang drew both on the intellectual breadth and encyclopedic scholarship of the Zhu Xi school and on the freshness and vitality of thought stimulated by Wang Yangming. Indeed, it is unlikely that he could have commanded such a range of institutional issues as he did in his Plan had it not been for the monumental histories and encyclopedic compilations of Neo-Confucians, of more than one school in the Song, Yuan, and Ming periods, from which he quotes so freely. Nor could he have been so incisive about key issues had he not learned much from the "utilitarian" thinkers of the Song (Li Gou, Ye Shi, and Chen Liang) as well as from the actual experience of the Dong-lin and Fu-she movements in the late Ming.

No one is more conscious than Huang of his indebtedness to earlier writers, some famous and others comparatively obscure, who had wrestled with the same problems. In certain cases, indeed, it is quite apparent that his solution for a given problem was anticipated by others. It is also true that other men of his own time shared Huang's views. They were by no means generally accepted, yet, among men with an intellectual inheritance similar to his, the same Confucian ideals inspired similar sentiments in regard to critical questions of the day. Among them Gu Yan-wu is an outstanding example. He says, in his letter to Huang after reading *Waiting for the Dawn*, that his own views are in agreement with "six- or seven-tenths" of what is set forth therein. A reading of Ku's essays on "Commanderies and Prefectures" (*jun xian lun*) and "Taxes in Money" (*Qian-liang*), as well as relevant passages in his great work *Rizhi lu*, confirms that his views were close to Huang's on many major issues. Other contemporaries, such as Lii Liu-liang (1620–1683) and Tang Zhen (1620–1704), are likewise outstanding exponents of the people's welfare against despotic rulers and oppressive institutions.

In this perspective, then, one can still say that Huang's work is the most eloquent and comprehensive statement of its kind in Chinese political literature. It draws together the ideas that others, in the past or present, had expressed in scattered or unsystematic form, and, while his discussion of certain problems is sometimes less exhaustive than the treatment of them by others (here the comparison to Gu Yan-wu is particularly apt), the balance that Huang achieves between general principles and their historical application adds considerably to the force of his presentation. It is for this reason, perhaps more than any other, that *Waiting for the Dawn* has proved the most enduring and influential Confucian critique of Chinese despotism in the late imperial age as well as the most powerful affirmation of a liberal Confucian political vision in premodern times.

Epilogue

In my conclusion to the above essay, I have presumed to speak of *Waiting for the Dawn* as an "early modern classic." Whether or in what sense it could be so classed many readers would have reason to doubt, especially here where it is placed in the impressive company of John Locke. It would be hard to overrate the importance of Locke as a major landmark in early modern thought and politics in the West and even, by extension, among the Western influences on Asia. Huang Zongxi's importance in late nineteenth- and early twentieth-century China was significant among reformist and republican thinkers and to a limited degree among liberal elements in twentieth-century Japan, but it was short lived and soon became submerged in the flood of Western influences that overtook all of East Asian thought and politics in the twentieth century. From this standpoint, Hegel, Rousseau, Marx, and Weber are more likely to have been read by educated East Asians, most of whom would not even have heard of Huang. But no less would this be true of many influential Western writers about China in the early to mid-twentieth century.

Part of the problem is that today education in East Asia is dominated by the economic, scientific, and technological rush toward the global market, which leaves little room for reading classics of any kind. But at least lip service is paid to tradition as, in some way, defining national identity and also possibly as a resource in deciding what ends are to be served by these new modern means. As China sooner or later comes to reassess the meaning of what is called "Chinese" Socialism, I believe it will want to reexamine works such as Huang's *Mingyi daifanglu* as major efforts to survey and reevaluate the Chinese tradition in broad, long-range terms, and I think that it will find therein much to think about. At the same time, however, other co-inhabitants of the same globe should be engaged with the Chinese in this process and should acquaint ourselves with this and other "modern classics" so as to be prepared for informed discourse with them.

A complete translation may be found in Wm. Theodore de Bary, *Waiting for the Dawn* (New York: Columbia University Press, 1993).

Note

1. See the Ming founders' raw assertion of their own personal will as binding law. Wm. Theodore de Bary and Irene Bloom, eds., *Sources of Chinese Tradition*, 2nd ed. (New York: Columbia University Press, 2000), 780–784. Hereafter abbreviated *SCT* in the text.

The Tale of Genji as a Japanese and World Classic

Haruo Shirane

THE TALE OF *Genji*, or the *Genji monogatari*, was written in the early eleventh century by a woman named Murasaki Shikibu. We know very little about the author except that she was the daughter of a scholar-poet, that she came from the middle ranks of the aristocracy, and that she served, at some point, as a lady-in-waiting to the empress, for whom she probably wrote at least part of this lengthy narrative. The title *The Tale of Genji* comes from the surname of the hero, who is the son of the emperor regnant at the beginning of the narrative and whose life, marriage, and relationships with various women are described over the course of the first forty-one chapters. The remaining thirteen chapters are primarily concerned with the affairs of Kaoru, Genji's putative son.

Murasaki Shikibu's creation of highly individualized characters in a realistic social setting and her subtle presentation of inner thought and emotion have encouraged critics to call the *Genji* the world's first psychological novel. The appearance of a lengthy masterpiece of vernacular fiction toward the beginning of a literary tradition is indeed highly unusual. The Chinese tradition, for example, begins with poetry, history, and philosophy, all of which become classic genres. Vernacular fiction, which has a problematic place in the tradition, does not emerge until much later, and the novelistic masterpiece of Chinese fiction—*A Dream of Red Mansions* (*Honglou meng*), or *The Story of the Stone*—does not appear until the late eighteenth century (1792), about the same time that the novel comes into its own in the Anglo-European tradition.

The Japanese, following the Chinese model, considered poetry, history, and philosophy to be the classic literary genres. But literary masterpieces failed to materialize, at least initially, from either history or philosophy, both of which had to be written in Chinese, the official language of religion and government. Of the three ideological centers—Buddhism, Confucianism, and Shintoism—two (Buddhism and Confucianism) are borrowed from the continent, and the third, Shintoism, the indigenous religion, while containing a body of intriguing myths, did not develop a self-conscious textual tradition. There is, in short, no Old Testament, no Plato, no Confucius. The impact of Buddhism and Confucianism, whose texts were considered literary classics by the Japanese priesthood and intelligentsia, cannot be underestimated. But these centers of thought did not directly give birth to great literature, at least not in the beginning.

Nor do we find epics, drama, or tragedy, the literary genres associated with the wellsprings of the Western literary tradition. Instead, there is poetry and, in particular, *waka*, the thirty-one syllable lyric, which was composed and exchanged by all educated Japanese from the ancient period onward. *Waka* was overwhelmingly private in nature and had little concern for politics, philosophy, or the larger humanistic issues that we normally associate with the Great Ideas, but it functioned superbly as a vehicle of aesthetic consciousness and led to an outstanding tradition of fiction, drama, essays, epics, and literary diaries, all of which are highly lyrical and poetic and of which the *Genji* is perhaps the most outstanding example.

The Tale of Genji also emerged out of a tradition of folk narratives, which can be traced back to the early histories and which had developed by the tenth century into a tradition of vernacular tales and Buddhist anecdotes. Of the two native genres, folk narratives and Japanese poetry, the latter took absolute precedence. Japanese poetry in fact was the only native, vernacular genre to be considered serious literature in Murasaki Shikibu's day. One consequence was that *The Tale of Genji* was not recognized as a classic in its own time.

Buddhism condoned storytelling for its use as parable, as a vehicle for transmitting higher truths, but it fundamentally distrusted prose fiction. Buddhist writers repeatedly condemned prose fiction for deceiving the reader, distorting facts, and encouraging immoral acts. Later medieval Buddhist anecdotes depict Murasaki Shikibu as suffering in hell for having written excessively of amorous affairs and of having "fabricated a tissue of lies." The early Anglo-European novel, which initially came under similar attack, defended itself by pretending to be a form of history, a kind of biography, or, as in the case of *Robinson Crusoe*, an authentic document. Probably for similar reasons, to borrow the prestige and apparent authenticity of the histories, Murasaki Shikibu gave her narrative a strong historical cast, interweaving historical names, places, and events, to the extent that parts of *The Tale of Genji*, which was written in the early eleventh century, can be regarded as a historical novel set a hundred years earlier. The title itself evokes the past, for the practice of conferring the surname of Genji, or Minamoto, upon a prince and thereby making him a commoner—which the emperor does in the opening chapter to provide the hero with political protection and opportunity—had ceased by the early tenth century. In an age in which the Fujiwara clan monopolized all phases of the imperial government, it was inconceivable for a Genji to gain power, let alone control the throne, as the Shining Hero eventually does.

In a famous discussion of fiction in the middle chapters of *The Tale of Genji*, the hero attacks *monogatari*, or vernacular tales, for being deceptive and worthless, but in the end he is persuaded, as Murasaki Shikibu no doubt hoped her readers would be, that there was more truth to be found in this admittedly fictitious tale than in the highly esteemed histories. It was, however, *The Tale of Genji*'s poetic qualities that first earned it literary prominence.

When the *Genji* was finally recognized as a classic in the medieval period, from the early thirteenth century onward, it was recognized not as a work of prose fiction per se but as a sourcebook for poetry, a guide to the poetic diction, imagery, and sensibility required for composing poetry, which was de rigueur for all educated Japanese. Fujiwara no Shunzei, the leading poet of the late twelfth century, publicly remarked that "any poet who was not well versed in *The Tale of Genji* was to be deplored." Indeed, without an intimate knowledge of the *Genji*, the subtle allusions upon which medieval poetry and linked verse, or *renga*, depended could not be comprehended. *The Tale of Genji* also lived in the popular imagination, in oral and written narratives, in Japanese drama, particularly the Nō plays of the late medieval period, and in the visual arts, where it graced everything from scroll painting to furniture engraving. But it was the medieval poet-scholars who were responsible for preserving, annotating, and explicating Murasaki Shikibu's masterpiece for future readers. In the premodern period alone, there are over a thousand commentaries.

One of the obvious attractions that the *Genji* holds for modern readers, particularly for those concerned with today's undergraduate curriculum, is the fact that it is a major classic by a woman. In Murasaki Shikibu's day, as in previous centuries, men devoted themselves to writing prose in Chinese, the official language of religion and government. (The only prose writing that was taken seriously was historical and philosophical writing, all of which was done in Chinese and little of which is read today.) One consequence was that women, who were not obligated to write in a foreign language and who were in fact discouraged from doing so, were the first to create a substantial body of prose texts in the vernacular. If Virginia Woolf lamented the silence of Shakespeare's sister, Japan's Shakespeare was a woman with many literary sisters. In the tenth century, vernacular prose, particularly literary diaries, belonged to women to the extent that the leading male poet of the day, Ki no Tsurayuki, pretended to be a woman in order to write a literary diary in Japanese—a reversal of the George Eliot phenomenon.

Male scholars, however, were the first to write vernacular tales, or *mono-gatari*, though they did so anonymously, for such writing was considered a lowly activity directed only at women and children. These early vernacular tales, which begin with the *Taketori monogatari* (*The Tale of the Bamboo Cutter*, early tenth century), tend to be highly romantic, fantastical, and dominated by folkloric elements. Women, by contrast, wrote highly personal, confessional literature based on their private lives and centered on their own poetry. The author of the *Kagerō nikki*, the first major literary diary by a woman, wrote out of a profound dissatisfaction with contemporary *monogatari*, which, in her view, were "little more than gross fabrications." Standing at the crossroads of literary history, Murasaki Shikibu was able to combine both traditions. *The Tale of Genji* carries on the *monogatari* tradition in its larger plot and its amorous hero. But in its style, details, psychological insight, and portrayal of the dilemmas faced by women in aristocratic society, *The Tale of Genji* remains firmly rooted in the women's tradition.

It was a plot convention of the vernacular tale that the heroine, whose family has declined or disappeared, is discovered and loved by an illustrious noble. This association of love and inferior social status appears from the opening line of the *Genji*: "Which imperial reign was it? Of the many consorts who were in the service of the emperor, there was one who was not of particularly high status but who received the special favor of the Emperor" (translation mine).

In the opening chapter, the emperor regnant, like all Heian emperors, was expected to devote himself to his principal consort (the Kokiden lady), the lady of the highest rank, yet he dotes on a woman of considerably lower status, a social and political violation that eventually results in the woman's death. Like his father, Genji pursues love where it is forbidden and most unlikely to be found or attained. In the fifth chapter, Genji discovers his future wife, the young Murasaki, who has lost her mother and is in danger of losing her only guardian when Genji takes her into his own home.

In Murasaki Shikibu's day, it would have been unheard of for a man of Genji's high rank to take a girl of Murasaki's low position into his own residence and marry her. In Heian aristocratic society, the man usually lived in his wife's residence, either in the house of her parents or in a dwelling nearby. As a rule, the wife did not leave her family after marriage. She received her husband at her own home, reared her children there, and continued to be supported by her family. Though political power lay in the hands of men, the succession to marital residences remained matrilineal. The prospective groom thus had high stakes in marriage, for the bride's family provided not only a residence but other forms of support as well. When Genji takes a girl with absolutely no political backing or social support into his house and marries her, he openly flouts the conventions of marriage as they were known to Murasaki Shikibu's audience. In the *monogatari* tradition, however, this action becomes a sign of excessive, romantic love.

A number of other sequences in the *Genji*—those of Yūgao, Suetsumuhana, Tamakazura, the Akashi lady, Oigimi (Agemaki), and Ukifune—start on a similar note. All of these women come from upper- or middle-rank aristocratic families that have, for various reasons, fallen into social obscurity and must struggle to survive. The appearance of the highborn hero signifies, at least for those surrounding the woman, an opportunity for social redemption, an expectation that is usually fulfilled in the earlier *monogatari*. Murasaki Shikibu, however, focuses on the difficulties that the woman subsequently encounters either in dealing with the man or in making, or failing to make, the social transition between her own class and that of the highborn hero. The woman may, for example, be torn between pride and material need, or between emotional dependence on the man and a desire to be more independent, or she may feel abandoned and betrayed—all conflicts explored in Heian women's literature. In classical poetry, which had a profound influence on the *Genji*, love has a similar fate: it is never about happiness or the blissful union of souls. Instead, it dwells on unfulfilled hopes, fear of abandonment, deep regrets, and lingering resentment. One of the most prominent poetic stances in the *Kokinshu*, the first imperial anthology of Japanese poetry (early ninth century) is that of the lonely woman. As the medieval aesthetic term *sabi* (which comes from the word *sabishii*, or "lonely") suggests, loneliness is not only a state of being; it is part of a larger aesthetic consciousness that finds melancholy beauty in loneliness.

As mentioned above, *The Tale of Genji* has often been called the world's first psychological novel, a notion reinforced by Arthur Waley, who transformed *The Tale of Genji* both stylistically and socially into a Victorian novel. The label of novel is obviously meant to be a compliment, but it can be misleading. First of all, *The Tale of Genji* need not be read from front to back as a single monolithic work. *The Tale of Genji* was not conceived and written as a single product and then published and distributed to a mass audience as novels are today. Instead, the chapters were issued in limited installments to a small aristocratic audience, possibly to a single reader (the empress). Furthermore, the chapters probably did not appear in the order that we have them today. In all likelihood, the *Genji* began as a short story, and in response to reader demand, Murasaki Shikibu produced another story or sequel.

The *Genji* is probably best appreciated as Murasaki Shikibu's oeuvre, or corpus: a closely interrelated series of texts that can be read either individually or as a whole and that is the product of an author whose attitudes, interests, and techniques evolved significantly with time and experience. For example, the reader of the Ukifune story (the last five chapters, devoted to Ukifune) can appreciate this sequence both independently and as an integral part of the previous narrative. It is thus possible for undergraduates to read only a part of *The Tale of Genji* and still appreciate many of its finer qualities. In fact, it is sometimes better to start with the later, more mature sequences and then, having acquired a taste for the narrative, go back to the earlier chapters.

Japanese poets were well aware that meaning is dependent on context and that the significance of a thirty-one-syllable *waka* could be profoundly altered by the prose context or by contiguous poems. An entire poetic genre—*renga*, or linked verse—eventually grew out of the pleasure derived from deliberately changing the meaning of a preexisting verse by adding another verse to it. In a similar fashion, Murasaki Shikibu altered the significance of her existing text, or body of texts, not by rewriting but by adding and interlacing new sequences. To take a larger example, love, glory, and *miyabi* ("courtliness"), the secular ideals assumed in the earlier volumes, are placed in relative and ironic perspective in the latter chapters by the emergence of their opposite: a deep-rooted desire to renounce the world and achieve detachment.

That *The Tale of Genji* is an evolving narrative, however, does not mean that Murasaki Shikibu ignores or forgets the earlier stages of the narrative. The author links many of the women by blood or physical appearance, in the form of surrogate figures. For example, in the opening chapter, after losing the Kiritsubo consort (Genji's mother), the emperor finds consolation in Fujitsubo, a lady of similar countenance. Genji, longing for his deceased mother, is likewise drawn to his father's new consort. Frustrated by Fujitsubo's stiff resistance and the barriers that separate them, he eventually finds a substitute and a wife in the young Murasaki, who is Fujitsubo's niece and almost identical in appearance. In each case, the loss of a woman leads the man to find a surrogate who is similar in appearance, or closely related, or both. The notion of the surrogate lover enabled Murasaki Shikibu not only to explore one of the great themes of the *Genji*—the pseudoincestuous nature of male/female relationships—but to move smoothly from one new sequence to the next.

An equally significant form of linkage exists between characters who are *not* associated by blood or appearance but who bear common social, spiritual, and emotional burdens. Perhaps the most revealing of these analogous relationships involves Asagao, Princess Ochiba, and Oigimi, three royal daughters who appear in three different parts of the *Genji*. Owing to an unfortunate turn in family circumstances, all three women have been placed in difficult positions. But despite the obvious rewards of marriage, each one rejects the advances and generous aid of a highborn, attractive noble: Genji, Yūgiri, and Kaoru, respectively. None of these women is directly related to the other. Nevertheless, each successive sequence explores, with increasing intensity, the problem of honor, pride, and shame in regard to the spiritual independence of a highborn but disadvantaged lady.

The *Genji* can also be thought of as a kind of *bildungsroman*, in which the author reveals the development of the protagonist's spirit and character through time and experience. In the *Genji* this growth occurs not only in the life of a single hero or heroine but over different generations and sequences, with two or more successive characters. Genji, for example, gradually attains an awareness of death, mutability, and the illusory nature of the world through repeated suffering. By contrast, Kaoru, his putative son, begins his life, or rather his narrative, with a profound grasp and acceptance of these darker aspects of existence.

The same is true of the mature Murasaki, the heroine of the first half, and Oigimi (in Waley, Agemaki), the primary figure of the last part. By the beginning of the middle chapters, Murasaki has long assumed that she can monopolize Genji's affections and act as his principal wife. Genji's unexpected marriage to the high-ranking Third Princess (in Waley, Nyosan), however, crushes these assumptions, causing Murasaki to fall mortally ill. Though Oigimi never suffers the way Murasaki does, she quickly comes to a similar awareness of the inconstancy of men, love, and marriage, and she rejects Kaoru even though he appears to be the perfect companion. Building on the earlier chapters, Murasaki Shikibu makes a significant leap, moving from a narrative about the tribulations of love and marriage to one that explores a world without men.

The form of the *Genji* is closely bound to its aesthetics. Beauty in the West has often been associated with the eternal, the sublime, with the uplifting, and in form it has been often tied to unity and balance. In Heian literature, however, beauty is found in the fleeting, in the uncertain, in the fragmentary, and in the inherently sorrowful aspects of the world. The cherry blossoms—the quintessential image of Japanese aesthetics even today—were loved by Heian poets not only because the delicate, multipetaled flowers reminded them of the glories of this world but because the same blossoms, in a matter of days, turned color, faded, and scattered in the wind like snowflakes, a sorrowful reminder not only of the brevity of life and fortune but of the uncertainty and fickleness of the human heart. In the *Genji* the essence of nature and human life tends to be grasped in terms of their end, in their dying moments rather than in their birth or creation. The dominant season of the *Genji* is autumn, when nature, in all its melancholy hues, seems to wither and fade away.

In one of the opening chapters of the *Genji*, the young hero discovers in a rundown residence on the outskirts of town a fragile young woman named Yūgao, or Evening Glory. Unable to resist her beauty and charm, he whisks her off to a deserted mansion where they spend the night together. Suddenly, in the darkness, she is seized by an evil spirit (presumably that of the Rokujō lady) and expires in the hero's arms. The hero comes, as he does elsewhere, to an understanding of his love not in its fulfillment but in its all-too-sudden and incomprehensible loss. Indicative of the symbolism that permeates the *Genji* is the woman's name, Yūgao, a gourdlike plant (suggesting her lowly origins) whose beautiful white flowers, at the height of summer, bloom in the dusk and fade before the sunrise.

Perhaps the most important critical concept in Japanese poetry from the classical period onward is the notion of *yojō* or *yosei*, which has two broad meanings. On the one hand, *yojō* refers to poetry or art as an expression or product of excessive, irrepressible emotions. When we compare Genji to the heroes of the Western classics, to Achilles and Odysseus, a strikingly different set of human values emerges. Genji does not triumph through strength and courage, by cunning and intelligence, by resisting temptation, or through acts of benevolence and insight. In fact, he fails in almost every one of these categories. Instead, heroism lies in his capacity not only to be deeply moved and rendered vulnerable but to express that inner weakness and deep emotion through aesthetic means, through poetry, painting, music, and other aesthetic forms.

Yojō also means overtones, what is beyond the referential meaning of words, what is implied rather than stated. Visually, *yojō* implies that the shadows—for example, the dusk and early dawn—have more allure and depth than light or darkness. Musically, *yojō* suggests that the faint echoes, the reverberations that linger in the ear, are often more moving than the melodic notes themselves. *Yojō* also implies that the fragrance, wafting on a gentle breeze, is often more memorable than the flower itself. Such is Kaoru, the Fragrant One, whose bodily scent reaches into the houses of unsuspecting women. The name borne by Oborozukiyo, the daughter of the Minister of the Right, with whom Genji is caught sleeping in the early chapters, literally means "The Evening of the Misty Moon." As in Japanese poetry, the softly enshrouded moon is more erotic and seductive than a brightly shining crescent.

Yojō also refers to the intertextual fabric of poetry. *The Tale of Genji* is not only an exquisite weave of poetry and prose but is interwoven with elaborate allusions to Chinese poetry and literature, to Buddhist scriptures, and to *waka*. Many of the places in the *Genji*—Suma, where Genji is exiled, or Uji, where Kaoru discovers two beautiful sisters—are *utamakura*, famous place-names in Japanese poetry, with rich clusters of associations that are woven into the drama. *The Tale of Genji* unfolds over seventy-five years, three generations, four imperial reigns, and presents over five hundred characters, yet it gravitates toward intensely emotional and meditative scenes in which the language, rhetoric, and themes of poetry are foregrounded and in which the primary reference is not to an "external" world so much as to other literary and poetic texts. (It is thus no accident that the *Genji* was first regarded as a classic of poetry.)

The notion of *yojō*, or overtones, also extends to the structure of the *Genji*, in which the aftermath, the lingering echoes, and the memories are often more central to the narrative than the event of action itself. The opening chapter, for example, describes the tragic love affair between the emperor and Genji's mother. The greater part of the chapter, however, is an extended meditation on the death of the lover, climaxed by poetry and allusions to Yang Kueifei and "The Song of Sorrow" by Bo Juyi, Japan's favorite Chinese poet. In the manner of lyrical narratives, the tone is elegant, poetic, and uplifting, even though the subject matter is tragic. These scenes belong to a familiar topos, the lament (*aishō*), which can be traced back to the elegies by Kakinomoto no Hitomaro (d. 709) and other *Manyōshū* (c. 771) poets. The meditations on personal loss—due to either death, separation, or abandonment—also derive from the women's tradition. If the earlier *monogatari* written by men revolved around action and plot, the literary diaries by women, often written in memoir or autobiographical form, ruminate on the consequences and significance of the past.

Western literary criticism, from the time of Aristotle onward, has stressed formal unity and balance, particularly beginnings, middles, and ends. But in *The Tale of Genji*, as in much of Japanese literature, the fragment or the part is often more aesthetically important than the whole. Literature is more akin to a trailing cloud, to use a recurrent image from the *Genji*, than a figure carved in stone. It is revealing that we do not know if the *Genji* is in fact finished. The last chapter, "The Floating Bridge of Dreams," suggests both an end and a new beginning, and it is no more closed than a number of other earlier chapters. The ending, or a lack of it, has disturbed some Western scholars, but Japanese critics have never made it an issue, for the notion of an open, unbound text is a given, just as is the poetics of overtones, fragmentation, and uncertainty.

Note

There are two English translations, complete or nearly so. Arthur Waley's appeared in installments more than half a century ago and is available in Modern

Library. Edward Seidensticker's was published by Alfred Knopf in 1976. A selection from the latter translation, about a fifth of the whole, was published by Vintage in 1985. Earlier essays on the *Tale of Genji* by Donald Keene and Edward Seidensticker may be found in *Approaches to Oriental Classics* (1958), 186–195; and *The Great Ideas Today* (Chicago: Encyclopedia Britannica, 1987), 286–291.

Passion and Poignancy in *The Tale of Genji*

Wm. Theodore de Bary

O PENING LINES ARE usually significant clues to almost any classic
work, and this is no less true of the *Genji*. Lady Murasaki's first words
are uncertain but nevertheless indicative: "In whatever reign it might have
been" (*izure no on toki ni ka*). Beginning on such an indefinite, questioning
note (*ka*), the *Tale* could be about almost any time or place. Then, after this
indefinite start comes an anonymous reference to a low-ranking court lady
whose favor by the emperor exposes her to the jealousy of higher-ranking
court women; in other words, instead of being introduced to a typical heroine whose noble character commands our attention if not respect, we meet
a lady who simply attracts our natural sympathies. There is some necessary
specificity of narrative detail, but rather than fixing our attention on that
particular scene or social context, the story appeals primarily to ordinary
human sentiments. In this case, the grand Imperial Court of Lady Murasaki's time simply serves as a stage for eliciting universal human feelings that
provide the essential themes of the novel.

In this opening passage, the narrator shows interest in a character of
somewhat marginal status. The context is courtly, aristocratic, hierarchical, and imperial (out of which contextual details professional critics or historians can make whatever they wish), but the author herself, and I think
most ordinary readers, recognize the essential poignancy of the human
situation being described—the conjunction of love, loss, and suffering.

My own teacher Ryūsaku Tsunoda once defined the Japanese sense of beauty in a rather offhand remark as "love touched by death." By this I think he meant "loss" in general and not just physical death. I don't think he had the *Genji* specifically in mind, but it certainly fits. Love and loss proves to be a major theme of the *Genji*. True, it is about much else as well, but given the very amplitude of the story and its diversity of incidents, we must necessarily focus here on what is most revealing of our chosen theme.

For me, one of the most telling passages is an early episode in which Genji, at an idle moment, is casually conversing with close friends about the women they have known who have most attracted them. These include a variety of types. Physical beauty is of course an obvious subject of conversation, but the discussion ranges over other aspects of human affectivity that join the psychological to the physical and less often the sentimental and sensual to the practical.

In a way typical of the Japanese proclivity for indirection, the conversation that sets the tone for the whole of *The Tale of Genji* takes place as if by happenstance: on a rainy night when nothing much is going on, Genji's good friend Tō no Chūjō catches him sorting through some old letters and suspects that he might find in them some intriguing secrets of Genji's most intimate life. It ends up in an exchange of views, among them and other companions, concerning different women they have known, each of whom has some attractive features but each of whom also has some offsetting and off-putting defect.

The terms in which the discussion is couched are those given by the aristocratic court culture: categories of social class, to each of which attaches the presumption that it represents a certain standard of high-class taste or virtue. Initially at least, the question is assumed to be whether the individuals being described are truly "classy" or not, but the judgment is usually that they fall short somehow—whether by society's standards or by more fundamental human ones.

Traditionally, this episode has been spoken of in Japanese as *shina no sadame*, wherein *shina* can be understood as "quality," "qualities," or "goods" and *sadame* as "judging," "determining," or "rating." Although described here as a very casual, if not desultory, process, the scene is one that reflects the strong Japanese penchant for erecting hierarchies of qualitative judgment or standards of quality, and although the manner is loose and low key, one should not be surprised to learn, as the *Tale* unfolds, that this "idle talk" in fact anticipates much that is to follow.

Tō no Chūjō prefigures this when he leads off with the observation: "I have at last discerned that there exists no woman of whom one can say 'This is perfection,' 'This is indeed she.'" The rest of this long rambling *Tale* relates how Genji's own search for perfection brings similar results, but with a much deeper awareness of the ambiguities in these relationships.

Intimations of this appear early on in Genji's comments on a judgment offered by Tō no Chūjō, who says: "I divide women into three classes. Those of high rank and birth are made such a fuss of and their weak points are so completely concealed that we are certain to be told that they are paragons. About those of the middle class everyone is allowed to express his own opinion, and we shall have much conflicting evidence to sift. As for the lower classes, they do not concern us."[1]

The completeness with which Tō no Chujō disposes of the question amuses Genji, who says, "it will not always be so easy to know into which of the three classes a woman ought to be put. For sometimes people of high rank sink to the most abject positions; while others of common birth rise to be high officers, wear self-important faces, redecorate the inside of their houses and think themselves as good as anyone. How are we to deal with such cases?" (23).

The range of possible outcomes is further projected in a comment by Uma no Kami: "However high a lady may rise, if she does not come of adequate stock, the world will think very differently of her from what it would of one born to such honors; but if through adverse fortune a lady of the highest rank finds herself in friendless misery, the noble breeding of her mind is soon forgotten and she becomes an object of contempt" (23).

Tō no Chūjō goes on:

> No doubt the perfect woman in whom none of those essentials is lacking must somewhere exist and it would not startle me to find her. But she would certainly be beyond the reach of a humble person like myself, and for that reason I should like to put her in a category of her own and not count her in our present classification. But suppose that behind some gateway overgrown with vine-weed, in a place where no one knows there is a house at all, there should be locked away some creature of unimagined beauty—with what excitement should we discover her! The complete surprise of it, the upsetting of all our wise theories and classifications, would be likely, I think, to lay a strange and sudden enchantment upon us.   (23)

Here adverse circumstances may confound one's normal expectations, and we become aware that subjective factors enter into the "objective" picture to complicate and compound the judgment.

"The conversation went on. Many persons and things were discussed." Uma no Kami contends that perfection is equally difficult in other spheres:

> But when the mistress is to be selected, a single individual must be found who will combine in her person many diverse qualities. It will not do to be too exacting. Let us be sure that the lady of our choice possesses certain tangible qualities which we admire, and if in other ways she falls short of our ideal, we must be patient and call to mind the qualities which first induced us to begin our courting.   (23)

If these other perspectives thus complicate the "objective" picture, this final remark suggests that the most fundamental difficulty still lies in the realm of subjectivity: the emotional complications that beset every loving relationship. Among these, jealousy is a prime factor. The games that lovers play with each other and the strategies they adopt all affect how one perceives or looks for a "perfect solution," which always remains elusive. The problem is already aired in this early conversation, but it is perhaps most vividly acted out later in the case of the young Evening Glory (Yūgao). A beauty hidden in the poorest, most unpromising circumstances, she is rescued from her shabby surroundings by Genji and installed in a more pleasant pavilion only to be struck dead by the vengeful spirit of another of Genji's lovers, Lady Rokujō, whose humiliation and embitterment, as ghostly disembodied karma (or unappeased obsession), works its own violence on Evening Glory and puts an end to this unlikely affair.

Jealousy and personal insecurity assume great prominence in *Genji*, equal almost to the intensity of love itself, because the court aristocracy is polygamous and a double standard for men and women contaminates things. The "perfect wife" is expected to suppress her own monogamous feelings and act with tolerance and forbearance toward her husband's promiscuous impulses. As Tō no Chūjō puts it: "when all is said and done there can be no greater virtue in a woman than this: that she should, with gentleness and forbearance, meet any wrong whatever that falls to her share." So obvious and unexceptional was this idea to the young gentlemen present that Genji himself dozes off in the midst of it and, as the narrator observes, takes no exception to what Tō no Chūjō is saying.

Genji, however, might well have been more alert had he not already resigned himself to the idea that perfect love was impossible to find. At the end of this long evening, the story concludes:

> All this while Genji, though he had sometimes joined in the conversation, had in his heart of hearts been thinking of one person only [his first wife, Princess Aoi] and the more he thought the less could he find a single trace of those shortcomings and excesses which, as his friends had declared, were common to all women. "There is no one like her," he thought, and his heart was very full. The conversation indeed had not brought them to a definite conclusion, but it had led to many curious anecdotes and reflections.
>
> So they passed the night, and at last, for a wonder, the weather had improved. After this long residence at the palace Genji knew he would be expected at the Great Hall and set out at once. There was in Princess Aoi's air and dress a dignified precision which had something in it even of stiffness; and in the very act of reflecting that she, above all women, was the type of that single-hearted and devoted wife whom (as his friends had said last night) no sensible man would lightly offend, he found himself oppressed by the very perfection of her beauty, which seemed only to make all intimacy with her the more impossible.   (27)

In other words, there was nothing wrong with his own No. 1 wife, Princess Aoi herself. It was rather her perfection that made her unapproachable and drove his restless heart to look elsewhere.

If we leap past the intervening incidents in Genji's subsequent affairs, much later in the *Tale* we find him taking stock of his amatory adventures in a way that he mistakenly thinks will be reassuring to Murasaki, his young protégé and later wife, who is now ailing. He reviews his affairs with other women, as if by citing their flaws he is thereby comparing them unfavorably to her. Little does he think of them as infidelities; they were simply diversions for him and imply no lack of appreciation for her. This is how he puts it to her:

> What a strange life mine has been! I suppose few careers have ever appeared outwardly more brilliant; but I have never been happy. Per-

son after person that I cared for has in one way or another been taken from me. It is long since I lost all the zest for life, and if I have been condemned to continue my existence, it is (I sometimes think) only as a punishment for certain misdeeds that at all times still lie heavily on my mind. You alone have always been here to console me and I am glad to think that, apart from the time when I was away at Akashi, I have never behaved in such a way as to cause you a moment's real unhappiness. . . . However, you are very observant, and I cannot believe you are not perfectly well aware.   (651)

To this Murasaki replies, as the ideal long-suffering wife should, by bearing with her husband: "I know that to any outside person I must appear to be the happiest of women, fortunate indeed far beyond all my deserts." Then she adds a few words that reveal her true feelings: "But inwardly I am wretched . . . every day" (651).

Try as she might, there is no way Murasaki can hold back her true feelings. All she can do is break down in uncontrollable sobbing. Genji tries to console her, but he has no idea what he has let loose within her heart. Her hero, her ideal, who should be the soul of sensitivity and sensibility, is indeed upset but still uncomprehending. He tries to divert and distract her by talking about other women he has known who did not measure up to her, as if these back-handed compliments would take the sting out of his philanderings. Instead it only makes things worse. He recalls Lady Rokujō: "Despite all that happened, I always think of her as the most brilliant creature that was at court. Never have I encountered a sensibility so vivid and profound and this, as you can imagine, made her a most fascinating companion. But there can never have been anyone with whom it was more impossible to have relations of a permanent kind." Eventually Murasaki does regain control of herself and carries on in a dutiful way. The author, however, has let us know what is really going on.

Most of this exchange is described in the language of daily life experience rather than in overtly philosophic or religious terms. Yet it should not be difficult to see in all this the underlying tensions that had arisen in Japanese culture owing to the continuing interaction between native traditions and the influx of Buddhism and Confucianism, especially Buddhism in both its original formulations and its Mahāyāna adaptations. If this early idle chat among Genji and his companions focuses on the nature of desire and the possibilities for its satisfaction, the Four Noble Truths and Noble

Eightfold Path of Buddhism, with their radical questioning of desire and pessimistic view of the possibilities for its satisfaction, must have been in the back of their minds, as well, of course, as in the narrator's. Nor can the portrayal of intense passions encountered in the *Genji* have been oblivious to the turn taken by Mahāyāna Buddhism as it reckons with the qualified reality of the sensual world and concedes after all that the passions too can be a means to enlightenment. The concession to such feelings would also serve prospectively as an adaptation to the received Japanese tradition by Lady Murasaki's time.

For a classic example of the latter, we might turn to the *Manyoshū*, an imperially sponsored collection of native Japanese poetry, as much a classic for the Japanese as the Confucian *Book of Odes* was to the Chinese. As an example of how closely akin the *Genji* is in feeling to the *Manyoshū*, we may take a poem composed by an earlier court lady, Princess Nukada, in answer to a question posed by Emperor Tenji to his prime minister Fujiwara Kamatari, who had played a major role in the great Taika reform that attempted to convert the Japanese system to the up-to-date model of a unified Chinese bureaucratic state. Although the issue has nothing to do with government policy, it is in sharp contrast to some critics who read the *Manyoshū*, with its imperial sponsorship, as having a strong ideological (that is, political) subtext. In the *Manyoshū*, the poem is introduced as follows:

> When the Emperor Tenji commanded Fujiwara Kamatari, Prime minister, to judge between the luxuriance of the blossoms on the spring hills and the glory of the tinted leaves on the autumn hills, Princess Nukada decided the question with this poem.

> When, loosened from the winter's bonds,
> The spring appears,
> The birds that were silent
> Come out and sing,
> The flowers that were prisoned
> Come out and bloom;
> But the hills are so rank with trees
> We cannot see the flowers,
> And the flowers are so tangled with weeds
> We cannot take them in our hands.
> But when on the autumn hill-side

We see the foliage,
We prize the yellow leaves,
Taking them in our hands,
We sigh over the green ones,
Leaving them on the branches;
And that is my only regret—
For me, the autumn hills.[2]

If there is political significance to this, it lies in the Japanese court being "the high court" in which such "delicate" aesthetic matters would be judged. The prestige of the court is much involved in its standing as the arbiter of high culture.

As for the poem itself, it fits the pattern of the *Manyoshū*: a strong attention to the natural world, the passing of the seasons and attendant emotions, and the pervasive nostalgia for past moments of intense longing—in short, the aesthetic response to life. Later writers and critics have identified this same feeling in the *Genji* as *mono no aware*,[3] variously translated as "the sadness or pathos of things" but here rendered as the "poignancy of things," because it is concerned with the recollection of a momentary experience of intense beauty and deep feeling. Thus it encapsulates a spiritual experience that responds on one level to the Buddhist sense of impermanence and ephemerality and on another to the distinctive involvement with nature characteristic of Shinto as well as with the passionate response to life that becomes a hallmark of both the Japanese aesthetic and Japanese religion.

In the *Genji* itself, this aesthetic feeling appears against the background of a more traditional Buddhist conception of the religious life as "leaving the world" or "leaving home," that is, breaking one's attachments by the formal act of withdrawal to monastic seclusion. This possibility occurs to many of the principals in the story, including Genji and Murasaki. Generally, however, traditional monastic discipline is not considered a viable option. Although Murasaki thinks of the religious life as a possible surcease for her sufferings, she will not do this without Genji's permission, and he is unready to face life without her. That she obeys him, despite all the pain he has caused her, tells us that she is still bound by her primary attachment to him as a dutiful wife.

When Genji (and others like him) contemplate a monastic retreat, they doubt that they can succeed in breaking off their attachments to the world.

This is not only because they are emotionally dependent on others (as in Genji's case) but because, as Genji sometimes puts it, in his own way he still feels a genuine concern for those he would be abandoning. Even in monastic seclusion, he would be worrying about them (and, indeed, from a human point of view that would not be seen as such a bad thing).

There are enough such cases in the *Tale* that we have reason to believe that the author takes the same view of formal religion as no real solution to the problem of desire. Part of the problem for Murasaki, however, is that human feelings, no matter how painful they may sometimes be, have a value that goes beyond any of the desires spoken of in the Four Noble Truths of early Buddhism. Just as in the Mahāyāna, the passions themselves can be made conducive to enlightenment; in the Japanese case, they can attain the level of a religious experience in themselves.

At this point, we would do well to consider how Murasaki deals with the matter when she has Genji speak for herself about the liberating function of literature. In another one of those casual encounters that prove to be so revealing, Genji happens to catch one of the court ladies in the midst of reading a novel, and at first he is inclined to dismiss fiction as frivolous literature. Later he qualifies this judgment and ends up taking it very seriously: "There is, it seems, an art of so fitting each part of the narrative into the next that, though all is mere invention, the reader is persuaded that such things might easily have happened and is as deeply moved as though they were actually going on around him."

He continues:

> "So you see as a matter of fact I think far better of this art than I have led you to suppose. Even its practical value is immense. Without it what should we know of how people lived in the past, from the Age of Gods down to the present day? For history-books such as the *Chronicles of Japan* show us only one small corner of life; whereas these diaries and romances which I see piled around you contain, I am sure, the most minute information about all sorts of people's private affairs. . . . " He smiled, and went on, "But I have a theory of my own about what this art of the novel is, and how it came into being. To begin with, it does not simply consist in the author's telling a story about the adventures of some other person. On the contrary, it happens because the storyteller's own experience of men and things, whether for

good or ill—not only what he has passed through himself, but even events which he has only witnessed or been told of—has moved him to an emotion so passionate that he can no longer keep it shut up in his heart. Again and again something in his own life or in that around him will seem to the writer so important that he cannot bear to let it pass into oblivion. There must never come a time, he feels, when men do not know about it. That is my view of how this art arose."

(500–501)

There are several points in these observations that may help us come to some conclusion about the *Genji*. First of all, in his discussion of the novel Genji is no doubt made to speak for the present author to express self-consciously what she thinks she is doing as she writes. Second is the idea that fiction, though an invention, best tells us about ordinary life; reading it one is "deeply moved" as though these "inventions" were actually going on around one.

It is not so much that the novel may actually preserve the facts of life and history, as *Genji* concedes, and thus serve as a veritable record of a certain time and place; more important is that the author, instead of simply telling "a story about the adventures of some *other person*," writes "because the story-teller's own experience of people and things, whether for good or ill was moving him [or her, in this case] to an emotion so passionate that he can no longer keep it bound up in his heart. Again and again something in his own life or in that around him will seem to the writer so important that he cannot bear to let it pass into oblivion" (501).

"Oblivion" might satisfy the need for a kind of detachment if one could actually put love, loss, and grief out of one's mind. But Murasaki, as Genji's creature in the novel (that is, adopted and brought up in court by him) was not free; she was only at a loss for words, sobbing uncontrollably in her grief. As the author, however, Murasaki could give voice to that grief in literature that is timeless. True liberation for her means cherishing the deepest of one's feelings as being profoundly meaningful in themselves and, by putting them into words, preserving them for, and sharing them with, all posterity.

At this point, one can relive, and perhaps even create, a reality that defies the vicissitudes of time. Impermanence and "emptiness" are overcome in a moment, and that is what gives such poignancy to the experience, which now breathes and feels with an intense reality of its own. Time stands still at that moment. "Love is touched by death," or better, "death is outdone by love," with deep pain or passion now recollected as poignantly beautiful.

Notes

1. Murasaki Shikibu, *The Tale of Genji*, trans. Arthur Waley (New York: Modern Library, 1935), 23; *The Tale of Genji*, trans. Royall Tyler (New York: Viking, 2001), 22–23. References to these editions will hereafter be cited in the text.
2. *Nippon Gaku Jutsu Shinkō Kai* (Chicago: University of Chicago Press, 1994).
3. Wm. Theodore de Bary, *Sources of Japanese Tradition*, 2nd ed. (New York: Columbia University Press, 2001), 1:244, 1:398, 1:418–419.

17

THE PILLOW BOOK

Wm. Theodore de Bary

I T I S N O T A B L E that two of the undoubted classics of the Japanese
cultural tradition have been written by women: Murasaki Shikibu's *Tale of
Genji* (*Genji Monogatari*) and Sei Shōnagon's *Pillow Book* (*Makura no sōshi*).
It is also striking that they appeared at almost the same early moment in
history, the products of the same age, the same aristocratic society, and a
culture that drew on similar religious traditions, both indigenous and imported. No less striking, however, is the marked difference between what
became equally classic models; the one, *The Tale of Genji*, a narrative spread
over a vast canvas of time and range of human experience, taking its time
to probe deeply into the depth of human feelings, and the other, the *Pillow
Book*, no story at all but timeless in its momentary reflections on much the
same life, restlessly pursuing its insatiable appetite for new aesthetic perceptions. The difference between the two, so apparent in their style of writing, was already intimated in Murasaki's unadmiring comments on Sei
Shōnagon as a person:

> Sei Shōnagon has the most extraordinary air of self-satisfaction, yet
> if we stop to examine these Chinese writings of hers that she so pre-
> sumptuously scatters all over the place, we find that they are full of
> imperfections. Someone who makes such an effort to be different
> from others is bound to fall in people's esteem, and I can only think
> that her future will be a hard one. She is a gifted woman, to be sure,

yet if one gives free reign to one's emotions, even in the most inappropriate circumstances; if one has to sample each interesting thing that comes along, people are bound to regard one as frivolous. And how can things turn out well for such a woman?[1]

Readers of the *Pillow Book* will see enough therein of Sei Shōnagon's cockiness and her supreme confidence in her own judgments, often unallayed by compassionate sentiments, to recognize much of what Murasaki reports of her. What may be less evident is the acute irony involved in Murasaki's own boldness in passing judgment on Shōnagon—on the latter's own home ground no less—in chiding her for her incompetence in "Chinese writings," given that Sei's own family, the Kiyowaras, had long been recognized as hereditary custodians and supreme authorities in all matters Chinese.

Against Murasaki's contrarian judgment, it will seem even more ironic and unexpected that the *Pillow Book* itself should belie the fate predicted for its author by Murasaki when she says: "Things could not turn out well for such a woman." Instead, things turned out extremely well for the *Pillow Book*, and that it could survive circumstances initially quite adverse to its perpetuation tells us something of its intrinsic strengths. As a collection of random notes that did not conform to any established category of literature, the inherent appeal of its contents enabled it eventually to become a model for the informal writings known in Japan as *zuihitsu*. The *Pillow Book* appeared long before printing became available, and thus it would not have survived had it not exerted enough appeal for many individuals to have found it worth the effort to copy out by hand.

What made it worth that effort—and still makes it attractive to us as readers? The *Pillow Book* lacks many of the recognized features of the traditional classic, especially unity of time and place, plot, and sustained narrative. Yet this is, at the same time, what renders it both traditional and classic: the strong sense of place, of local color, of particularity and endless variety, to which Shōnagon responds with her own acute sensibility. It may irritate and even offend so deep a sensitivity as Murasaki's, but it is precisely the insistent self-revelation of Shōnagon herself that is endlessly attractive and impressive. Considering the formidable handicaps and disabilities that she and Murasaki both suffered in the male-dominated class system of Heian Japan, in her own way, simply by asserting herself, Shōnagon triumphed over them.

As Murasaki testifies, Shōnagon "gave free rein" to her own feelings and held nothing back, unconstrained by the polite conventions of her time or even by her conscious inhibitions. Sometimes this may seem a kind of hypocrisy on her part, as when she catches herself giving vent to feelings in conflict with the social and cultural norms of her day, which she is at one and the same time conscious of yet not bound by in her writings. This should not be taken to mean that Sei Shōnagon is engaged in social protest—that she is an early but premature advocate of women's liberation from an oppressive social system. Shōnagon is engaged in self-liberation, not social or class protest, and this is probably why she has not been claimed as a feminist by later scholars of women's resistance to the political and social discrimination so pervasive in their society.

Ivan Morris has explained Shōnagon's situation and cultural environment as one dominated by good taste, and one can understand her success as taking advantage of the predominant aesthetic culture to break through her social limitations. He writes:

Not only did the rule of taste extend to every sphere of life and apply to the smallest details, but (with the single exception of good birth) it took primacy over all else. Artistic sensitivity was more highly valued than ethical goodness. Despite the influence of Buddhism, Heian society was on the whole governed by style rather than by any moral principles, and good looks tended to take the place of virtue. The word "yoki" referred primarily to birth, but it also applied to one's beauty or aesthetic sensibility; the one implication that it lacked was one of ethical rectitude. For all their talk about "heart" and "feeling," this stress on the cult of the beautiful, to the virtual exclusion of any concern for charity, sometimes lends a rather chilling impression to the people of Genji's world.[2]

Here the world that Morris writes about is no less Shōnagon's than Murasaki's, but we also know that what Murasaki saw of Shōnagon left a "chilling impression" on her. Murasaki's own depth of feeling led her to perceive a certain sharpness in her opposite number. Thus despite the accuracy of what Morris says about their shared world and about Heian society in general, it may not be quite the whole truth of the matter when we see how these two react so differently to it.

Part of what needs to be considered here is the role of religion, particularly Buddhism. Morris says, this time about Shōnagon herself:

> Contemporary literature suggests that for many Heian aristocrats religion had become mere mummery. The temples had become crowded with visitors, but the motives that brought them there often had little connection with the Buddhist faith. This is a subject that lends itself to satire, and . . . no one has treated it more pungently than Sei Shōnagon, whose mordant wit was, as far as we can judge, uninhibited by any religious feelings.[3]

Morris goes on to quote a memorable passage from the *Pillow Book* in which Shōnagon says: "A preacher ought to be good looking. For if we are properly to understand the most worthy sentiments of his sermon, we must keep our eyes fixed on him while he speaks; by looking away we may forget to listen. Accordingly an ugly preacher may well be a source of sin."[4]

The thing to note here is Shōnagon's frankness in admitting the actual conflict that she experiences at that moment. Her observation is psychological and confessional; she does not express any real doubt about the "worthy sentiments" she is sure the preacher has to offer but only how she may be distracted from them. It may be true, as Morris says, that Shōnagon's "wit is . . . uninhibited by any deep religious feelings," but the apparent conflict is actually obviated by the religion itself.

To understand this, we have to go back to the sources of Heian religiosity itself, and for this a well-known quotation from Kūkai (774–835) may serve our purpose. Kūkai was the leading exponent of Esoteric Buddhism in the form of the True Words (Shingon) Sect, which probably gave Heian culture its most distinctive cast as well as its inherent ambiguity. "Esoteric" signifies that it was a mystery religion, and "True Words" means that despite its inherent mystery—that it is not definable in words—words of a kind still can convey some suggestive meaning. Words may be problematic, but they still can perform some kind of magical communication.

Here the teachings of Mahāyāna Buddhism through its doctrine of expedient or convenient means (*hōben*) convert its sense of compassion into some tangible form. Thus, it could adapt itself to the traditional tastes of the Japanese.

The law [*dharma*] has no speech, but without speech it cannot be expressed. Eternal truth [*tathatā*] transcends color, but only by means of color can it be understood. Mistakes will be made in the effort to point at the truth, for there is no clearly defined method of teaching, but even when art does not excite admiration by its unusual quality, it is a treasure which protects the country and benefits the people.

In truth, the Esoteric doctrines are so profound as to defy their enunciation in writing. With the help of painting, however, their obscurities can be understood. The various attitudes and mudras of the holy images all have their source in Buddha's love, and one may attain Buddhahood at sight of them. Thus the secrets of the sutras and commentaries can be depicted in art, and the essential truth of the Esoteric teaching are all set forth therein. Neither teachers nor students can dispense with it. Art is what reveals to us the state of perfection.[5]

By Sei Shōnagon's time, Heian society was deeply involved with Esoteric Buddhism, and many of her contemporaries, accepting that Beauty is Truth, could understand how she could easily be distracted by appearances while still trying to understand what the preacher was saying. Ideally, the two should go together, but often they did not. In that situation, it would not be quite true that Shōnagon was, as Morris put it, "uninhibited by any religious feelings." She is uninhibited in expressing herself but still conflicted by the essential ambiguity of her situation, even understood in Buddhist terms, as a problematical subordination of morality to art.

What remains true in Morris's characterization of the Heian view is that "not only did the rule of taste extend to every detail of life and apply to the smallest of details, but it took primacy over all else. Artistic sensitivity was more highly prized than ethical goodness." This might also apply to Shōnagon, but it does not mean that she was unreligious, and on the contrary there are many incidents related in the *Pillow Book* that suggest otherwise.

In the incidents to be cited here, it is essential to recognize how religious ritual, whether performed at temples, shrines, or in palaces, had an aesthetic importance inseparable from its other professed functions. A common early word for governance was *matsurigoto*, the literal meaning of which was "attending to sacred rituals," which is indicative of the ceremonial conduct of government and its exercise through customary religious forms more than through open political debate. Such governance might then be noted for its lack of emphasis on what is public in the sense of stated policy or standards of public morality. In modern times, we might take this as a lack of transparency in government, which would be true of the Heian insofar as most political maneuvering was conducted in private, behind closed doors. But in a culture that responded to elegance and beauty above all, the latter, not political debate, would be the most evident, transparent, and prestigious—"public"—values.

The first illustration that I shall give of this is Shōnagon's attendance at a ritual performed at the Kamo Shrine, which combined strong natural and local features (river and mountains) with its functions as tutelary to the imperial dynasty. Shōnagon recalls her attendance at the special festival held there for the Sacred Dance of the Return.

> I remember one such evening. As the smoke rose in slender wisps from the bonfires in the garden, I listened to the clear, delicate, charmingly tremulous sound of the flute that accompanied the sacred dances. The singing also moved me greatly. Delighted by the scene, I hardly noticed that the air was piercingly cold, that my robes of beaten silk were icy, and that the hand in which I held my fan was almost frozen.   (147)

It is clear that Shōnagon was caught up in a kind of transcendent experience that so lifted her out of her bodily self and senses that she was transported to a higher spiritual plane. One could regard this simply as "aesthetic," but its association with shrine rituals and the cult of the imperial house, which claimed divine origins and sanctions, suggests that some religious and political connotations are also implicit and fused in the experience.

A similar fusion of aesthetic and religious elements is found in Shōnagon's frequent mention of her experience of visits to Shinto shrines and Buddhist temples and of her attendance at palace rituals. Addicted as she was to such regular and repeated observances, she was on the lookout for impromptu happenings that could give fresh significance and charm to what otherwise tended to become familiar and dull routine. One such experience is reported on a visit to a famous pilgrimage site, Hase Temple, east of the old capital at Nara. She knows the rituals well, but she also appreciates it when something unexpected happens:

Once I went on a pilgrimage to Hase Temple. While our rooms were
being prepared, our carriage was pulled up to the foot of the long
steps that lead up to the temple. Young priests, wearing only their
sashes and under-robes, and with those things called high clogs on
their feet, were hurrying up and down the steps without the slightest
precaution, reciting verses from the Sacred Storehouse or such scraps
from the sutras as come into their heads. It was very appropriate to
the place and I found it charming.   (126)

What was "very appropriate to the place," that is, what fitted with her own
sense of place at the temple, was also reminiscent of similar experiences at
the Imperial Palace. She continues:

Presently a priest told us that our rooms were ready and asked us to go
to them directly; he brought us some overshoes and helped us out of
our carriage. Among the pilgrims who had already arrived I saw some
who were wearing clothes inside out, while others were dressed in
formal style with trains on their skirts and Chinese jackets. The sight
of so many people shuffling along the corridors in lacquered leather
shoes and short clogs was delightful and reminded me of the Palace.
                                                                    (126–127)

As Shōnagon continues her account of the temple visit, her sense of the
sublime is often tinged with irony (which I would not call "satire" or "ridicule," since it was not actually at the expense of the religious): "On the way
to our rooms we had to pass in front of rows of strangers. I found this very
unpleasant; but, when I reached the chapel and got a view past the dog-
barrier and right up to the sanctuary, I was overcome with awe and wondered how I could have stayed away for so many months. My old feelings
were aroused and they overwhelmed all else" (127).

What Shōnagon saw looking up the stairway to the icon at the top was
an image of the temple's main object of worship (*honzon*), more precisely the
Bodhisattva Kannon, commonly known as the "Goddess of Mercy." As the
most popular object of devotional worship and pilgrimage in Japan (not to
say East Asia), she attracted innumerable devotees of all classes and kinds,
which explains why Shōnagon found herself, the paragon of elite taste, in the
presence of crowds she would consider uncouth, unrefined, and unpleasant.
Still, if her sense of propriety and good taste dominated the social situation,

it did not have the last word, as her "old feelings" toward the compassionate Bodhisattva "overwhelmed" all else.

The account of her temple visit further testifies to her genuine religiosity, again, alongside other observations prompted by her keen sense of taste and proper form:

> Now the bell rang for the recitation of the sutras. It was very comforting to think that it rang for me. In the cell next to ours a solitary gentleman was prostrating himself in prayer. At first I thought that he might be doing it because he knew we were listening; but soon I realized that he was absorbed in his devotions, which he continued hour after hour. I was greatly moved. When he rested from his prayers, he started reading the sutras in a loud, fervent voice. I was wishing that he would read still more loudly so that I might hear every word; but instead he stopped and blew his nose—not in a noisy, unpleasant way but gently and discreetly. I wondered what he would be praying for so fervently and hoped that his wish might be granted.
>
> Sometimes the booming of the temple bell became louder and louder until I was overcome with curiosity about who had asked for the readings. Then someone would mention the name of a great family, adding, "It is a service of instruction and guidance for Her Ladyship's safe delivery." An anxious period indeed, I thought, and would begin praying for the lady's well-being.   (128)

In these cases, it is not a matter of Shōnagon's being completely absorbed in her own religious feelings. She shares them with others, as she joins herself to the compassion of Kannon.

> The service continued all night, and it was so noisy that I could not get to sleep. After the matins I finally dozed off, only to be woken by a reading of the sutra consecrated to the temple Buddha. The priests were reciting loudly and raucously, without making any effort to sound solemn. From their tone I gathered that they were traveling monks and, as I listened to their voices, which had awakened me so abruptly, I found myself being strangely moved.   (129)

These examples should suffice to show that Shōnagon was not simply a snob or a cool-headed, cold-hearted critic offering her snap judgments of others but was instead a highly cultivated woman deeply sensitive to others' feelings. What is most remarkable about her, and what renders the *Pillow Book* such a classic treasure, is the keenness of her observation and ability to capture the given moment in very precise words. Her manner of speaking is quite different from Murasaki's, but she has her own gift for making the moment memorable. As Murasaki redeemed her own sufferings by making them live forever in the *Genji*, Shōnagon had the same aspiration in the *Pillow Book*. She recalls a moment at court:

> After accompanying the Emperor, Korechika returned to his previous place on the veranda beside the cherry blossoms. The Empress pushed aside her curtain of state and came forward as far as the threshold. We were overwhelmed by the whole delightful scene. It was then that Korechika slowly intoned the words of the old poem,
>
> The days and the months flow by,
> But Mount Mimoro lasts forever.
>
> Deeply impressed, I wished that all this might indeed continue for a thousand years. (16)

Her wish has been fulfilled with the survival of the *Pillow Book* as a classic for well over a thousand years. For all this, however, modern scholarship has not always appreciated Murasaki's and Sei Shōnagon's exceptional contributions to Japan's cultural sensibilities. In at least one recent and prominent case, these authors go unmentioned because the current trend found them irrelevant to the demand for social literature as gender protest. In a project sponsored by the Tōhō Gakkai of Japan (a highly reputable academic organization promoting East Asian studies) for "Women in Japanese Buddhism," focusing on the ancient and medieval periods, there is no mention at all of these two remarkable women who spoke for Japanese sensibilities beyond all gender limitations.[6] We may be confident, however, that this momentary neglect or oversight will fade before the *Genji* and *Pillow Book* ever do.

Notes

1. Ivan Morris, *The Pillow Book of Sei Shōnagon* (New York: Columbia University Press, 1967), xii–xiv. Further references to this edition will be cited in the text.

2. Ivan Morris, *The World of the Shining Prince: Court Life in Ancient Japan* (New York: Knopf, 1964), 198.

3. Ibid, 106.

4. Ibid, 106–107.

5. Wm. Theodore de Bary, *Sources of Japanese Tradition*, 2nd ed. (New York: Columbia University Press, 2001), 1:155.

6. *Bulletin of the Institute of Eastern Culture*, ACTA Asiatica, no. 97 (Tokyo: Tōhō Gakkai, 2009).

18

KAMO NO CHŌMEI'S "AN ACCOUNT OF MY HUT"

Paul Anderer

K AMO NO CHŌMEI was born in 1153, and at the age of fifty, he tells us, he renounced the world and became a Buddhist monk. He was of a hereditary line of Shinto priests, and in better times may well have succeeded his father as a priest at the Kamo Shrine in Kyoto. But the late twelfth century was among the most strife-torn and transforming of all periods in Japan, and thus that was not to be.

In 1212, ten years after he took the tonsure and assumed a Buddhist name and after he adopted the life of a recluse in the mountains,[1] Chōmei wrote a brief essay. His "Account of My Hut" (*Hōjōki*) seems to have a simple, almost fragile literary structure, yet it has proved to be among the most resilient and enduring of all Japanese texts. Indeed, when we recall how frequently Japanese writing—whether a thirty-one syllable lyric or a Nō play or a narrative of over a thousand pages—coheres around the site of a hut, of a small sequestered dwelling, in the mountains or a strand of desolate beach, at a discrete remove from the pressures of politics and society, we begin to understand the range and importance of Chōmei's account. We might also adjust our sense of a literary "monument," of a "classic" work of canonical stature, to accommodate other understandings of how literary strength or spiritual value can be recognized or measured.

The "Account of My Hut" has been variously described, but to begin simply we can say that it is written in two parts. The first is an illustration of suffering in the world. Here the writing is reminiscent of the apocalyptic

Buddhist commentaries and parables popular at the time, and it finds a visual analogue in those medieval picture scrolls depicting a desiccated world haunted by hungry ghosts. The second part, though nostalgic and often brooding in tone, is also a celebratory record of how the author recovered, under specific conditions, at a particular place, what he calls "peace," or else minimally, "absence of grief." It is an account, finally, of a cultural survivor who has witnessed dramatic and ultimately far-reaching changes. No modern Tokyo writer, sipping coffee under a naked light bulb while recollecting the glow of fireflies, had greater material cause for nostalgia than did Chōmei.

Plainly, this short, diary-like rendering we know as "An Account of My Hut" offers no thorough historical record of occurrences in the second half of the twelfth century (which saw the advent of the medieval age and the rise to power of the provincial military or samurai class, accompanied by warfare and widespread disorder). But neither does Chōmei ignore completely the sights and the consequences of that history, as does much later medieval writing, where concrete reference to worldly distress seems but a lapse of concentration, so strong is the meditative urge. The "Account," to be sure, is the work of a cleric whose adopted faith teaches most fundamentally that the world is a place of suffering and that the things of the world are illusory, inconstant, impermanent. It is work, moreover, that, from beginning to end, means to be instructive (when Chōmei claims that he is writing to please himself, as though he had no audience, he is affecting a familiar stance taken, among others, by Sei Shōnagon when she wrote her *Pillow Book* ca. 996). Yet the didactic tone is modulated, where it does not break off altogether. The will to transmit abstract religious truth fades away, and in its place we find another impulse: to speak in a personal, lyrical way of suffering and a path toward tranquility. In this sense, the "Account" is no mere tract that heaps scorn on this "cracked husk of a world" but is rather a guide directing us to a remote mountain hut, where in solitude Chōmei reveals affection for all that the world has torn and scattered—for a whole culture uprooted, unhoused, and in need of shelter, however fragile or temporary.

For many, it seemed, religion itself was to provide that shelter. In fact, a number of popular Buddhist revival movements had emerged and were enthusiastically embraced in Chōmei's day. Their popularity sprang, no doubt, from the sheer scale of change, wherein people of every place in society were daily faced great uncertainty. This historical predicament was given heightened significance in the notion of *mappō*, or the "last days of the Law." According to Buddhist chronology, in this phase the world would lapse into degeneracy, laws and rites would be imperfectly observed, and merely ordinary suffering would yield to chaos. This age was to have begun fifteen hundred years after the Buddha's birth, and so by a numerical estimate in 1052, and was to continue for an indefinite period. This put Chōmei and his culture squarely within a sick, decadent cycle and gives a distinctly religious aura to that litany of disasters by which the "Account" begins.

And so the Fire that sweeps the capital, which was a historical fact and can be documented, assumes figural significance as an inevitable inferno brought on by the vanity of the city dwellers. The Whirlwind, given realistic detail as "roofs of bark or thatch [that] were driven like winter leaves in the wind," also reminds the author of "the blasts of Hell" and is of such uncommon force that "it must be a presage of terrible things to come." The Moving of the Capital, which too was a historical occurrence, seems a pure sign of instability and the unexpected, provoking both anxiety and a painful comparison between these days and a better past, when rulers were wise and forbearing and people presumably did not "all feel uncertain as drifting clouds." With the Famine there is the graphic scene of bodies decomposing along the banks of the Kamo River and of an infant, unaware that its mother is dead, still sucking at her breast, yet it also totalizes the author's vision, as he sees that the world is one of "foulness and evil." Finally, the Earthquake seems to signal the end, as "mountains crumbled and rivers were buried, the sea tilted over and immersed the land"; as for damage throughout the capital, "not a single mansion, pagoda, or shrine was left whole." Considered the most benign of the four elements, the earth itself had thus broken apart to afflict the people. With this, Chōmei concludes his litany of disaster and extraordinary suffering, drawing out the ultimate lesson: "the vanity and meaninglessness of the world."

As mentioned earlier, Chōmei's language in this section has parallels in other religious or secular writings of this general period. In the monk Genshin's *Essentials of Salvation*, for example, a widely known catechetical text, the Hell that awaits karmic evildoers is described as horrifyingly as is Chōmei's Kyoto-Hellfire. Just as the heavenly rewards awaiting those who attain salvation, in Genshin's portrayal, assume a certain this-worldly form, so too Chōmei compares them to the pleasures of his hut. Also, in the warrior tales, and notably in *The Tale of the Heike*, which grew from oral stories that had begun to circulate in Chōmei's day, we find episodes of fire, earthquake, and moving capitals, examples of unnatural disaster and disease, with the reiteration that clearly "the world was fixed on the path of chaos" or, again, that "for men of sensitive soul, the world now seemed a hopeless place." Also to be noticed about the *Heike*, whose theme is that of impermanence and the fall of the mighty and whose subject is the historical struggle between the Heike and the Genji clans, is that the reach toward a certain epical breadth is often interdicted by lyrical intensity ("the blood stained the sand like dark maple leaves"). Here, as in Chōmei's "Account," a way out, a path toward salvation, follows the path of the exile, haunted by the loss of past glory. Here, too, tranquility is recovered in the quiet of a mountain retreat, where the former empress, now a Buddhist nun, waits for death "on a velvety green carpet of moss."

When Chōmei concludes his opening section with a reflective passage on "Hardships of Life in the World" and when he tells us that in his fiftieth year he renounced the world and took Buddhist orders, we are at once given certain biographical facts as well as the sketch of a literary archetype. For even in better times, indeed, in some of the memorable writing of the lost Heian golden age, we regularly come across the figure of an emperor abdicating or a love-stricken courtier withdrawing to the outlying hills and the contemplative life, even though many such world-weary figures never finally make their vows or eventually return at intervals to the colorful complications of the city.

In that sense and just when he seems most "original," setting off on his own solitary path and leaving the vanities of culture and society behind, Chōmei moves modestly but with grim, focused determination along a literary path previously taken. Then he fashions a hut "where, perhaps, a traveler might spend a single night." It is this kind of path, this type of dwelling, that will carry and shelter Saigyō and later Bashō along their own protracted periods of exile and wandering. Here too we identify the traveling priest who, in some out-of-the-way but culturally resonant place in nature, will discover the heroes and heroines of many Nō plays. The hut that Chōmei builds is made of wood and thatch. But it assumes shape because of certain cultural materials that Chōmei knew and used and sought to rescue.

Like other influential medieval literati, Chōmei was a writer (an essayist, compiler of miracle stories, travel diarist, but primarily a poet) and a monk. Literature, and especially poetry, came thus to be practiced and preserved as a religion. And the poet's life, like the monk's life, was one of seclusion or exile. It was spare, unadorned, and, in any practical sense, marginal and precarious. Yet it did have formidable precedents. Genji himself was exiled to a forlorn dwelling on Suma Beach, a dark but crucial chapter in Murasaki's great narrative, one of its several illustrations of karma leading even the brightest of lives into darkness. And besides the figure of Genji in this scene is that of Bo Juyi, the most influential of all Chinese poets for classical writers in Japan, who himself built a hut on Mount Lu (just as beyond Bo Juyi emerges the figure of the Indian recluse-sage Vimalakīrti).

This is exile, then, but an enabling deprivation. Lacking color, variety, and action, its very *blandness* (a trait widely celebrated in Taoist and later Chan or Zen texts) generates other insights, other tastes. These Chōmei attempted to identify in his *Mumyōshō* (Notes Without a Name), one of the most famous of all medieval treatises on poetry and aesthetics. Chōmei himself had written poetry in a so-called new style notable for its "mystery and depth," or *yūgen*, an aesthetic category of crucial importance to medieval culture. But here, in the question-and-answer form typical of such discussion, Chōmei feigns ignorance and asks what "new style" poetry and its alleged "mystery and depth" might possibly mean. The answer, his own of course, but deferentially attributed to his master, the priest-poet Shunei, gives no definition but rather a series of metonymical illustrations:

on an autumn evening, for example, there is no color in the sky nor any sound, yet although we cannot give any reason for it, we are somehow moved to tears. . . .

again, when one gazes upon the autumn hills half-concealed by a curtain of mist, what one sees is veiled yet profoundly beautiful; such a shadowy scene, which permits free exercise of the imagination in picturing how lovely the whole panoply of scarlet leaves must be, is far better than to see them spread with dazzling clarity before our eyes. . . .

it is only when many meanings are compressed into a single word, when the depths of feeling are exhausted yet not expressed, when an unseen world hovers in the atmosphere of the poem, when the near and common are used to express the elegant, when a poetic conception of rare beauty is developed to the fullest extent in a style of surface simplicity—only then, when the conception is exalted to the highest degree and the words are too few, will the poem, by expressing one's feelings in this way, have the power of moving Heaven and Earth within the brief confines of a mere thirty-one syllables, and be capable of softening the hearts of gods and demons.   (269)

In the atmosphere of all that Chōmei writes, in the contours of his fragile hut and the misty views of autumn twilight it provides, what is it if not the old lost world of the Heian court that "yet hovers like an unseen world," waiting to be apprehended? Nature immediately and clearly surrounds Chōmei in the mountains, but it is the distant world of a fading culture that he consciously gathers about him:

On mornings when I feel short-lived as the white wake behind a boat, I go to the banks of the river and, gazing at the boats plying to and fro, compose verses in the style of the Priest Mansei. Or if of an evening the wind in the maples rustles the leaves, I recall the river at Jinyō, and play the lute in the manner of Minamoto no Tsunenobu. If still my mood does not desert me, I often tune my lute to the echoes in the pines, or pluck the notes of the Melody of the Flowering Stream, modulating the pitch to the sound of the water.

What Chōmei sees in nature are not "unmediated visions" generated by the force of the poet's free imagination. Setting out on an "ambitious journey," Chōmei passes through the fields of Awazu, there to "pay my respects to the remains of Semimaru's hut"; crossing the Tanagami River, he visits the tomb of still another Heian poet, Sarumaru. These are lyrical movements in prose, through sights and sounds recorded by other wanderers. Even "the hooting of owls," a startling sound suggestive of the stark isolation of the mountain, contributes to Chōmei's "endless pleasure," because Saigyō had also heard and sung of the owl's "eerie cries." Far beyond Chōmei's hut, in the city, the world rages and people fall victim to a dizzying flux. But inside the hut, where on a shelf rest his books of poetry and music and extracts from the sacred writings, and beside the shelf a folding koto and a lute, or in the nature that immediately surrounds his hut, Chōmei lives both in solitude and in the company of a tradition he willfully places in all he hears and sees.

Throughout the medieval period, it is the poet who most movingly illuminates this forlorn, tumble-down, autumnal scene. But it is in the prose-poetry of Chōmei's "Account" that within this scene, if dimly and in monochrome, emerges a human figure—a medieval portrait of the artist, though here an old man. The "Account" warns us of disaster and hardship in the world. And it reveals the path of renunciation, which leads into nature and the crude but comforting arrangement of a hut ten feet square. Still, it is

Chōmei himself, the aging poet-priest, who is the hidden, and so in the terms of medieval aesthetics, the truly valuable subject of this "Account."

Chōmei is "hidden" insofar as he does not stand forward in this work and present a whole life for our scrutiny and judgment, which seems to be the dramatic burden that St. Augustine or Rousseau bear. His are modest claims: "I seek only tranquility. I rejoice in the absence of grief." When he tells us what he knows, of the world, of human dwellings, and finally of attachment, Chōmei reveals himself as an all-too-human monk. He is weak both by the standards of the world he has renounced and weak before his religion's imperative, since he remains attached to what is, after all, illusory.

But Chōmei is strong in a way that is comprehensible, given the history that he experienced. He knew that much of the past was gone and that much else would not last. He mourned what was lost and gathered about him what was left. In a hut on Toyama in 1212, he recorded the exact site, the day-to-day moments, where he eked out his own, and his tradition's, survival.

Note

1. Buddhist monks are not normally recluses (hermits). They often live in monastic communities.

19

The Tale of the Heike

Paul Varley

T HE TALE OF *the Heike* is a lengthy war tale (416 pages in the translation into English by Helen McCullough) that recounts the rise and fall
of the warrior house of Taira (or Heike) in Japan in the late twelfth century,
culminating in the Gempei War of 1180–1185 fought by the Taira against the
Minamoto (or Genji).[1]

The version of the *Heike* that has been most widely read for many centuries is a 1371 text attributed to an itinerant, blind storyteller named Kakuichi.
It is the product of a long process of both written and oral development. According to the best scholarship, the original *Heike* was written by a courtier
named Yukinaga sometime about 1220, a quarter of a century or so after the
events with which it deals. During the later thirteenth and early fourteenth
century, it was greatly expanded in size and fictionally embellished, especially by blind storytellers like Kakuichi, who accompanied themselves
with lute-like musical instruments called *biwa*. The accretions to the original *Heike* that we attribute to these storytellers were designed in particular
to appeal to the dramatic expectations of the storytellers' audiences.

Although usually categorized as a war tale, the *Heike* deals with much
more than just warriors and their battles. It is a rich evocation of life in Japan
during the tumultuous period of transition from ancient to medieval times,
focusing primarily on the affairs of the courtier and warrior aristocrats who
were the principal actors of the age. The war tales as a literary genre are
loosely structured and episodic. But the *Heike*, virtually alone among them,

also possesses narrative unity because of its powerful and consistently maintained theme of the decline and destruction of the Taira. This sad, ultimately pathetic story must be seen against prevailing attitudes in Japan— at least at the aristocratic level of society—during the years that ushered in medieval times, which brought the warrior or samurai class to national leadership after a long period of growth in the provinces.

The medieval Japanese believed that, beginning in the late eleventh century, the world had entered the age of *mappō*, or the "end of the Buddhist Law," a time of decline and disorder. To the courtier class, it seemed that not only the Buddhist Law but also the "Imperial Law"—rule by the emperor with the assistance of his courtiers in Kyoto—was in sharp, perhaps irreversible decline. Under such circumstances, it appeared that only warriors, with their coercive powers, might be able to restore order to the country.

Acceptance of the idea of *mappō* was accompanied by the stirring of fervent religious belief in salvation, especially in the form of Pure Land Buddhism, which was based on the promise of the Buddha Amida to save all beings who placed their faith in him by transporting them upon death to a Pure Land paradise in the western realm of the universe. In historical fact, the Pure Land sect was just being established as an independent sect of Buddhism by the priest Hōnen in the final years of the Taira-Minamoto conflict of the late twelfth century, and the sect did not become widely popular until the thirteenth century. In this sense the *Heike*, in which we find one character after another imploring Amida to be saved, is clearly more a product of the thirteenth than the twelfth century.

In addition to its bleakness of outlook based on conviction that the world had entered the age of *mappō*, the *Heike* is suffused with an acute awareness of impermanence (*mujō*): that all things are fleeting, ephemeral, and ever changing. Although impermanence is fundamental to the Buddhist view of life, it is presented with particular intensity in the literature of the medieval age. Thus the *Heike* begins with the famous statement that "the sound of the Gion Shōja bells echoes the impermanence of all things; the color of the *sala* flowers reveals the truth that the prosperous must decline. The proud do not endure, they are like a dream on a spring night; the mighty fall at last, they are as dust before the wind" (23).

It is the Taira who have prospered, who have become mighty and proud, and who will inevitably fall. The Taira chieftain Kiyomori, having led his clan, although warriors, to preeminence as ministers at the emperor's court in Kyoto, is described as being guilty of sins and crimes that are "utterly beyond the power of mind to comprehend or tongue to relate" (23). He has treated members of both the imperial family and the courtier class abominably and has, against all precedent, made himself the grandfather of an emperor by marrying his daughter into royalty.

The *Heike* is the story of the tragedy of the Taira. But "tragedy" cannot be understood in any classical Western sense. The course of decline and ultimate destruction of the Taira, once begun, is governed by an unrelenting fate (*unmei*), and the Taira themselves become the merest pawns in the functioning of this great, dark force. In this regard, the *Heike* divides roughly into two parts. In the first part, up to the death of Kiyomori in 1181 (he literally boils to death in a fever), we feel little more than contempt for the haughty and arrogant Taira, who believe that "all who do not belong to [our] clan must rank as less than men" (28). But the Minamoto have already begun their rebellion in the provinces against the Taira—the Gempei War started in the eighth month of 1180—and there is no question, from this point, that the Taira will in the end be completely destroyed, so completely that at the finish of the book it is stated: "Thus did the sons of the Heike vanish forever from the face of the earth" (425).

In the second half of the *Heike*, the Taira, heretofore despised, increasingly elicit our sympathy as they suffer defeat after defeat at the hands of the Minamoto. In 1183, they are driven from Kyoto and thereafter are hunted (by the enemy) and haunted (by memories of their former glorious existence in the capital). Fleeing from lost battles, they find themselves "drifting on the waves of the western seas" (404), "drawn onward by the tides" (255), and "in aimless flight" (370).

Like most of the war tales, the *Heike* is primarily concerned not with the victors of medieval warfare but with those, such as the Taira, who lose out. As the fate of the Taira moves steadily toward oblivion, the fortunes of the Minamoto rise. Yet the author of the *Heike* (to speak of him in the singular, for convenience) never shifts his focus from the Taira and their somber story. Even the Minamoto chieftains who appear most importantly in the *Heike*, Yoshinaka and Yoshitsune, are prominent losers, victims of the suspicion and jealousy of the supreme Minamoto commander, Yoritomo. At the same time, Yoritomo, founder of the Kamakura Bakufu and, by any standard, one of the great victors in Japanese history, appears in the *Heike* as a remote, indistinct figure.

The tragedy of the Taira, as they are driven inexorably toward their destruction, is made more poignant by the portrayal of them as elegant, refined, and courtier-like. Thus we find Kiyomori's brother Tadanori, shortly before he is killed in battle, imploring the famous poet Fujiwara no Shunzei to include even one of his poems in a forthcoming imperially authorized anthology. Tadanori claims that he will "rejoice in [his] grave and become [Shunzei's] guardian spirit" (247). And when the slayer of the youthful Taira general Atsumori at the battle of Ichinotani discovers a flute in a brocade bag at Atsumori's waist, he cries out: "There are tens of thousands of riders in our eastern [Minamoto] armies, but I am sure none of them has brought a flute to the battlefield. Those court nobles [that is, the Taira] are refined men!" (317). Even the dashing Minamoto chieftain Yoshitsune, who is destined to go down in history and legend as probably the most famous and best loved of all Japanese samurai, is described in the *Heike* as, in appearance and bearing, "not the equal of the dregs of the Heike" (357).

Perhaps the best example in the *Heike* of a Taira who is portrayed much like a court noble is Koremori, the grandson of Kiyomori and father of Roku-dai, the "last of the Taira." We first encounter Koremori, apart from passing references, in the early stages of the Gempei War, where he shows himself to be an inept military commander. When the time comes for the Taira as a group to depart from Kyoto, Koremori alone among the clan's leaders cannot bring himself to take his wife, the daughter of a courtier, and children with him to face the hardships that undoubtedly lie ahead. He leaves his wife "prostrated . . . in a passion of weeping" and his two children and the ladies-in-waiting "shrieking and screaming without caring who heard them" (245).

As the Taira are forced to move from one place to another, defeated in their battles with the Minamoto, Koremori becomes increasingly despondent and suffers a constant agony of yearning for the capital. He finally absconds from the Taira camp at Yashima on Shikoku Island and, making his way to Mount Kōya, shaves his head and becomes a Buddhist monk. This is in preparation for committing suicide, which he does by drowning himself after making a pilgrimage to Kumano.

While on the pilgrimage, Koremori encounters a monk at a retreat who remembers him from the former glory days of the Taira. The monk recalls in particular a celebration in the capital years earlier for Retired Emperor Goshirakawa, which was attended by the leading Taira and at which the youthful Koremori danced: "[Koremori] emerged [from among the Taira], dancing 'Waves of the Blue Sea,' with a sprig of blossoming cherry tucked behind his headgear. His figure was like a flower coquetting with the dew; his sleeves fluttered in the breeze as he danced; his beauty seemed to brighten the earth and illumine the heavens" (348). Here, on the eve of his suicide at age twenty-seven, Koremori is remembered in a setting that the *Heike*'s author has clearly taken from the *Tale of Genji*, likening Koremori to the Shining Genji himself, the fictional prototype of the cultured Heian courtier.

In a sense, the courtier-like Taira serve as surrogates in the *Heike* for the courtier class itself, which is losing out to the warriors as the new rulers of the country. But, in combining the qualities of the cultural (*bun*) and the military (*bu*), the Taira also set a standard as courtier-warriors that was very much admired by later samurai leaders, especially during the Muromachi period (1336–1573).

Many memorable women appear in the pages of the *Heike*, including Giō and Hotoke, court dancers who are brutally exploited by Kiyomori for his sensual pleasure but who ultimately achieve spiritual fulfillment as nuns; the Minamoto partisan Tomoe, who was both a "remarkably strong archer, and as a swordswoman . . . was a warrior worth a thousand, ready to confront a demon or god, mounted or on foot" (291); and Kiyomori's widow, the Nun of Second Rank, who leaps into the sea with her grandchild, the seven-year-old Emperor Antoku, in the climactic naval battle of Dannoura in 1185, which marked the destruction of the Taira and the end of the Gempei War.

But many other women in the *Heike*, especially those who have married into or serve the Taira, are consigned to the roles of waiting for and mourning their men. Grandmothers, mothers, wives, daughters, and nurses, they are the secondary victims of the battlefield casualties of the Gempei War. These sad personages are essentially stereotypes, the creations of storytellers, who typically either become Buddhist nuns to pray for the souls of dead warriors or commit suicide, usually by drowning, in an agony of grief over the warriors.

Stereotypes abound as well among the male characters in the *Heike*. Indeed, apart from the leading performers in the tale such as Kiyomori, Yoshinaka, Yoshitsune, and Koremori, most of the warriors are stock figures representing the values that were most esteemed by the samurai class—selfless loyalty to one's lord, military prowess in the "way of the bow and horse," an exaggerated regard for personal honor, a bold and ferocious fighting spirit, and pride in family traditions. There are, in addition, stock villains among the warriors in the *Heike*—although they are far fewer in number—who disgrace their samurai status through acts of cowardice, betrayal, and the like.

We also find in the *Heike* recurrent narrative devices and themes that were used by its storyteller authors, often extemporaneously, to develop and enhance their recitations. Two of these devices were "dressing the heroes," or descriptions in minute detail of the armor and weapons of the leading warriors as they entered battle, and the "naming of names," prebattle declamations by the heroes in which they recited in booming voices their family lineages and family and personal achievements and, in the process, sought both to bolster the morale of their troops and to intimidate their opponents psychologically.

Still another common narrative device was the description of a battle in terms of "summary" and "scenes," that is, the presentation first of a general overview of a battle and its contending armies and then the recapitulation of a series of close-up encounters among smaller groups or between individual warriors. Although this division of a battle into summary and scenes was a device convenient to the storyteller's art, it also cohered, in fact, to the actual conditions of warfare in the late twelfth century. The main participants in a battle in this age were mounted warriors who, after an exchange of arrows and a charge, quickly broke ranks to seek worthy opponents— opponents of equal or higher rank—with whom to engage in essentially one-to-one combat.

Among the narrative themes that appear frequently in the *Heike* are those of the loyal retainer or servant following his lord in death, the warrior bidding farewell to a lover or wife before leaving for battle, and—a theme already discussed—the female survivor either committing suicide in grief or taking Buddhist vows to pray for a lover, master, or kinsman killed in battle. A particularly interesting theme, which appears twice in the *Heike*, is that of the older warrior who spares (or wishes to spare) a younger enemy because the younger enemy reminds him of his son. This theme is the basis, for example, of the "Death of Atsumori," one of the most cherished stories in the *Heike*.

In this story, a Minamoto adherent, Kumagai no Naozane, attacks and wrestles the Taira general Atsumori from his horse at the battle of Ichinotani, wrenching off Atsumori's helmet to cut off his head. To his amazement, Naozane finds himself gazing at a youth "sixteen or seventeen years old, with a lightly powdered face and blackened teeth—a boy just the age of [his] own son . . . and so handsome that Naozane could not find a place to strike" (317). Naozane would willingly free Atsumori but is forced to kill him to prevent his being captured—and more poorly treated—by others on the Minamoto side. Much of the appeal of this story lies in Atsumori's courtier-like appearance and in Naozane's discovery, discussed earlier, that Atsumori possesses a flute.

Throughout the *Heike* there are references to the "luck" of the Taira "running out," and the last chapters of the book are devoted to the final, awful retribution that fate has ordained for them. The Minamoto were not content with crushing the Taira militarily at the battle of Dannoura, which claimed the lives of many Taira leaders; they also killed most of the other leaders they took as prisoners and even tracked down and murdered surviving male children of the clan. Thus, for example, the Taira commander at Dannoura, Kiyomori's second son, Munemori, and his grown, warrior son were executed, and another of Munemori's sons, the eight-year-old Fukushū, was torn from the breast of a nurse and beheaded.

This brutal conduct did not reflect any particular perversity of the Minamoto but was dictated by the harsh laws of the "way of the warrior." Throughout their history, the samurai followed the law of the vendetta: a warrior "must be determined not to live with the slayer [of a parent or lord] under the same heaven" (*Book of Rites*). A corollary to this law was that victors in battles were virtually compelled to exterminate remaining male kin to prevent them from carrying out acts of revenge against the victors in the future. Taira no Kiyomori had ignored this need for extermination and, yielding to the persuasive pleas of women, had allowed the youthful Yoritomo and Yoshitsune of the Minamoto to live after Kiyomori caused the death of their father in 1160. According to the *Heike*, Kiyomori, angrily regretting his error twenty years later, after Yoritomo had launched the Gempei War, blasphemously forswore on his deathbed any posthumous tributes to him, instead demanding of his wife, who sat attending him, to "build no halls or pagodas after I die; dedicate no pious works. Dispatch [a] punitive force immediately, decapitate Yoritomo, and hang the head in front of my grave. That will be all the dedication I require" (211).

The last chapter of the *Heike*, "The Initiates' Chapter," is thought to have been created at a date much later than the other twelve chapters, and it is not included in some versions of the *Heike*. It contains, however, some of the work's loveliest and most moving passages. It recounts the final, pathetic years of Kenreimon'in, the imperial lady who was both the daughter of Kiyomori and the mother of the tragic young Emperor Antoku. The chapter's story is simple. Kenreimon'in, agonized with grief over the virtual extermination of the Taira—especially the death of the "Former Emperor"—and filled with guilt that she did not drown with so many of her kinsmen and kinswomen at Dannoura, becomes a nun and retires to a Buddhist temple at Ōhara, a remote place in the mountains a short distance to the northeast of the capital. She is visited there by Retired Emperor Goshirakawa, tells him of the religious practices she is engaged in, and recites with much feeling the account of the decline and destruction of her family. Some time after the retired emperor's visit, Kenreimon'in falls ill and dies, praying fervently for rebirth in the Pure Land.

The language and tone of "The Initiates' Chapter" are very much like those of the fictional and historical tales of the Heian period, including the *Tale of Genji*. There are many other passages scattered through the *Heike* of similar language and tone, including those that tell of the wandering of the Taira after their expulsion from Kyoto. Such passages, and "The Initiates' Chapter" as a whole, establish a literary link between the *Heike* and the mainstream of Heian prose writing. They also contribute a sense of sadness and nostalgia based on the classical Heian aesthetic of *mono no aware*, which may be translated as "sensitivity to things," especially the perishable beauties of human life and nature.

The complex textual and tonal qualities of "The Initiates' Chapter" can be illustrated by the description it contains of the hut (or "hermitage," in the McCullough translation) that Kenreimon'in has constructed for herself at Ōhara:

The crudely thatched cryptomeria roof seemed scarcely capable of excluding the rain, frost, and dew that vied with the infiltrating moonbeams for admittance. Behind, there were mountains; in front, barren fields where the wind whistled through low bamboo grass. The bamboo pillars, with their many joints, recalled the manifold sorrows of those who dwell apart from society; the brushwood fence, with its loose weave, brought to mind the long intervals between tidings from the capital. (431)

The chief purpose of the hut is to provide an austere setting in which Kenreimon'in can pray not only for her personal salvation but also for the redemption of the Taira clan, which although guilty of grave sins has also been the collective victim of catastrophic forces, described variously as fate, bad karma, and the will of the gods, that are utterly beyond the comprehension and control of humans. We are told that Kenreimon'in was "zealous . . . in reciting the sutras and invoking Amida's name so that they (the Taira dead) [might] achieve enlightenment."

The hut, then, is a place for the gravest, most serious kind of business, involving release from the toils of what Buddhism regards as an unceasingly sorrowful and suffering existence, salvation, and, ultimately, enlightenment. Yet the hut's setting is pictured in words that also finely evoke the sensibilities of the Heian poet to the perishable, sad beauties of nature as implied in *mono no aware*. And the hut itself—like the hut in Kamo no Chōmei's *Hōjōki* ("An Account of My Hut")—is representative of a central image in the aesthetics of deprivation, the aesthetics of the lonely (*sabi*), withered (*kare*), and cold (*hie*) that evolved in the medieval age.

The *Heike*, we know from modern scholarship, is largely fictional, but for most of its existence it has been regarded as largely historical, a generally reliable account of the exciting, violent years that led Japan into its medieval age. In any case, no other work of fiction or history is comparable to the *Heike* as a source from which the Japanese over many centuries have derived their sense of the character and ethos of the samurai class. The stories of the *Heike* have been told and retold by countless generations and in countless forms, including the Nō, puppet, and Kabuki theaters; historical novels; the radio; cinema; and television. The appeal of these stories and the characters in them seems to be timeless.

Notes

The best translation of the *Heike* into English is the one cited in this chapter: *The Tale of the Heike*, trans. Helen Craig McCullough (Stanford, Calif.: Stanford University Press, 1988).

1. The Taira and the Minamoto had, by the late twelfth century, become multi-branched clans living in many parts of Japan. The Taira who play the leading roles in the *Heike* were simply one branch, from Ise province, of this great clan. The leaders of various branches of the Minamoto rose against the Ise Taira in the Gempei ("Gem" or "Gen" for "Genji" and "Hei" or "Pei" for "Heike") War, and some Taira branches from the eastern provinces and elsewhere joined the Minamoto against the Ise Taira.

20 (A)

KENKŌ'S *ESSAYS IN IDLENESS*

Donald Keene

*E*SSAYS IN IDLENESS (*Tsurezuregusa*) is a collection of essays and observations that range in length from a sentence or two to several pages. The title is derived from a phrase in the preface where the author reveals that he has spent whole days "with nothing better to do" (*tsurezure naru mama ni*) jotting down whatever thoughts happened to enter his head. The work belongs to a tradition known in Japan (following Chinese examples) as *zuihitsu*, or "following the brush," meaning that the author allowed his writing brush free rein to scribble down anything it chose.

The author of *Tsurezuregusa* is most commonly known by his Buddhist name, Kenkō. His name before he took Buddhist orders is usually given as Urabe no Kaneyoshi but also sometimes as Yoshida no Kaneyoshi, presumably because he at one time resided in the Yoshida district of Kyoto. The Urabe family were hereditary Shinto diviners, but this background did not keep Kenkō from pursuing Buddhist studies. The dates of his birth and death have yet to be definitively determined, but it is generally agreed that he was born in 1283 and died in 1352 or somewhat later. As a young man he served at first in a nobleman's household. Later, after his talents were recognized, he was granted official rank, enabling him to serve at the court, where his skill at composing poetry was prized. The knowledge of court precedents and distaste for novelty characteristic of *Tsurezuregusa* may reflect the years he spent in the conservative milieu of the court. At some time before 1313, Kenkō took orders as a Buddhist monk. It is not known why he took this step, but there are strong suggestions in the poetry he composed around this time of an increasing disenchantment with the world.

Even after he took orders, however, Kenkō did not reside in a temple but lived by himself at various places around the capital, occasionally traveling elsewhere. During his lifetime, he enjoyed a considerable reputation as a poet and was even known as one of the "four heavenly kings" of the poetry of his time. Some of his poems were included in imperially sponsored anthologies, but they are no longer so highly esteemed. The poems, written in the conservative traditions of the Nijō school of poetry, are apt to strike modern readers as being tepid if not downright boring.

Tsurezuregusa was by far Kenkō's most important literary achievement. We do not know just when he wrote the preface and the 243 essays that make up the work. Some scholars have suggested that many years elapsed between the composition of the first and last of the essays, but it is more common to date the work between the years 1330 and 1332. This was not a propitious time for a work of reflection. In 1331, the Emperor Go-Daigo staged a revolt against the Hōjō family, who had ruled the country as surrogates of the shoguns in Kamakura, but he was defeated and exiled the following year to the lonely Oki islands in the Sea of Japan. The Hōjō family subsequently set up another imperial prince as the emperor. In 1333, Go-Daigo returned from exile, and this time he and his supporters succeeded in overthrowing the Hōjōs. These events often divided families because of conflicting allegiances, but they hardly ruffle the surface of *Tsurezuregusa*; it neither grieves over the turbulent times nor rejoices over the victories of one side or the other but presents instead the reflections of a strikingly civilized man.

At first glance, there seems to be no apparent order to the 243 sections. According to one old tradition, Kenkō wrote down his thoughts as they came to him on scraps of paper that he pasted to the walls of his cottage. Years later, the distinguished poet Imagawa Ryōshun, learning of this unusual wallpaper, had the various scraps of paper removed and arranged them in their present order. This account was long accepted, but modern critics tend to reject it, because they can detect subtle connections linking one section to the next that suggest associations in the writer's mind that would probably not have occurred to another person. At least four clusters of essays were unmistakably composed in sequence, and other links have been found. The oldest surviving text, dated 1431, bears the title *Tsurezuregusa*, but we cannot be sure that this title was given by Kenkō himself. The present arrangement of a preface and 243 numbered sections goes back only to the seventeenth century.

Tsurezuregusa seems to have been unknown to anyone but the author during Kenkō's lifetime. It was first given attention by the poet and critic Shōtetsu (1381–1475), to whom we owe the 1431 text, but the popularity of the work dates only from the seventeenth century. In 1603, the haiku poet Matsunaga Teitoku (1571–1633), who had previously been instructed in *Tsurezuregusa* by a scholar of the old school, offered lectures to the general public on the work, breaking the tradition of secret transmission of the traditions surrounding the classics. *Tsurezuregusa* subsequently became one of the books that every educated Japanese was expected to have read, and Kenkō's thoughts affected many people. The influence of *Tsurezuregusa*, especially on the formation of Japanese aesthetic preferences, can hardly be exaggerated.

Buddhist thought naturally supplied the background for much of what Kenkō wrote. Specifically Buddhist doctrine is sometimes expressed, but more typical of the work are the general Buddhist beliefs that colored Kenkō's thinking—that the world is no more than a temporary abode and that all things in this world are impermanent. Kenkō also describes the full cycle of birth, growth, sickness, and death, followed by rebirth: "With the falling of the leaves, too, it is not that first the leaves fall and then young shoots form; the leaves fall because the budding from underneath is too powerful to resist." But the predominant tone is provided by Kenkō's conviction that worldly achievements and possessions are without lasting significance in a world that is itself no more than transitory. Many passages in *Tsurezuregusa* convey this belief, including: "The intelligent man, when he dies, leaves no possessions." "If you have power, do not trust in it; powerful men are the first to fall. You may have possessions, but they are not to be depended on; they are easily lost in a moment." "When I see the things people do in their struggle to get ahead, it reminds me of someone building a snowman on a spring day, making ornaments of precious metals and stones to decorate it, and then erecting a hall to house it."

Kenkō again and again reproached the man who delays taking the Great Step of entering the Buddhist priesthood until he has achieved desired success:

My observation of people leads me to conclude, generally speaking, that even people with some degree of intelligence are likely to go through life supposing they have ample time before them. But would a man fleeing because a fire has broken out in his neighborhood say to the fire, "Wait a moment, please!"? To save his life, a man will run away, indifferent to shame, abandoning his possessions. Is a man's life any more likely to wait for him? Death attacks faster than fire or water, and is harder to escape. When its hour comes, can you refuse to give up your aged parents, your little children, your duty to your master, your affection for others, because they are hard to abandon?

And again: "You must not wait until you are old before you begin practicing the Way. Most of the gravestones from the past belong to men who died young."

Such passages are testimony to the depth of Kenkō's religious convictions. Sometimes he also finds unusual implications in Buddhist doctrine, as when he traces the close relationship between impermanence and beauty, a particularly Japanese aesthetic principle. "If man were never to fade away like the dews of Adashino, never to vanish like the smoke over Toribeno, but lingered forever in this world, how things would lose their power to move us! The most precious thing in life is its uncertainty." Other Buddhists rarely suggested that impermanence itself was valuable; like the ancient Greeks who declined to call a man happy until he was dead, the uncertainty of life was frequently called a source of grief. But unless (like Kenkō) the Japanese had appreciated impermanence, they surely would not have displayed such love for cherry blossoms, which hardly bloom before they fall, and their preference for building houses of perishable materials such as wood and paper, rather than of brick or stone, was surely not due only to a fear of earthquakes. The falling of the cherry blossoms is regretted in innumerable poems, but the very brevity of their blossoming imparts a special beauty and makes them more precious than hardier flowers.

Ironically, wooden statues and temples erected in Japan a thousand years ago survive, despite the perishable nature of the materials, but the Japanese made no conscious effort to achieve the permanence of marble. Whatever has survived has also aged, and this faded quality, the reminder of impermanence, has been prized. Kenkō quoted with approbation the priest Ton'a, who said: "It is only after the silk wrapper has frayed at top and bottom and the mother-of-pearl has fallen from the roller, that a scroll looks beautiful." Kenkō constantly warned of the shortness of life and the close presence of death, and he urged people to hasten in the path of Buddha, but he also found in the shortness of human life the source of its poignancy. His delight in the worn, the obviously used, contrasts with the Western craving for objects in mint condition and the desire to annihilate time by restoring works of art to so pristine a state as to make people exclaim: "It might have been painted yesterday!" The Japanese craftsman who repairs a broken or chipped bowl fills in the cracks with gold, as if to emphasize the ravages of time.

Kenkō's preference for objects that reveal the effects of impermanence was accompanied by a similar preference for the irregular and the incomplete. "In everything, no matter what it may be, uniformity is undesirable. Leaving something incomplete makes it interesting, and gives one the feeling there is room for growth." Again: "It is typical of the unintelligent man to insist on assembling complete sets of everything. Imperfect sets are better."

No doubt most people in Kenkō's time preferred to own complete sets rather than odd volumes, but as anyone knows who has ever confronted the grim volumes of a set of the Harvard Classics or the complete works of Sir Walter Scott, they do not invite browsing. Asymmetry and irregularity not only allow the possibility of growth but the participation of the outsider; perfection tends to choke the imagination.

Kenkō's love of the imperfect led him to stress also the importance of beginnings and ends: "Are we to look at cherry blossoms only in full bloom, the moon only when it is cloudless? To long for the moon while looking on the rain, to lower the blinds and be unaware of the passing of the spring— these are even more deeply moving. Branches about to blossom or gardens strewn with faded flowers are worthier of our admiration." Even in Japan a fondness for the imperfect has usually not caused people to rush to see cherry blossoms before they open or to wait until they are scattered before paying a visit, and in the West the climactic moments—when Laocoön and his sons are caught in the serpent's embrace or the soprano hits the much-awaited high C—have been given the greatest attention. But for Kenkō the climax, whether the full moon or the full flowering of the cherry trees, was less suggestive than the beginnings and ends: the full moon and the cherry blossoms at their peak do not suggest the crescent moon or buds, but the crescent and the buds (or the waning moon and strewn flowers) can evoke with poignancy the full cycle. In Japanese poetry, hoped-for love affairs and regretted affairs that have ended are often treated, but hardly a poem expresses the pleasure of requited love.

Irregularity and incompleteness accord with another element of Japanese aesthetics emphasized by Kenkō: simplicity, the art of suggesting more than is stated. "A house which multitudes of workmen have polished with every care, where strange and rare Chinese and Japanese furnishings are displayed, and even the grasses and trees of the garden have been trained unnaturally, is ugly to look at and most depressing." It is easier for us to assent to this opinion than it would have been for Western readers of a century ago. In the West, the house "which multitudes of workmen have polished with every care" was for long considered beautiful, as we know from photographs showing the profusion of treasures with which the drawing rooms of the rich were adorned. Gardens where even the trees and plants have been trained unnaturally still attract visitors to the great houses of Europe.

Kenkō elsewhere stated: "People agree that a house which has plenty of spare room is attractive to look at and may be put to many different uses." By a curious coincidence, this preference is now a commonplace of decorators in the West, for whom "less is more" has replaced richness of effect as an ideal. No doubt Kenkō's tastes were formed by earlier traditions, but he was probably the first to define these tastes, and when *Tsurezuregusa* came to be generally circulated it surely influenced the tastes of later Japanese.

Kenkō exercised even greater influence with his descriptions of the proper behavior of the well-bred man. Indeed, *Tsurezuregusa* is a kind of manual of gentlemanly conduct. "A man should avoid displaying deep familiarity with any subject. Can one imagine a well-bred man talking with the airs of a know-it-all, even about a matter with which he is in fact familiar? ... It is impressive when a man is always slow to speak even on subjects he knows thoroughly, and does not speak at all unless questioned." Kenkō often contrasted his gentleman with the insensitive, boorish people who make up most of society: "The man of breeding never appears to abandon himself completely to his pleasures; even his manner of enjoyment is detached.... When the well-bred man tells a story he addresses himself to one person, even if many people are present, though the others too listen, naturally." "You can judge a person's breeding by whether he is quite impassive even when he tells an amusing story or laughs a great deal even when relating a matter of no interest." "The well-bred man does not tell stories about prodigies." "When a person who has always been extremely close appears on a particular occasion reserved and formal towards you ... some people will undoubtedly say, 'Why act that way now, after all these years?' But I feel that such behavior shows sincerity and breeding."

Early in the work, Kenkō states the cultural qualifications of a gentleman:

A familiarity with orthodox scholarship, the ability to compose poetry and prose in Chinese, a knowledge of Japanese poetry and music are all desirable, and if a man can serve as a model to others in matters of precedent and court ceremony, he is truly impressive. The mark of an excellent man is that he writes easily in an acceptable hand, sings agreeably and in tune, and, appearing reluctant to accept when wine is pressed on him, is not a teetotaler.

These abilities continued until recent times to be the marks of a gentleman in Japan.

Kenkō's insistence on the importance of knowing precedents and court ceremony accounts for his inclusion of the least interesting parts of the text of *Tsurezuregusa*. He clung to each usage sanctified by tradition, even though some were surely meaningless even in his day. He wrote: "It is best not to change something if changing it will not do any good," but he gives no instances of desirable changes. Instead, he laments each violation of precedent and praises each act of fidelity to the old ways. He describes, for example, how an official, deciding that the file chest in his office was unsightly, ordered it to be rebuilt in a more elegant style. Other officials, familiar with court precedents, voiced the opinion that the chest was not to be altered without due consideration: "This article of government property, dating back many reigns, had by its very dilapidation become a model." Kenkō enthusiastically approved the final decision not to remodel the chest.

His nostalgia for the past is eloquently described in various sections, notably: "When I sit down in quiet meditation, the one emotion hardest to fight against is a longing in all things for the past." Such feelings made him treasure even the least important tradition. He was impressed by the Abbess Genki, who remembered from childhood that the "bell-shaped windows in the Kan'in Palace were rounder and without frames." For Kenkō, even a window whose shape was slightly at variance with tradition was indicative of the degeneracy of the age. He was dismayed that no one knew any longer the proper shape of a torture rack nor the manner of attaching a criminal.

Various essays devoted to precedents and correct usage were omitted from eighteenth- and nineteenth-century editions of the work, evidence that they had lost their interest, but they are no less typical of Kenkō than the more celebrated essays. He so startles us again and again with his insights into the characters of people, the nature of beauty, the passage of time, and other eternally moving subjects that we are likely to forget that he was acutely aware of belonging to a particular age. He feared that people of his time might be so involved in the turbulent changes that affected everyone as to destroy by ignorance or indifference the civilization that had been created in Japan. It probably seemed just as important to him to preserve the correct nomenclature for palace ceremonies as to preserve the old texts or works of art that had survived from the past. His work is not systematic, and its pages even contain contradictions, but it is central to an understanding of Japanese taste. Kenkō was not the first to be aware of the principles he enunciates, but he gave them permanence by his eloquent and affecting presentation.

Note

A full translation of the *Tsurezuregusa* has been made by Donald Keene and published under the title *Essays in Idleness* (New York: Columbia University Press, 1967).

KENKŌ AND MONTAIGNE IN TANDEM

James Mirollo

T HIS IS A very brief and tentative reply to the following questions: What is the pedagogical and personal value of juxtaposing an Eastern and Western classic, whether in your classroom or your study (or at your bedside)? In a course syllabus, should the Eastern and Western texts be taken up together in clusters or in tandem, based on thematic or genre affinities?

To juxtapose the essays of Kenkō and Montaigne is to discover, once again, how frustrating and wonderful such encounters of classics can be. The wonder comes from recognizing startling similarities, the frustration from learning that each classic resides elusively within its own impenetrable culture. Thus you learn both more than you did before and how much more you need to know. Aside from the surprising similarities and the disconcerting differences, however, there is a third lesson to be grasped, and that is how the encounter illuminates qualities and features of the thinking and writing of each author that you might not have noticed otherwise. In my own case, Kenkō has taught me how Montaigne is both more admirable and more deficient than I might realize when reading him alone. And perhaps the same insights might occur to an open-minded Kenkōite.

To begin with the similarities, particularly with regard to form and content, there is the personal essay. Montaigne wrote his essays several hundred years later than Kenkō wrote his, and he wrote more of them, and much longer ones. But he and Kenkō, importantly, share in promoting the fraudulent assumption of that genre: first, that the essays are casual jottings written in idleness and not worth your serious consideration, and second, that they record rather than represent these fleeting thoughts. Don't you believe it. These so-called nonsensical thoughts have been carefully filtered through a highly esthetic, literary sensibility that is both innate and refined by intensive reading of their predecessors. Their minds are stuffed with other classics of their cultures, which they quote or refer to incessantly, especially poetry. Montaigne admitted he was addicted to poetry, and Kenkō makes clear that he shared the same disease. If you still think an essay is a species of automatic writing, just try writing one. Or better, please don't.

Kenkō

What a strange, demented feeling it gives me when I realize I have spent whole days before this inkstone, with nothing better to do, jotting down at random whatever nonsensical thoughts have entered ones head.[1]

Montaigne I, 8: "On Idleness"

Lately when I retired to my home, determined so far as possible to bother about nothing except spending the little life I have left in rest and seclusion, it seemed to me I could do my mind no greater favor than to let it entertain itself in full idleness and stay and settle in itself, which I hoped it might do more easily now, having become weightier and riper with time. But I find—

Ever idle hours breed wandering thoughts   LUCAN

—that, on the contrary, like a runaway horse, it gives itself a hundred times more trouble than it took for others, and gives birth to so many chimeras and fantastic monsters, one after another, without order or purpose, that in order to contemplate their ineptitude and strangeness at my pleasure, I have begun to put them in writing, hoping in time to make my mind ashamed of itself.[2]

As to wondrous similarities of content, once you get over the initial shock of recognition, you discover that these have to do with the passions and foibles of our common humanity. Both of our authors write about vanity, greed, lust, appetite, and the hunger for happiness. Kenkō's 175 and Montaigne's II, 2, for example, are about drunkenness, and both begin by denouncing it as a loathsome vice but end up by excusing it somewhat: Kenkō because it is socially enhancing, and besides, drunks can be pretty amusing; Montaigne because it is the last sensual indulgence possible for old age.

But the Japanese Buddhist and the French Catholic also coincide in their philosophical awareness of mortality, or transience, and impermanence. Kenkō, famously in his Buddhist way, records the passing season and warns against clinging to the world, while simultaneously, it should be noted, seeming to revel in its sadness.

Kenkō 189

You may intend to do something today, only for pressing business to come up unexpectedly and take up all of your attention the rest of the day. Or a person you have been expecting is prevented from coming, or someone you hadn't expected comes calling. The thing you have counted on goes amiss, and the thing you had no hopes for is the only one to succeed. A matter which promised to be a nuisance passes off smoothly, and a matter which should have been easy proves a great hardship. Our daily experiences bear no resemblance to what we had anticipated. This is true throughout the year, and equally true for our entire lives. But if we decide that everything is bound to go contrary to our anticipations, we discover that naturally there are also some things which do not contradict expectations. This makes it all the harder to be definite about anything. The one thing you can be certain of is the truth that all is uncertainty.[3]

Montaigne III, 2

Others form man; I tell of him, and portray a particular one, very ill-formed, whom I should really make very different from what he is if I had to fashion him over again. But now it is done.

Now the lines of my painting do not go astray, though they change and vary. The world is but a perennial movement. All things in it are in constant motion—the earth, the rocks of the Caucasus, the pyramids of Egypt—both with the common motion and with their own. Stability itself is nothing but a more languid motion.

I cannot keep my subject still. It goes along befuddled and staggering, with a natural drunkenness. I take it in this condition, just as it is at the moment I give my attention to it. I do not portray being: I portray passing.[4]

At other times, Kenkō becomes the stern moralist reminding us to not waste our time in useless activity, even though such activity looks fairly necessary to a non-Buddhist. Montaigne too is preoccupied with uncertainty, inconsistency, and bewildering variety and diversity.

Kenkō 242

Man is eternally swayed by the pleasing or displeasing circumstances around him, thanks to his constant preoccupation with pleasure and pain. Pleasure is liking and loving. We never cease our pursuit of this happiness. The pleasure we desire first of all is that of fame. There are two kinds of fame: glory derived from one's conduct, or from one's talents. The next pleasure desired is that of lust, the third of appetite. None of man's other desires can equal these three. They arise from a perverted view of life, and cause innumerable griefs. It is best not to seek them.[5]

Montaigne III, 13

I have a vocabulary all my own. I "pass the time," when it is rainy and disagreeable; when it is good, I do not want to pass it; I savor it, I cling to it. We must run through the bad and settle on the good. This ordinary expression "pastime" or "pass the time" represents the habit of those wise folk who think they can make no better use of their life than to let it slip by and escape it, pass it by, sidestep it, and, as far as in them lies, ignore it and run away from it, as something irksome and contemptible. But I know it to be otherwise and find it both agreeable and worth prizing, even in its last decline, in which I now possess it; and nature has placed it in our hands adorned with such favorable conditions that we have only ourselves to blame if it weighs on us and if it escapes us unprofitably.[6]

Note how in book III, essay 13 he fairly agrees with Kenkō about "passing time" profitably but tends to see time as a gift of nature that we scorn (more on his "nature" later).

Kenkō 108

If some man came and informed you that you would certainly lose your life the following day, what would you have to look forward to, what would you do to occupy yourself while waiting for this day to end? In what does the day we are now living differ from our last day? Much of our time during any day is wasted in eating and drinking, at stool, in sleeping, talking, and walking. To engage in useless activities, to talk about useless things, and to think about useless things during the brief moments of free time left us is not only to waste this time, but to blot out days that extend into months and eventually into a whole lifetime. This is most foolish of all.[7]

One important difference in their attitudes to time is Kenkō's preoccupation with beginnings and endings, as opposed to Montaigne's very Renaissance focus on "ripeness." The speed with which Kenkō's blossom trees decay perhaps forced him to value the early and late stages of growth. But unlike Montaigne, he did not transfer that interest to human growth and decay, and certainly not to old age.

It is surely on the topic of sensual pleasure that Kenkō and Montaigne most obviously disagree. At times they are like two chatty birds who alight on the same branch for a bit and then fly off in different directions. But on the subject of one of those sensual pleasures, the love of women, they are as remote as can be from each other. For it is Kenkō who, as in the European romantic literary tradition, records the joys, sorrows, and mysteries of erotic feeling. Whereas Montaigne, the heir to the great French literary tradition of courtly love, will have none of it.

Montaigne I, 33: "To Flee from Sensual Pleasure at the Price of Life"

But as for pushing the contempt of death to the point of using it to withdraw ourselves from the honors, riches, dignities, and other favors and goods which we call those of fortune, as if reason had not enough to do to persuade us to abandon them without adding this

new burden on her, I had never seen this either commanded or practiced until I came across that passage in which Seneca advises Lucilius, a powerful personage and a man of great authority with the
emperor, to give up his voluptuous and pompous existence and retire
from worldly ambition to some solitary, tranquil, and philosophical
life. Lucilius alleged some difficulties, to which Seneca replied: "My
advice is that you either quit that life you lead, or quit life altogether. I
so indeed counsel you to follow the milder way, and untie rather than
break the knot you have so badly tied; provided that if it cannot be
otherwise untied, you break it. No man is such a coward that he would
not rather fall once than remain forever tottering." I should have
found this advice in keeping with Stoical harshness; but it is more
strange that it should be borrowed from Epicurus, who writes things
just like it on this subject to Idomeneus.[8]

In part, as we can see in the excerpt from I, 33, Montaigne is wary of Stoic
injunctions to squelch the passions, but as we also note in book II, essay 11,
his is a macho view of sexual intercourse, for he even brags (in "Of Cruelty") that he can resist desire when reason so commands, except of course
when reason is suddenly surprised by the beast of lust.

Montaigne II, 11

Those who have to combat sensual pleasure like to use this argument
to show that it is wholly vicious and unreasonable: that when it is at its
greatest pitch it masters us to such an extent that reason can have no
access. And they cite the experience of it that we feel in intercourse
with women,

> Anticipated joy the body feels, And Venus now prepares to sow
> the woman's fields [Lucretius];

Where it seems to them that the pleasure transports us so far beyond ourselves that our reason could not possibly then perform its
function, being all crippled and ravished away in pleasure.
I know that it can go otherwise, and that we may sometimes, if we
will, cast our soul back to other thoughts at this very instant. But we
must tense and stiffen it vigilantly. I know that it is possible to master

the onset of this pleasure; and I am well versed in this; and I have not found Venus so imperious a goddess as many chaster men than I attest her. I do not take it for a miracle, as does the queen Navarre in one of the tales of her *Heptameron* (which is a nice book for one of its substance), or for an extremely difficult thing, to spend entire nights with every opportunity and in all freedom, with a long-desired mistress, keeping the faith one has pledged to her, to be content with kisses and simple contacts.

I think the example of the chase would be more appropriate. Even as there is less pleasure in it, so there is more transport and surprise, whereby our reason, stunned, loses the leisure to prepare and brace itself against it, when after a long quest the beast starts up suddenly and appears in a place where perhaps we were least expecting it.[9]

Note too the shot he takes at the Queen of Navarre's *Heptameron*, a collection of tales inspired by Boccaccio but very different from the Italian in its attitude to spiritual love. Montaigne takes his literary cues if not his amorous lifestyle from the Roman love poets, especially Ovid, for whom love is lust, period, and women are the objects of a chase or Lucretian fields to be sown.

It is a relief to turn from Montaigne's sexism to Kenkō's fetishism if only because it is obviously and admittedly more of a recipe for his kind of poetry than an encouragement of asymmetrical relations between the sexes. Besides, Kenkō, unlike Montaigne, really seems to like women or at least to represent them as other than objects of unbridled desire.

Kenkō 9

Beautiful hair, of all things in a woman, is most likely to catch a man's eye. Her character and temperament may be guessed from the first words she utters, even if she is hidden behind a screen. When a woman somehow—perhaps unintentionally—has captured a man's heart she is generally unable to sleep peacefully. She will not hesitate to subject herself to hardships, and will even endure cheerfully what she would normally find intolerable, all because love means so much to her.

The love of men and women is truly a deep-seated passion with distant roots. The senses give rise to many desires, but it should be possible to shun them all. Only one, infatuation, is impossible to control;

old or young, wise or foolish, in this respect all seem identical. That is why they say that even a great elephant can be fastened securely with a rope plaited from the strands of a woman's hair, and that a flute made from a sandal a woman has worn will infallibly summon the autumn deer. We must guard against this delusion of the senses, which is to be dreaded and avoided.[10]

It starts out being about a woman's beautiful hair and then goes on to describe being in love from a woman's point of view. It even asserts the mutuality of love between men and women before the usual warning against the delusion of the senses. Here again, as elsewhere, Kenkō is seemingly ingenuous in charming us with his subject, then telling us not to go there, a ploy that Montaigne would have denounced as a breach of faith with the reader and with his own integrity.

In Kenkō's essay 105 we read an astonishing evocation of a romantic scene, with a couple conversing and the author wishing he could hear more than the snatches of talk that reach him.

Kenkō 105

The unmelted snow lying in the shade north of the house was frozen hard, and even the shafts of a carriage drawn up there glittered with frost. The dawn moon shone clear, but its light was not penetrating. In the corridor of a deserted temple a man of obvious distinction sat beside a woman on a doorsill, chatting. Whatever it was they were discussing, there seemed no danger they would run out of things to say. The woman had a charming manner of tilting her head towards the man, and I caught an occasional, enchanting whiff of some exquisite perfume. The scraps of their conversation reaching me made me long to hear the rest.[11]

This essay, a prose poem really, recalls one of the foundational lyrics of European love poetry, by Sappho, which established the thematic convention of what we now call triangulated desire. An important difference, however, is that Sappho's speaker is driven madly jealous by the sight of one of the duo chatting with her beloved, whereas Kenkō's persona looks upon his lovers with the bemused longing of a poet, straining to hear them but not necessarily to be one of them. As usual with Kenkō, the setting, the atmosphere, and the picturesque scene is what really matters to him. One imagines a Japanese scroll painting or a nocturnal version by Watteau or Fragonard. And like other prose painters, Kenkō encourages the reader (or viewer) to imagine his or her own painting of the scene (in my own case where to locate that frosted carriage as the key image, what with its suggestion of time suspended and motion paralyzed).

On the themes of human nature and the natural world, our two authors sometimes converge but mostly diverge. Unlike Kenkō, who despite his several indoor scenes seems to live outdoors, Montaigne could not care less about external nature. There was a window in the tower where he composed his essays, but he apparently never looked outside. Surrounded by books and painted quotations from books, he was content to quote others and their evocations of Greco-Roman nature myths. Kenkō, in addition to writing about moonlight, snow, heat and cold, and blossoms budding and falling, expressed a Buddhist concern for animals as a valued part of creation. Apart from one famous reference to his cat, Montaigne, essential soldier that he thought himself to be, cherishes only his horses. Despite his travels and frequent exposure to the natural world, his essays are fundamentally indoor creations.

To Kenkō's notion of human beings as a potentially miraculous species, of the same stuff as heaven and earth, Montaigne opposes a more limited view based on his skepticism. All he can know, he argues, is himself. If steadily observed, that self will turn out to be both unique and typical. Know thyself, and you will also know others.

Finally, to return to my earlier question about how rubbing Kenkō and Montaigne together sends off sparks of fresh awareness of their strengths and weaknesses, let us focus on their attitudes to political and social reality. Both are fond of the past, reveling in historical anecdotes and frequently citing exemplary past events. They were connected to and utterly familiar with the life of the court, though Kenkō seems to have been far less critical of it than his Renaissance counterpart. Montaigne, witness to savage religious wars, the discovery and exploitation of the Americas, and the invention of printing, was rarely able to enjoy that solitude he praises constantly. In the preface to the first printed edition of his essays, he addresses the reader as though he or she had in hand a manuscript circulated privately rather than a book that reader had purchased.

Montaigne was also responsible for managing the estate that his father had bequeathed to him, but he wrestled with a good deal of guilt over not maintaining it well and failing to produce a male heir. In sum, the world was very much with Montaigne, which was why he sought in vain to have the private life he craved, or so he said. When you read Kenkō, you realize that, in contrast, despite Montaigne's project to render himself, he remains elusive. We know what he thought but not always what he felt.

Quite different, Kenkō parades his feelings, sentiments, joys, and sorrows in response to nature and human nature. But one looks in vain for any public awareness of how his Buddhist-shaped "take" on the world influences contemporary political and social reality. I am not asking him to be a Confucian, as Ted de Bary might point out. I am just noting that for someone who seems to tell us so much about how he feels and how we should feel—about how fleeting our environment and our passing moments are—Kenkō remains the consummate artist, the creator of a wonderful world, but perhaps not our world. Too bad for us. In contrast, Montaigne's world—as I indicated earlier—with its evocations of religious strife, imperialist incursions, technical dislocation, and psychological hang-ups, looks more than suspiciously like our own times. Too bad for Kenkō!

So what to do? My advice is that when you teach Kenkō you should keep the windows open, and when you take up Montaigne you should close them! To read them on your own, you should take up the essays of Montaigne in New York and explore Kenkō in Vermont, as I do every year.

Notes

1. Kenkō, *Essays in Idleness*, trans. Donald Keene (New York: Columbia University Press, 1998).
2. *The Complete Essays of Montaigne*, trans. Donald M. Frame (Stanford, Calif.: Stanford University Press, 1958), 21.
3. Kenkō, *Essays in Idleness*, 162.
4. Montaigne, *Essays*, 610.
5. Kenkō, *Essays in Idleness*, 200.
6. Montaigne, *Essays*, 853.
7. Kenkō, *Essays in Idleness*, 91.
8. Montaigne, *Essays*, 162.
9. Ibid., 313.
10. Ibid.
11. Kenkō, *Essays in Idleness*, 88.

THE POETRY OF MATSUO BASHŌ

Haruo Shirane

MODERN HAIKU DERIVES from the seventeen-syllable *hokku*, or opening verse, of *haikai*, or comic linked verse. In the early Edo period, when Matsuo Bashō (1644–1694) began his career as a *haikai* poet, the seventeen-syllable *hokku* was regarded primarily as the beginning of a linked verse (*renga*) sequence, which usually consisted of thirty-six or a hundred links (5/7/5, 7/7, 5/7/5, 7/7, etc.) composed alternately by one or more poets. Bashō considered himself to be, first and foremost, a comic linked-verse poet and made a profession as a *haikai* teacher, but he often composed independent *hokku*—commonly referred to by modern readers as haiku— for which he is primarily known today and which lie at the heart of his prose narratives.

In a linked-verse session, the author of the *hokku* was required to include a *kigo*, a seasonal word, which functioned as a greeting to the gathered poets and established a special line of communication between the poet and the audience—a pipeline that proved crucial to the independent *hokku*. In the course of poetic history, the seasonal words used in classical poetry (the thirty-one syllable *waka* and later orthodox linked verse, or *renga*) had come to embody particular emotions, moods, and images. Thus, the word "spring rain" (*harusame*), which always meant a soft, steady drizzle, brought sweet thoughts; the long, oppressive "summer rain" (*samidare*) meant depression; and the cold and sporadic "early winter showers" (*shigure*) became associated with the uncertainty and impermanence of life. The importance of seasonal words in the *hokku* is evident in the following poems from the beginning and end of Bashō's *The Narrow Road to the Deep North* (*Oku no hosomichi*).

yuku haru ya	The passing of spring:	
tori naki uo no	Birds cry, and in the eyes	
me wa namida	Of the fish are tears.	(1689)

hamaguri no	A clam being parted	
futami ni wakare	From its shell at Futami—	
yuku aki zo	The passing of autumn.	(1689)

The two respective seasonal words, "the passing of spring" (*yuku haru*) and "the passing of autumn" (*yuku aki*), indicate more than the temporal dimensions of the poems; in the classical tradition they are strongly associated with the sorrow of separation, particularly that caused by a journey. In the first poem, nature at large—here represented by a bird and a fish—reveals its sorrow at the departure of spring. Through the connotations of the seasonal word, the same poem also expresses Bashō's sorrow at leaving behind his friends. In the last poem, the departure of autumn (and implicitly that of Bashō) becomes as difficult and painful as prying apart the shells of a clam.[1] On the surface, the two poems appear to depict only nature, but the seasonal words, coupled with the larger context, underscore a recurrent theme of *The Narrow Road to the Deep North*: the sorrow of the eternal traveler.

Haikai deliberately employs contemporary language and subject matter, which classical poetry (the thirty-one syllable *waka*) was forbidden to use. *Haikai* is also informed by a sense of the comic, which usually derives from humorous subject matter, verbal play, or parody of traditional poetry and literature. Ichū, a *haikai* theorist of the Danrin school, once stated that "a poem that draws on the literary tradition and at the same time parodies it is *haikai*." The same is true of much of Bashō's poetry, though in a more subtle manner than in earlier *haikai*. A good example is Bashō's famous frog poem, which marks the beginning of his mature poetry, of the so-called Bashō style.

furu ike ya	An ancient pond—	
kawazu tobikomu	A frog leaps in,	
mizu no oto	The sound of water.	(1686)

Kawazu ("frog"), a seasonal word for spring, was a popular poetic topic, appearing as early as the *Manyōshū* (mid-eighth century). The following *waka* appears in a section on frogs (vol. 10, no. 2161–2165).

kami tsu se ni	On the upper rapids
kawazu tsuma yobu	A frog calls for his lover.
yū sareba	Is it because,
koromode sasumimi	His sleeves chilled by the evening,
tsuma makamu toka	He wants to share his pillow?

By the Heian period (the late eighth to the late twelfth century), the *kawazu* became almost exclusively associated with the blossoms of the *yamabuki* (kerria), the bright yellow mountain rose, and with limpid mountain streams, as in the following poem from *Kokinshū* (early ninth century).

kawazu naku	At Ide, where the frogs cry,
Ide no yamabuki	The yellow rose
chirinikeri	Has already scattered.
hana no sakari ni	If only I had come when
awamashi mono o	The flowers were in full bloom!
	(Spring II, no. 125, Anonymous)[2]

In medieval poetry, the poet was often required to compose on the poetic essence (*hon'i*) of a given topic, which, in the case of the *kawazu*, became its beautiful voice. In a fashion typical of *haikai*, or comic linked verse, Bashō's poem on the frog works against these traditional associations. In place of the plaintive voice of the frog singing in the rapids or calling out for his lover, Bashō gives us the plop of the frog jumping into the water. And instead of the elegant image of a frog in a fresh mountain stream beneath the bright yellow rose, the *hokku* presents a stagnant pond. According to *Kuzu no Matsubara* (1692), one of Bashō's disciples suggested that the first line be "A yellow rose—" (*yamabuki ya*), an image that would have remained within the associative bounds of traditional poetry. Bashō's version, by contrast, provides a surprising and witty twist on the classical perception of frogs.

This is not to say that Bashō rejects the seasonal association of the frog with spring. The *kawazu* appears in spring, summer, and autumn, but in the seasonal handbooks used by both Bashō and his readers, the frog is listed in the category of mid-spring, along with other insects and reptiles that emerge then from underground hibernation. As a seasonal word, the frog thus deepens the contrast or tension between the first half of the poem, the image of an old pond—the atmosphere of long silence and rest—and the second part, a moment in spring, when life and vitality have suddenly (with a surprising plop) returned to the world.

In Bashō's time, the seasonal words in *haikai* formed a vast pyramid, capped at the top by the key seasonal topics (*kidai*) of the classical tradition—the cherry blossoms (spring), the cuckoo (summer), the moon (autumn), and the snow (winter)—which remained the most popular topics even for early Edo *haikai* poets. Spreading out from this narrow peak were the other seasonal topics derived from classical poetry. Occupying the bottom and the widest area were the *kigo*, which literally numbered in the thousands by Bashō's day, used by *haikai* poets. In contrast to the seasonal topics at the peak, which were highly conventional and conceptual, those that formed the base were drawn from and directly reflected contemporary life. Unlike the elegant diction at the top of the pyramid, the new, ever-expanding words at the base were earthy, sometimes vulgar, and drawn from a variety of "tongues," particularly those of popular Edo culture and society.

Bashō's place in *haikai* history can be defined as an attempt to tread the "narrow road" between the complex and rigidly defined aesthetic order centered on traditional seasonal topics and a strongly antitraditional movement that sought to break out and explore new topics, subject matter, and poetic language. As the frog poem suggests, Bashō draws on the classical tradition not in order to return to it but to provide it with new life. Indeed, for those aware of the cluster of associations that have accumulated around the seasonal words, the beauty of Bashō's poetry often lies, as it does in the frog poem, in the subtle and ironic tension between the traditional associations and the new presentation.

It has often been noted that the effect of the frog poem derives from the intersection of the momentary and the eternal, of movement and stillness. The two parts of the poem, divided by the cutting word, interpenetrate, the sound of the frog accentuating the stillness of the ancient pond and the quiet atmosphere highlighting the momentary. A similar effect can be found in the following poem in *The Narrow Road to the Deep North*.

shizukasa ya	How still it is!
iwa ni shimiiru	Into the rock it pierces—
semi no koe	The cicada shrill. (1689)

In this summer poem, the cries of the cicada, which seem to sink into the surrounding rocks, deepen the profound feeling of silence. According to one modern commentator, the spirit of the speaker becomes one with the voice of the cicada and penetrates the rocks, arriving at a deep, inner silence.[3] In a number of *hokku* written by Bashō at this time, a small, vulnerable, or fragile creature—a cicada, a frog, a cricket, etc.—is cast against a temporally or spatially unbounded setting, creating a feeling of "loneliness" (*sabishisa*), a poignant and tender mood that is savored and appreciated for the inner peace and quiet communion it brings with nature.[4]

Shikō, one of Bashō's foremost disciples, once noted that "loneliness and humor are the essential style of *haikai*." "Humor is the name of *haikai*, and loneliness the essence of its poetry" (*Zokugoron*). Bashō referred to this unique combination as *sabi*, which is to be distinguished from *sabishisa* ("loneliness"), a medieval poetic and aesthetic ideal that represents only part of *sabi*. Kyorai, another of Bashō's prominent disciples, reminds us of the distinction between the two: "*Sabi* is the complexion of a verse. It does not mean a tranquil and lonely verse. *Sabi* exists in both lively and quiet verses" (*Kyoraishō*). As the word *haikai*, which literally means "comic," suggests, *haikai* was originally comic verse. In early Edo *haikai*, the comic element derived almost entirely from the parody of classical poetry (*waka* and orthodox linked verse), from the playful destruction of the aesthetic world created by classical tradition. Many of Bashō's earlier poems are in fact amusing and clever displays of wit that make light of the conventions of classical poetry. However, Matsuo Bashō's mature poetry, which begins from the period of the frog poem, transformed *haikai* into a serious form that embraced larger human and worldly concerns even as it retained its comic roots. The *haikai*, or comic, element in Bashō's mature poems usually derives from a sense of "newness" (*atarashimi*) or the unexpected, which brings a smile rather than the laughter typical of earlier *haikai*. In the frog poem, it is the unexpected, sudden plop of the frog that provides the comic overtone.[5] The solemn opening line, "An ancient pond—" (*furuike ya*), however, tempers and internalizes this comic aspect, making it part of a highly meditative poem. This ironical movement or tension, which is both serious and light, profound and minor, is *sabi*, a hallmark of Bashō's mature style.

Bashō and his disciples speak broadly of two fundamental kinds of *hokku*: the "single-topic" (*ichimotsu shitate*) *hokku* and the "combination" (*toriawase*) *hokku*. The "single-topic" *hokku* treats only one subject, as in the following examples by Bashō.

kegoromo ni	In fur robes,
tsutsumite nukushi	They are warmly wrapped—
kamo no ashi	The feet of the wild duck. (1693)

bii to naku	Crying "Bee—,"
shirigoe kanashi	The sadness of the trailing voice.
yoru no shika	A deer at night. (1694)

Both poems describe a single topic, the feet of a wild duck and the voice of the deer, albeit in a surprising and fresh manner.

The "combination" (*toriawase*), by contrast, combines two or more different images into one *hokku*. Bashō's disciples further divided the "combination" into two types: those "outside the circumference," which bring together two (and sometimes more) images that traditionally have not been found together, and those "inside the circumference," which combine images that have been associated with each other in the classical tradition. Bashō once said that "combinations that emerge from within the circumference are rarely superior, and all of them are old-fashioned" (*Udanohōshi*). As we have seen, in classical poetry the frog was usually combined with fresh water and the yellow rose (*yamabuki*) to form an elegant and bright image. Bashō's poem effectively goes outside that circumference, but had Bashō used "A yellow rose—" (*Yamabuki ya*) instead of "An ancient pond—," as one of his disciples suggested, he would have stayed within the circumference.

Sometimes a "combination" of distant, extracircumference images is held together by an intermediary image, as in the following poem by Bashō.

aoyagi no	Branches of the willow
doro ni shidaruru	Drooping down into the mud—
shiohi kana	The tide is out. (*Sumidawara*, 1694)

The gap between the two elements of the "combination," the "willow" (*aoyagi*) and "low tide" (*shiohi*), two classical images never associated in the poetic tradition, is bridged by the earthy, nonclassical image of "mud" (*doro*). The *haikai*, or comic, element derives from the vernal, feminine image of the elegant willow, admired for its gracefully drooping branches, being unexpectedly soiled by the mud on the bay bottom.

Bashō's distant "combinations" are closely associated with the "fragrant links" (*nioi-zuke*) that he regarded as an aesthetic and literary ideal in *haikai* linked verse. The following example is from a thirty-six-link verse sequence in *Sarumino* (*The Monkey's Raincoat*, 1691).

sō yaya samuku	A priest returning to a	
tera ni kaeru ka	Temple as he grows cold?	(Bonchō)

saruhiki no	A monkey trainer,	
saru to yo o furu	Passing through life with a monkey—	
aki no tsuki	The moon of autumn.	(Bashō)

In the first verse, a priest has come back from a chilly day of begging for alms, and in the second verse a monkey trainer, fated to pass his days with a monkey, is juxtaposed to an autumn moon, an image of loneliness. The two scenes are completely unrelated to each other on both the referential and rhetorical levels, yet they are linked by a common mood, by the solitary and humble sadness of two individuals who stand outside the warm embrace of society. The second verse (by Bashō) probes the chilly atmosphere and loneliness of the previous verse (by Bonchō) even as it stands at a distance. To use *haikai* terminology, the new verse "lets go" (*tsukihanasu*) of the previous verse even as it catches its "fragrance" (*nioi*).

The same kind of "fragrant" link can be found within the confines of a single *hokku*, as in the following verse by Bashō.

kiku no ka ya	Chrysanthemum scent—	
Nara ni wa furuki	In old Nara the ancient	
hotoketachi	Statues of Buddha.	(1694)

The chrysanthemum, which blooms amidst the bright colors and leaves of autumn, possesses an old-fashioned but refined fragrance. The dignified and elegant statues of the Buddha that fill the temples in the old capital of Nara have no overt connection to the scent of chrysanthemums—the statues are not surrounded by flowers—yet the overtones of the two parts overlap: both possess an antique, elegant atmosphere that is at once familiar.

The "distant combination" can take the form of a question and an answer, one of the formats from which Japanese linked verse first arose. The following poem was written shortly after Bashō fell ill on a journey.

kono aki wa	Why have I aged
nande toshi yoru	This autumn?
kumo ni tori	A bird in the clouds.

(1694)

According to one of Bashō's disciples, the speaker, hampered by the vicissitudes of old age, looks enviously at the bird in the floating clouds, symbolic of eternal travel. The bird in the clouds also reflects the speaker's loneliness. Whatever connection one finally decides to draw, the reader must leap from one mode or state to another (in this instance, from a subjective, lyrical statement to an objective description).

The "combinations" found in Bashō's *hokku* do not usually employ simile or metaphor proper, in which a direct transference is made between one image and another. Instead, Bashō relies on selective juxtaposition, in which the connections are only suggested. The *hokku* usually juxtaposes either two antithetical items or two similar elements. In either case, the combination is usually unexpected and "new"—that is to say, it works against traditional associations, shedding new light on both sides of the "combination" and often joining a classical topic with a nonclassical image or phrase.

The notion of "fragrance" (*nioi*) also applies to the relationship between Bashō's prose and the embedded poetry. Like the two parts of the *hokku*, the poem and the surrounding prose often highlight each other even as they can be read and appreciated independently. The linking by "fragrance," or overlapping overtones, also occurs between poetry and painting. Instead of the poem simply reflecting the content of the painting or sketch on which it appears, we often find the two juxtaposed, creating a montage effect, in which the poetry and the painting are joined only by "fragrance."

The *toriawase* (combination) is usually made possible by the "cutting word" (*kireji*), one of the formal requirements of the *hokku*, which severs the semantic, grammatical, or rhythmic flow of the poem. The "cutting word" frequently takes the form of the exclamatory particle *ya* at the end of the first or second line or the exclamatory particle *kana* at the end of the poem.[6] According to Bashō, any of the seventeen syllables of the *hokku* can function as a "cutting word" as long as it "severs" the poem. In the frog poem, the *ya* (translated by a dash) at the end of the first line splits the poem into two parts, causing the two halves to reverberate against each other. In typical Bashō fashion, the "cutting word" sets up an opposition or parallel between a visual image and an auditory sensation.

The "cutting word," like the seasonal word, vastly increases the complexity and power of the seventeen-syllable *hokku*, which is commonly recognized as the shortest poetic form in world literature. The cutting word, however, can only be effective if the recipient makes it so. In linked verse, the *hokku*, or opening verse, was followed by a second verse that drew on or emerged out of the overtones of the first verse. In the independent *hokku* (that is, the haiku), the reader must perform the same task in his or her imagination. To "cut" a verse is to entrust the final meaning to the reader, to allow the audience to participate actively, an aesthetic process similar to the cadenza in pre-Romantic music, in which the composer leaves part of the musical notation blank for the performer. It is no accident that Matsuo Bashō once said, "those verses that reveal 70 or 80 percent of the subject are good. Those that reveal 50 to 60 percent, we never tire of."

Many of the literary characteristics of Bashō's *hokku* are also to be found in his literary travel journals, where much of his best poetry appears. In addition to hundreds of *haibun* (poetic prose) vignettes and essays, Bashō wrote a series of more extended works (all available in English translation), *Nozarashi kikō* (*Record of a Weather-Exposed Skeleton*), *Kashima mōde* (*A Visit to Kashima Shrine*), *Oi no kobumi* (*Record of a Travel-Worn Satchel*), *Sarashina kikō* (*A Visit to Sarashina Village*), *Oku no hosomichi* (*The Narrow Road to the Deep North*), and *Saga nikki* (*The Saga Diary*), all of which are based on journeys to various parts of Japan. Most of these journeys, particularly the one that led to *The Narrow Road to the Deep North*, Bashō's masterpiece, involve a search for or visit to *utamakura*, famous places in Japanese poetry.

Like seasonal words, *utamakura* ("poetic places") were aesthetic clusters, which, as a result of their appearance in famous poems, possessed rich overtones. When used in a poem (or, as Bashō often did, in prose), the established associations radiated out from the *hokku*, providing depth to the seventeen-syllable verse. From as early as the classical period, *utamakura* became popular topics for classical poetry, and like seasonal topics, they assumed fixed associations that the *waka* poet was required to employ. Relying on poetry handbooks, classical poets could easily write about places that they had never seen, just as they composed about aspects of nature that they had never encountered. Bashō broke from this tradition, and in a manner that deliberately recalled certain poet-priests of the classical and medieval past—Nōin, Saigyō, and Sōgi—he journeyed to numerous *utamakura*, where the present met, sometimes in ironic and violent disjunction, with the literary past. If, for most classical poets, the *utamakura* represented a beauty that transcended time and place, Bashō's travels brought him face to face with the impermanence of all things. This tension between the unchanging and the changing, between literary tradition and intense personal experience, and between classical diction and the contemporary language lies at the heart of both Bashō's prose and poetry.

The following is from *Record of a Weather-Exposed Skeleton.*

akikaze ya	The autumn wind!
yabu mo hatake mo	Nothing but thicket and fields
Fuwa no seki	At Fuwa Barrier.

Fuwa Barrier (in present-day Gifu prefecture), originally one of the three main checkpoints in Japan, was abandoned in the late eighth century, but it continued to exist in literature as an *utamakura*, immortalized by the following poem in *Shinkokinshū* by Fujiwara no Yoshitsune.

hito sumanu	The shingled eaves
Fuwa no sekiya no	Of the guard post at Fuwa,
itabisashi	Where no one lives,
arenishi nochi wa	Have collapsed, leaving only
tada aki no kaze	The winds of autumn.

(Msc. 2, no. 1599)

Coming upon the guard post at Fuwa (which literally means "Unbreakable"), the speaker in Bashō's poem finds that even the building has disappeared, leaving only thickets and open fields swept by autumn winds. The *hokku* follows the "poetic essence" (*hon'i*) of Fuwa Barrier (the pathos of decay) as well as that of the "autumn wind" (loneliness). But these classical associations, which are embodied in Yoshitsune's *waka*, are re-presented in a new and striking manner, using nonclassical diction: "nothing but thickets and fields," a phrase that subtly contrasts the present with the poetic past.

Bashō repeatedly told his disciples that they "should awaken to the high and return to the low" (*takaku kokoro o satorite, zoku ni kaerubeshi*). Matsunaga Teitoku, the founder of Edo *haikai*, defined *haikai* as linked verse with *haigon*, vocabulary that classical poetry had excluded as being vulgar and "low" (*zoku*). The use of *haigon* (literally "*haikai* words") transformed *haikai* into a highly popular form that could be enjoyed by all classes. At the same time, however, *haikai*'s poetic "liberation," particularly the free use of *haigon*, threatened the literary life of *haikai*, making it more a form of amusement than a serious literary genre. Bashō was the first major poet to bring a heightened spiritual and literary awareness to *haikai*, to infuse the "high" (*ga*) into the "low" (*zoku*) of *haikai*, or rather, to seek the high in the low, a pursuit that ultimately transformed the *hokku* into a powerful poetic form. As the frog poem suggests, Bashō sought to find the new in the old, the high in the low, the profound in the trivial, the serious in the comic.

"Awakening to the high" also meant exploring and sharing in the spirit of the "ancients," the superior poets of the past. The long and difficult journeys to *utamakura* were a means of communing with the spirits of the great poets of the past, of sharing in their poetic experience. For Bashō, the great figures were Li Bo, Hanshan, Du Fu, and Bo Zhuyi in the Chinese tradition and Saigyō, Sōgi, Rikyū, and Sesshū in the Japanese tradition—most of whom, significantly, had been recluse poets or artists. The work of these "ancients" was bound together, in Bashō's mind, by a common literary spirit, in which the best of *haikai* should share. It was not enough, however, simply to imitate and borrow from the "ancients," whose "high" (*ga*) art—particularly Chinese poetry, *waka*, and *renga*—had become, by Bashō's day, aristocratic, refined, and exclusive. One must also—and here Bashō parts company with his medieval predecessors—return to the "low" (*zoku*), to the popular, to everyday life, to immediate personal experience, and to the language and "tongues" around us, all of which continue to change from day to day. It was only by "returning to the low" that one could create poetry with "newness" and lightness, which were critical to the life of *haikai*. For Bashō, it was ultimately the harshness of travel on foot, which combined the pursuit of *utamakura* with the vicissitudes of everyday life, that became the quintessential means of "awakening to the high and returning to the low" and that led to much of his finest poetry.

Notes

1. Futami, Bashō's destination and a place known for clams, is also a homonym for "shell" (*futa*) and "body" (*mi*).
2. The phrase "the frogs cry" (*kawazu naku*) functions as an epithet (*makurakotoba*) for Ide (in the present-day Kyoto prefecture), a place famous for its frogs.
3. Ogata Tsutomu, in Ogata Tsutomu, ed., *Haiku no kaishaku to kanshō jiten* (Obunsha, 1979), 82.

4. Another famous example is:

shizukasa ya	How quiet it is!
e kakaru kabe no	On a wall, where a picture hangs,
kirigirisu	A cricket. (Genroku 4, 1691)

5. Another example of the unexpected is:

hototogisu	A cuckoo
kieyuku kata ya	Fading into the distance—
shima hitotsu	An island.

The poet, standing on the shores of Suma Bay, hears the sound of a *hototogisu* (cuckoo), and as he watches it fade into the distance, it suddenly becomes a small island, presumably Awajishima, a small island across from Suma. In contrast to the first two lines, which have the lyricism of *waka*, the last line possesses the element of *haikai* in the unexpected transfer between an aural and a visual image.

6. The eighteen standard *kireji* established by Muromachi *renga* masters and generally followed by Edo *haikai* poets include four imperative *verb* endings, four auxiliary verbs, and one speculative adverb.

21(B)

MATSUO BASHŌ

Donald Keene

BASHŌ IS THE best-known Japanese poet not only in his own country but throughout the world. About a thousand of his haiku survive, a relatively scant output for someone who spent most of his life as a haiku poet; a professional Japanese haiku poet today would not find it difficult to turn out that many poems in a single year. Haiku, at first glance, seems extremely easy to compose—all one has to do is arrange a bare seventeen syllables into three lines of five, seven, and five syllables. The ease of composition attracts many Japanese today. It is estimated that a million amateurs belong to haiku groups, each headed by a recognized master. They regularly meet, and the haiku they compose are published in the group's magazine. Yet of the many tens of thousands of haiku composed by such groups each year, probably not more than a handful will be remembered the following year. It is tempting to say that composing a successful haiku, far from being easy, is unusually difficult. Not a word—not even a syllable—can be wasted, and, while obeying certain conventions, it must seem refreshingly new.

The restriction on the number of syllables tends to make a haiku difficult to understand, because words necessary for ready comprehension have been omitted. The poet, whatever he wishes to communicate, must depend on the reader to intuit and complete what he has not overtly expressed. Sometimes a haiku is prefaced by a title or by a brief statement of the circumstances of the composition that makes it easier to comprehend. For example, the travel diary *Exposed in the Fields* (*Nozarashi Kikō*), written by Bashō in 1684, contains this haiku:

te ni toraba kien	Taken in my hand it would melt
namida zo atsuki	My tears are so hot—
aki ni shimo	This autumnal frost.

One notes first of all that the initial line is in eight instead of the pre-scribed five syllables. Bashō rarely violated the syllable count unless something in a poem was of such importance to him that he simply had to break the rules. This haiku, then, probably had a special meaning for Bashō. But why, we may wonder, should he have taken frost into his hand, and why did it make him weep? Without help from the poet, the reader is likely to be puzzled, though he may be moved even by the literal sense of the words—the poet takes in his hand a very easily perished substance, and its disappearance makes him weep. But if one knows the circum-stances that inspired Bashō to write the haiku, it becomes far more affect-ing. Just before he wrote the haiku in his diary, Bashō related that he had returned to his home in Iga after spending ten years in Edo: "At the begin-ning of the ninth month I returned to my old home. The day lilies in the northern hall had been withered by the frost, and there was no trace of them now. My brother's hair was white at the temples and his brow was wrinkled. 'We are still alive,' he said. 'Pay your respects to Mother's white hairs!'"

It is clear from this passage that the "autumnal frost" was a lock of the white hair of Bashō's mother, who had died the previous year. That is why his tears were so hot. But why did he mention the day lilies that had with-ered in the northern hall? Commentators inform us that it was customary for an aged mother to live in the northern wing of a house, and that such women, relieved of household duties, frequently cultivated plants such as day lilies. Bashō's reference to the day lilies also alluded to Chinese poems that mentioned them in the same connection. Such an allusion was not an affectation; Bashō, by linking his grief to the grief expressed by poets in China on losing their mother, deepened his own experience.

If one is unfamiliar with the Chinese and Japanese writings to which Bashō at times alluded, some haiku will seem obscure, but the use of allu-sions was one way of surmounting the limitations of seventeen syllables. A few key words, borrowed from a poem of the past, could expand a haiku by reference to the content of a predecessor's work. It is possible to enjoy even such haiku without knowledge of the allusions, but if they are understood we can appreciate the additional richness that has been obtained.

Bashō's haiku may be ambiguous even when the surface presents no apparent problem of interpretation. His most famous haiku seems absolutely clear:

furuike ya	The old pond
kawazu tobikomu	A frog jumps in
mizu no oto	The sound of water.

Masaoka Shiki (1867–1902), the celebrated poet and critic of haiku, insisted that "the meaning of the haiku about the old pond is nothing more than what appears on the surface; there is no other meaning." Shiki's preferred stance when composing haiku was to describe as objectively as possible what he observed or felt without borrowing overtones from the literature of the past. This accounts for his belief that Bashō's haiku on the frog, a poem he admired, contained no more than what appears on the surface. But this haiku lends itself to other interpretations. The first line, for example, is perfectly clear but if carefully considered is rather puzzling. Why should Bashō have felt it necessary to stipulate that the pond was old? Is not every pond old? Why should he have wasted two precious syllables on the adjective *furu* ("old")? It may be because Bashō wanted to emphasize the unchanging nature of the pond, which gives the haiku its quiet, horizontal base. Suddenly a frog jumps into the pond, a vertical intersection of the unchanging by the momentary, marked by the splash of the water that defines both. Is that what Bashō actually had in mind? If so, did he hope that we would share with him the epiphany brought on by the sound of the water? Shiki declared that "the special feature of this haiku is that it hides nothing, does not use the slightest artifice, has not one word that is broken or twisted." We may disagree.

Kagami Shikō, one of Bashō's disciples, related how Bashō happened to compose this haiku: "It was just the kind of day when one most regrets the passing of spring. The sound of frogs leaping into the water could frequently be heard, and the Master, moved by the remarkable beauty of the scene, wrote the second and third lines of a haiku describing it. . . . Kikaku, who was with him, suggested as a first line 'The yellow roses,' but the Master settled on 'The old pond.'" If this account is to be trusted, not one but many frogs jumped in, repeated violations of the peacefulness of the setting. We will never know Bashō's intention, but such ambiguity is part of the appeal of his poetry.

A line in a haiku by Bashō can be often be interpreted in different ways:

kareeda ni	On the withered branch
karasu no tomarikeri	A crow has alighted—
aki no kure	Nightfall in autumn.

Does the last line mean "nightfall in autumn" or "the last [days] of autumn"? Either or both are possible. The crow that has alighted on the withered branch is the "now" of the poem, and its dark presence is equated with the coming of night in autumn. But surely it is not a twilight in early or mid-autumn, when the bright red leaves always associated with this season in Japanese poetry were at their height. The season is the end of autumn, when the red leaves have scattered, leaving bare branches. The scene is in monochrome: a black crow has perched on a whitened branch at the time of day and in the season of year when colors disappear. The long middle line suggests that Bashō suddenly realized that the moment the crow alighted on the withered branch a day and a season had ended.

Even in translation many of Bashō's haiku can be enjoyed, but the loss of the original sounds deprives the reader of a part of the meaning. The sounds of the previous haiku, especially the *k-r* consonants in the words *kareeda*, *karasu*, and *kure*, add to the darkness of the mood.

A celebrated haiku makes use of the special, mournful sound of the vowel *o*, rather in the manner of Edgar Allen Poe:

natsukusa ya	The summer grasses—
tsuwamonodomo ga	For many brave warriors
yume no ato	The aftermath of dreams.

Here the repeated *o* sounds (six of the seventeen syllables) create a solemnity that underlines the sadness of the death of brave warriors.[1] Another haiku describes silence in sound:

shizukesa ya	How still it is!
iwa ni shimiiru	Stinging into the stones,
semi no koe	The locusts' trill.

Only through sound can silence be known. The stillness of the mountains is interrupted by the prolonged din of the cicadas, but when they stop, the silence is overpowering. In this haiku, the vowel *i* occurs seven times out of seventeen in the poem. The *i* is the sound of the cicadas.

Four stages of this haiku have been preserved. They suggest Bashō's dissatisfaction even with versions that other poets would be delighted to have composed.[2] The first was:

yamadera ya	Mountain temple—
ishi ni shimitsuku	Seeping into the stones
semi no koe	Cicada voices.

Yamadera, the popular name of the Risshakuji, is a temple in Yamagata that Bashō visited, but *yamadera* otherwise means "mountain temple," the scene of the haiku. The term *shimitsuku* is used to describe a liquid seeping into another substance. The haiku says that the cries of the cicada permeate the stones. The second version is stronger:

sabishisa ya	What loneliness—
iwa ni shimikomu	Penetrating the rocks
semi no koe	Cicada voices.

Loneliness was akin to the medieval concept of *sabi*. It was not necessarily disagreeable; the Buddhist monk found peace in solitude. The verb *shimikomu* is more intense than *shimitsuku*, penetrating rather seeping into the boulders. The rocks are also more impressive than the stones of the first version. But Bashō was still not satisfied. The third version was:

sabishisa no	Into the loneliness
iwa ni shimikomu	Of the rocks penetrate
semi no koe	Cicada voices.

Here the loneliness is not the general atmosphere of the landscape but a condition fostered by the rocks. Bashō's fourth and final version reads:

shizukesa ya	How still it is!
iwa ni shimiiru	Into the rocks stab
semi no koe	Cicada voices.

The substitution of *shizukesa ya* for *sabishisa ya* was crucial. Loneliness was a conventional topic of poetry, but mentioning silence, despite the din of the cicadas, was a masterstroke. The verb *shimiiru* is the strongest of all. It suggests that the cries of the cicada do not merely penetrate the rocks but stab deep into them.

Bashō's haiku include various examples of synesthesia, the transference of an impression from one sense to another:

Kiku no ka ya	Chrysanthemum scent—
Nara ni wa furuki	And in Nara all the old
hotoke tachi	Statues of Buddha.

The musty scent of chrysanthemums is equated with the dusty, peeling statues in the old temples but also with Nara, a city living in its past. Scent and sight are interchanged. Bashō composed this haiku at the time of the chrysanthemum festival in the ninth month. It thus evokes both the time of composition and the musty past.

The senses of sight and hearing are joined in another haiku:

Umi kurete	The sea darkens—
kamo no koe	The voices of the seagulls
honoka ni shiroshi	Are faintly white.

Here, the cries of the seagulls against the black sky seem like flashes of light.

To create such poems was not easy, even for Bashō. In his *Sarashina Diary*, he related how, as he lay one night in his room at an inn, he attempted to beat into shape the poetic materials he had garnered during the day, groaning and knocking his head in the effort. A priest, imagining that Bashō was suffering from a fit of depression, tried to comfort him with stories about the miracles of Amida Buddha, who had vowed to save all men, but he only succeeded in blocking Bashō's flow of inspiration. Groaning and knocking probably accompanied the creation of many of his haiku. The successive revisions he made to the wording and even the underlying meaning of a haiku enable us to trace his efforts to reach the exact center of the perception he described.

Not all of Bashō's haiku were polished and revised. If, during his travels, he was a guest at someone's house or at a temple, he felt obliged to compose a haiku of salutation and thanks, rather like signing a guest book. Such haiku were dashed off easily and seldom revised, but they too have charm. At the house of a rich man, his host in Obanasawa, Bashō wrote:

suzushisa wo	Making the coolness
wa ga yado ni shite	My abode, here I lie
nemaru nari	Completely at ease.

Bashō mentioned coolness as a compliment to a host whose house was pleasantly cool in the summer. He and the host had not previously met, but he felt completely at home, as he conveyed by using the word *nemaru*, from the local dialect, meaning to rest comfortably. The use of this word may have indicated his hope he might converse with the host as intimately as someone who spoke the same dialect.

During his *Oku no Hosomichi* (*The Narrow Road to Oku*) journey, Bashō composed poems at almost every place he stopped, but not at Matsushima, the place he most wanted to see. He related at the outset, while making preparations for travel: "To strengthen my legs for the journey I had moxa burned on my shins. By then I could think of nothing but the moon at Matsushima." On arrival, however, Bashō seems to have been stunned into silence by its beauty. This was not his only such experience. During his travels he passed Fuji many times, but his only haiku on the mountain was:

kiri shigure	Fog and rain showers:
Fuji wo minu hi zo	A day one can't see Fuji
omoshiroki	Is interesting.

Although Bashō did not compose a haiku at Matsushima, his prose description is a highlight of the diary:

No matter how often it has been said, it is nonetheless true that the scenery of Matsushima is the finest in Japan, in no way inferior to Tung-ting or the West Lake in China. The sea flows in from the southeast forming a bay seven miles across, and the incoming tide surges in massively, just as in Zhe-zhiang. There are countless islands. Some rise up and point at the sky; the low-lying ones crawl into the waves. There are islands piled double or even stacked three high. To the left the islands stand apart; to the right they are linked together. Some look as if they carried little islands on their backs, others as if they held the islands in their arms, evoking a mother's love of her children. The green of the pines is of a wonderful darkness, and their branches are constantly bent by winds from the sea, so that their crookedness seems to belong to the nature of the trees. . . . What man could capture in a painting or a poem the wonder of this masterpiece of nature?

Somewhat later in the journey, Bashō visited Kisagata, a place of great scenic beauty where, recalling Matsushima, a great number of islands were scattered in the sea. Here he composed this haiku:

Kisagata ya	Kisagata—
ame ni Seishi ga	Seishi sleeping in the rain,
nebu no hana	Mimosa blossoms.

This haiku, in the manner of older schools, has a pun at its core. The word *nebu* (or *nemu*) means "to sleep" and is used in this sense with what precedes—Seishi is sleeping. But its homonym means "mimosa," and that goes with what follows—mimosa blossoms. The pun was not intended to be humorous but to add to the complexity. Bashō had been dazzled at Matsushima by its unclouded beauty. Now he is at Kisagata. It is an equally lovely place, but seen in the rain it is somehow melancholy. The sight recalls Seishi (Xi Shi), a pensive Chinese lady who was famous for her seductive frowns. Mimosa, a delicate summer flower, recalls the delicate Seishi.

Some haiku are openly funny:

natsugoromo	My summer clothes—
imada shirami wo	I still haven't quite finished
toritsukusazu	Picking out the lice.

There are probably no hidden meanings behind this haiku!

Toward the end of his life, Bashō insisted on the importance of "lightness" (*karumi*). The term seems to have meant simplicity, as opposed to the complexity of the haiku like the one about Seishi. His last few haiku, composed shortly before his death, are plainly expressed and almost unbearably moving.

kono michi wa	Along this road
yuku hito nashi ni	There are no travelers—
aki no kure	Nightfall in autumn.

kono aki wa	This autumn
nan de toshi yoru	Why do I feel so old?
kumo no tori	A bird in the clouds.
aki fukaki	Autumn has deepened:
tonari wa nani wo	I wonder what the man next door
suru hito zo	Does for a living.
tabi ni yande	Stricken on a journey
yume wa kareno wo	My dreams go wandering about
kakemeguru	Desolate fields.

These haiku are almost entirely in the colloquial language. Bashō, at the very end of his life, seems to have rejected the literary language of his earlier poems. These are so direct and unadorned as to be almost painfully beautiful.

Bashō is celebrated not only for his haiku but for his poetic prose. Indeed, the fifth of his travel diaries, *Oku no hosomichi* (*The Narrow Road to Oku*), is probably the most widely read work of Japanese classical literature, although all five diaries rank as masterpieces of "diary literature," a peculiarly Japanese genre. In no other country has the diary played so important a part, from the first examples in the ninth century to the present. In Bashō's third travel diary, *Oi no Kobumi* (*Manuscript in My Knapsack*), written in about 1690, he acknowledged his debt to his predecessors, the diary writers of the past:

Nobody has succeeded in making any improvements in travel diaries since Ki no Tsurayuki, Chōmei, and the nun Abutsu wielded their brushes to describe their emotions to the full; the rest have merely imitated. How much less likely it is that anyone of my shallow knowledge and inadequate talent could do better. Of course, anyone can write in a diary, "On that day it rained . . . it cleared in the afternoon . . . there is a pine at that place . . . the such-and-such river flows through this place," and the like, but unless a sight is truly remarkable one shouldn't mention it at all. Nevertheless, the scenery of different places lingers in my mind, and even my unpleasant experiences at huts in the mountains and fields can become subjects of conversation or material for poetry. With this in mind I have scribbled down, without any semblance of order, the unforgettable moments of the journey, and gathered them together in one work. Let the reader listen without paying too much attention, as to the ramblings of a drunkard or the mutterings of a man in his sleep.

Bashō's first four travel diaries, though definitely not the ramblings of a drunkard, may seem unfinished despite their beauty, because the prose and the haiku have not been well blended. Bashō had yet to acquire his mastery of the art of combining in a seamless manner events of a journey with the haiku composed on the way. *The Narrow Road to Oku*, his account of a journey to the northern provinces in 1689, took him four years to write, even though in a modern edition it runs to perhaps twenty-five pages. Undoubtedly Bashō revised the text many times before he was willing to let it out of his hands.

The work opens with a celebrated passage:

The months and days are the travelers of eternity. The years that come and go are also voyagers. Those who float away their lives on ships or who grow old leading horses are forever journeying, and their homes are wherever their travels take them. Many of the men of old died on the road, and I too for years past have been stirred by the sight of a solitary cloud drifting with the wind to ceaseless thoughts of roaming.

The opening words were adapted from a work by Li Bo, but nobody considered this plagiarism. On the contrary, such borrowing was not only tolerated but deemed essential; a literary work without allusions seemed lightweight. But *The Narrow Road to Oku* is not a pastiche assembled from the writings of the great poets of the past; it is the record of an actual journey, and people today still follow Bashō's footsteps along his course, though the passage of three hundred years has obliterated or coarsened most of the sights he described.

The haiku in *The Narrow Road to Oku* include some of his most famous. The first, written just before he started on his journey, is the most difficult to understand without a commentary:

kusa no to mo	Even a thatched hut
sumikawaru yo zo	May change with the dweller
hina no ie	Into a doll's house.

This translation is approximate. The background of the haiku was apparently Bashō's sale of his house to a man with small daughters. At the time of the annual Feast of Peach Blossoms, dolls would be displayed in the house now that girls lived there, but Bashō was a bachelor and as long as he had lived in the house dolls had never been displayed. The thatched hut will change into a doll's house.

The next poem, the first of the journey, is much easier:

yuku haru ya	Spring is passing by!
tori naki uo no	Birds are weeping and the eyes
me wa namida	Of fish fill with tears.

Grief over the passage of spring was, of course, often expressed in poetry. Bashō could not have been wholly serious in declaring that there are tears in the eyes of fish, though he may have felt such empathy for other creatures that he felt they shared his grief. The first line of this haiku would be echoed in the last line of the final haiku of the journey, *yuku aki zo* ("autumn is passing by").

The Narrow Road to Oku consists of prose passages describing places Bashō visited, together with poems inspired by each. Because most of Bashō's journey took place during the summer, the haiku naturally have summer as their season, though summer haiku had been composed relatively seldom. A curious result of the popularity of *The Narrow Road of Oku* is that today more summer haiku are composed than for any other season.

The haiku, good at the beginning of this diary, get even better as the journey proceeds. The prose is marvelous from the start. Perhaps the most affecting section of the entire diary occurs about halfway through. Bashō visits a monument that survives from the eighth century. The text inscribed on the stone relates the circumstances of the building and repairing of a castle that had stood nearby. It is not in the least of literary interest, but it moves Bashō profoundly:

Many are the names that have been preserved for us in poetry from ancient times, but mountains crumble and rivers disappear, new roads replace the old, stones are buried and vanish in the earth, trees grow old and are replaced by saplings. Time passes and the world changes. The remains of the past are shrouded in uncertainty. And yet, here before my eyes was a monument that none would deny had lasted a thousand years. I felt as if I were looking into the minds of the men of old. "This," I thought, "is one of the pleasures of travel and of living to be old." I forgot the weariness of my journey and was moved to tears of joy.

Wherever Bashō went on his travels, he searched for places mentioned in the poetry of the past. Often nothing remained, but this monument was proof that even if mountains crumble and rivers dry up, written words will survive. Later on in the journey, at Hiraizumi, he recalled lines by Du Fu that insist that nature is hardier than any work of man:

It was at Palace-on-the-Heights that Yoshitsune and his picked retainers fortified themselves, but his glory turned in a moment into this wilderness of grass. "Countries may fall, but their rivers and mountains remain; when spring comes to the ruined castle, the grass is green again." These lines went through my head as I sat on the ground, my bamboo hat spread under me. There I sat weeping, unaware of the passage of time /

natsukusa ya	The summer grasses
tsuwamonodomo ga	For many brave soldiers
yume ni ato	The aftermath of dreams

Bashō was moved to tears by Tu Fu's poem, but perhaps more important was his earlier discovery that the written word lasts even longer than mountains and rivers.

The Narrow Road to Oku has inspired many poets. Bashō was acclaimed by his successors as the "saint of haiku," and he was revered not only for his haiku and his diaries but as a man of great goodness who lived in near poverty and inspired the love of many disciples. It may be imagined what consternation was caused when in 1943 the diary of Sora, Bashō's companion on The Narrow Road to Oku journey, was discovered and published, revealing serious discrepancies between the accounts of Bashō and Sora describing the same sights. Worshippers of Bashō refused to believe he could have told a lie, but Sora's diary is so devoid of literary pretense that one can only suppose it is true.

For example, when the two men arrived at Nikkō, Bashō was so moved by the name of the place (*nikkō* means sunlight) and by its associations with the Tokugawa shoguns who have their mausoleum there that he wrote:

ara tōto	How inspiring,
aoba wakaba ni	On the green leaves, the young leaves
hi ni hikari	The light of the sun.

But Sora's diary stated that it rained on the day that they visited Nikkō. Bashō evidently sacrificed truth to beauty. Again, Bashō described with wonder the marvelous interior of the Konjikidō (Golden Hall) of the Chūsonji, but Sora prosaically related that they could not find anyone to open the hall and therefore had to leave without seeing the famous sculptures.

The believers in the "saint of haiku" in desperation insisted that Sora had either lied or was forgetful. Only after years had passed did they and other scholars decide that *The Narrow Road to Oku* actually was enhanced by Bashō's departures from the facts. This proved that he was more concerned with the artistic effect of the diary than with mere accuracy.

Although Bashō is without doubt the greatest haiku poet, at times he has been criticized. In 1893, Masaoka Shiki, aged twenty-six, wrote a series of short essays on Bashō, which included these remarks: "Let me state at the outset my conclusion: the majority of Bashō's haiku consists of bad verses and doggerel; those that might be termed superior amount to no more than one out of dozens. No, even if one searches for barely acceptable haiku, they are as rare as morning stars." Shiki, about to start a school of haiku on his own, seems to have felt that the best way to establish his credentials as the champion of a new kind of haiku was to attack the reputation of the master. Of course, he hoped that his intemperate comments would startle people, but his real enemy, as he later disclosed, was not Bashō but his numerous followers, whom Shiki blamed for the decline in the vital importance of the haiku. The followers of Bashō showed no awareness of the changes that had occurred in Japan during the past three hundred years, and their incompetent guidance of amateur poets had reduced haiku composition to being nothing more than a means of earning a profitable income. Shiki successfully established his school, and many other schools proliferated, but the reputation of Bashō remained untarnished. His poetry will surely last as long as there are people who can read Japanese.

Notes

1. If the second line were *heitai tachi ga*, an expression of identical meaning, the poem would be destroyed by the unsuitably cheerful sounds.
2. I have tried to make the translations as literal as possible.

22

CHIKAMATSU

Donald Keene

I N THE LATE nineteenth century, when the Japanese first became aware
of the glories of Western literature, they felt impelled to discover a "Japanese Shakespeare." Their choice for this honor was Chikamatsu Monzaemon (1653–1725). Western readers who read translations of Chikamatsu's
plays and hope that they will equal or at least resemble Shakespeare's are
likely to be disappointed; there was only one Shakespeare. The plays of
Chikamatsu, however, not only present a vivid portrayal of a unique age in
Japan but may even seem more modern than Shakespeare's. The characters
in his tragedies, particularly those set in his time, are not about kings and
generals but the common man.

Chikamatsu lived in a country that was virtually sealed off from the rest
of the world. Fear that proselytizing by Western priests might be the pre-
lude to colonization by foreign powers caused the Japanese government in
the seventeenth century to prohibit foreigners from entering the country
under penalty of death—and prohibit Japanese from ever returning if they
left the country. The only exceptions to this decree were some Chinese and
a handful of Dutch traders permitted to engage in commerce at the port of
Nagasaki. Contacts between the Japanese and these foreigners were extremely limited, and whatever books the Dutch brought with them from
Europe were subject to strict censorship for fear that they might contain
Christian doctrine.

Chikamatsu never read a foreign play and knew nothing about the theater outside his country. Because his plays grew out of earlier Japanese drama and were written without foreign influence, their content and manner of presentation naturally differed from plays performed in Europe. Chikamatsu's domestic tragedies, often caused by a lack of money and similar worldly concerns (as opposed to battles over dynastic succession and the like), may surprise us by a modernity not encountered in Western drama for another century or more, but others of his plays may surprise us by a violence or unbridled fantasy that seems to belong to a more primitive theater. But this seeming modernity or primitiveness is misleading and means mainly that Chikamatsu's theater did not follow the same course of development as in Europe.

Another important difference dividing Chikamatsu from European playwrights was that he wrote some of his major works for the puppet theater. The special demands of this theater obliged Chikamatsu at times to write in a manner that weakens their literary value. Scenes of mayhem or supernatural feats, however exciting in a puppet performance, may seem absurdly exaggerated when read in translation. Chikamatsu's history plays abound in larger-than-life actions performed by the characters. In the first act of his most successful play, *The Battles of Coxinga* (1715), occur two moments that would be intolerable if performed realistically by actors. In the first act, the villain Ri Tōten gouges out his left eye. He offers the eye on a ceremonial baton to a Tartar envoy as a pledge of his loyalty to the king of Tartary. Later in that act, the loyal Go Sankei performs a Caesarean operation on the dead empress in order to deliver an heir to the throne. The stylization of puppets makes such scenes not only endurable to the audience but even more moving than the same actions performed by an actor.

The second act of the same play features a battle between Coxinga, the half-Japanese hero, and a tiger. This scene when performed by actors is bound to be funny, because the audience can detect the actor inside the tiger skin, but on the puppet stage a tiger is no less realistic than a human being, and thus the combat can be exciting.

In the third act of *The Battles of Coxinga*, Kinshōjo, the wife of a Chinese general, tells her brother Coxinga, who has asked permission to enter the general's castle, that if his request is granted by her husband, she will drop white powder into a conduit that flows into the Yellow River, but if his request has been rejected, she will color the water with rouge. Shortly afterward, rouge-tinted water flows down to the river. The narrator (a feature of the puppet theater) describes Coxinga's superhuman fury: "His feet rush forward furiously up the rapids of the river. When he reaches the moat at his destination, he leaps across, climbs the inner wall, tramples down wattled fences and lattice railings, and finally arrives at a spring within the garden of the women's apartments."

Coxinga on arriving in the garden learns that the reason the water was red was not due to any admixture of rouge but to the self-inflicted wound in Kinshōjo's breast. She says: "If I begrudge my life and fail to help my parents and my brother, it will be a disgrace to China." She tells her husband, urging him to open the castle gates: "Now that I have stabbed myself, no one will slander you by saying that you acted under your wife's influence."

Such extreme behavior was well suited to puppets, which can leap over walls or slash themselves more easily than actors; the skill of the puppet operators in fact was best displayed in such scenes. Kinshōjo fears that if she fails to help her parents and brother, this will disgrace not only herself but her country. She knows also how demeaning to her husband it would be if people said that he allowed Coxinga to enter the castle because of his wife's intercession. She reveals in her final words to her husband her awareness of a social concern that every member of the audience would have shared: what will people say if we admit Coxinga? The fear of what people may say is a persistent theme of Japanese literature even when a person's elevated status would in a Western drama make him indifferent to the gossip of others. Kinshōjo's gesture may seem excessive to readers of the play, but we know that in performance it deeply moved audiences. The Battles of Coxinga was Chikamatsu's most popular play and has been performed ever since, by actors as well as by puppets.

The appeal of The Battles of Coxinga was first of all the skill of Chikamatsu's writing, particularly in the various conflicts he depicted: between a loyal subject and a traitor in the first act, between Coxinga and a tiger (Coxinga subdues the tiger with help from the god of the Great Shrine of Ise), between Kinshōjo and the Chinese soldiers who wish to keep Coxinga out of the castle, and finally, the fight with the Manchus ending in Coxinga's triumph.

The play also intrigued audiences, cut off from the outside world, with the exotic glimpses it provided of China. The bizarre food offered by Chinese ladies to Coxinga's Japanese mother must have amused audiences but probably also made them feel that simple Japanese food was preferable to the complicated dishes that the Chinese ate.

Needless to say, Chikamatsu's depiction of China was inaccurate in every allusion to Chinese history or customs, down to the defeat of the Manchus by Coxinga's forces, but it provided the pleasures of exoticism and the patriotic feeling that a Japanese (Coxinga was half Japanese and born in Japan) was the equal of a Chinese, even though Japan was a much smaller country.

Chikamatsu's history plays, with the exception of *The Battles of Coxinga*, are seldom performed. They are long, taking as many as ten hours to perform in full, and seldom have unified plots. However, Chikamatsu probably considered these plays to be his most important, and in his day they constituted the major part of a day at the theater. They are also far more numerous than his domestic plays, which were based not on Japanese history but on recent events. However, today the domestic plays are now performed far more often than the history plays and are usually considered to include his masterpieces.

The Love Suicides at Sonezaki (1703), his first domestic play, was so great a success that it restored the fortunes of the theater for which it was written. This play was completed very quickly; the first performance was only a month after the events that inspired it. However, the popularity of this play and others that concluded with the double suicides of the lovers led to a vogue for double suicides by young couples who had been influenced by the plays. The government stepped in and forbade the performance of any plays that contained the words "double suicides" in their titles or that depicted such suicides.

The ban on double suicides led to a revival of the popularity of the history plays, though they now often contained scenes depicting life among the common people as well as the heroics of the warrior class. The invention about this time of puppets operated by three men led to a great refinement in their movements, and the unspectacular domestic plays lost favor with audiences that craved the complexity in the actions of the puppets that were now possible. *The Love Suicides at Sonezaki* was not performed for over two hundred years until its revival in 1953. It is now the most popular play in both the Kabuki and puppet theaters.

In his domestic plays especially, Chikamatsu showed that he was an artist of subtlety and imagination. Unlike his history plays or the classical European dramas, with their kings, princesses, and the like, Chikamatsu's domestic plays have for their heroes low-ranking samurai or shopkeepers whose sweethearts are most often prostitutes. There was in fact a close connection between the plays and the licensed quarter where prostitutes of different ranks catered to customers in surroundings of artistic beauty.

For men of the time, the licensed quarters provided an area of freedom in an otherwise constricted society. The government, which allowed no political freedom, allowed sexual freedom as a way of defusing possible social tension. The merchant, who might be obliged to toady to samurai in his daily life, in the licensed quarter could dally with women of the quarter on an equal footing. The samurai, but not the merchant, was embarrassed to be seen in the "bad quarters," as they were called by the government. The boastful Tahei in *The Love Suicides at Sonezaki* declares: "A customer's a customer, whether he's a samurai or a merchant. The only difference is that one wears a sword and the other doesn't."

The licensed quarters inspired not only the theater but the popular fiction and art of the time. The *ukiyoe* prints had their inception in pictorial evocations of the prostitutes. Though these beautiful women in magnificent robes command attention, most were available to any man who could pay the fee. Numerous handbooks to the licensed quarters rated the prostitutes, both high and low class, according to their beauty and talents.

The licensed quarters, so elegantly pictured in the *ukiyoe*, also had an undeniably sordid aspect. Women were sold to brothels by their desperately poor families and remained there until their contracts expired. They were like serfs, forbidden to leave the quarter. Although they wore splendid clothes, they had no choice but to lie with men even if they found them physically repulsive. It is true that the *tayū*, the highest rank of courtesan, had the privilege of refusing men who displeased them, and even when they accepted a large fee might do nothing more than offer a man a cup of saké, but extremely few women attained this rank, and at any rate the *tayū*'s glory was short lived.

The ideal household of the Tokugawa period, as envisioned by the Confucian philosophers, must have been boring. A man had the duty to his ancestors of perpetuating the family line; a wife was therefore indispensable. Even if he did not love his wife and seldom even spoke to her, he could not easily desert a useful person who not only gave him children but looked after them. A man who yearned for more interesting company than was available at home felt free to divert himself with prostitutes whenever he chose and felt that this behavior was appropriate. Infidelity to one's wife was not counted as a sin, provided the man merely amused himself with prostitutes and did not fall in love. If he violated this unwritten code by falling in love with a prostitute, it was likely to lead to disaster, particularly if he was reluctant to leave his wife. Eventually, he would have to make a choice between the two women, and this was bound to be painful. In *Love Suicides at Amijima*, the wife Osan, realizing that despite all his protests to the contrary her husband Jihei has fallen in love with a prostitute, says with anger: "The year before last we lit the first fire in the *kotatsu* and celebrated by sleeping here together, pillow to pillow. Ever since then—did some demon or snake creep into my breast that night?—for two whole years I've been condemned to keep watch over an empty nest."

Osan loves her husband and misses his love. As an ideal wife, she deserves it, by the standards of the time, and she is ready to give up her savings so that Jihei can buy up the contract of the prostitute he loves. The grateful Jihei, however, realizes that if he redeems the prostitute he will either have to maintain her in a separate establishment, which is far beyond his means, or bring her home. "Then what will become of you?" he asks. Osan answers, "Yes, what shall I do? Shall I become your children's nursemaid or the cook? Or perhaps the retired mistress of the house?"

The problem is insuperable; the husband's love for the prostitute can only result in tragedy. But if his life is one of torment, despite the pleasures he has enjoyed in the licensed quarter, the lot of his wife was infinitely harder. This was true not only of this play but of Japanese society at that time. One gets the impression from Chikamatsu's plays that a wife normally never said anything to her husband except possibly during moments of great emotional stress. In a conversation with a friend about the puppet theater, Chikamatsu remarked:

> In writing for the puppet theater, one attempts first to describe the facts as they actually occurred, but while so doing one also writes things that are not literally true, in the interests of art. In many of my recent plays, many things have been said by female characters which no real women would utter. Such things fall under the heading of art: it is because they say what could not come from a real woman's lips that their true emotions are revealed. If in such cases the author were to model his character closely on a real woman and not allow her to reveal her feelings, such realism, far from being admired, would destroy any interest in the work.

It was commonly said that a woman had no home of her own for three generations: as a child she served in her father's home; as a wife she served her husband; and if she survived the husband, she lived in her son's home. Her greatest pleasure, it would seem, was after she acquired a daughter-in-law to torment. If a wife felt so lonely when her husband was away for years at a time that she had an affair with another man, even if this was accidental, the penalty was death, usually administered at the hands of the aggrieved husband. Chikamatsu's plays about the samurai class, such as *The Drum of the Waves of Horikawa* and *Gonza the Lancer*, have infidelity and its punishment as the central theme. A husband might not actually have wanted to kill his wife for her crime, but this is what society expected of him.

Chikamatsu's plays have often been characterized as embodying the conflict between *giri* (obligation) and *ninjō* (human feelings). The conflict may take the form of a man's personal desires (his love for a prostitute) and his obligation to his wife and family. *Giri* was not necessarily stern-voiced duty calling a man away from the inclinations in his heart. Often it was a natural response, directed toward another person primarily out of gratitude. But when critics speak of the theme of *giri* in Chikamatsu's tragedies, they are generally referring to instances when a fear of what society will think, or a feeling of obligation to another person, compels someone to give up what he most desires. In the play *Yosaku from Tanba*, a lady-in-waiting rejects her long-lost son, though it pains her exceedingly, because of *giri* to the princess she serves; if it were known that the lady had an illegitimate son, this might reflect adversely on the princess.

The Love Suicides at Amijima is built around these two facets of human nature: the prostitute, out of *giri* to Osan, attempts to break with Jihei, the man she loves, who is Osan's husband. Osan, when she learns of the prostitute's self-sacrifice, is ready because of *giri* to give her possessions to her husband so that he can buy up the prostitute's contract. But Jihei is unable to control his *ninjō*. *Giri* not softened by *ninjō* may seem inhuman: it denies the individual's right to happiness at the expense of society. *Ninjō* unchecked by *giri*, however, is not only self-indulgent but in the end can destroy society.

How faithful was Chikamatsu's portrayal to his times? Should his domestic tragedies be accepted as mirrors of Tokugawa society? Most were based on actual events. Chikamatsu, hearing about the love suicides that took place in Osaka at Sonezaki, set to work immediately and completed the play in two weeks. His audiences would have known about the lovers who committed suicide at Sonezaki from gossip or from cheaply produced pamphlets sold in the streets, but they would not have known what caused the pair to kill themselves. In order to make a drama out of what today would be no more than an item in the popular press, Chikamatsu had to invent plausible reasons for the lovers' deaths. Scholarly research has revealed that the villain Kuheiji, the direct cause of the tragedy, never existed; he was created by Chikamatsu in order to make the suicides plausible.

Tokubei, the hero, could not have appeared in a play by Shakespeare except in a comic role. He works as a clerk in a shop that sells soy sauce. His sleeves are stained with the sauce. He loves Koharu, a prostitute who is not of high rank. He is good natured and somewhat stupid. He trusts Kuheiji with the money even though the audience knows from its first glimpse of Kuheiji that he is not to be trusted. Tokubei confronts Kuheiji with the promissory note he has written, but Kuheiji has cleverly foreseen this and laughingly tosses away the note. Tokubei attempts to challenge Kuheiji with his fists, but the latter has five companions and Tokubei is alone. If this were a samurai movie, Tokubei would certainly have disposed of the six men without trouble, but in fact he is soundly beaten. At the end of the scene the crestfallen hero declares: "Before three days have passed I, Tokubei, will make amends by showing all Osaka the purity at the bottom of my heart." This he does with his suicide.

The prostitute, Ohatsu, is stronger than Tokubei. It is she, rather than Tokubei, who first proposes that they die together. Needless to say, the words exchanged by the lovers were invented by Chikamatsu, as were the passages sung or spoken by the narrator. The most beautiful passage in all of his plays is sung as the lovers travel on their final journey:

> Farewell to this world, and to the night farewell.
> We who walk the road to death, to what should we be likened?
> To the frost by the road that leads to the graveyard,
> Vanishing with each step we take ahead:
> How sad is this dream of a dream!

As Tokubei walks he gradually becomes taller, perhaps because of the beautiful poetry that describes his journey. He has become a man capable of killing the woman he loves and then himself. Both Tokubei and Ohatsu, despite their humble professions, are ennobled and redeemed by the purity of their love. The play concludes with the narrator telling us: "No one is there to tell the tale, but the wind that blows through Sonezaki Wood transmits it, and high and low alike gather to pray for these lovers who beyond a doubt will attain Buddhahood. They have become models of true love."

From a commonsensical point of view, it might seem that the lovers' suicide had snuffed out the lives of two people whose nobility had at last been revealed. From the standpoint of Aristotle's *Poetics*, the fate of a shop clerk and a prostitute could not inspire pity and terror. But Chikamatsu, alone among the dramatists of his time, predicted salvation for the dead lovers because of the purity of their love; other writers promised at best that the victims would be long remembered. Chikamatsu not only justified their act but assured in the future world the happiness that the lovers were denied in this life.

Note

Quotations in this chapter are taken from Donald Keene, *Four Major Plays of Chikamatsu* (New York: Columbia University Press, 1961).

23

SAIKAKU'S *FIVE WOMEN WHO LOVED LOVE*

Wm. Theodore de Bary

*F*IVE WOMEN WHO *Loved Love* was written by a citizen of Osaka for the amusement of the townspeople in the new commercial centers of seventeenth-century Japan. From the few surviving records of Ihara Saikaku we know that he was not only a popular novelist but also a poet of wide reputation in his own day, a playwright and commentator on theater life, and something of a vagabond who had closely observed life as it was lived in parts of the country other than his own. Being so cosmopolitan, he was all the more truly a citizen of Osaka. The things that fascinated him in his native city he also found in others—back alleys and slums as well as gay theaters and teahouses; beggars, peddlers, and the lowliest prostitutes, along with merchant princes and famous courtesans. But in writing about them as he did, with such a rare combination of sympathy and detachment, Saikaku gave expression to a feeling of which the inhabitants of Osaka were probably more conscious than other townspeople: that they were citizens with a new importance to society and a new outlook on the world, one that showed the way to a richer and happier life than medieval Japan had known. This came to be known as the *chonin-dō*, "the way of the townspeople," in contrast to *bushidō*, "the way of the warrior," which has been so widely publicized in recent years that it has come to appear to many as the sole embodiment of Japanese tradition.

If Saikaku, as a spokesman for the new citizenry, did not compose a "Marseillaise" to inspire his fellow townsmen in a struggle against the old order, it is partly because fighting was one of the things that they wished to free themselves from. They were engaged together not in a class struggle but in pursuit of individual happiness—something for which little allowance had been made in the stern and unsparing life of medieval fighting men. Indeed, this was almost revolutionary in its implications for a society that had long lived as though in a graveyard, overcast by the seemingly endless tragedy of war, haunted in its literature and drama by specters of the dead, and steeped in the pessimistic view that traditional Buddhism took toward life in this world.

We must understand, however, that this "new" outlook was not just a sudden effusion of the human spirit responding to changed conditions of life and breaking clearly with its past. On the contrary, certain attitudes most characteristic of Osaka in Saikaku's time quite plainly reflect its religious heritage as much as its newfound prosperity. Especially is this true of the theme treated in Saikaku's first great novels: the search for happiness in love. What at first sight seems no more than the universal preoccupation of man is soon seen to have a special quality, an extraordinary intensity akin to religious feeling. These townspeople went about making love as if it were a way of life in itself, as if, amid the uncertainties of the world, love alone would endure. "In Love We Trust" might well have been the inscription on their coins, which were just coming into general circulation at that time.

There is here, no doubt, a defiant rejection of the traditional Buddhist view that all is dust and subject to corruption, that nothing escapes the universal law of change. But the protest bears a strong resemblance to one that had already come from within Buddhism itself, proclaiming salvation through loving faith in the Buddha Amida, whose abiding mercy and redemptive power alone could be relied upon to rescue men from the suffering of this world. Osaka itself had long been a stronghold of this new faith, and in the far more worldly atmosphere of the seventeenth century, though the people of that city looked increasingly to human love for happiness, it was still with the same sense of desperation and utter self-abandonment that was characteristic of Amida's devotees. Thus, Saikaku's heroines, forsaking the security of their homes and the "good things of life" to pursue some ill-fated affair, impress us less with their lusty relish for life than with their final unworldliness.

It is in this sense that we see a profound connection between the two seemingly disparate meanings of the word *ukiyo*—the Buddhist "world of sadness" and the "floating world" of fashion and pleasure inhabited by

Saikaku and his friends. They knew well enough that this new world was no more lasting than the old. Still, Saikaku, who sensed most keenly the vanity and pathos of existence in the Floating World, had not less but rather still more lively an appreciation of its ephemeral attractions and the wealth of experience that this new age opened to all. Certainly the pleasures of these townsmen were richer and more varied than any known before to ordinary Japanese, for success in commerce gave them the means to develop some of their other talents and the leisure to enjoy them. The warrior class, with all its past exploits, had nothing to compare with the entertainments of the city, and the Floating World lay before their wondering eyes like Cleopatra on her barge, luxuriating in an infinite variety of goods from exotic places, an endless life of salad days, and an elusive but unchangeable charm.

Wherever one found merchants and tradesmen in those times, there were sure to be signs of this new life described by Saikaku—busy markets, side lanes lined with little shops, the dignified establishments of moneychangers, great warehouses, teahouses frequented by smartly dressed people, theaters, restaurants, bathhouses, brothels, and streets full of peddlers, panhandlers, jugglers, freaks, and dancing shows. But in Saikaku's time, no city was the equal of his own as a paradise for townspeople. Kyoto was still too conscious of its splendid past to live as Osaka did—for the present alone. The imperial court remained, making feeble pretense at its ancient elegance, and with it an aristocracy that did much to give Kyoto society its style and tone, even if it had the power to do little else. Meanwhile, the warriors of the nation were establishing a new capital at Edo (now Tokyo), a fast-growing city with a political as well as commercial future. But under the watchful eyes of the shogunate, with a large warrior population to accommodate, and with much of its effort devoted to the building of a new city, the townsmen of Edo were not at first so free to go their own way, to create a new life and make the most of it.

Osaka, perhaps, had less of a future in the political life of the country, but this fact served in part to stimulate its growth along independent lines. The city had once seemed to have such a future, and when the Tokugawas took away their hope in it, the men of Osaka had another cause for resentment against the established order. Osaka had long been a city of commercial importance and was, along with the country at large, enjoying unprecedented prosperity when Toyotomi Hideyoshi chose it as his personal seat. There in 1583 he built the most formidable and elaborate fortified castle Japan had ever seen and planned extensive improvements in the city to make it the military, political, and economic heart of the nation. This it was indeed for the remaining fifteen years of his life. Then, not long after Hideyoshi's death, Tokugawa Ieyasu determined to erect his new capital at Edo, where he built a castle even more imposing than Hideyoshi's and started work on a metropolis that in time was to rival, and then outdo, Kyoto and Osaka in importance.

Ihara Saikaku was born in Osaka in 1642. Nothing is known about his early life and very little even about his later years. His wife died young, leaving him with a blind daughter, who also died within a few years. It is said that Saikaku's grief led him to place his affairs in the hands of an assistant, but instead of retiring to some religious sanctuary as might have been expected, he devoted himself to travel and writing. We may judge from his novels that his journeying about Japan in those early years provided him with a rich store of information from which to draw for local color and charming incidents. His knowledge of places, peoples, and things was, for a novelist, probably equal to that which the famous actor Sakata Tojuro expected of his own profession: "The art of an actor is like a beggar's bag and must contain everything, whether it is important or not. If there is anything not wanted for immediate use, keep it for a future occasion. An actor should even learn how to pick pockets."

Saikaku first won literary recognition as the leading disciple of Soin, a writer of *haikai* (seventeen-syllable epigrammatic verses linked into long poems) who headed the liberal Danrin school of poetry. As the chief exponent of this school in Osaka, Saikaku was influential in the movement to free poetry from rigid adherence to conventional forms, to enlarge the scope of its subject matter, and to have it read in a natural style. His predilection for commonplace themes, drawn from the daily life of the people, won for him the contempt of the famous poet Bashō, who found Saikaku's verse vulgar and uninspired, but it made him enormously popular for a time in Osaka. Saikaku was especially famous for his marathon poetry performances before assembled friends and admirers.

When these public orgies exhausted for the moment Saikaku's appetite for expression in the limited, if not inflexible, *haikai* form, he turned to writing fiction, finding this medium perhaps better suited to the development of his subject matter because it permitted a far wider range of expression than did epigrammatic verse. In these same years, Saikaku also tried his hand at playwriting and at recording his observations on theater people of his time, especially the personal charms of young actors and amusing details of their private lives. But it was the novel form that gave full scope both to his rich poetical imagination and to his talent for realistic observation of the life of his time.

Saikaku's first novel, *Koshoku ichidai otoko* (*A Man Who Loved Love*), tells of a man who roamed around the country working at all sorts of trades and making love to thousands of women and hundreds of young boys. It is considered by many Japanese to be his most realistic novel, while *Five Women Who Loved Love* is thought more imaginative and poetic. The former is likened to *The Tale of Genji*, some even arguing that Saikaku used *Genji* for his model. But whatever Saikaku may have owed to earlier literature, including tales of the Floating World (*ukiyo-zoshi*), which were popular in his own time, he did much to create a type of literature new to Japan, and at the same time he gave the common people an equivalent for the *Genji* in terms of their own experience. The hero of his first novel was as handsome and accomplished a lover as Prince Genji, but instead of luxuriating in the magnificent surroundings of the court, he found his pleasure where Saikaku's readers looked for theirs: in teahouses, brothels, bathhouses, theaters, and the homes of commoners. The heroes and heroines of his other romances, including *Five Women Who Loved Love*, bear much less resemblance to people in Murasaki's *Tale of Genji*, yet we often find them aping the latter. When some young bucks of Kyoto spend an evening at a teahouse, passing judgment on the beauty and dress of the girls who come by, they do in their own way what Genji and his friends did in discussing the virtues and desirability of various court ladies.

Not all of Saikaku's novels concern the love of men and women, as do the two already mentioned. But much of what he had to say in other novels is suggested in these. There is, for instance, the matter of men who loved men, which became the subject of a later series, the *Nanshoku ōkagami* (*Mirror of Manly Love*). In the early Tokugawa period, prohibitions were placed on this practice by the shogunate, but it continued to flourish in places where the latter's influence was too weak to enforce compliance, some of them places where an individualistic and warlike tradition was still strong and men scorned the love of women as effeminate. Satsuma was one of these places, and the last of Saikaku's five women had to win her man from Satsuma away from the love of young boys.

It is perhaps as a reward for her success that Saikaku lets this girl, alone among his heroines, enjoy a happy ending to her story. The others all die, commit suicide, or enter a nunnery, but she and her lover are brought back in triumph for a marriage in her father's home, where there is wealth enough for her mate to dream, still, of buying up all the theaters in Japan, with all their pretty male actors.

What drew Saikaku to this subject was not simply the realistic writer's desire to mirror his society or describe impartially the varieties of love practiced in his time. Such a cool detachment would have been quite spurious with him, for Saikaku's sharp objectivity implied no dulling of his human sympathies or his moral sensibility. Nor could he delve into the inmost secrets of human life only to expose them to ridicule or snickering prurience. Saikaku was obviously fascinated by the variety and complexity of human love, but, retaining always a sense of its intrinsic dignity, of love in its most exalted form as leading to self-denial rather than self-gratification, he is both a discriminating and compassionate judge of his fellow men. Thus it is not the sensual aspects of homosexual love that he takes up but the theme of heroic devotion or base disloyalty.

There is another kind of love that, as we might expect, figures even more prominently in Saikaku's writings: the love of money—of riches generally, but in particular of coined money, which was a new object of love in those days and worth writing about in itself. In the *Eitai-gura* (*Treasury for the Ages*) he says: "It is not plum, cherry, pine, and maple trees that people desire most around their houses, but gold, silver, rice, and hard cash." The whole book is devoted to showing how men go about satisfying this desire, as is another, *Seken mune-zanyo* (*The Calculating World*). While *Five Women Who Loved Love* is written mostly about people enjoying the pleasures of already-earned wealth, two of its heroes do have to figure out how to go about acquiring it, and we know from them something of what Saikaku thought was essential to the making of money: frugality, persistence, a ready mind for figures, mastery of the abacus, a pleasant manner, honesty, and imagination.

Most of these virtues had not been made much of before. The businessmen's creed was new, and Saikaku was its first publicist in Japan. It was developed largely by a class of merchants and moneylenders, called *kami-gata-mono*, who had become active in the Kyoto-Osaka region during the sixteenth and seventeenth centuries. These were the men whose resourcefulness, we are told, created the merchant guilds (*za*) in Japan, the free ports, free markets, the use of gold and silver as legal tender, paper money, and bills of exchange. Among them were some who had gone abroad in search of fortune and, when ordered home by the shogunate, had brought back to the port cities a new sense of freedom, an acquaintance with other ways of life, and especially a better knowledge of trade and money handling. From them, we may imagine, the people of these cities learned to look outward and ahead rather than inward and back, as did the framers of the Tokugawa seclusion policy.

To them also Saikaku must have owed much of his curiosity about the world and his taste for the exotic. Ancient exoticism had captured the Japanese mind, during the first flush of Buddhism and Chinese learning, but it later languished in a medieval dungeon of introspection and antiquarianism. Saikaku was one of those who brought it back to life in literature. He was fascinated both by the great variety of wealth in his own country and the innumerable treasures of foreign lands. The known world was, indeed, hardly enough to satisfy his thirst for the exotic. He followed the map to its limits when he had a dissolute company of pleasure seekers play "naked islanders such as are mentioned on maps of the world." And when he came to the end of this book, to the treasure of a man from the Ryukyus, Saikaku could not be happy with such precious gifts as the silks of China and jewels and incense wood of the Indies. He had to have wonders from a Daoist paradise and the palaces of the gods.

Saikaku's enormous appetite for the wonders of the world earned for him the nickname Oranda Saikaku (Holland Saikaku). This did not mean, so far as we know, that Saikaku had any special acquaintance with the Dutch, who were then the only foreign traders allowed into Japan, or that he was in fact a student of Dutch learning. Rather it meant that people thought him unconventional enough to have a taste for things foreign or strange.

The heart of his nonconformity was not, however, his exoticism. It was his adherence to the way of the townspeople and his belief that, in the cities at least, successful businessmen were the real aristocrats, while high birth and military prowess counted for little. This belief is expressed in one way by what he says in the *Treasury for the Ages*: "It makes no difference whether a man is of humble birth or of fine lineage. The genealogies of townspeople are written in dollars and cents. A man who traces his ancestry to Fujiwara Kamatari [a noble of the highest court rank] but who lives impoverished in the city will be worse off than one who leads a monkey through the streets to earn his living." And the same belief is expressed in another way in Saikaku's stories of the warrior class, such as the *Buke-giri monogatari* (*The Warrior's Sense of Duty*). Though ostensibly written to popularize the way of the warrior, these stories leave a final impression of the warrior class as use-less, misguided, and worthy of sympathy rather than admiration.

Still, it is with the individual that Saikaku is ultimately concerned, not the substitution of one type of class thinking for another. Even among the townspeople, whom Saikaku loves, there is no general title to admiration and success. The virtues of industry and frugality can easily be corrupted to make men overscrupulous and stingy, as in the example of Moemon, who economizes on his coat sleeves, does not buy a hat when he comes of age to wear one, and sleeps with an abacus under his pillow to keep track of the money he makes in his dreams. But, somewhat like Gengobei, Moemon is one minute a ridiculous clerk and the next a daring hero who runs off with the most beautiful lady in town. Saikaku is as loath to confine his people in rigid characterization as in tight social classes. They are consistent only in their need for happiness and their weakness in pursuit of it. The reader must be quick if he is to follow the unpredictable course of human behavior and learn its secrets.

Saikaku is not one to accommodate a Western reader's taste for consis-tency in other matters, either. Time and place mean nothing to him except as they serve to create a mood. He will stop the sun in its course if he needs a sunset at the beginning and at the end of a picnic; he rushes the seasons to get the appropriate atmosphere for a certain scene. Sometimes people seem to be everywhere at once, and Gengobei, as a street singer, impersonates himself as if he had already become a legend. One woman is successfully seduced while asleep; a man spends the night with a young friend but wakes to find it all a dream and his friend long since dead. Nothing is too implau-sible for the logic of mood and emotion.

But his readers would probably not have held Saikaku accountable for such contradictions and inconsistencies. Many of Saikaku's characters were already known in popular drama and song, and he was obliged to respect in some degree the associations people had with their names, to make them do some of the things for which they were already celebrated. It did not matter whether these things fitted poorly into the rest of the story; the thrill of identifying an old hero or favorite actor was enough. We should also bear in mind that Saikaku wrote *Five Women Who Loved Love* in some haste. It was the second of five books published within a period of only twelve months, and he probably spent little time trying to straighten out its inconsistencies.

There is another set of conventions that the Western reader may be surprised, this time pleasantly, to find disregarded by Saikaku: those deriving from what some consider the excessive Japanese sense of politeness and discretion. Their absence in Saikaku may be due in part to the fact that his stories move too swiftly to allow for lengthy circumlocutions or polite explanations of what people do. Saikaku is customarily forthright himself—a quality that he probably shared with most other townsmen of the time—and his characters are generally direct in going about what they wish to do. In *Five Women Who Loved Love*, this is most noticeable in the impetuosity of his heroines. They do not wait to be wooed by the men of their choice or stand by timidly while customary procedures decide their fate. In each case, the heroine makes the advances, forces the issue, and decides what must be done in a crisis. And when her impetuosity leads to ruin for herself and her lover, as most often happens, it is the heroine again whose unchastened spirit dominates the final scene at the execution ground.

For Saikaku, this boldness is what makes a woman great, more than her beauty. Nevertheless, his heroines are weak as well as strong, and he does not spare them the consequences of their weakness—in most cases, death. This ultimate retribution is not brought about merely to satisfy conventional morality; nor is it, on the other hand, held up as the final injustice done by society to a girl more sinned against than sinning. Death may be too extreme a penalty to pay for such offenses, but offenses they are nonetheless. To Saikaku the moral order as karmic retribution is as hard and inescapable a fact as human passion.

In this respect, despite the reputation he was later to acquire as a skillful teller of erotic tales, Saikaku is a keener and more effective judge of human foibles than many a writer whose purpose is more obviously moralistic. Saikaku never appears as the doctrinaire proponent of a particular moral philosophy. He does not, like the playwright Chikamatsu, lend his talents to the movement that popularized Confucian ethics in the seventeenth and eighteenth centuries. The moral law prevails, but Saikaku cannot pretend that his heroines are easily reconciled to it. His five women remain wholly themselves—temperamental, volatile, passionate, unpredictable.

In Saikaku's story, Osan's only regrets are for herself. Her elopement with Moemon, with its elaborate hoax to make people think them dead, proves a miserable affair; she is a wretched fugitive, without the strength for flight through the wilderness, and is sustained only by Moemon's promise of an early chance to go to bed together. Moemon returns to the scene of his crime not in the hopes of redemption but because he must hear what people are saying about him and because he is homesick for Kyoto after weeks of pleasureless life in the country. In the end, both must die—a poignant death, because they are not ordinary lovers and everyone pities their frailty—while the war between passion and prudence goes on. Reason wins no false victory; it succeeds only in showing men as they are, at their best and at their worst.

But with Saikaku the consequence of sin is not always death. Sometimes there is an alternative in the Buddhist monastery, where a ruined lover can pray for the soul of his beloved and hope to be reunited with her in paradise. The monastery is, in fact, such a ready alternative that it seems to have become simply a place for escaping from the world. It is not a place one goes to escape oneself. This is because the lover remains a lover and goes to the monastery in order to remain faithful to his love. There is little consciousness of personal sin, no estrangement from God or repentance. In death, the lovers are defiant because the world is against them; in the monastery they are resigned, confident that they will have ultimate victory over the world.

What Saikaku's characters are more conscious of than personal sin, as others know it, is a kind of Perduring Original known as karma or *inga*, the chain of moral causation that conditions one's life in accordance with one's past actions. Strictly speaking, it was possible by one's actions to lighten the burden or add to it, as one chose. In practice, however, the overcoming of sin and the acquisition of merit depended upon the individual's capacity for enlightened conduct. It came to be recognized that few men were sufficiently enlightened to cope with the weight of karma accumulated through innumerable previous existences. Thereupon a savior appeared in the Buddha Amida, who had vowed that his great accumulation of merit should be applied to the salvation of all men, so that they might, without any merit of their own, share with him the pleasures of the Western Paradise. Redemption was then free for the asking, not a reward for good conduct in this life.

For this reason, when Saikaku's lovers speak of their misfortunes as due to karma, to them it is almost the equivalent of Fate, because they feel helpless under its crushing weight. In some cases there is a further complication arising from a Buddhist superstition called *shushin*: a curse that falls upon someone who refuses to gratify the love of another. Thus, unequal to karma, threatened perhaps by the curse of a disappointed lover, and feeling desperately the urge to seize a brief moment of bliss in this dreary world, Saikaku's five women plunge headlong and headstrong into love, into death, into the cloister—with the name of Amida on their lips and in their souls a faith that salvation depends on the Buddha's love, not upon what they do themselves.

We may believe that they are real people as well as Saikaku's creatures. We know enough about the life of his society and the celebrated cases of ill-fated lovers to recognize them as people of his own time. Yet what Saikaku has to tell us about them takes a form much different from the realistic novel to which we are accustomed. This is a work of poetry and imagination, not simply of skilled observation. Saikaku is no social scientist. He is indeed a sorcerer, whose powers are unexpectedly used to bring all of life out into the light of day, after his friends, in their search of fugitive pleasures, have turned day into "a kingdom of eternal night."

24

KAIBARA EKKEN'S *PRECEPTS FOR DAILY LIFE IN JAPAN*

Mary Evelyn Tucker

Introduction: Learning of the Mind-and-Heart

Kaibara Ekken (1630–1714) was regarded by his contemporaries and by later generations as a major figure in Japanese intellectual history during the Tokugawa period (1603–1868).[1] Well versed in the writings of the Chinese Neo-Confucians, especially Zhu Xi (1130–1200), he strove to transmit their spiritual essence and practical implications to the Japanese of his day. In the teachings of Zhu Xi, he saw a system of personal cultivation, intellectual investigation, political organization, and cosmological orientation that provided a broad context for thought and a functional basis for action that he perceived as essential for his time. Ekken was also deeply influenced by the philosophy of *qi* of Luo Qinshun (1465–1547), and he developed a vitalistic naturalism based on material force.

His philosophy found expression spiritually in the "learning of the mind-and-heart" (C.: *xinxue*; J.: *shingaku*), a form of interior self-discipline that began with reverence and gratitude to Heaven and Earth as the source and sustainer of life. It proceeded to a recognition of one's personal deficiencies and outlined a program of self-examination and reflection. The ultimate aim of this self-cultivation was to realize one's unity with the vital energy of Heaven and Earth and all things. Clearly familiar with the earlier expression of *xinxue* in the *Heart Classic* of Zhen Dexiu (1178–1235) and with later Chinese and Korean commentaries on this text, Ekken formulated a version of self-cultivation that drew extensively on these earlier writings while trying to make their ideas comprehensible to the Japanese.

Kaibara Ekken's teachings on spiritual cultivation thus lie within the broad tradition in East Asian Neo-Confucianism of the learning of the mind-and-heart, which has been discussed by Wm. Theodore de Bary. According to de Bary, this learning arose amid the teachings of the Song Neo-Confucians, as efforts to articulate an alternative to Buddhist doctrines of the mind and to develop an appropriate method for the cultivation of the mind-and-heart.[2] This was a Neo-Confucian response to the intensive methods of disciplining the mind advocated by the Buddhists, particularly within the Chan (Zen) sect. While initially related to the "Learning of the Emperors and Kings" as a means of governance, it was primarily understood as a mode of self-governance. It thus came to have a universal application for both educated leaders and commoners.

Its appeal as a teaching also transcended national and cultural boundaries, extending to the Mongols and other non-Han Chinese as well as to the Koreans and Japanese. Being both traditionalist and reformist, its rich humanistic character and religious tone distinguishes it as an important mode of East Asian moral and spiritual cultivation. Ekken developed his own form of *shingaku* (The Learning of the Mind-and-Heart) intended for all classes and occupations of people. As the foundation of his system of education, it figures prominently in the *Precepts for Daily Life in Japan* (*Yamato Zokkun*) and in his other ethicoreligious treatises (*kunmono*). Learning of the mind-and-heart was also an important movement for several Tokugawa teachers, including Ishida Baigan.[3]

Precepts for Daily Life in Japan begins by establishing the context for Neo-Confucian spiritual discipline in an overarching religious context combined with specific moral practices. Ekken outlines the general cosmological framework for his *shingaku* teachings and suggests the appropriate method of self-cultivation for humans in this framework. These two themes of cosmology and ethical practice are interwoven throughout the text and provide its fundamental unity. Despite Ekken's rambling and repetitious style, it is well suited to the inculcation of Ekken's teaching for a wide audience. Similarly, the use of polite conversational Japanese in contrast to the stylized conventions of Chinese-style prose (*kanbun*) distinguishes his writing from other Confucians of the same period. By their very repetition, certain key ideas can be identified as constituting the principal components of Ekken's teaching: namely, the religious impetus, the learning imperative,[4] personal integration, and modes of practice.

The Religious Impetus: Gratitude to Heaven and Earth

In the preface and throughout the *Precepts for Daily Life in Japan*, the religious motivation for self-cultivation is clearly expressed. Ekken believes that the special quality of human life is due to the fact that all human beings receive the mind-and-heart of Heaven and Earth. Given a capacity for reflective moral behavior, humans have a Heaven-bestowed nature that sets them apart from the plant and animal world and marks them in a special way as children of Heaven and Earth. This unique status of humans brings with it both privileges and responsibilities. The human being is extremely fortunate to have been born a human and must develop his or her Heaven-bestowed nature by serving Heaven and Earth. To this end, an individual practices filiality and reverence toward Heaven and Earth, considering them as one's great parents and the source of all life and blessings. This religious sense of profound indebtedness to the cosmos for the gift of life, sustenance, and support is at the root of Neo-Confucian spiritual practice as seen in the *Precepts for Daily Life in Japan*.[5] Moreover, it is also part of the larger process of Neo-Confucian cultivation, namely, the attainment of sagehood through the realization of one's moral nature as linked to Heaven and Earth and all things. The recognition of this potential for a profound experience of identity with ultimate reality becomes both the impetus and the goal of cultivation.

By receiving the mind-and-heart of Heaven and Earth, the human becomes a natural vessel for nurturing virtue. As such, one is the "spirit of the universe," or the "soul of creation" (*banbutsu no rei*). Through human beings the great consciousness and compassion of the heavenly mind-and-heart may be expressed in the creative and nurturing capacities of moral practice. Humans receive with their Heaven-bestowed nature a rational, moral sense, expressed through the primary virtue of humaneness (C.: *ren*; J.: *jin*), that gives them a capacity for nourishing life in the same way as does the vast heavenly mind-and-heart. For humans, this implies an extension outward in concentric circles of a profound love for other people as well as a compassion for birds and beasts, trees and plants.

This fundamental virtue of humaneness encompasses the other principal virtues or constants, namely rightness, decorum, wisdom, and trustworthiness. In order to avoid too general and diffuse a sense of morality, this virtue is particularly emphasized in the context of the "five relationships": between lord and retainer, parent and child, husband and wife, older and younger siblings, and friends. These establish a model for interpersonal relations through a mutual bonding of human emotions to a sense of reciprocal obligation as a guide to human behavior.

In order to realize their responsibilities as human beings, Ekken believes that people must know the "Way of the human" and adopt it. Guidelines exist for following this path, and they should be sought out. There arises, then, an overriding need to know the Way so as to discover and discern the most authentic mode of human behavior. This can be called the "learning imperative" of Neo-Confucian spirituality. It is the source of the constant emphasis on learning and on education in the Confucian tradition. In *Precepts for Daily Life in Japan*, this is the subject of the first two chapters on the "Pursuit of Learning."

Here the pursuit of learning becomes the transformation of the self through moral and spiritual cultivation, the subject of chapters 3 and 4, on the "The Discipline of the Mind-and-Heart" (*shinjutsu*). The last four chapters of the text are principally concerned with modes of practice based on the steps of internal cultivation outlined in the first four chapters.

The Learning Imperative: The Basis, Method, and Extension of Knowledge

As these titles indicate, Ekken's first two chapters are primarily concerned with the "Pursuit of Learning" through a method of education and self-cultivation based on the essential teachings of the *Great Learning* and later Neo-Confucian texts and commentaries on the same subject. This substructure emphasizes the importance placed in Neo-Confucian education on the need for sequence and method in learning, as does Zhu Xi's preface to the *Great Learning*.

The Basis: Balancing Subjective and Objective

For Ekken, the basis of learning is in establishing a dynamic balance between subjective and objective knowledge. Overemphasis on one or the other poles of knowledge can lead to a distortion of learning as a moral process. For this reason, while Ekken is critical of the subjective tendencies of Buddhism, Daoism, and of the Lu-Wang School of the Mind, he does not believe that a purely rational or empirical approach is satisfactory either. Those who are overly subjective tend to sink into quietistic or solipsistic practices, while those who stress rationality and objectivity are inclined to become technically adept at external investigation while ignoring the process of inner cultivation. Instead, Ekken emphasizes a balancing of subjective and objective knowledge, leading to an expression of that knowledge in action.

With regard to subjectivity in knowing, Ekken, following Zhu Xi before him, states that learning begins with things close at hand. There is no need to search for an abstract wisdom when one can rely on one's own innate knowledge of the good in trying to understand the teachings of the sages—their subjective capacity for "good knowing" (C.: *liangzhi*; J.: *ryochi*). This affirmation of the potential of all humans for discernment and the confirmation of the goodness of that innate nature are at the heart of Neo-Confucian learning and self-cultivation.

Along with this dynamic reliance on subjectivity, there is a recognition of the need for objectivity so as to avoid the danger of depending exclusively on one's own perceptions or opinions. Ekken stresses the importance of learning from teachers, friends, and the sages of the past. It is difficult to master even small arts without a teacher. Even the sages learned by studying with a teacher. It is essential to select good teachers and to respect them fully. In addition to teachers, people should learn and consult with trusted friends who will objectively point out their shortcomings and correct their mistakes. The biases of one's own disposition can thus be rectified. Ekken is, however, aware of the need for a constant reevaluation of Confucian scholarship, for he wishes to avoid an uncritical acceptance of its ideas.

In order to bring together the objective and subjective standards of knowledge, two factors are indispensable for Ekken. The first is establishing a resolute goal or aim for one's learning, and the second is adopting humility as the foundation—imperatives reiterated throughout the text.

For Ekken, establishing a goal is essential for all later progress. Within the context of Neo-Confucian self-cultivation, the ultimate goal for Ekken was understood to be the attainment of sagehood, namely the full realization of one's own nature and the experience of oneness with Heaven, Earth, and all things. Perhaps in an effort to maintain a sense of the accessibility of such a goal and to stress the availability of Neo-Confucian practice for all classes of people, he speaks less about this ultimate goal than simply about the transformation of one's nature through moral cultivation. Human nature is weak, and thus consciousness of a larger goal is essential. Without such a goal one may waver, become lazy, or be distracted by ephemeral things. For Ekken, establishing a goal means having a resolute aim and being constantly diligent toward this end. Thus he calls for a firm will, which is single minded and not divided or faltering. Dedicated effort of the will is the basis of study and the dynamic motive behind the learning imperative.

Lest a person become self-absorbed in this resolute drive toward a goal, Ekken advocates humility as a correlative principle for the learning process. Thus a person should take pleasure in questioning others, listening carefully to instructions, and welcoming admonishment. People should be modest about their knowledge or accomplishments and be quick to correct their errors when necessary. Ultimately, Ekken follows the important directive of Confucius to learn for oneself, not to impress others. This was a cornerstone of Zhu Xi's teachings and was continually cited by Neo-Confucians in China, Korea, and Japan.

Ekken urges those involved in learning to avoid illiterate people who dislike all forms of scholarly endeavor and thus err in their subjective prejudices. He says scholars should not argue angrily with such people, as it will only intensify their antagonism toward all scholarly endeavor. Many uneducated people dislike learning because frequently scholars are arrogant and disdainful of them. He makes a special plea for sincerity and humility in learning so that Japan may become an enlightened nation of Noble persons. Ekken continually returns to these two principles of resoluteness and constant humility as the basis of all learning.

The Method: Integrating Knowledge and Action

The essential method of the learning imperative involves steps for integrating knowledge and action. These are the fundamental principles originally stated in the *Mean* (*Zhongyong*) and emphasized by Zhu Xi, namely, study widely, question thoroughly, think carefully, judge clearly, and act seriously. "By first delving into the Way and its principles in our own hearts, and then widely searching out the principles in all things, we will apprehend a truth in the center of our own being." This requires an investigation of both the past and the present by a reliance on the books of the sages and on the teachings of other people. Similarly, questioning thoroughly serves as a method for resolving doubts and clarifying principles. Thinking carefully means reflecting with discretion so that one will acquire knowledge for oneself. Judging clearly means investigating right and wrong and distinguishing between good and evil. The first two steps involve the specific "external" activities of studying and questioning, while the latter two revolve around the more reflective internal activities of assimilating what one is learning through dispassionate reflection. This involves "getting it for oneself" (C.: *zide*; J.: *jitoku*), so essential to Neo-Confucian self-cultivation, which has its natural culmination in the fifth directive, to act seriously by being sincere in words and careful in action.

More specifically, Ekken outlines the proper method of daily study as learning with a teacher in the morning, reviewing in the afternoon, studying again in the evening, and reflecting on mistakes at night. Referring back to a passage from the *Record of Rites* that was often stressed by Zhu Xi, he encourages the student to be conscientious through daily renewal. This means trying to eliminate the mistakes of the previous day through examination, thereby facilitating a return to goodness.

He continually urges students to make an effort in their youth to use time wisely, giving careful attention when one is young to learning characters and to understanding the meaning of words so that one's education will progress steadily. At the same time, one should have a calm, natural approach in order to know how to wait and be open to wisdom. If students are conscientious in their youth yet are patient with gradual progress, anyone can succeed in achieving the goal of intellectual and moral development, which applies to all classes of people and all walks of life.

Similarly, people can be educated by the methods established in Zhu Xi's *Elementary Learning* and the *Great Learning*. According to Zhu Xi, the *Elementary Learning* begins when a child reaches the age of eight, while the *Great Learning* begins at the age of fifteen. Ekken summarizes the teachings as follows:

> What they were taught was to have filial piety toward their parents, respect their seniors, and serve their lord; the way to receive guests, sweep the rooms, prepare food and drink, advance and withdraw in the presence of notable people, and respond to questions and requests; and they were also taught the skills of the six arts for daily use, namely, ritual, music, archery, driving [a horse or chariot], reading, and arithmetic.

While the *Elementary Learning* is concerned with two essential virtues (filiality and respect), with external decorum (serving, sweeping, preparing, etc.), and with basic skills (six arts), the *Great Learning* concentrates on the truths of governing the people through self-discipline.

Ekken is especially concerned with explicating the method of the *Great Learning*, namely, the three guiding principles and eight steps, so that their essentials can be understood and practiced by most Japanese people. The eight steps embrace a comprehensive program of social-political involvement (bringing peace to all under Heaven, effecting order in the state, and regulating the family), moral and spiritual discipline (cultivating oneself, rectifying the mind, and making the will sincere), and intellectual realization (extending knowledge and investigating things). These are the essence of the method of Neo-Confucian education and are discussed throughout the text as the core elements underlying both the pursuit of learning and the "Discipline of the Mind-and-Heart" (*shinjutsu*).

The Extension of Knowledge: The Investigation of Things

After outlining the basis and method or program of learning, Ekken discusses the importance of the extension of knowledge through the investigation of things. Here he elaborates on both his general directives and his more specific instructions for a curriculum of study. Investigating things means examining the truth of objects and events, beginning with moral virtues and relations close at hand and moving outward. Extending knowledge implies a careful examination of the mind-and-heart so that one will arrive at an authentic self-knowledge. These two poles, then, of internal reflection and external investigation are the pivotal points of the process of the *Great Learning* and are essential to all Neo-Confucian spiritual practice. While Ekken is primarily concerned in this text with moral and spiritual cultivation, he observes that merely investigating human relations or virtue as a separate entity is not sufficient. It must be seen in relation to the dynamic life process of nature itself. People must also study the Way of Heaven and Earth as the basis of the human Way. The cosmological context and the role of principle (*li*) within material force (*qi*) is, for Ekken, essential to an understanding of the root from which truth emerges. Without understanding the cosmology, one cannot recognize the natural principles inherent in human beings. This connection becomes the metaphysical basis for Ekken's efforts to investigate objects in the natural world. He thus extends the idea of investigating principles from a primarily ethical concern to an empirical and naturalist enterprise as well.

Ekken further notes that one should take an open-minded approach to investigation. To do so, one should realize that there is no one way to investigate principles (ethically or empirically). Rather, there are a variety of approaches and numerous layers to be examined in one's studies. Taking up Confucius's directive to study for oneself rather than for others, Ekken urges the reader not to be concerned with impressing people or with seeking honor or fame through learning but to investigate principle with vigor, perseverance, and sincerity.

Following these general directives, Ekken gives more specific instructions on investigating things and extending knowledge through a curriculum of study. He suggests which books should be read by beginning students and which ones should be used for more advanced studies. The Four Books and the Five Classics naturally form the heart of a Neo-Confucian program for learning. Reading the Four Books is like listening to the teachings of the sages directly. To fully understand their meaning, he urges the student to consult the commentaries on the Four Books as well as those on the Five Classics. Next he suggests reading the books of the Song Neo-Confucians: Zhou Dunyi and especially the Cheng brothers and Zhu Xi.

After these have been read thoroughly, Ekken urges the student to look at the histories, especially the *Zuozhuan* (*Zuo's Commentary on the Spring and Autumn Annals*), *Shiji* (*Records of the Grand Historian*), and Zhu Xi's *Tongjiangangmu* (*Outline and Details of the Comprehensive Mirror*). These serve as guides to government by helping one understand the past so as to lead intelligently in the present. The historical records of Japan are similarly of assistance in this respect. Ekken also includes collected works and literature in his list of books to be consulted. He warns against dilettantism, however, saying that merely trying to read widely is not enough. Rather, people should keep in mind the overarching concern to understand moral principles in order to extend knowledge and practice it in daily life. Thus, as in all Neo-Confucian programs of education, breadth should be balanced by selectivity and restraint.

Personal Integration: The Discipline of the Mind-and-Heart

Chapters 3 and 4 describe the purpose and the method of moral and spiritual cultivation involved in the learning of the mind-and-heart. To rectify the mind-and-heart, one must first make one's will sincere in loving good and disliking evil. Then a person will be able to maintain and express the seven emotions (happiness, anger, sadness, enjoyment, love, hate, desire) in correct proportion. With a balancing of emotions, an effective social-political activity can be undertaken while maintaining a deep spiritual harmony.

Discernment, Resolution, Balance: Human Mind and Way Mind

At the core of Neo-Confucian moral and spiritual cultivation is the learning of the mind-and-heart that arose among the Song masters and was formulated in the *Heart Classic* of Zhen Dexiu. Ekken relies on the first quotation in the *Heart Classic*, which was originally taken from the *Classic of History* and attributed to the sage king Yu: "The human mind is precarious, the Way mind is barely perceptible. Be discerning and unified in mind; hold to the Mean." He begins his discussion, as does Zhu Xi, by advocating a method that combines intellectual discernment, volitional effort, and emotional and aesthetic balance.

Ekken first notes the importance of distinguishing between the human mind and the Way mind. The human mind is seen as the seat of emotions and desires, while the mind of the Way is the root of moral principles and virtues. Recognizing the difference between the two is the beginning of moral and spiritual cultivation. This process of discernment is difficult both because of the unstable nature of the human mind, which is connected to physical forms and precariously balanced between selfish and unselfish desires and because the subtle nature of the mind of the Way is hidden in the depths of the heart.

In discerning between the two, one can begin to learn how to control the human mind and preserve the Way mind. This is the fundamental basis of moral and spiritual discipline. This process of distinguishing between the human mind and the moral mind is what is referred to by the phrase "having utmost refinement." The next phrase, "singleness of mind," indicates the resolution to unify the will so that the Way mind is dominant and the human mind does not run rampant (that is, so that selfish desires do not dominate the human mind). Finally, "holding fast to the Mean" implies achieving a balance of the emotions and the senses so that they are neither excessive nor deficient.

Moral Purification and Emotional Control

Ekken cites three major obstacles to the practice of the learning of mind-and-heart: selfish desires and evil thoughts, a biased disposition, and faults.

All of these obstacles must be carefully eliminated in order to progress in virtue. Selfish desires he describes as pleasures of the senses, namely, greed for fame, profit, sex, or possessions. Evil thoughts he sees as oppressing people, arguing angrily with others, boasting about ourselves, criticizing or slandering others, and flattering or deceiving people. A biased disposition means the partiality with which one is born, namely, having a rough and boisterous nature, a soft or weak nature, a dull or greedy nature. Faults refer to unwitting mistakes or habits that one should reform quickly. He emphasizes that it is extremely important to purify oneself of these deficiencies, or attempts at spiritual cultivation will be useless.

In connection with moral purification, Ekken concerns himself with the question of how one controls the emotions yet expresses them so as to live morally but also humanely. He aims at an authentic integration of the person so that the emotions are not suppressed or eliminated but are restrained when appropriate and expressed when appropriate. He wishes to avoid the extremes of puritanism or libertarianism. Specifically, he cites the directive in the *Classic of Changes* to restrain anger and contain the desires, considering these two to be the deadliest of the emotions. The will must act as the master of the emotions so that it can control them rather than be controlled by them. When such control is achieved, a person will be better able to practice virtue with a sense of ease and with the assurance that his emotions will be expressed naturally and spontaneously in response to specific circumstances.

Modes of Practice

After purification and emotional balancing, one can then effectively practice virtue, beginning with love and respect toward others. Ekken identifies the virtue of humaneness with the life-principle in the universe. Compassion is the great virtue of Heaven and Earth as well as the principle of life. He also says that humaneness is a heart that loves and sympathizes with others; in other words, a heart that gives life to things as do Heaven and Earth. He speaks of an order and sequence in extending humaneness, namely, from family outward to relatives, retainers, and friends but also to animals, fish, birds, insects, trees, and vegetation. From the lower forms to the higher forms of life all are worthy of love, respect, care, and nourishment, which allows for no separation between ourselves and others. He also discusses the importance of reciprocity, which is the ability to imagine others as ourselves and to treat them accordingly.

Ekken describes the culmination of this path of virtue as the practice of hidden virtue, which does not seek recognition or repayment from others. Such hidden virtue is concerned with the public good rather than any private gain. He portrays this virtue in the following passage:

> In order to have compassion and kindness toward others, grieving with their sorrows and rejoicing in their happiness, we should give priority to the widowed, orphaned, and childless, bring relief to the hungry, give clothes to those who are cold, help the tired and sick, repair roads and bridges, eliminate things which harm people, and do things which benefit them—making peace among people; praising their goodness; concealing their faults; overlooking their small mistakes; developing and utilizing their talents; not being angry at people indiscriminately; not having resentments against them; stopping the angry disputes of others; not slandering people even slightly; not despising, depriving, or hindering others; fostering their virtue; reproving their errors; not injuring birds, animals, insects, or fish; not killing recklessly; not cutting plants and trees wantonly. All this is hidden virtue.

If people choose such a generous and public-spirited path, they will be in accord with reason, with the will of Heaven, and with the human heart. In so doing they will have a broad tolerance toward others and will not harbor resentments or agonize over mistakes. Instead, they will move with an inner calm in the rigorous practice of hidden virtue and humaneness.

Consequently, Ekken emphasizes the virtue of reverent mindfulness as something that should be constantly cultivated. He notes how this virtue, which implies both moral seriousness and religious reverence, had consistently been the touchstone of the learning of the mind-and-heart of the sages. Rulers should have hearts that are morally serious and sympathetic toward others. They should give people what they need and not selfishly indulge their own pleasures. If the rulers love the people with sincerity, the people will definitely sense this and be happy.

Ekken also speaks of reverence as a constant state of mindful respect, while he sees harmony as a calm enjoyment. By reverence he means that people should be mindful of themselves and others in relation to Heaven and Earth. By harmony he suggests that people be content with their position in life, make an effort at their vocation, and avoid striving after external goals or seeking trivial satisfactions. Ekken speaks of this state of reverent, joyful contentment as a natural quality that is enriched by harmony with external things.

Thus he says that by contact with the wind and the flowers, the snow and the moon, the original contentment of the heart is deepened. That is because the reverent contentment of the heart reflects the natural harmony of the universe. Birds fly, fish leap, birds chirp, animals cry out, vegetation flourishes, flowers bloom, fruit is produced—these are all expressions of the will of Heaven and the natural delight of all things. Appreciating this, the Noble person is not led astray by desires but reverently nurtures the natural contentment of the heart, which is part of the ceaseless fecundity of the universe.

Spiritual Harmony and Intellectual Illumination

For Ekken, when a person comes to this stage of integration, the mind-and-heart will be illuminated, clear, and not vacillating in discerning right from wrong. Through the acquisition of true knowledge, the mind will indeed be the master of the body and the controller of the emotions and senses. Heavenly principles will grow within, as human desires decrease; thus a person's nature will become fully realized. The result will be an inner calm that reflects the peaceful harmony of the workings of Heaven. Microcosm and macrocosm will mirror each other in the inner harmony of the individual. In Neo-Confucianism, this can be expressed as attaining sagehood. Through an arduous effort at discernment, purification, and practice, the individual can experience himself as a vital part of the larger, cosmic processes. It is toward this end that Ekken advocates his "Discipline of the Mind-and-Heart," based on a dynamic naturalism articulated as a philosophy of qi.

Ekken's *Precepts for Daily Life in Japan*, as the most developed of his ethicoreligious treatises, serves as an appropriate summary of Ekken's teachings. When considered in conjunction with his philosophical treatise, the *Taigiroku (Record of Great Doubts)*, one can see how his naturalist metaphysics provides a dynamic basis for his ideas on cultivating the self in relation to change in the natural order. Finally, one can appreciate, as an example of Tokugawa Neo-Confucianism, Ekken's considerable efforts to spread the education of the mind-and-heart among the people at large.

Notes

1. See also my *Moral and Spiritual Cultivation in Japanese Neo-Confucianism: The Life and Thought of Kaibara Ekken* (Albany, N.Y.: SUNY Press, 1989). For further information on Kaibara Ekken, see my *The Philosophy of Qi: The Record of Great Doubts* (New York: Columbia University Press, 2007). See also Olaf Graf, *Kaibara Ekken* (Leiden: E. J. Brill, 1942), 284–330.
2. Translation of *Precepts for Daily Life in Japan*, from my *Moral and Spiritual Cultivation in Japanese Neo-Confucianism*, 149.
3. Translation from ibid., 160.
4. *Classic of History (The Shou-King) Counsels of Great Yu*, in *The Chinese Classics*, trans. James Legge (Oxford: Clarendon Press, 1865), 3:61–62.
5. Translation of *Precepts for Daily Life in Japan*, from my *Moral and Spiritual Cultivation in Japanese Neo-Confucianism*, 192.

25

The Contemporary Meaning of T'oegye's Ten Diagrams on Sage Learning

Michael C. Kalton

Introduction

Yi T'oegye's *Ten Diagrams on Sage Learning* (*Seonghak sipdo*) stands as one of the masterpieces of Neo-Confucian thought. In ten diagrams, he leads us from a grand vision of the cosmos into ethics and the question of how we should educate ourselves and spiritually cultivate our inner lives to realize the fullness of our natural endowment, concluding by describing just what a well-lived day might look like. More than two decades ago, I had the great privilege of translating and commenting on this insightful and wise crystallization of T'oegye's lifetime of learning and spiritual cultivation.[1] Since then, T'oegye's diagrams and understanding of life have been a quiet but continual presence in my mind, even as I extended my investigation into contemporary systems thinking and environmental concerns.

In many ways, we live in a world that no one in T'oegye's sixteenth century could have imagined. The concepts that were central to their understanding of the world—the Supreme Ultimate, *li* (理), *dao* (道), *qi* (氣), and many others—are little used now, and psychological categories such as the Four Beginnings and Seven Feelings are no longer central concerns as we consider the proper ordering of our lives. Even our concerns and problems seem new and distinctive: our ancestors never imagined anything like modern economies, globalization, or the radical environmental crisis of sustainability. T'oegye meant to teach his audience the meaning of the world and how we humans should cultivate and conduct ourselves accordingly. Can we still learn from him, given the very changed circumstances of our times, or is his *Ten Diagrams* only of historical interest, a record of the thoughts of a good and wise man who belongs to a past age?

My own experience has been that this is a voice not only of the past but of the present as well. As an intellectual, I have found that the background understanding and ways of thinking that I learned from my work on T'oegye constantly leads me to new, deeper, and often unexpected understandings as I wrestle with contemporary materials, questions, and problems. T'oegye's description of the inner life of the mind and heart still is full of insight, and his suggestions on appropriate cultivation are much to the point for our contemporary world. In this chapter, I will follow the order of T'oegye's *Ten Diagrams*, discussing the meaning of each and how it relates to the much changed circumstances of the twenty-first century.

Diagram 1: The Supreme Ultimate

What is the nature of existence?

This question for Neo-Confucians was practical rather than speculative: they assumed that we needed to understand the origins and depths of the universe in order to know how to live. T'oegye begins with Zhou Dunyi's *Diagram of the Supreme Ultimate* to frame the most essential knowledge we need as human beings (see the frontispiece, on page ii).

The central message of this diagram is that a single, formative unity runs through and encompasses all existence. The same original circle is purposefully repeated; the Supreme Ultimate does not become multiple even as it becomes the ground of a multiple existence. Whatever is going on here, whatever forms and events emerge, there is in the depths of all existence a unity, a oneness that means that everything takes place interdependently, in terms of everything else. Contemporary systems theory has arrived at a very similar understanding, as is evident in both the physical and life sciences. On whatever scale of consideration, whether it be the formation of galaxies and planets, the evolving structure of an ecosystem, or the transforming social and economic lives of a community, every sort of process is deeply shaped by a web of interdependent relationships.

This understanding, so graphically represented by the repeated circles of the *Diagram of the Supreme Ultimate*, has critical practical consequences: Therefore the sage, "with respect to Heaven and Earth is at one with their character, with respect to the sun and moon is at one with their brilliance, with respect to the four seasons is at one with their order and with respect to the spirits is at one with the good fortune and the misfortune [which they mediate]."[2] The superior man in cultivating these qualities enjoys good fortune, while the inferior man in violating them suffers misfortune.[3] This is a mighty proposition: Zhou is claiming in the broadest terms possible that whether things work out well or ill in human life hinges on this quality of being *at one* with the relational network to which we belong.

T'oegye picks up on this theme, for it discloses "the Mandate," the most fundamental directive for life: "When the day of reaping the fruits arrives and one completely returns to the Single Origin, he will have arrived at the condition described as having 'exhaustively comprehended principle, fully realized his nature, and so completely fulfilled the Mandate.'"[4] Our shared "Single Origin" mandates that our lives are complete only when we are at one with many-layered dynamic system within which we exist, from the universe to the earth; to the everyday society of our associates, friends, relatives, families; and the encompassing processes of the natural world about us. In the language of self-cultivation and practice, the imperative is to *fit* with appropriate responsiveness to all of these throughout all the affairs of our daily lives.

It is nothing other than this Mandate with which we now wrestle as we try to achieve a "sustainable" way of human life, for nothing can long last if it does not fit.

Diagram 2: The Western Inscription

For his second diagram T'oegye reaches for Zhang Zai's *Western Inscription*, which calls forth the most powerful motivating force in Confucian society to support our quest to live at one with the shared life coursing through Heaven and Earth. Confucians reflected deeply on the family, understanding it as the shared flow of a single life force; consequently filial piety, the proper alignment of feelings and conduct within this shared life, became both a powerful motive and the criterion for the rightness of one's life. In the *Western Inscription*, Zhang Zai calls on this deep feeling by celebrating the cosmic and global flow of life as weaving all creatures into a single family: "*Qian* [Heaven] is called the father and Kun [Earth] is called the mother. I, this tiny being, am commingled in their midst; therefore what fills up all between Heaven and Earth, that is my body, and that which directs Heaven and Earth is my nature."[5] His conclusion, modeled on the family, is an unprecedented expansion of the relationships that count: "All people are from the same womb as I, all creatures are my companions."[6] The accompanying diagram makes this the central organizing statement: "All others and I, the people and other creatures, are brothers; their principle is all one."[7]

For Neo-Confucian philosophers who saw *li*, a single formative and organizing principle (理) flowing through all things, this statement of the familial unity of all life was more than a metaphor. And contemporary science, understanding genes as the formative organizing factor passed down an evolving family of life, strongly enforces a similar understanding. On Earth, all life does indeed belong to a single family tree, and branches of the family are closer than one might think: mice and humans, for example, share 85 percent of the same genes. The contemporary community is excited by the implications of this knowledge for enhancing medical research, but unlike the *Western Inscription*, we have not yet thought deeply about its moral implications.

Nor did the Confucians in fact pay much attention to the nonhuman branches of the family tree. While the *Inscription* describes accurately a family of life, its consequential focus quickly shifts to the human community: "All persons in the world who are exhausted, decrepit, worn out, or ill . . . are my own brothers who have become helpless and have none to whom they can appeal."[8] It was beyond imagining at the time that polar bears or dolphins or eagles or bluefin tuna or whales might also fall into the category of the "exhausted and decrepit," the "helpless" that stand in need of our attention. They could not suspect that the very atmosphere that "fills up all between Heaven and Earth" could be modified by humans in ways that would shift the character of the life-giving seasons.

We are yet far from realizing and practicing the implications of even the human race constituting a single family, let alone the care and fellow feeling that should go with recognizing the interdependent family of life that relates us to all living beings on earth. But caring for this larger family has become the neglected imperative of our times. Both the best insight of T'oegye's second diagram and the best understanding of contemporary life sciences points to the fact that the exhausted and decrepit creatures that perish due to the scope of our exploitation of the Earth "are our own brothers who have become helpless and have none to whom they can appeal." None other than us, that is.

Diagrams 3, 4, and 5: Learning (學)

The next three diagrams address the question: how should we educate ourselves to live appropriately responsive lives? In the contemporary world, the overriding reason given for education is to "equip us to compete in the global market." For traditional Confucians, in reality education may well have been not that much different, a matter of equipping young men to further their family's well-being by competing in the civil-service exams. But that was never the publicly announced or ideal purpose of education. Instead, education was conceived in terms of the Mandate: it was to ensure and enhance our fit as life-giving members of the community. This ideal motivated the most serious *tohak* (道學) Neo-Confucians such as T'oegye, separating them and making them harsh critics of the civil service exam–oriented system of their time. One wonders what they would have to say today, when education prepares us for "success" in a global market economy that drains the larger community of life on a scale that the Confucians could never have imagined.

Confucians were always aware of the fact that our individual life exists only as a participation in a larger systemic flow of life, that we live in and through a matrix of interdependent relationships. Thus the essence of the education that they envisioned centered on relationships. The famed Five Relationships of the Confucian tradition appear prominently in the center of the *Diagram of the Elementary Learning* and again in the *Diagram of the Rules of* [Zhu Xi's] *White Deer Hollow Academy*. These basic relationships, encompassing family, friendship, and public service, reflect the inherently social character of human nature. But however familiar and even inherent in our nature such sociability might be, Confucians also regarded these relationships to be the most important instruction for the young and—as evident in the Academy Rules—as a matter for ceaseless reflection and pondering thereafter. Being central to the flow of communal life, nothing could be more important.

China was in the midst of the strife and civil dissolution known as the Warring States period when Mencius wrote of the Five Relationships. Indeed, it is not too much to say that the deep social character of Confucian thought originated as a profound response to conditions during a time when human relationships were in critical disarray. What then would the Confucian response be to a time where the critical disarray has infected our relationships with a myriad of species in the interwoven community of life?

Both science and the evidence of our daily experience reveal an environmental crisis that can be solved only through a relational understanding, reflection, and self-cultivation as deep and profound as Confucius and Mencius directed to the social crisis of their time.

Zhu Xi and T'oegye never doubted that the single life-giving pattern of the universe wove itself into our nature and related human nature to the world at large. But only the sage is so perfected that the relationships patterned into human nature spontaneously and reliably shape and guide activity. The rest of us have other, more distorting tendencies to deal with. So further on in his *Introduction* Zhu explains: "The ordinary man is foolish and ignorant; the desire for things beclouds his vision and causes his inborn good qualities to decline, and he is content to thus do violence to himself and throw himself away. The sage, pitying this [miserable condition] set up schools and established teachers in order to fertilize the roots and make the branches arrive at their full growth."[9] This conviction caused the Cheng-Zhu school to place great emphasis on the need for education—an emphasis reflected in T'oegye's devoting three of his ten diagrams to the topic.

In the contemporary world we also emphasize the need for education, with main attention to our ever-growing economy. In this context, the "desire for things," mentioned above by Zhu Xi as a major distorting influence, is conceived of as a high value. Economists tell us the desire to possess ever more is a market-enhancing and appropriate response, one inherent in our economic nature. So we can understand why nowadays so much education is directed toward maximizing profit but almost none toward rectifying "the desire for things." In fact, an entire industry, advertising, is now devoted precisely toward maximizing and shaping ("educating") that desire.

The classic *Tae hak* (大学), the fourth of T'oegye's diagrams, holds the final goal of learning to be no less than the proper ordering or "tranquility" of the whole world. The *Zhongyong* (中庸) suggests that a proper ordering of human feelings can bring it about that "Heaven and Earth assume their proper order and all things will be nurtured and flourish."[10] Now that human learning and technological power have reached a condition where the order and nurture of the living world indeed hang in the balance, the goal and content of our education process has become critical. "Consumer" has become the most widely shared human identity, and the economic thought that guides entire nations assumes that the "desire for things" forms the essence of our profit-maximizing human nature. The next diagram will present a far deeper, wiser, and more life-giving view of human nature.

Diagram 6: How the Mind Combines and Governs the Nature and the Feelings

This section, which discusses three diagrams, delves into understanding the dynamics of our inner life in terms of the complex structure of our responsiveness. The first diagram outlines the life-giving world framework within which our own responsive natures are formed. The second of these three diagrams clarifies the traditional Mencian affirmation that our natural dispositions are in themselves perfectly fitting; because we inherently fit within the system, we should expect its life-giving qualities to be part of our own nature.

Many people now regard nature as good in this sense, and the adjective "natural" is often used as the equivalent of "good, safe, fitting, life-giving." But those who view nature this way often exclude human society, thinking we humans are somehow outside of nature, and thus our actions are liable to be unnatural and suspect. T'oegye's analysis in this second diagram would suggest that this view of the matter is mistaken. If we consider the way the entire system is interwoven, *fit* is the essential character of the weaving. This is true whether one thinks in terms of the all-encompassing unity of *li/dao* (Supreme Ultimate) or in contemporary terms of the dynamic process of co-evolution.

Certain sorts of feelings in humans, the Seven Feelings (joy, anger, grief, fear, love, hate, desire) were often associated by Confucians with going astray. But T'oegye's analysis ranks them in this second diagram along with the feelings that Confucians thought of as inherently good. On this level of consideration, there is a fitness in all our inborn tendencies. They are natural and have their place, just like everything else in nature.

But human society rarely appears to be an unalloyed manifestation of fitting, life-enhancing conduct. What, then, goes wrong? This is the question T'oegye addresses in the chapter's third diagram. His basic answer is the perennial Confucian view: self-centeredness distorts the appropriate manifestation of our dispositions. Neo-Confucians gave this explanation further depth by associating it with *ki* (氣), material force, the stuff of all concrete and thereby particularized existence. Perfect clarity of *ki* allows for undistorted relational dynamics and perfect responsiveness, because the appropriate dispositions of our natural endowment are functioning with full integrity. More turbid *ki* conditions people who get "blocked up" in the individuality of their persons, distorting the dynamics of their inherently relational existence through an inappropriate self-centeredness.

T'oegye ventures further: his third diagram suggests that different sorts of feelings relate differently to the *ki* of our individuality. The Four Beginnings (humanity, rightness, propriety, wisdom) had long been considered the constitutive core of our natural dispositions; as inherently social dispositions, they were regarded as emblematic of the goodness or fittingness of human nature. The Seven Feelings (anger, joy, etc.), by contrast, are closely related to maintaining the well-being of our physical individuality and thus are much more liable to slip over into an ill mode of centering on self at the price of relationships. T'oegye describes this difference in his famous formula: "If one considers the Four Beginnings, principle issues and material force follows in accord. . . . As for the Seven Feelings, material force issues and *li* mounts it."[11]

T'oegye's reflection here insightfully explores one of the most fundamental dynamic tensions of living systems, that between the well-being of the parts and the well-being of the whole system. The parts of a single organism are inherently shaped only for fit, for all parts work together for the well-being of the whole organism. But an ecosystem or a social system is made up of many whole organisms, and the fitness of these organisms involves taking care of themselves as well as with fitting in with all the other members of the system. The dynamics of such a system are much more complex than simple cooperation, for they must also take in the competition among creatures.

In a system of natural mutual constraint, living creatures try to maximize their own lives but are fittingly limited by others in an interdependent dance of predator and prey, plant and herbivore, herbivore and carnivore. In a balanced ecosystem, the dynamic pursuit of individual gratification is interwoven into a relational whole, a fluctuating system of life that nonetheless achieves a basic equilibrium and furnishes a fitting life and well-being to the many creatures that constitute it. Individual-oriented instincts, the equivalent of the Seven Feelings, are not a problem in the natural world, because everything else in the system works to constrain such behaviors in an interlocking network. The human case is far different, for we have managed to escape the network of mutual constraint that marks the natural world.

Much like the natural world, human society self-organizes in ways that include mutual constraints on individual self-maximizing conduct. We achieve this through our cultural and legal systems; the educational emphasis on the Five Relationships in the earlier diagrams are a clear example of how a society seeks to constrain individual self-seeking. But our power of speech and thought, and therefore of contriving novel strategies, is such that we can easily devise ways around constraints when we are so inclined. The unconstrained profit-seeking strategies that led to the worldwide financial crisis of 2008–2009 are an example on a global scale of the human capacity to damage the system upon which we all depend in order to maximize personal profit. As Confucius observed, if you set up laws but do not teach people to feel shame, they are of no use.[12] What fits us into a life-giving flow of common life is partly systemic, but it also depends to a unique degree upon the cultivation of the individual mind-and-heart.

Confucians had deep insight into the extent to which systemic social relational fit is inherent in our inborn dispositions. T'oegye added an interesting further dimension when he noted that these dispositions, conceptualized as the "Four Beginnings," are self-moving along relational (social) lines (*li*), an important difference from the feelings that move us to take care of ourselves (the Seven Feelings). Contemporary economic theory has led many to a superficial view of humans as inherently self-interested; Confucian learning does a service in balancing that picture, calling attention to an instinctive sociability that is evident all around us if we but look for it.

In the human case, then, the life-giving order of a networked society and world pivots on sets of inherent dynamics that pull in different directions, the one involving an appropriate relational fit, the other directing us to take care of ourselves. The latter is also appropriate and necessary (cf. the second diagram) but can get out of hand and distort relationships in a way that diminishes the life of all, including our own selves.

Confucians, including T'oegye, thought that if we got this right, the world would be in proper, life-nurturing order. But in this, they missed a critical consideration: with their intense focus on human-to-human relationships, they never imagined that human-to-nonhuman relationships could present an equal or perhaps even more threatening problem.

The structural dynamic of this problem is much as T'oegye has described, except in this case it is human society's collective instinct to take care of itself that is in tension with dispositions to fit and enjoy a life-giving relationship with the natural world. Now the disordering factor is not just inappropriate self-centeredness but an inappropriate centeredness on our whole species at the expense of the larger community of life. A short-sighted and anthropocentric form of the Four Beginnings can, in fact, inspire ferocious insistence upon economic development for humans even at the expense of the extinction of whole species. There may be a fairly strong social instinct in human beings to take care of one another, but that seems to fall off quickly when it comes to nonhuman life.

Here the Cheng-Chu emphasis on the necessity of learning (学) becomes critical. The exhaustive investigation of the dynamic patterning of the affairs of life (理) cannot stop at matters such as the Five Relationships, unless learning enables us to understand them in the inclusive framework of the whole Earth. The modern power with which we make our own living ("the economy") operates on such a scale that it affects the way all creatures in the earth, air, and water are able to go about making their livings. This, and its consequences, can be understood only by study. We may indeed be deeply shaped for an interdependent relational existence, but what this requires of us is far more challenging, complex, and removed from our immediate instincts than could have been imagined in earlier centuries.

Diagram 7: The Explanation of Humanity (仁说)

In the *Diagram of the Supreme Ultimate*, we saw that the Mandate is the imperative that we fit with the dynamic pattern (理) of not only human relationships but of the entire relational system to which we belong. This section investigates this dynamic pattern and the way it constitutes context for our spiritual self-cultivation.

The *Book of Changes*, in its hexagram for spring (復, literally "return" of the life force) describes the character of Heaven and Earth (the cosmos) as "continually producing life" (生生).[13] Zhu Xi goes further, seeing the humane (仁), life-giving dispositions of the human mind-and-heart as just our way of sharing in the life-producing dynamism of the cosmos. The life-giving quality of humanity is then a quality of the universe first, and it thereby becomes a quality of humans: "Humanity is the mind of Heaven and Earth whereby they produce and give life to creatures, and this is what man receives as his own mind."[14]

The cycle of the four seasons had long been correlated with the Four Beginnings, the social dispositions that constitute the essential dynamic of the mind-and-heart, and Zhu Xi notes how the seasons and our social dispositions are really only differing manifestations of this single life-giving force that flows through the seasons:

> The mind of Heaven and Earth has four characteristics: they are origination, flourishing, benefiting, and firmness, and origination runs

throughout all. As they move in rotation, we have the cycle of spring, summer, fall, and winter, and the generative force of spring runs throughout all. Therefore in the mind of man there are likewise four characteristics: they are humanity, rightness, propriety, and wisdom, and humanity encompasses them all.[15]

This understanding of both the natural world and the inner life of our minds-and-hearts derives from deep reflection on the experience of an agricultural society. In the minds of our contemporary urban cultures, the place of the seasonal growth cycle has been replaced by the vision of an ever-growing industrial feedback loop of raw materials, productivity, and consumption. It is not surprising, then, that we should more easily think of profit maximization or acquisitiveness as the fundamental dynamic of the human mind-and-heart. Many thinkers of the last century even imagined that this was the essential dynamism of the whole life system, as in Social Darwinism or the more recent "selfish gene" theories.[16]

We now see and experience that the difference between the agriculturally informed vision and the industrial vision has become a pressing and urgent matter for the future of the entire system of life. In the industrial world, we have our eyes on the GNP and we calculate the flow of goods and services, to which the Earth simply furnishes an endless supply of raw materials. Zhu Xi explicates a far different kind of circulatory system:

Thus although Heaven and Earth and man and other creatures each are different, nevertheless in reality there is, as it were, a single circulatory system running through them. Therefore if one personally realizes this mind and can preserve and foster it, there is nothing that the principle of the mind does not reach and one naturally loves everything. But if one's capacities are small and [this mind] is beclouded by selfish desires, then its flowing forth is cut off and there are those to whom one's love does not reach.[17]

This difference of understanding cuts to the heart of our contemporary sustainability crisis: a beclouded, short-sighted, and self-centered human mind can cause spreading death as it heedlessly stops the flow that is the life-giving dynamic of the world. Although we now mainly inhabit large cities rather than rural areas, the agricultural understanding of the patterned, dynamic flow of life is critically important, for all other considerations depend on maintaining that flow. Without it, the GNP and the rest of the humanly constructed world become meaningless.

Diagram 8: The Study of the Heart-and-Mind

The *Diagram of the Study of the Heart-and-Mind* (see p. x) lays out for us the essential features of the terrain of our inner life and the stages of its cultivation as these appear against the background of the Neo-Confucian view of the world. Not surprisingly, its assessment of the dynamics of our inner life is rather different from the view of what is appropriate to human nature as described by contemporary economic thinkers.

The mind-and-heart is the relational conduit through which life flows as we interact appropriately with the family of our fellow creatures. Feelings are the motivating force that shapes our initial responsiveness in this relational network, so feelings become a central object of spiritual cultivation. The various phrases in the diagram indicate aspects of our feelings and the cultivation appropriate to them. The distinctive role of the mind-and-heart is to preside over the feelings-led responsiveness as we participate in the flow of life, and thus it occupies the central circle in this diagram and is inscribed with the words, "the master of the entire person."

The diagram portrays the interior life of the feelings as divided into two distinctive aspects, the "Human Mind" and the "Dao Mind" or "Mind of the Dao." These expressions come from a brief but very influential passage in the *Book of Documents*: "The human mind is perilous, the mind of the Dao is subtle; be discerning, be undivided. Hold fast the Mean!"[18] As is evident in the way that these categories structure this entire diagram, this passage came to epitomize the Confucian view of the essential task of self-cultivation. The text that accompanies the diagram clarifies: "This does not mean that there are two kinds of mind; but since in fact man is produced through the material force that gives one physical form, no one can be without the 'human mind'; and [at the same time] origination [as a human being] is from the nature, which is the Mandate [of Heaven], and this is what is referred to as the 'mind of the Dao.' "[19]

We have already encountered this tension between physical individuality and the mandate for systemic fit in relation to T'oegye's sixth diagram. This inherent individual/social tension gives rise to two complementary facets in cultivating the full integrity of our inner life. The "perilous" Human Mind easily slips into inappropriate forms of self-centeredness. We must struggle to keep the powerful instincts by which we take care of our own well-being selves within proper bounds. On the other hand, the problem with the Dao Mind is that the feelings that weave all life together are very "subtle," especially in comparison to the robust demands of our individual physical bodies. The characteristic cultivation of this side of our inner life calls for a heightened alertness and careful nurturing of dispositions too easily neglected.

The mastery of the mind-and-heart in presiding over these dynamics of our inner life is described in the lower part of the diagram as the exercise of "mindfulness." Both Zhu Xi and T'oegye regarded mindfulness as the central feature of all spiritual self-cultivation, and the remainder of the *Ten Diagrams* is devoted to this practice.

Diagram 9: Admonition on Mindfulness (Reverence)

The ninth diagram focuses specifically on what is involved in mindfulness, the exercise of appropriately presiding over the dynamic inclinations of the mind-and-heart. Where earlier diagrams brought out the flow of life as what is ultimately at stake in cultivating the mind-and-heart, here the focus closes in on the practice of a discerning awareness of the motivations that guide and inform the way that we respond to the constantly shifting situations of daily life. Small misaligned currents can carry us far from a life-giving fit: "If one should falter for a single moment, selfish desire will put forth ten thousand shoots." And, "if there is a hair's breadth disparity, Heaven and Earth will change their places."[20]

This sounds exaggerated to those accustomed to thinking of morality as a matter of making choices between good and evil: great evil, we think, happens because very evil people choose great evil. Confucians are much more aware of how great wrongness can unfold from seemingly minor inappropriate actions.

Mindfulness means maintaining a self-possessed, focused state of mind. "Concentrate on one thing without departing" occupies the central place in this diagram: "Let your mind be undivided as it watches over the myriad changes." And, "when you encounter some affair, attend only to it; do not set off about something else." There is great optimism about the life-giving potential of simply paying close attention to what we are doing, but the optimism is tempered by a keen awareness that however available guidance may be, it cannot help if we do not attend to it. And the phrase "without departing" draws attention to how subject we are to distracting influences. Self-possession and the ability to pay attention are two sides of the same coin, but they draw on somewhat different sides of cultivation practice. Various forms of disciplined conduct, such as propriety in dress, speech, and behavior, feed into the ability to maintain a self-possessed frame of mind, while meditative practice, nurturing a profound inner quietness, enhances the ability to pay close attention in the more active situations of our complex lives.

The cultivation of mindfulness recommended in this diagram addresses a problem that has become even more difficult in the contemporary world. We have entire industries—advertising, media, entertainment—largely devoted to distracting us. We learn "multitasking" as a strategy for lives that have become so busy and stuffed with so many activities that the diagram's advice, "because of two do not divide your mind into two" sounds quaint and impractical. But how life giving are the responses of our preoccupied minds-and-hearts? On scales both large and small, personal and global, there is a price to be paid for inattention and distraction, and that price seems to steadily grow larger. Deep in a global recession, we now ask how we could have allowed the most inappropriate kinds of financial practices to ramify to a point where the global financial system threatened to melt around us. Future generations may well wonder how we could let the polar icecaps melt and the climate change around us without decisive action. Surely the practice of mindfulness would challenge us to realign lives of mindless production and consumption that drain the life vitality from the communities—human and nonhuman—to which we belong.

Diagram 10: Rising Early and Retiring Late

This final diagram describes a model day lived mindfully. A model day in the life of a semiretired Confucian scholar-official in an agrarian society seems set in an entirely different world than that of the fast-paced, hectic, demanding urban life of this century. But though the external characteristics of the lifestyles have changed greatly, the nature of the challenge of self-cultivation has not changed at all. We are still human, still engaged from rising until bedtime with a flow of situations to which we must respond, and we must cultivate ourselves so that we will respond appropriately, in a life-giving way. From T'oegye's time to our own, that has always been the human situation, and that is the subject of this diagram.

The day presented in this diagram is shaped by a deep conviction that we live in a world of dynamic, interlocked, relational unity, so that everything is shaped in terms of everything else; there is always a relational shape to all affairs and situations that renders some ways of conducting ourselves more appropriate than others. And our minds-and-hearts, which belong not just to our own persons but, in a deeper sense, to this whole relational system, are informed with the sensitivity to read the situation, be guided aright, and respond in a life-giving way. T'oegye refers to this always available guidance in his remarks accompanying the diagram: "Indeed, the uninterrupted flow of the Dao throughout the affairs of daily life is such that there is nowhere one can go that it is not present; thus there is not a single foot of ground in which principle is absent."[21]

If indeed guidance is surrounding us always and everywhere, a mode of life that fosters a habit of close and responsive attentiveness ("mindfulness") seems appropriate. But the mind-and-heart presides over a situation that is both inward (our feelings) and external (affairs). The mastery of mindfulness is precisely the quiet attention to the interplay between these two as situations give rise to feelings that motivate, guide, and shape our activity.

Neo-Confucians anticipated a natural rhythm of quiet and activity that could be turned usefully to each of these aspects. Quiet provides the context in which to cultivate the deep inward calm and harmony of our emotions. Then, in activity, careful focus on what is happening would call forth the most fitting kind of feelings or motivational response. This rhythm is built into the day depicted in this diagram. "Over the cyclic alteration of activity and quiet, the mind alone presides; it should be possessed in quiet and discerning in activity."[22] And again: "When the matter has been responded to and is finished, then be as you were before, with your mind clear and calm."[23]

Now this rhythm seems not only hard to attain but even beyond the imagination of many. We are constantly overloaded with information from sources near and far, constantly on call or calling from cell phones, or plugged into iPods, constantly stimulated. In such a setting, the advice to "be as you were before, with your mind clear and calm," sounds like irony. When, indeed, are our minds "clear and calm"? We have global awareness, but we do not know what to pay attention to until disaster strikes. We multitask but seem never to catch up, and what gets done is frequently not well done.

The major message of the tenth diagram for contemporary daily life, then, would be: SLOW DOWN! Especially the relational, social side of our dispositions (the "Four Beginnings"/Dao Mind) has become stressed and starved for time and development as we hasten to maximize our production and consumption (the "Seven Feelings"/Human Mind). An inner hunger for deeper, more thoughtful, more meaningful relationships with families, friends, colleagues, and community runs through industrial societies as they climb the steep path to economic development. And a deeper appreciation and relationship with the natural living world about us has become an urgent imperative in exact proportion to the way our fast-paced search for human comfort has mindlessly drained life from the rest of our living community.

T'oegye's *Ten Diagrams* explores for the contemporary mind the human ramifications of existing in what science tells us is a relational web. It raises for us challenging questions regarding the way that we live that T'oegye could not have imagined: advertising, entertainment, constant stimulation, multitasking, the plugged-in life, economic growth, and the whole meaning of "development." The Dao Mind/Human Mind categories pick up a tension inherent in our systemic social-individual lives and suggest deep problems in our contemporary way of thinking about development or personal fulfillment. Contemporary institutions that foster and emphasize what T'oegye spoke of as the "Seven Feelings" are problematic not because they do not fit into T'oegye's worldview but because they do not fit with the systemic, relational nature of existence and the condition of life on our planet.

A thorough contemporary reading of T'oegye's *Ten Diagrams* raises many unsettling questions about the institutions, values, and perhaps even the whole way of life that we now take for granted. We should be grateful that the framework within which he worked out his ideas about education, cultivation, and an appropriate mode of life is so similar to our best knowledge of the world today. In reading T'oegye's ideas, we are brought to confront our own inconsistencies and contradictions between what we know about the world and the way we live. But even more valuable, in the techniques of cultivation that Neo-Confucians investigated so deeply, there is a deep wisdom concerning how to go about living in accord with the mandate to *fit* into the community of life.

Notes

This is a shortened version of a paper originally prepared for the International T'oegyehak Conference, Daegu, Korea, August 2009.

1. Michael Kalton, *To Become a Sage: The Ten Diagrams on Sage Learning by Yi T'oegye* (New York: Columbia University Press, 1988). Most references in this paper will be to this translation and commentary, hereafter referred to as *Ten Diagrams*. The complete text of this book, as well as T'oegye's original Chinese text, is available for downloading on my Web site: http://faculty.washington.edu/mkalton.

2. *Book of Changes*, commentary on Ch'ien hexagram.

3. *Ten Diagrams*, 38.

4. Ibid., 42. The subquotation is a reference to *Book of Changes*, "Remarks on Certain Trigrams," chap. 1.

5. *Diagram of the Western Inscription*, in *Ten Diagrams*, 51.

6. Ibid.

7. Ibid., 53.

8. Ibid., 52.

9. Ibid.

10. *Zhongyong*, chap. 1.

11. *Ten Diagrams*, chap. 6, pp. 126–127.

12. *Analects* 2.3.

13. *Book of Changes*, hexagram no. 24, and "Appended Remarks," part 2, chap. 1.

14. *Diagram of the Explanation of Humanity*, in *Ten Diagrams*, 144.

15. Ibid., 147.

16. Cf. Richard Dawkins, *The Selfish Gene* (Oxford: Oxford University Press, 1976).

17. Yǔlei 95.86–89a.

18. *Book of Documents*, part 2, 2.15.

19. *Ten Diagrams*, chap. 8, p. 160.

20. *Admonition on Mindfulness*, in *Ten Diagrams*, chap. 9, p. 178.

21. *Ten Diagrams*, chap. 10, p. 195.

22. Ibid., 193.

23. Ibid.

26

THE MEMOIRS OF LADY HYEGYŎNG

JaHyun Kim Haboush

THE MEMOIRS OF *Lady Hyegyŏng*, known in Korean as *Hanjungnok* (*Records Written in Silence*), or *Hanjung mallok* (*Memoirs Written in Silence*), is a collection of four autobiographical narratives written by Lady Hyegyŏng from 1795 to 1805. Lady Hyegyŏng was born in 1735 in Seoul, the daughter of Hong Ponghan (1713–1778), of the illustrious P'ungsan Hong family. In 1744, she married Crown Prince Sado (1735–1762). They were both nine years old, and the nuptials did not take place until five years later. Prince Sado was appointed prince regent and, save for several crucial areas, assumed a role in governing. Lady Hyegyŏng bore him two sons and two daughters. One son died in infancy; the other became King Chŏngjo (r. 1776–1800).

One hot day in July 1762, King Yŏngjo ordered his son, Prince Sado, to enter a rice chest of about four feet square, which was then sealed. And there in the chest, Prince Sado died eight days later. This incident, the only publicly known filicide in the five-hundred-year Chosŏn dynasty (1392–1910), cast a terrible pall over those who were involved in the tragedy and lived through it. Most conspicuous among them were King Yŏngjo, whose long and brilliant reign was deeply compromised by this inhumane filicide; Sado's son, King Chŏngjo, whose reign even surpassed that of his grandfather in brilliance and accomplishment yet who, all his life, battled the shame and grief that his father's tragic death left behind; and other ministers and tutors, some of whom took their own lives or suffered political upheaval because of their relationships to Prince Sado.

As his wife, Lady Hyegyŏng was profoundly affected by the prince's death and its repercussions. Nonetheless, as was the case with women in Chosŏn, she was mostly hidden from public view. Had it not been for her memoirs, Lady Hyegyŏng, like countless other women whose husbands, fathers or sons were involved in political incidents, would have been dimly perceived as someone who suffered silently behind the scenes. Breaking that long silence, however, Lady Hyegyŏng wrote four sets of memoirs in which she narrates not only her own life but also the affair of Prince Sado from her own perspective and renders judgment on all concerned.

In so doing, Lady Hyegyŏng accomplished a great feat rare for women prior to the modern era anywhere in the world. Narration is a mode of expression but also a mode of empowerment. Until recently, in most societies, women did not narrate their own lives, not to mention the lives of others. Autobiographies by women were few, and those written tended to be private and domestic. In Europe or in Japan, for instance, women's autobiographies were confined to the interior or domestic aspect of their lives. That a woman narrated a royal filicide, the most public of incidents, an event that can be described as the ultimate in male power rivalry, makes Lady Hyegyŏng's *Memoirs* unique in autobiographical literature. Moreover, despite the paucity of descriptions of the incident of Prince Sado in official historiography, not only does Sado reign supreme as a tragic figure in the popular imagination of contemporary Korea, but he is imagined as he is depicted in *The Memoirs of Lady Hyegyŏng*. In this sense, her autobiography was turned into a history, either as an alternative to the official history or a more persuasive version of it.

When Lady Hyegyŏng wrote her memoirs, there was neither an accepted tradition nor a well-defined genre for writing women's memoirs. I would like to place *The Memoirs of Lady Hyegyŏng* in the context of Chosŏn Korean literary culture, which developed out of dual linguistic traditions— classical Chinese and Korean. I will also speculate on the cultural significance of the genres that Lady Hyegyŏng used. She did not have a ready-made form available to her, and so for each memoir she resorted to a genre from classical Chinese prose and used it for her own purposes. As the memoirs move from the personal to the public, so do the genres in which the memoirs are written, from autobiography to historiography.

The written culture of Chosŏn Korea, from the time the Korean script was devised in the mid-fifteenth century until early in the twentieth century, consisted of writings in classical Chinese and vernacular Korean.

Classical Chinese functioned as something like a sacral or universal language of East Asia, similar to Latin in Europe. Educated men in East Asia, that is, in China, Japan, Korea and Vietnam, felt themselves to be members of a civilization rooted and conducted in classical Chinese. From the seventeenth century, the output of vernacular writing increased vastly both in volume and in variety in Korea. But its popularity did not diminish the prestige of the classical Chinese tradition, and Korea enjoyed a diglossic effervescence in its written culture. Though this diglossia is often described in a dichotomous framework—that is, discourse in Chinese was conducted by men, was canonical (Confucian), public, universal, and hegemonic, whereas discourse in Korean was practiced by women and was local, private, domestic, and subversive—the relationship between the two traditions was much more complex. Men began to write in Korean as well as in Chinese. Also, there was substantial interplay between the two: each tradition influenced, appropriated, and challenged the other. Thus, the intertextuality of a text written in one language often transcended the limits of that language and extended to the other. *The Memoirs of Lady Hyegyŏng* grew out of this complex diglossic culture. On the one hand, Lady Hyegyŏng could write in the linguistic medium that was thought to be primarily female. On the other hand, she could appropriate and privatize the genres and themes that were male and public in classical language.

The structure of the *Memoirs* is quite intriguing. The four memoirs were not conceived of nor composed as a single work. They were written on separate occasions for specific audiences in defense of specific causes and individuals. Despite their separateness, the memoirs do constitute a certain integral whole. It is noticeable that they move from the personal to the public. While the first three memoirs describe at length the emotional turmoil and political repercussions of the Sado incident, the incident itself is only referred to cryptically. So when that story is finally narrated in the last memoir, it functions almost as does the solution in a detective story, in that it answers many questions that arise but are left unanswered in the course of reading the first three memoirs.

The first memoir, written in 1795, when Lady Hyegyŏng had just reached her sixtieth birthday, was addressed to her nephew, the heir of her natal family, the Hongs. It is in the form of an epistle. It contains advice and exhortations to the younger generation, but its main body is a self-narration followed by a postscript devoted to short remembrances of members of her family. It begins with her remembered childhood. In fact, a description of childhood is rare in any literature dating from this period.

She had one older and three younger brothers, and she grew up as the only daughter, apparently the favorite of her parents. She presents her childhood as a perfectly happy one, with loving parents, bright and affectionate siblings, and prosperous and harmonious relations, even though her family was not wealthy.

This childhood abruptly came to an end. In 1743, the royal house sent out an edict announcing that it was seeking a bride for the crown prince and that *yangban* families—aristocratic scholar families—with eligible daughters were to submit the names of those daughters for the three-step selection process. This was a method used in choosing spouses for royal children. It was done when the children were about eight or nine, although the nuptials would not take place until they were about fifteen. The custom was designed to let the outsiders become familiar with court life. Hyegyŏng's father submitted her name. Hyegyŏng first went into the palace for the first presentation when she was nine years old. With the remembered eye of a curious child, she captures vivid impressions of the royal family and the palace, providing a unique record of the process of selecting the spouse of a royal child.

The selection process sounds a little like a beauty pageant. The king and the queen were present, evaluating each girl. The royal child, for whom the selection was being made—in this case, Prince Sado—was not allowed to be present. Even by the second presentation, it was obvious that Lady Hyegyŏng had been chosen: when she returned home, her palanquin was carried by palace servants. This was the first instance of the palace taking possession of Hyegyŏng's life. A messenger carrying the formal message announcing her selection accompanied Hyegyŏng home, and her parents received the message with due respect. Her relationship to her parents and relatives changed immediately. "From that day, my parents changed their form of address to me; now they spoke to me exclusively in respectful language." The Korean language has several levels of honorifics, and parents use the informal form when conversing with children, while children use the formal form with parents. But now Hyegyŏng was designated the Crown Princess Consort. So the change in form of address was a sign that her public status preceded her private relationship.

Hyegyŏng also turns a longing gaze on the house that she was leaving behind. She recounts a very touching scene: her mother making a skirt for her.

Just after the second presentation, her mother burst into tears and said, "I never got to dress you in pretty clothes. In the palace you won't be able to wear ordinary clothes. I had better make something pretty for you now, just as I always wanted to." Grieving all the while, my mother made me a skirt of double red silk and made me wear it before the final presentation. I wept, and I wore it.

Hyegyŏng idealized her childhood, probably because she was forced to leave it early. Her remembrance of it is always accompanied by a sense of loss. In fact, her abruptly ending childhood becomes a metaphor both for everything that ends before it runs its natural course and for unfulfilled promises. This sense of unrequitedness defines sadness for her.

After the final presentation, Hyegyŏng was housed at the bridal pavilion, a detached building outside the palace wall, until the wedding ceremony, which was held two months later, in February 1744. Her parents also stayed at this pavilion. This arrangement was a concession on the part of the royal family to Korean custom, in which the wedding ceremony took place at the bride's house. The first part of the wedding ceremony took place at the bridal pavilion, and it was followed by the grand ceremony, later the same day, at the palace. On the following day, a ceremony of bowing took place, in which the new bride bowed to the king. Afterward, accompanied by her mother, Hyegyŏng paid respect to the ladies of the older generations. She settled into her residence, a house within the Crown Prince Residence. Then her mother had to leave. Hyegyŏng was presented to the Royal Ancestral Temple, and her life as the Crown Princess Consort began.

Life at court was governed by ritual and ceremony. Hyegyŏng was expected to perform her part, but mostly in the domestic sphere. There were four people of the older generations that she had to serve: Yŏngjo, Queen Chŏngsŏng, and Queen Dowager Inwŏn, Yŏngjo's stepmother—who are referred to as the Three Majesties—and Lady Sŏnhŭi, Sado's mother. Yŏngjo and Chŏngsŏng were estranged from one another, and Lady Sŏnhŭi, despite her lower status, was the king's favorite companion. In any case, Hyegyŏng was expected to pay respect to Queen Dowager Inwŏn and Queen Chŏngsŏng on every fifth day and to Lady Sŏnhŭi on every third day. Hyegyŏng brought her nurse and several maidservants with her to the palace, and they helped her to do her duty. There were also a number of princesses, Prince Sado's sisters, most of whom were born of Lady Sŏnhŭi.

She seems to have gotten along with them, although it required a certain tact on her part.

Things seemed to be going well for her. Early in 1749, when Prince Sado and Hyegyŏng were both fourteen years of age, their nuptials took place. In 1750, she gave birth to a son. Although this son died two years later, another was born in 1752 to the immense joy and relief of the royal elders and Hyegyŏng's parents. This son would later become King Chŏngjo. She repeatedly says that he was the most bright, good, and handsome of living beings. Though this was obviously the statement of a loving mother, judging by what he accomplished, he must have been an exceptional child. Two daughters followed, Princess Ch'ŏngyŏn in 1754 and Princess Ch'ŏngsŏn in 1756. Prince Sado, soon after he turned fourteen, was appointed a prince-regent and given heavy duties in governing. Hyegyŏng's natal family also prospered. Her father passed the civil-service examination and, under royal patronage, moved into a position of power, eventually becoming prime minister. Her brothers excelled in their studies, and her parents had another daughter, over whose birth Hyegyŏng was very happy.

At some point, however, the tone of Hyegyŏng's memoir becomes perceptibly dark and anguished. First, her mother died in 1755. Ordinarily, married women mourned their mothers for a year, but Hyegyŏng's mourning for her mother was seen as a private matter and had to be shortened. In 1757, Queen Chŏngsŏng, and Queen Dowager Inwŏn passed away within a month of each other. As women married into the royal family as legal consorts, the three ladies seem to have developed a sense of affinity and sympathy across generations, and Hyegyŏng expresses a sense of loss and loneliness at their passing.

Her anguish, however, seems unaccountably profound and mysterious. Sometime around 1756, she begins to cryptically refer to Prince Sado's illness. She says things like "the deep worry, which burned in my heart like a flame, grew worse, and I really lost my desire to live." Again: "I would rather not discuss the depths of my disquiet and nervousness during this period." Of her father she writes: "He was profoundly troubled by the state of things at court. We spent our days in deep gloom. Things grew even harder. I longed for oblivion." Then in 1762, she says: "Things grew still worse. My desire to do away with myself, and thus to attain a blissful ignorance, became ever so strong." Then finally: "On the thirteenth day, Heaven and Earth clashed and the sun and the moon turned black." This was the day that Prince Sado was put into the rice chest. What has been going on? *The Memoir of 1795* does not say more on the topic; indeed, as mentioned above, she does not explicitly narrate the event until her last memoir, written ten years later.

The Memoir of 1795 is written as an apologia for herself and her father, defending their choices to live on after Prince Sado's death. Widows were not expected to follow their husbands to the grave in Chosŏn Korea, but this was a special case. Prince Sado had been put to death by his father, and to be indebted for her life to the king who had killed her husband carried compromising implications. But, on the other hand, had she chosen to die, it would have implied a protest against the royal decision or have deepened the suggestion that Prince Sado had been guilty. Neither would have furthered her son's legitimacy. Lady Hyegyŏng presents this as the ultimate example of the conflict between the demands imposed by her different roles. She presents her decision to live as a decision to choose the most public of her duties, in this case, the course that benefited dynastic security. This coincided with her maternal duty. That this obligation had a prior claim does not obliterate the fact that she failed to discharge her wifely duty to follow her husband. That, of course, was the source of her shame. She says: "Wishing to repay the throne and to protect the Grand heir, I gave up the idea of killing myself. Nevertheless, how can I ever forget, even to the last moment of my consciousness, the shame of not having known the proper end and my regret over my long and slow life." At the same time, she implies that it was also her ultimate sacrifice, born of her devotion to the public cause. In fact, the choice between personal honor and public cause is a familiar theme in her narration. She defends the rest of her family in the same manner—that the choices they made also required deep compromises of personal honor but that they did so for public cause. She, in fact, presents her narrative as an "elaborate drama of honor," a drama of her class and milieu.

The last three memoirs were written after her son Chŏngjo had died and are addressed to King Sunjo, her grandson, who ascended the throne as a minor and thus began his reign under a queen dowager's regency. These memoirs are more public, each a little more so than the previous one. The second memoir, written in 1801, is a defense of her younger brother, Hong Nagim, who was executed during the first major persecution of Catholics. The charges against Hong Nagim were unsubstantiated and it seems in all likelihood unfounded. Lady Hyegyŏng attributes the outcome entirely to an acrimonious interfamilial feud. This memoir is written in a form resembling a petition/memorial. Lady Hyegyŏng's *Memoir of 1801* privatizes a mode of writing that had been reserved exclusively for public discourse. Availing herself of her position as the grandmother of the king, she appropriates this genre and uses it for testimony in Korean.

The Memoir of 1802, the third, presents a moving portrayal of Chŏngjo as a son obsessed with restoring honor to his ill-fated father. Lady Hyegyŏng recounts that in his unrequited obsession, Chŏngjo drew up a plan in which he would fulfill his dream of restoring honor to his father and the dishonored members of his maternal family. He died before he could enact this plan. Recounting Chŏngjo's filial devotion, she appeals to Sunjo. In this way, Lady Hyegyŏng privatizes the genre of biography as well as its subject. This memoir is the biography of a filial son rather than that of a king who was, in fact, one of the most brilliant rulers of the Chosŏn dynasty. And it is written by the mother of this filial son and is addressed in turn to her grandson, upon whom filiality presumably weighed just as heavily.

The Memoir of 1805 finally presents the incident of Prince Sado. With Lady Hyegyŏng's claim that it recounts a truthful history of the royal filicide of the crown prince, it enters into the realm of historiography. But in several crucial ways, her narrative differs from conventional historiography. This memoir is again addressed to her grandson. Befitting its public subject matter, she speaks to him as a senior member of the royal family would speak to a royal descendant. Also, her narrative is a first-person, eyewitness account based on her own recollections. In fact, the authenticity and value of her account lie precisely in her claim that she alone witnessed the event and that she alone knew the truth. And she professes that the reason for writing was her duty to transmit to Sunjo this knowledge about his ancestors. In other words, she wants to establish "public history" with her private memory. In so doing, she eschews the customary indirection in describing the failings of the king or the royal family. It is as if she believed that the only redemption for them and the other players involved in the incident lay in her portrayal of them in their full human complexity and imperfection, causing an enduring pain.

It is a remarkable story. As each player fulfills his or her sorrowful destiny, terror and sadness become unbearable. The psychological persuasiveness of her memoirs comes from Princess Hyegyŏng's keen observation, apparently related to her status as an outsider, someone born and raised outside the palace. And she focuses her keen outsider's gaze, which she used in commenting on the rigors of court life, on the causes of the deepening conflict between father and son.

She narrates the story of the father-son conflict in two modes. In one mode, she evokes the cosmic realm—ultimately, human motives and human emotions are mysterious and beyond human comprehension. She uses this mode when she discusses the reasons for Yŏngjo's harshness toward his own son sometimes despite himself. She acknowledges that he had his own demons to fight, but she leaves these strange impulses unexplained. Most of the time, however, she narrates in the realm of human comprehensibility.

When Sado was born, Yŏngjo was overjoyed. He had been without an heir since the death of his first son, Prince Hyojang, in 1728, a year that was marked by another disaster. There had been a rebellion in the south, and though it was soon pacified, Yŏngjo never forgot the terror of thinking that he might have lost his royal mantle. He redoubled his efforts to bring prosperity to the country. He was also anxious to secure his successor.

Contravening the custom that the heir be formally invested as crown prince at about seven or eight years of age, Yŏngjo appointed Sado the crown prince when he was a mere fourteen months old and installed him in the Crown Prince Residence, complete with tutors and military guards. Sado's residence was very far from the residences of Yŏngjo and Lady Sŏnhŭi. Although the prince's removal happened before she entered the palace, Hyegyŏng presents this distance as the seed of trouble. The parents spent less and less time with their son, and the prince spent most of his time in the company of eunuchs and ladies-in-waiting, hearing gossip and tales of scandal. The physical distance created a psychological barrier between father and son. Prince Sado began to fear his father, while Yŏngjo, who had placed so much hope in his late begotten son, began to feel apprehensive over his development.

Princess Hyegyŏng also remarks on their different personalities: Yŏngjo was articulate and bright. He was penetrating in observation and quick of comprehension, whereas Prince Sado was reticent, slow, and deliberate of movement. She cites as an example that when Yŏngjo asked him the most ordinary questions, the prince answered very slowly and hesitantly. This tried Yŏngjo's patience.

This is how Hyegyŏng found them when she entered the palace. She says that she was struck by the strictness of life at court. Prince Sado was only nine, but he did not dare to sit in front of his father except in a prostrate position, just as officials did. He referred himself as "your servant." From the beginning, she sensed that something was amiss. The prince never finished his morning toilet on time. She says that on those days when they were supposed to visit the elders, she was ready on time, but she had to wait for him for quite some time. She thought it peculiar and wondered whether he was somehow ill. Then Sado grew terribly afraid of thunder. When it thundered, he lay on the ground on his face, covering his ears with his hands.

Yŏngjo began to humiliate his son in front of people. He would test him in front of a large crowd and, when the prince answered incorrectly, would ridicule him. Prince Sado's appointment as prince-regent created additional conflict. Yŏngjo hoped that Sado would be able to alleviate some of the pressures he felt and responsibilities he bore, but Sado, fearful of paternal disapproval, was ineffectual. Yŏngjo faulted Sado for incompetence. But, however, if Sado did make a decision, Yŏngjo would scold him for acting without consulting him. Hyegyŏng relates that there was no way that Sado could please his father.

At some point, Sado began to react to his father. Yŏngjo wrongly accused him of drinking—this was during the prohibition against alcohol—and Sado in reaction began to drink. Yŏngjo scolded him for his unkempt attire. Sado developed what Hyegyŏng refers to as "clothing phobia"—a difficulty or inability to get dressed. In order to get dressed, he destroyed many sets of clothing, and he often physically hurt those who helped him dress. This behavior grew steadily worse. Hyegyŏng had to have dozens of sets of clothing on hand.

Space is an important metaphor in Hyegyŏng's narration of Sado's deterioration. The Yi royal family did not casually venture outside the palace wall. Royal visits to Yi ancestral tombs were one of the few common outings. Since coming of age, Sado wished to be included in the entourage, but this was rarely permitted to him. Then, through his sister's mediation, he received royal permission to go to Onyang, a hot spring, south of Seoul. Hyegyŏng says that though Sado had been badly off, outside the palace wall he became instantly better. He played the role of a concerned future ruler effectively, earning praise from the population on the way. Jubilant, he sent letters of greeting to his family. Once back in the palace, however, he retreated into his world of insanity.

In the spring of 1761, Sado began to leave the palace in disguise. The first time, he went to P'yŏngyang, the present capital of North Korea. He returned after several weeks. Going outside of the palace walls without prior arrangement was strictly forbidden. This was probably for security reasons, but the royal house also did not want its members to make overly frequent demands on the population. We do not know what Sado did on this trip, but there are intimations that he behaved rather badly. He picked up a couple of *kisaeng* (women entertainers) and some male cronies and brought them with him back to Seoul. He routinely was leaving the palace in disguise by now, and with several attendants he prowled the environs of the city. Inside the palace, he avoided staying in his official quarters. He dug an underground space in which he built a house with three small rooms just like the inside of a grave, and he spent many hours inside this subterranean chamber.

Sado also grew violent. In 1757, he began to kill people. The first was a eunuch on duty. Sado showed the bloody, severed head to Hyegyŏng and some ladies-in-waiting. As the court watched in shock, horror, and dismay, Sado descended into destructive violence. Those he killed were mostly people in service at his residence. Many ladies-in-waiting, including Sado's favorite concubine, were injured. Hyegyŏng says that she feared for her life and her son's. This state of terror continued until Lady Sŏnhŭi, Sado's mother—alarmed by a rumor indicating that Sado had attempted patricide—urged Yŏngjo to protect the safety of the dynasty by carrying out the final act. Sado was placed in the chest in July 1762. He died eight days later, on a day of torrential rain and thunder.

In narrating Sado's deterioration and breakdown, she states that his transgressions were caused by mental illness and that this was directly attributable to a profound sense of rejection and injury by his father. In this sense, she is intent on constructing an apology for Sado. She does not condone his transgressions, but she implies that even his transgressions were testimony to the depth of his suffering. The underlying theme is that he lost his battle to meet his father's demands not because he did not want to comply but because he desired so intensely to live up to his father's expectations. The constant paternal disapproval was too great to bear. As for Yŏngjo, Hyegyŏng is less forgiving. He was simply too harsh on his son. Completely departing from the official historiographical view, she presents her opinion that Yŏngjo's cruelty was responsible for Sado's madness. Nevertheless, she also offers sympathy for his pain in the end, when, to restore order, he had to put his son to death. She thus offers a historian's compassion and consolation to all. But her historical vision was that of a private person, and it was vastly different from the official historiography. In the last memoir, there is a curious exchange of the public and the private. The history of a ruler and his heir is recounted as the story of a father and son by the son's wife. Here is an extreme case of the privatization of an impersonal and public genre. At the same time, it exteriorizes and historicizes her private memory as public history.

What is the cultural meaning of *The Memoir of Lady Hyegyŏng*'s progression in genres from autobiography to historiography? In studies of Western autobiography, it has been posited that a sense of the discrete self is a precondition for writing autobiography. Women autobiographers are seen a little differently. The female sense of self is viewed as more relational, defined by its relationships to the persons surrounding the self, and autobiographies by women show this. The autobiographers talk not only of themselves but frequently of persons around them at great length. In her memoir, a great deal of attention is devoted to defending her father and her family. Writing the last memoir, in which she narrates her husband's madness and death, was her way of asking her husband's forgiveness for not following him into death. Since she did not follow him, she should at least record his suffering as accurately as possible so that he will be judged fairly by history.

At the same time, through the act of writing, the author desires to recompose and discover herself. By writing her memoirs, she seeks to understand the discrepancy between her beliefs and her experiences. She grew up believing in a correspondence between the moral order and human affairs. This was repeatedly challenged. She probed her doubt and disillusion over this discrepancy, sometimes expressing a sense of betrayal by fate. In the last memoir, she somewhat resolves the conflict between belief and experience. She does not claim any greater understanding of the mystery of the workings of Heaven than she did when she wrote the first memoir. But rather than displaying a sense of outrage or betrayal, here she seems to acquiesce to the idea that Heaven must have its own way of operating even if it cannot be discerned. Lady Hyegyŏng acknowledges that if the working of each sphere—the personal, the social, the human, and the cosmic—are quite complicated separately, the relationship between them is even more complex. She does not deny that there is a correlation between them, but she concedes that ultimately these forces are mysterious and not immediately apparent. So while she validates the moral order, she does not demand its transparency in individual lives.

In the same vein, she upholds the primacy of the social order. Individual considerations, no matter how compelling, must be subservient to the public cause. This view is accompanied by full sympathy for the human condition and respect for individual endeavors regardless of results. Thus she offers sympathy to all of those who, in 1762, voluntarily or involuntarily, had to do what it took to uphold the social order. This cost each of them a great deal. While it meant different things to different people, the event caused all of them deep pain. She describes the pain and struggle of each of them, including her own, and she offers them a historian's consolation. As she transforms pain and sorrow into writing, the boundaries between autobiography and historiography, a discrete sense of self and a relational sense of self, are almost completely blurred.

Note

This essay is in part taken from the author's introduction to *The Memoirs of Lady Hyegyŏng* (Berkeley: University of California Press, 1966), 1–32; and "Private Memory and Public History: The Memoirs of Lady Hyegyŏng and Testimonial Literature," in *Creative Women of Korea*, ed. Young-Key Kim-Renaud (Armonk, N.Y.: M. E. Sharpe, 2004), 122–141.

27

THE SONG OF THE FAITHFUL WIFE CH'UNHYANG

Rachel E. Chung

*T*HE SONG OF *the Faithful Wife Ch'unhyang* has often been called "the Romeo and Juliet of Korea" for its depiction of the passion and poignancy of young love. And surely its charming portrayal of the playful intimacy and eroticism in young conjugal love, complete with affectionate bickering and sweet-nothing make-ups, is second to none in all of East Asian literature. Still, the overall theme of the work rests not so much on the enduring love of the two young people as on the role of self-realization in the fulfillment of that love.

The psychological richness of the Ch'unhyang story comes from the complex, fully developed personality of the heroine, who undergoes a test of persecution and suffering in which she comes face to face with abandonment as well as death. Life asks of her: for what and for whom do you keep your integrity and faithfulness when both your love and Heaven itself have abandoned your cause? With that question, the story of Ch'unhyang helps illuminate the important Korean concept of *han*—to be defined not simply as a deeply held resentment against some injustice or unhappiness but rather as the grief of a finite being holding itself together under the demands of an infinite universe. In Korean culture, *han* is a catalyst and a powerful driving force toward a transcendent worldview. Unlike in the Book of Job, however, in the *Song of Ch'unhyang*—and indeed much of Korean literature—this worldview is arrived at not by hearing the voice of God in all its power and unfathomable majesty but by the experience of suffering through self-sacrifice and humaneness to the very end, to come out its "other side." It is a profoundly Neo-Confucian spirituality, and the human journey there is the source of comedy and tragedy so often indissolubly infused together in the Korean literary ethos.

The development of *han* as an ethos, under the influence of Zhu Xi's Neo-Confucian ideology on which Korea's Chosŏn dynasty (1392–1910) was firmly founded, will be an important area for future study, helpful for an understanding of both the trajectory of Korean Neo-Confucianism over the course of a uniquely long-lasting dynasty and of its spirituality and aesthetics. For the moment, it will suffice to note that the *Song of Ch'unhyang* is one of the so-called Songs of the Five Moral Relations that form the mainstay of *p'ansori*, the genre of popular Korean opera that had its beginnings in the early eighteenth century.[1] The Five Moral Relations refer to affection between parent and child, rightness between ruler and minister, differentiation between husband and wife, precedence between older and younger, and trust between friends, as mentioned in Mencius.[2] In the reform-minded Chosŏn era, the focus on the Five Moral Relations as the cornerstone of Neo-Confucian ethical practice and social renewal was intense; by the sixteenth century, these were not only a well-established part of the "core curriculum" for advanced and popular education alike but also the object of independent interpretations by scholars, as in the widely respected and ever popular *Primer for Youth* (*Tongmong sŏnsŭp*), with its unusual emphasis on the *reciprocal* nature of human relationships.[3]

Among the Songs of Five Moral Relations, the *Song of Ch'unhyang* represents the relationship between husband and wife.[4] Ch'unhyang is the fifteen-year-old daughter of a scholar-official father—since passed away—and a retired courtesan. The young Master Lee, the only son of the newly appointed governor to the city of Namwŏn (and of same age as Ch'unhyang), falls in love with her and enters into a secret "marriage" after pledging never to abandon her. But after only a year of perfect happiness together, Lee finds himself having to follow his father back to the capital without her. Though he promises to come back for her and they exchange tokens of faith, all communication ceases once he is gone. In the meantime, Pyŏn, the new governor of Namwŏn, is a dedicated womanizer set on having Ch'unhyang for himself. He assumes her compliance to be a natural and foregone conclusion, given her status as the daughter of a former courtesan, and he loses no time in commanding her to serve him. When she refuses his repeated persuasions and threats and instead gives him a blistering remonstration for his depraved ways, he orders her flogged and imprisoned for insolence to an official. On the eve of her impending death, young Master Lee—who in the meantime has devoted himself to his studies, won the coveted top prize in the civil-service examinations, and been appointed a secret censor (*amhaeng ŏsa*) to Ch'unhyang's own Chŏlla province by the king's personal command—arrives looking every bit a penniless beggar. Finding Ch'unhyang's love for him unchanged in spite of her long sufferings and his own "changed circumstances," he announces the arrival of the secret censor, sets the city affairs straight, saves Ch'unhyang, and in time reports her conduct to the king, who confers on her the honor of Exemplary Woman.

Despite the main plot focusing on the lovers, the *Song of Ch'unhyang* does not present a merely one-dimensional idealization of the faithful and otherwise faultless Confucian womanhood. Rather, contained within it are complex, nuanced attitudes toward class, gender relations, the corruption of officials, and laws governing status, sexuality, and even filiality—the whole web of Neo-Confucian values, tensions, and conflicts that by this time had acculturated Chosŏn popular consciousness for several centuries. As literature driven by such accumulated *han*, every character in the *Song of Ch'unhyang*—even the most minor ones—as well as the narrative material itself are imbued with a certain "saturated awareness" of the tragicomic nature of life, held together in turn by the basic premise of Neo-Confucian community compacts "to encourage virtue and shun evil (*kwŏnsŏn ching'ak*)." To take a random scene as an example, the young Master Lee comes upon some farmers singing in the fields as he travels about incognito. In one we hear:

> Almost done, almost done
> *Ŏlŏlŏl sangsa-dyuiyŏ*
> This li'l field almost done.
> *Ŏlŏlŏl sangsa-dyuiyŏ*
> Hurry planting this li'l field,
> *Ŏlŏlŏl sangsa-dyuiyŏ*
> Everyone go—each to his own,
> *Ŏlŏlŏl sangsa-dyuiyŏ*
> Barley and sweet rice to eat.[5]
> *Ŏlŏlŏl sangsa-dyuiyŏ*
> Get beneath the straw mats—[6]
> *Ŏlŏlŏl sangsa-dyuiyŏ*

You-know-what, you-know-that—
Let's beget some baby farmers at that.[7]

Within the story, the song is a trifling detail that could easily be left out of a performance without being missed. But typical of the *p'ansori* genre there is a poignancy even in such passing "human scenery," here specifically in the farmers' abject suffering intermingled with their sense of irony and resigned good humor. There is hope in the song (of work "almost done" as well as of a good harvest year) founded on a shared community work ethic (finish planting together before each goes home) and humble dreams (lots of sweet rice to eat). But the hope is laced from the outset with awareness of the unlikelihood of their realization (what we have are barley rice and straw mats for blankets), and the farmers take comfort instead in simple, bawdy humor ("you-know-what, you-know-that"), which, too, in their case is not without a certain tragic perpetuation of their condition ("make us some baby farmers"). Nevertheless, in the affectionate deprecation of their offspring-yet-to-be as "baby animals" one senses more affirmation than bitterness or anger. Likewise Pangja, the nimble-mouthed manservant attached to young Master Lee, is described as "cool and full of fun, with a certain *je ne sais quoi* air to his figure, not prone to troubling anyone, but having no sense of dignity whatsoever, fluttering about here there everywhere without much thought, seemingly thick in the skull when really quick to sense." He brings a great deal of liveliness to the human interactions with his teasing but basically sympathetic ways—he acts, after all, as a go-between of sorts for the lovers. But his more unremarkable, passing remarks will let on his consciousness of being treated like a little errand boy by everyone, including young Master Lee, who might be of an age with his own son, had he had the means to have gotten married in his youth like everyone else.

Each of these secondary and peripheral characters in the story carry some source of pain and what might be deemed justifiable cause for resentment against a social order that disenfranchises them. Some critics in fact read the *Song of Ch'unhyang* and the *p'ansori* genre itself as social criticism only thinly veiled by the humor. There are those, for example, who stress not only the oppressive, corrupt nature of the power wielded by Governor Pyŏn but also the pain Ch'unhyang suffers at the hands of the good but fundamentally uncomprehending Master Lee. But while the frankness of the social criticism and its uncensored wide circulation are remarkable in and of themselves in the context of eighteenth-century Korea, it is not the purpose or even the undertone of the story. The social criticism here is only a natural by-product of the larger cosmological worldview in which imperfect human beings are called upon to coexist with one another in the world.

The constant puns and other plays on words are another expressive device of the tragicomic ethos and a signature element of the *p'ansori* genre. When Master Lee asks the farmers about the goings-on in Namwŏn, one of them answers: "What do we mere farmers know, but if we speak as we heard our town is a flood of *samang*" ("death," but it also can mean "four crazies"). When asked to explain, the farmer replies: "The magistrate is *jumang* ['drink-crazy'], his secretary is *nomang* ['old-crazy,' i.e., senile], his staff are *domang* [literally, 'escape,' but can also mean 'gambling-crazy'], and the people are *wŏnmang* ['resentment']—that's why it's likened to a flood of *samang*." The delicate balance between the sufferings of the common folk and their ability to rise above it with sense of humor hangs on the fast, lively rhythm of the clever sung/spoken puns. Among the more famous wordplays in the opera are the series of impromptu love songs exchanged between Lee and Ch'unhyang during their early days of wedded bliss. In one of them he tells her, "here, Ch'unhyang, listen. You and I being so affectionate [*yujŏng*], listen to this song on '*jŏng* [feeling],'" and launches into a virtuoso rhyming verse that begins with stately quotations of lines from famous Chinese poems ending in *jŏng* but ends with ever quicker iterations of the designated syllable in an increasingly humorous vein. As Lee develops his theme from *jŏng* every ten syllables, to every seven syllables, down to four, then almost hip-hop-like every other syllable, the meaning of the designated syllable also runs the gamut from the poetic to rustic colloquialisms that leave Ch'unhyang laughing and adoring his wit. And with such games their intimacy grows by leaps and bounds: "Here, Ch'unhyang, let's try playing at piggy back." "*Aigo*, how can we play at such an embarrassing thing? What will you do if my mother across the hall ever finds out?" "Your mother did a lot more than that in her younger days, they say. Stop hawing and let's play at piggy back."

Then carrying her on his back, he sings:

> "Come on, come on, let's piggyback,
> let's play, let's play at piggyback.
> Love, love, you're my love,
> aren't you a love, my very own love.

Yiyiyiyi, you're my love indeed.
No matter what, you're my love.
What would you eat, what'd you have to eat?
Round and round a watermelon—
crack its hard shell,
pour a bit o' sweetest honey,
throw the seeds out,
scoop its flesh all ripe and red and
have its tasty juicy stuff?"
"No, that I don't want."
"What would you, then, what'd you have?
Long and thick—an eggplant or a Chinese melon would you
    have?"
"No, that I don't want to eat."
"What would you, then? What'd you have?
Shall I give you cherries, or grapes,
tangerines in honey, or sugar sweet candy?
No matter what, ever my love,
what would you have, what'd you to eat?
Hairy and sour—an [unripe] apricot,
would you eat that to have a little Master Lee?"[8]
"No, that I don't want either."
"No matter what, ever my love,
walk over there, let's see your charm [in the back].
Walk over here, let's see your charm [in the front].
Ajang-ajang, take a little walk, let's see your charm in walking
    about.
Give me a smile—the charm of your mouth,
O no matter what, ever my love."

And Ch'unhyang is by now so comfortable and on such intimate terms
with him that she returns the favor by "carrying" him piggy back in turn
and singing impromptu bawdy songs of her own celebrating their love.

Ultimately, the *Song of Ch'unhyang* is a love story between two young
people. In *Romeo and Juliet*, lovers from two feuding families are driven to
suicide; here we have two lovers from different class statuses reaching toward a transcendent ideal of love and harmony by overcoming hardships,
overcoming the Self, and thereby in a sense overcoming even the limits of
the Neo-Confucian social order itself. Although the narrative avoids being

explicit on this point, by the story's end it is clear that the self-trust and self-respect each has won for himself and herself through their individual trials will be the foundation on which they will build a new life together as mature partners and contributors to society. It is particularly appropriate that such a Confucian ideal of Self-Other relations gets depicted in the *Song of Ch'unhyang*, because popular emphasis on filiality as the basis of virtue notwithstanding, the Confucian tradition held the relationship between husband and wife to be the beginning *and* chief among all human moral relations.[9]

Of course, there is a difference in the nature of the trials that the two lovers undergo.[10] For Ch'unhyang, who carries the conflict of social stratification from the moment of her birth, it is a battle to know what she's made of. She is beautiful, intelligent, well educated, and brought up to have the bearing and dignity of a scholar-official's daughter. At the same time, she cannot shake free of the social taint that comes from having a former courtesan for a mother. It is a label that accompanies her wherever she goes, and in the strict Confucian social order of eighteenth-century Chosŏn, where one's social status depended on the standing of the mother, she cannot realistically hope to become the formal first wife of a man of the scholar-official class, regardless of her personal merits. Although she is free to not register herself as a courtesan and later claims the rights of a married woman in defending herself against the attentions of Governor Pyŏn, it is a constant battle to negate the social expectations of her being an easy, "open" target. It was partly in defiance to this that she had decided—long before she had even met young Master Lee—to live the life of a faithful wife to one husband, whoever that man might be. That she believes she has found a true match in Lee makes it easier for her to commit herself, to trust in the strength of their mutual pledge in spite of the immanent risk in "marrying" a man of higher class without the approbation of his parents. But as the text makes it clear, her fidelity itself is by no means dependent on—or the result of—the strength of her love for Lee as an individual. The battle is rather within herself and perhaps also for her mother who, for all her worldly, talkative, sometimes vulgar ways, must suffer far more from the social contempt she has brought on not only herself but her beloved daughter as well. In that sense, the persecution she suffers at Governor Pyŏn's hands is a test not so much of her love for Lee as of her own innermost image of herself: when push comes to shove, who am I really? What am I made of?

It is said that children of criminals often go through life wondering if they've somehow inherited a "bad gene." Ch'unhyang must also have wondered, if only subconsciously, whether she really has what it takes to live a life of wifely chastity and fidelity—an ideal she probably holds higher because she was not privileged to take it for granted or to grow up seeing its workaday reality. *Would* she remain faithful when she has been abandoned after less than a year by a man who had pledged never to leave her? *Should* she remain faithful when no one seems to expect it of her and when she only gets flogged and imprisoned for it? *Is it right* to remain faithful when it means the ultimate betrayal of filial duty, leaving her mother childless and without support in her old age? Ch'unhyang does not ask whether it is right for a society to demand that women be faithful to one husband regardless of circumstance in order to be respectable; the *Song of Ch'unhyang* does not mean to be a *Madame Bovary* or *Anna Karenina*. Indeed, the perspective is entirely different. Here is a woman persecuted for trying to live up to expectations of womanhood from which she herself is exempt by birth. For her, faithfulness is a right to fight for as much as it is a responsibility and a burden, just as Zhu Xi had conceived of self-cultivation as a human right as well as human responsibility.

But is that enough of an answer in her struggle between life and death and with questions of "why not?" Why not repay betrayal in kind? Why not cherish one's life and body? Why not save her mother from a pitiable old age? More than simply a social construct, Ch'unhyang's endorsement of Confucian principles is founded on an underlying trust that the universe is Good and that she by nature *is* and ought to be an extension of that Good which transcends life and death, transcends the pain of love, and transcends also the conflicting claims of one's multiple human bonds. She may have absorbed this trust unconsciously as part of the Neo-Confucian cultural context in which she grew up, but she enters into a much deeper and more personal relationship with it in overcoming her own mortality, as symbolized by the dream where she visits faithful women of the past. In other words, she finds the wherewithal to die a faithful wife not through her own determination alone but by learning to "rest" on a universe that is Good.

For young Lee the trial is different. He has sometimes been cast as a sweet but thoughtless cad—couldn't he at least have written Ch'unhyang a few times during his absence to give her comfort and reassurance? But a test of silence is a universally established trope, and although in young Lee's case there was no one to command it explicitly—as for example Prince Tamino is commanded in Mozart's *Magic Flute* (1791)—it is clear he nevertheless understood implicitly the higher necessity of silence trumping the lovers' mutual desire for reassurance. It is possible that for an aristocratic blueblood like him Ch'unhyang is no more than a youthful first love for whom he feels much affection but not a life-and-death passion. But if we take him at his word, the test of silence was for him also a true test of his essence, learning patience and restraint, learning to trust Ch'unhyang, and above all learning to trust and obey Heaven's decree no matter what it might be.

What makes the *Song of Ch'unhyang* such an enduring classic is that neither Ch'unhyang nor Lee is presented as imperturbable paragons of Confucian virtue at the outset. Instead of responding with mild-mannered iron discipline to every circumstance, Ch'unhyang lets her passions be known. She might compose flawless poetry and speak in the most gentile manner when occasion requires, but when provoked she gives Pangja as good as she gets. She is sexy, sensual, and not afraid to share bawdy private jokes with her partner. She flies into a towering, throwing-things-around-level rage when she realizes Lee means to leave her behind, and when he is gone she frequently spends her days in tears of longing and despair. These might not register as faults in today's contemporary Westernized culture, but they certainly challenged eighteenth-century Confucian ideas of feminine virtue. She is scared in prison; she feels all the conflicting, "uncultivated," natural feelings any one of us might feel under similar circumstances. Lee, too, is shown in the beginning as a mixture of chivalry, arrogance, pride, cowardliness, impatience, silliness, naiveté, and so on. Both are supposed to have been brought up according to the highest standards of Confucian education and *noblesse oblige*, but Lee is not above fibbing to his father, and even filial Ch'unhyang saves the tastiest dishes for Lee instead of her mother.

These seeming contradictions in their characters have sometimes been criticized as a flaw of the *p'ansori* tradition. *P'ansori* was after all a popular art form, developed by multiple voices possibly in a somewhat pastiche fashion, to entertain the common folk. But in actuality the human and spiritual development Ch'unhyang and Lee undergo in the story is a major source of the work's enduring appeal, and not just in terms of its literary interest. The nineteenth and twentieth centuries was a time of unprecedented suffering for Koreans. Swept up in the storm of global imperial politics, Korea underwent by turns its first loss of independence, a devastating war, and the traumas of national division, Westernization, modernization, industrialization, and military dictatorship all at breakneck speed, posing again and again the question of Korean identity, its values and raison d'être. The *Song of Ch'unhyang*, itself brought into existence by the Korean collective popular consciousness of an earlier era, came to represent for generations upon generations of Koreans the pain, the determination, the hope in hopelessness, the ability to laugh at one's foibles, and most of all the still abiding faith in a moral universe despite all evidence to the contrary and despite even the recognition of their falling ever so short of Heaven's standards. The fact that a work like the *Song of Ch'unhyang* could be created not by the pen of a single educated author but by the collective consciousness of the common people perhaps speaks to the great achievement of the Chosŏn Neo-Confucian civil order.

Notes

1. Though often called an "opera" for its dialogue-based structure, *p'ansori* is sung by a single singer singing all the roles, including that of the narrator and even occasional commentator on the performance, creating multiple, almost postmodern perspectives on the story. The singer has only a drummer on an hourglass drum for instrumental accompaniment and a hand-held fan for prop. To sing just one opera from beginning to end could take as long as eight hours without a break, so although it often took singers years to master just one opera and to build up enough stamina to sing it through, it was also common practice to shorten the performance by leaving out parts of the work at the singer's discretion. Because of this and because *p'ansori* was traditionally passed down orally from master to master, there can be some differences of text and characterization associated with the various regional schools of style, which is carried through to the many later written versions as well.

2. Zhu Xi later emphasized the Five Moral Relations much more through such works as his *Elementary Learning* and the "Articles of the White Deer Grotto Academy."

3. Although its author was not even known for a time, this work came to be widely used by Chosŏn educators. By the mid-seventeenth century, the work carried a preface by the famed scholar and minister Song Siyŏl (1607–1689). King Yŏngjo (r. 1724–1775) later composed his own personal preface to it, demonstrating both its popularity and importance in the highest echelons of Chosŏn society. For an excerpt of *Tongmong sŏnsŭp* in English, see "Pak Semu: *Primer for Youth*," trans. James Jinhong Kim and Wm. T. de Bary, in *Sources of Korean Tradition*, ed. Yŏngho Ch'oe, Peter H. Lee, and Wm. Theodore de Bary (New York: Columbia University Press, 2000), 2:37–43.

4. The Songs of the Five Moral Relations refer to the *Song of Sim Ch'ŏng*, the *Song of the Underwater Palace*, the *Song of Ch'unhyang*, the *Song of Hŭngbo*, and the *Song of the Chŏkbyŏk River*, respectively.

5. Barley rice was the usual fare for poor farmers, whereas the much more expensive sweet rice would have been a rare, if not undreamed of, treat.

6. Straw mats (*kŏjŏk*) are cheap, rough material for outdoor use in the summer and hardly appropriate for bedding in the home.

7. The Korean word *saekki* translated here as "baby" is a term specific to baby animals rather than humans, though here it is used affectionately enough. Throughout this essay, all translations are my own, based on the version sung by Cho Sang-Hyŏn as recorded in *P'ansori Tasŏt Madang* [*Five Works of P'ansori*]: *Annotated P'ansori Texts* (Seoul: Korea Britannica, 1982).

8. "To have a little Master Lee"—i.e., to become pregnant.

9. See Zhu Xi's "Proclamation of Instructions" for community compacts, in *Sources of Chinese Tradition*, 2nd ed., ed. Wm. Theodore de Bary et al. (New York: Columbia University Press, 1999), 1:750. Students of Confucianism might be surprised to note that Confucius is attributed as having said of "Guan-ju," the first love song in the *Odes*, the following: "The *Guan-ju* is perfection. Now in its relation to man, the *Guan-ju* above is like Heaven; below it is like Earth. Mysterious and dark is the virtue it hides; abundant and rich the Way it puts into practice. . . . It is complete in its brilliancy and order. Oh great is the Way of the *Guan-ju*! It is that which connects all things and on which the life of human beings is dependent. The He and the Luo Rivers gave forth the writing and the diagram; the *lin* [Chinese unicorn] and the phoenix frequented the suburbs; by what means should this be brought about except by following the Way of the *Guan-ju*, and by taking the subject of the *Guan-ju* for a model? The writings of the Six Classics are not all devoted to exhaustive discussion, but they derive their matter from the *Guan-ju*. The subject of the *Guan-ju* is great! Vast and soaring, 'from the east to the west, from the south to the north, there is not a thought but does it homage.' May you exert yourself to emulate it, and cherish it in thought. Neither human beings between Heaven and Earth nor the origin of the Kingly Way are outside its compass." From *Han Ying's Illustrations of the Didactic Application of the Classic of Songs*, as quoted in *An Anthology of Translations: Classical Chinese Literature*, vol. 1: *From Antiquity to the Tang Dynasty*, ed. John Minford and Joseph S. M. Lau (New York and Hong Kong: Columbia University Press and the Chinese University Press of Hong Kong, 2000), 96.

10. According to the Five Moral Relations, there is to be differentiation between husband and wife.

28

READING AND TEACHING *THE TALE OF KIEU*

Conrad Schirokauer

L IKE OTHER TEXTS accepted as canonical, *The Tale of Kieu* (金雲翹傳) by Nguyen Du (阮攸) is celebrated as a classic in its own culture and addresses aspects of the human condition that transcend space and time. Once condemned by Marxists as "feudal" in origin and decadent in spirit, it is now embraced by the Vietnamese, who in 2007 turned it into an opera performed at Ho Chi Minh City's Military Zone 7 Stadium, with a cast of 515 actors and musicians, including eight prominent actresses who joined in playing Kieu.[1] Presumably this opera, like classic Western operas, made the most of *Kieu* as melodrama.[2] More modest but nonetheless significant was the performance in 2009 in Berlin of Augustin Maurs's "mini-opera" (three minutes/four musicians),[3] confirming that *Kieu's* appeal reaches well beyond the time and place of its creation in nineteenth-century Vietnam and even extends beyond the borders of any single artistic discipline.[4]

We can and should read (and hear) what it tells us about Vietnam and about ourselves, but at the same time we should be aware that, like other classics, it is also deeply embedded in the greater cultural world in which Vietnam participated, for this is a profoundly East Asian text in its philosophical framework, its Chinese source, its setting in Ming China, and its references and allusions. It is based on a minor Chinese "scholar-and-beauty novel" (才子佳人小說), a genre regarded as "hackneyed and artificial" and that "never enjoyed the slightest critical esteem in China,"[5] but it is written not in Chinese but in Nom (喃). "Nom," the name of this script, is itself written as a Sino-Vietnamese character that signals Vietnam's place in the south (南) of the Sinographic world, speaking (literally, "mouthing," 口) its own distinctive vernacular.[6] We are told by experts that works written in Nom

> share a certain romantic and poetic quality and an enchanting tenderness and melancholy that are characteristically Vietnamese. . . . The varying lilt of Vietnamese six-eight or seven-seven-six-eight verse is deeply moving for a Vietnamese, particularly in passages where a halting rhythm produced the effect of stifled sobs: here both reciter and listener may shiver compulsively with sensuous pleasure.[7]

As elsewhere in East Asia, vernacular literature like *Kieu* was accessible to those who did not command classical Chinese, and even for those who did, the vernacular facilitated self-expression. Some of the *Tale*'s wordings have entered current Vietnamese, but Nom is no longer in use. Instead, the language is now written in the modified Latin script devised by Alexandre de Rhodes (1591–1660), the Jesuit missionary from Avignon who had originally been intended for Japan but was reassigned to Vietnam when Japan proscribed Christianity. Unfortunately, this script is difficult to vocalize for those of us who have not studied Vietnamese, and the music of the language remains elusive to ordinary readers, even though the most accessible English translation, that by Huyn Sanh Thong, is bilingual, with pages in Vietnamese and English facing each other. The French prose translation by Xuan-Phuc and Xuan-Viet[8] and the English prose version by Le-Xuan Thuy can help us appreciate the dimensions of the task Huyn set himself in rendering the text into verse. There seems little prospect of the publication of a rival version in the near future, though *Kieu* may yet inspire a poet-scholar such as John Balaban, who has already enriched us by translating Ho Xuan.[9]

As it is, Huyn has produced a well-informed and thoughtful translation with notes that are essential reading, an informative introduction, and an all-too-short seven-and-a-half page discussion of historical background by Alexander Woodside.[10]

Text and Context

One goal in teaching this and other literary texts is to help students read wisely and well. We want them to enter into dialogue with the texts directly and experience them fresh. Therefore, unlike in my other classes, I limit discussion of background to bare essentials. However, not only the texts themselves but the teaching of them occurs in a context, and the latter, of course, includes most immediately what we have read in our course prior to *Kieu*. In my course, *Kieu* is assigned at the end of the semester, a position at least chronologically justified, for it is the most recent of our readings from traditional East Asia.

Although written in the early nineteenth century, *Kieu* clearly belongs with traditional Vietnamese and East Asian literature, before the intrusion of the West introduced new concepts and literary influences. The role of the French in the founding of the Nguyen Dynasty in 1802 is and was well known, but there is no hint of an impending Western political or cultural challenge in the writings of Ngyuen Du (1765–1820), who came to serve the new dynasty while remaining loyal at heart to the Le Dynasty (1418–1788) that his family had served as Confucian statesmen. Granted, cannons (the shooting, not the literary, kind) do appear twice in the *Tale* (lines 2271 and 2514—rendered as guns by Huyn), but we should note that Western cannons had been employed in China for two centuries prior and are not singled out by Du as at all new or exotic. There was no Vietnamese equivalent of Japan's "Dutch Learning." Any doubts about the vitality of traditional Sinocentric culture in nineteenth-century Vietnam can be dispelled by a visit to Hue, the site of the court that Du served, the buildings in which he presumably worked, and the hall where he received the commission appointing him envoy to Beijing. Indeed, Hue's architecture and Du's literary work stand as impressive monuments attesting to the vitality of traditional East Asian culture on the eve of its modern transformations.

Kieu is the most outstanding work in its genre, but it is neither first nor last of what are often called novels in verse or alternatively "narrative verse" (*truyen*, 傳), a literary form that students (and teachers) most likely will not have previously encountered but that has been traced back to the fourteenth-century "Story of the Virtuous Mouse." The titles of these works may be intriguing, but few will be tempted to explore the genre after reading in the most authoritative account of Vietnamese literature in English that "a few are readable, even charming, but many are very dull."[11]

Like the mouse protagonist of the first of these works, these novels in verse often featured animals and frequently served as safe vehicles for political criticism at a time when a poem implying political dissent could cost a man his life. Du was politically active as well as highly politically conscious. *The Tale of Kieu* includes lines that can and have been read as political criticism (955, 959), but it is not driven by politics. Yet it is not apolitical. Government first appears in the *Tale of Kieu* when, charged as a debtor, Kieu's father and brother are placed in cangues (a heavy wooden collar somewhat like a portable stocks) and the family's home is devastated by "buffalo faces and horse heads" (576–584), that is, the fiends who torture those condemned to a Buddhist hell but who are here on duty as *yamen* runners who "like bluebottles buzzed around the house" destroying and thieving.

> Fear gripped the household—cries of innocence
> Shook up the earth, injustice dimmed the clouds   (589–590)

Generally, the government is portrayed as being corrupt and untrustworthy. A partial exception is a magistrate so deeply moved by the beauty of Kieu's poetry that he reverses his original verdict and grants justice, but this exception offers little comfort to those who need to rely on morality or law rather than the beauty of words. Du, who at times turns caustic, certainly has no illusions about how government operates. On the other hand, at the end of Kieu's and the reader's long, turbulent journey, the man she loves as well as her brother pass the civil-service examinations and become officials. Du does not defend let alone glorify the status quo, but neither does his long poem seek to subvert the political order. The political system is part and parcel of the landscape of this masterpiece of "narrative verse," which transcends its genre, for it is a drama, or perhaps a melodrama, that seemed destined for the operatic stage while inspiring inclusion among the world's great epics.[12]

The Shape of the *Tale*

The *Tale* begins by setting out the cosmic and poetic framework of the poem. Since the class is reading Huyn's final version, we quote here from an earlier rendition, which retains the imagery of line 4, which is relegated to the notes in the final version.

> A hundred years—in this life span on earth,
> How apt to clash, talent and destiny!
> Men's fortunes change and even nature shifts—
> The sea now rolls where mulberry fields grew

> One watches things that make one sick at heart.
> Thus is the law: no gain without loss,
> And Heaven hurts fair women for sheer spite

Kieu is supremely beautiful and virtuous as well as most exceptionally talented in poetry, painting, and music. Very early in the text, she foreshadows
her own story: she has composed a song called "Cruel Fate" to "mourn all
women in soul-rending strains" (33–34). Kieu's romance with the young
student Kim starts with a fleeting glimpse during the Qingming Festival.
This occurred shortly after Kieu had been so deeply moved when she came
across the neglected grave of Dam Tien (淡仙, Dan Xian), a Chinese courtesan, that Dam's spirit responded in a whirlwind, leaving footprints on the
moss (60–132). Later that night, Dam Tien appears to Kieu in a dream and
reveals to her that she has been marked for a life of sorrow (185–223). Dam is
Kieu's kindred spirit as well as her link to the other world, where our fates
are shaped.

Despite the usual taboos and obstacles, Kieu's romance with Kim progresses into deep love confirmed yet unconsummated out of considerations
of age and propriety—but celebrated in a passionate tryst and an exchange
of solemn oaths.

> The stark bright moon was gazing from the skies
> As with one mouth they pronounced the oath.
> Their hearts' recesses they explored and probed
> etching their vow of union in their bones   (448–452)

The moon will follow the story as witness, companion, mirror (1199), and,
as in the East Asian calendar, marker of time.

We know from the start that Kieu and Kim's dream will not come true.
Throughout the poem, there are frequent mentions of the overwhelming
weight of Kieu's karma, but she and we are never told what she had done in
previous lives to earn her talents or deserve the suffering that is set in motion in an act of overwhelming Confucian self-sacrifice.

Kieu sells herself to rescue her father from the horrors of prison, and she
asks her sister to take her place and become Kim's wife. To all appearances,
it seems that she is selling herself to become a concubine, but the scoundrel
who makes the purchase, after having his way with her and pretending to
be her husband, turns out to be the agent of a common brothel. When she

learns the truth, Kieu attempts suicide, thereby frightening Dame Tu, the madam of the establishment, into making false promises. Instead of looking after Kieu as promised, Dame Tu conspires with a smooth unscrupulous villain to stage a false escape. After Kieu is caught attempting to flee, Dame Tu gains the upper hand. She thrashes Kieu within an inch of her life and forces her to confess and accept instruction.

> Because I badly lived an earlier life,
> Now in this world I must redeem past sins.
> My innocence is lost—a broken vase:
> My body shall pay off my debts to life　　　　　(1195–1199)

After three years in the brothel, she is rescued by a rich merchant, Tuc, who makes her his live-in concubine while his father is away. When his father returns, the old man "stormed and thundered in his towering wrath" (1389). Infuriated, he takes her to court, but, just like the magistrate, the father is won over by the power of her verse. However, her husband is too craven to inform his strong willed and well-connected wife ("her father ruled the Civil Office Board" [1530]), who resides in a distant province, of the existence of Kieu. When that woman nevertheless learns of her husband's concubine, she arranges for Kieu to be kidnapped. Without informing her husband and keeping her burning jealousy (1609) secret, she turns Kieu into her own household slave. The personality of the wife, the reaction of the weak husband when he encounters his wife's new servant but does not dare to acknowledge her, and Kieu's own thoughts and feelings give Du rich opportunities for reflecting on human personality and on the drama of life.

For a while, Kieu is allowed to serve in a shrine to Guanyin located in the grand house's garden (1913), but she remains under the thumb of Tuc's wife, whose jealousy remains unabated. Kieu finally escapes from this unbearable situation and finds a temple maintained by the nun Giac Duyen. But her trials are far from over, for Giac Duyen recommends her to a woman who forces Kieu to marry her nephew, who promptly sells her to another brothel. And so Kieu finds herself back in the filthy mud.

However, she is not to be kept down. She is rescued by the rebel leader Tu Hai, who marries her and establishes her as his consort. Kieu even gets to take "sweet revenge" (2352) and pass judgment on her tormentors (2315–2396). She shows mercy to Tuc's wife, but others are not so fortunate.

blood flowed in streams while flesh was hacked to bits . . .
All soldiers, crowded on the grounds, could watch
The scourge divine deal justice in broad day.

(2389, 2395–2396)

Xuan-Phuc and Xuan-Viet acknowledge that Kieu has been criticized for taking justice into her own hands, but they defend Du as not intending his heroine to be perfect and also point out that her weaknesses and flaws too are products of her karma.[13]

Kieu's tale is one of repeated betrayal, yet she never loses her ability to trust. She now makes the mistake of trusting a governor's promises of amnesty and honor if Tu Hai will only lay down his arms. Tu suspects a trap, but Kieu advises him otherwise. The results are disastrous. Once again Kieu is betrayed, and Tu Hai is killed.

When Kieu rejects the governor's offer of a reward for facilitating the government's victory and repulses his advances, he has her married to a tribal chief. Implicated in the betrayal and filled with guilt at "killing a man," she throws herself into the Qiantang River,[14] calling on Dam Tien to welcome her into the underworld (2620–2625). "Wandering in a grove of dreams," she encounters Dam Tien, who tells her that her ordeals are over:

Who can match your true heart, despite past sin?
Heaven has noticed it: a loving child,
You sold yourself; an altruist, you saved lives.
Your country and your people you served well
Such hidden merits have now tipped the scale.   (2716–2729)

Meanwhile, Gic Duyen has encountered the Daoist prophetess Tan Hop (introduced in verse 2406), who attributes Kieu's suffering partly to fate but also in part to Kieu herself, for following her passions. But Tan Hop concludes:

When judged for her past sins, Kieu must be charged
With reckless love, not with wanton lust   (2680–2681)

Tsan Hop concludes by asking Gic Duyen to prepare to rescue Kieu from the Qiantang River. "Year in, year out" the nun waits in her grass hut until, as prophesized, Kieu tries to drown herself. Rescued by Giac Duyen, Kieu joins her in her hut and leads a pure life until discovered by Kim, now an official and married to her sister. There is a joyful reunion. Kieu and Kim at last are joined in a marriage—but at her insistence it is a chaste one, to which Kim agrees:

> I thought you still attached to human love.
> But no more dust stains your mirror now
> Your vow can't but increase my high regard   (3172–3174)

Before we consider the concluding lines and draw our own conclusions about the meanings of Kieu's tale, it behooves us to consider the poetry. The interweaving of plot and themes shape the fabric of Kieu's tale, but it is language that provides the texture.

The Tale's Texture

While some of the texture can be sensed in Huyn's translations, it is necessary to consult his notes to understand how his decision to translate for denotation inevitably comes at the expense of connotation and color.[15] To the uninitiated, it is hardly obvious that "green pavilions" are whorehouses, frequented by "bees and butterflies," images first encountered in the role of suitors. Not until late in the poem (line 3098) are "bees and butterflies" finally released from the notes into the text itself. That butterflies can have multiple meanings is illustrated by the (mandatory?) appearance of Zhuang-zi's butterfly, which flutters in near the end of the poem (3200) with nary a bee, let alone a green pavilion, in sight.

While some of the images, like the ant inside the rim of a cup (1548) or the hapless eel who cannot help mudding his head (1148), are of Vietnamese origin, a great many are Chinese. Comparison of Kieu to Yang Gueifei begins early in the poem (line 226), with "cheeks like some pear blossoms drenched with rain" (from "Song of Everlasting Sorrow"), and reappears later, but the most widely used source is *The Classic of Poetry, Shijing* (詩經), which is drawn on some fifty times. A striking example is line 954, translated as "I hugged my humble lot as concubine," with a note (on 185) that tells us that "concubine" here replaces "little stars," an allusion to *Shijing* (poem 28), in which concubines are compared to little stars that must fade out before daybreak, unlike the first wife, who can stay with the lord the whole night. Or to cite just one more example: "they'd tryst and cling to-gether night and day" (1289, and also 3220) is a rendition of "they would stay together [exchange] peaches by night and plums by day," from poem 64.

Other references and borrowings abound. Tao Qian's Peach Blossom Spring appears very early and returns. We see Lu Sheng live a whole life in a dream only long enough to cook a pot of millet (1715). There are quotations from Meng Qiao, Sima Xiangru, Qi Kang (one of the seven sages of the Bamboo Grove), Su Shi, and others. For instance, when Kieu speaks in fear of Tuc's wife, she says, "her vinegar will burn worse than hell's own fire" (1352). The translator explains that this refers to the sour vinegar in which Empress Wu pickled the body of a palace lady that she had killed out of jealousy. The references range widely and even include one to Mencius, though he would hardly be happy that his text is drawn upon only to link eastern walls to improper love.[16]

Du's *Tale* is a treasure house of poetic expressions and literary lore that are largely Chinese in origin. These Chinese elements do more than pro-vide authenticity for a story set in China, though they certainly do that. The prominence of the *Classic of Poetry*, believed to have been edited by Confu-cius himself, may also have helped legitimize a narrative poem bound to offend Confucians. Linking the Vietnamese poem to the greater Sinocen-tric East Asian tradition serves to validate as well as enrich a text written in the vernacular. Beyond that, we can surmise that thinking and writing in these terms came naturally to a well-educated man such as Nguyen Du. It also serves to remind us that not among the least of the shared components of East Asian culture is a shared literary heritage: a font of poetic images, tropes, allusions, figures of speech, and quasi-historical lore. Recognition of these elements in turn enhances the pleasure as well as the comprehen-sion of the readers, and this includes students engaged in their first encoun-ter with East Asian and Vietnamese literature.

That rich and varied heritage is grounded in common ways of looking at a world in which philosophical frameworks and religious convictions form the base. With that in mind, let us turn to the concluding lines of *Kieu*.

Final Words and Reflections

The concluding stanza of the *Tale of Kieu* reiterates the disjunction between talent and destiny introduced in its opening and concludes:

> In talent take no overweening pride
> for talent and disaster form a pair:
> Our karma we must carry as our lot—
> Let's stop decrying Heaven's whims and quirks
> Inside ourselves there lies the root of good
> The heart outweighs all talents on this earth.

We may agree that "talent and disaster form a pair" (and there is a rhyme here that works in Vietnamese and in Chinese) even as we recognize that it is Kieu's talent for poetry and music that makes her so very special, that helps her endure suffering, and that, as in the case of the magistrate, rescues her from disaster, if only temporarily. Her art is even sufficiently powerful to move (though not to transform) Tuc's harsh wife. It remains a precious asset and never becomes a liability.

Beginning with her early encounter with Dam Tien and including her decision to drown herself in the Qiantang River, Kieu pours out her heart in poems too sublime to share with the reader, who is told only of her composing them. That may reflect the author's modesty, and, in elevating the reader's attention to such poetry of the imagination, it increases our appreciation of Kieu's talents all the more. It also puts her most deeply felt poetry on a par with the music of her lute, which we can hear only in our imagination. Such poetry and music resonate with cosmic mystery.

But we are told the heart outweighs talents and that Kieu's is a "guileless heart" (2467), impervious to contamination no matter what fate or karma determines a person's lot. As in the reference to dust accumulating on the mirror, there is an echo here of the *Platform Sutra*, but it may be more pertinent to point to Du's own lengthy poem, "Summons to the Souls," characterized by its translator as Amidist and all encompassing in its conviction that all people are worthy of salvation. That includes prostitutes, whose lot is described with great sympathy, in a stanza of their own. It ends with:

> Hail to the Buddha. Hail to the Law, Hail to the Clergy
> Hail to all those who have ascended the Lotus Platform![17]

Xuan Phuc's scholarly translation and study of Kieu[18] opens with a photograph of a statue identified as representing Avalokitesvara (Quan Am, Guanyin), but she never appears in person and her name occurs only once. No Buddhist deities figure in the poem, which, nonetheless, exudes the fragrance of Buddhism[19] and which is Buddhist primarily in the weight of the burden of karma and the faith in an ultimately just universe (as revealed in part by a Daoist prophetess).

It was a Chinese cliché to equate the loyalty that an official owed his ruler to that of a wife to her husband, and most commentators see Du's life story reflected in that of Kieu, for Du had passed the provincial examination as a young man and, continuing his family tradition, had briefly served the old dynasty. After avoiding office under the Tay Son, he reluctantly accepted service under the Nguyen. It is not far fetched to conclude that Du's own experience was a source of his empathy for Kieu when he read the original Chinese novel. The suggestion that the portrayal of the rebel Tu Hai shows Du's sympathy for the Tay Son Rebellion is somewhat dubious, because Du's poem associates Tu Hai with the notoriety of Huang Chao's rebellion against the Tang, but then again, Du is skilled at mixing the positive and the negative. Possibly *The Tale* suggests—even if only subliminally—that Du and the Le will be reunited, but such a reading seems implausible, and that is not how it was read in its day.

The Tale of Kieu is a moral tale in which filial piety plays a pivotal role and Confucian values form the ethical framework. As the two Xuans point out, at the start of her ordeal, Kieu thinks longingly first of Kim, but by line 2239[20] her parents come to mind first. Such devotion is close to the heart of Confucians but, like their Marxist antagonists, Confucian commentators have been critical of Du's novel in verse for their own moral reasons. Certainly, Kieu has engaged in very un-Confucian activities, not only in the sordid episodes in her life but in two marriages that were only disrupted by external circumstances. Du apparently is saying that a pure heart triumphs over the most demeaning adversity and remains unaffected by guilt or shame. Purity of heart outweighs Confucian norms.

The Tale has been read as the story of Vietnam itself, a tale of adversity and subjection at the mercy of forces it could not predict or control. This speaks to what appears to be a widespread perception of Vietnam's story as one of heroic response to victimization. This perception is historically one sided and misleading, but in its light, the ultimate lesson of *Kieu* may be that, in a world in which so many claim maximum victimization, adversity need not corrupt or embitter the spirit. The *Tale of Kieu* has been admired as a moral tale. If so, its ultimate moral lesson is that purity of heart and unbroken spirit are heroic achievements that even under the most difficult circumstances find expression in the poetry of music and the music of poetry.

Notes

1. See "'Kim Van Kieu': The First Billion Dong Traditional Opera," *VietNamNet Bridge.* http://english.vietnamnet.vn/lifestyle/2007/02/666650.

2. For *Kieu* as melodrama see Maurice Durand, *L'universe des Troyen Nom: The' Gioi cua Truyen Nom."* (Hanoi: École Francaise d'Extreme-Orient, 1998), 61. Pages 57–101 are an authoritative study of *The Tale*, including its poetic structure and reception. Durand (1914–1966) originally published this study in *Melanges sur Nguyen Du. Reunis a l'occasion du bi-centenaire de sa naissance* (1765; repr. Paris: École Francaise d'Extreme-Orient, 1966), which includes scholarly investigations of such issues as the kind of "lute" played by Kieu as well as broader interpretations and appreciations.

3. For a three-and-a-half-minute video, see http://www.youtube.com/watch?v=psdP72jJBMI.

4. According to Le-Xuan-Thuy, every Vietnamese is affected by its verses, "whose echo seems to flow like waves of deep emotion that gathers love in his heart." He goes on to say that "certain persons, mostly of the fair sex" use *The Tale of Kieu* to discover their future by opening it at random and reading its verses as horoscopes. Nguyen Du, *Kim Van Kieu*, trans. Le-Xuan-Thuy (1964; repr. Rockville, Md.: Swallow Press, 2006), 4. This prose translation is worth consulting but is unsuitable for classroom use.

5. See Eric Henry, "On the Nature of the Kieu Story," *The Vietnam Forum* 3 (1984): 61–98.

6. 喃 is unusual in that it is also a Chinese character ("to chatter, mumble") and perhaps stems from ancient Chinese perception of Vietnamese as babble. See Maurice M. Durand and Nguyen Tran Huan, *An Introduction to Vietnamese Literature,* trans. D. M. Hawke (New York: Columbia University Press, 1985), 16.

7. Ibid, 81.

8. Nguyen Du, *Kim Van Kieu*, trans. Xuan-Phuc and Xuan-Viet (Paris: Gallimard, 1961).

9. John Balaban, ed. and trans., *Spring Essence: The Poetry of Ho Xuan* (Port Townsend, Wash.: Copper Canyon Press, 2000).

10. Nguyen Du, *The Tale of Kieu: A Bilingual Edition*, trans. Huyn Sabh Thong (New Haven, Conn.: Yale University Press 1983). Unless otherwise indicated, references in the present essay are to this edition.

11. Ibid, 95. For a scholarly discussion of this genre, see Durand, *L'universe des Troyen Nom.* Also see Hoang Ngoc Thanh, *Vietnam's Social and Political Development as Seen Through the Modern Novel* (New York: Peter Lang, 1991), 44–57.

12. See Eric Henry, "On the Nature of the Kieu Story."

13. Nguyen Du, *Kim Van Kieu*, trans. Le-Xuan-Thuy, 187–188.

14. Near Hangzhou, associated with the martyrdom of Wu Tzu-hsū (伍子胥).

15. The notes in Li-Xuan-Thuy's translation are also very useful, although neither he nor Huyn provide scholarly identification of their sources.

16. *Mencius* (6, B1): "If by scaling the wall of your neighbor on the east and dragging off his daughter you would get a wife, while by not dragging her off you could not get a wife would you then drag her off?" *Mencius*, trans. Irene Bloom (New York: Columbia University Press, 2009), 134.

17. Nguyen Ngoc Bich with Burton Raffel and W. S. Merwin, trans. *A Thousand Years of Vietnamese Poetry* (New York: Alfred A. Knopf, 1975), 129–140, esp. 136.

18. Nguyen Du, *Kim Van Kieu, Roman-poeme. Texte nom, avec transcription, traduction, notes glossaire et index de variants establish par Xuan Phuc* (Brussels: Editions Thanh-Long, 1986).

19. See Dong-Ho, *Melanges sur Nguyen Du*, 245–256, identified as a translated excerpt from a larger as yet unpublished book entitled *Parfums de bouddhisme, de sagesse et de poesie dans la literature vietnamienne*.

20. See Nguyen Du, *Kim Van Kieu*, trans. Xuan-Phuc and Xuan-Viet, 130.

INDEX

Abhirati, 125–26

"absence of [purposeful] action." See wu-wei ("absence of [purposeful] action")

"Acropolis on the Hudson," 5

Adler, Mortimer, xii; "The Colloquium on Important Books," 12; educational reform, 35; Four Books and, 198; "Hundred Great Books," 7; People's Institute of New York and, 10

advertising, desire and, 340

aesthetics, 216–17; imperfection, 260; religion and, 235–38; simplicity, 261–62. See also beauty

"affectionate" (yujŏng), 369

agricultural versus industrial vision, 345–46

aishō (lament), 218

Al-Ghazālī, 2; Qur'ān and, 16; works as Asian classics, 22

Al-Harīrī, 22

All Men are Brothers. See Water Margin (Shui hu)

allegory: in A Dream of Red Mansions (Honglou meng), 178; Western versus Chinese, 172–73

Allegory and Courtesy in Spenser, 172

allusion, 288–89

American Library Association, 10

American Philosophical Society, xii

amhaeng ŏsa (secret censors), 367

amour propre, 85

Āmrapālī, 121

"An Account of My Hut" (Hōjōki), 242–43; as Asian classic, 25–26; deprivation, aesthetics of, 256; description, 241–42; disaster in, 243–44; importance, 241; nature in, 246; tone, 242, 242–43. See also huts, symbolism of; Kamo no Chōmei

Analects of Confucius: as Asian classic, 24; Ezra Pound and, xiii; Four Books, as one of the, 187; human experience, appeal to, 46; limitations, 16–17; Neo-Confucian version, 55–56; student response to,

Analects of Confucius (continued)
    44–45; Zhu Xi and, 55. *See also*
    Zhu Xi
animals, 338; in "narrative verse," 378
anxiety, freedom from, 82
aoyagi (willow), 280
Approaches to the Oriental
    Classics, xvi
The Arabian Nights, 166
archetypes, literary, 244
aristocrats, businessmen as, 316
Artha Śāstra, 23
Ārya Mahāyāna Sūtra, 120
Asia: "The Great Conversation"
    extended to, xii–xiii; traditions of,
    14–16
Asian classics: criterion for recognition
    as, 28; education, crisis in, 18–19; as
    extension of core curriculum, 39–40;
    necessity of, 40–41; "parity of
    treatment," 19–20; selecting, 15–21;
    suggested list, 22–26
The Assemblies of Al-Harīrī, 22
"At Yellow Crane Tower Taking Leave
    of Meng Haoran as He Sets off for
    Guangling," 157
atarashimi ("newness"), 279
Aṭṭār, Farid ud-Din, 22
attentiveness, 80
autobiographies. *See The Memoirs of*
    Lady Hyegyŏng
"Autumn Floods," 83–85
Avalokiteśvara, 113–14
Avataṃsaka scriptures, 126
Averroes, 2
Avicenna, 2
The Awakening of Faith, 25
"awakening to the high," 284–85

Ba tiaomu (Eight Items), 191
Balaban, John, 377
balance, 330
banbutsu no rei ("soul of creation"), 323
"Barely Tolerable" Universe, 125
Barr, Stringfellow, xi
Barzun, Jacques, 1, 10, 12
basic needs, Mencius on, 61
The Battles of Coxinga, 302–304
beauty, 216–17; impermanence and,
    260–61; Japanese sense of, 221; ritual
    as, 102; virtue, more important than,
    233–34. *See also* aesthetics
beginnings and ends, 261
Bell, Daniel, 34
Bennett, William, 30
betrayal, 382
Bhagavad Gītā, 23
Bible, universality of, 5–6, 9–10
bildungsroman novels, 215–16
biographies, 359
Biographies of Eminent Monks
    (Gao-seng juan), 110
biwa, 248
Black Jade (fictional character), 177,
    180–82
blandness, 245
Bloom, Allan, 30; Adler and, 35;
    cultural relativism and, 40
Bo Zhuyi: personal content of poems,
    152; social criticism, poems of,
    151–52; works, 150, 218
"bodhisattva ideal," 121
Bodhisattva Kannon, 113–14; as a Future
    Buddha, 116; temple of, 237–38
bodhisattvas: "inconceivable liberation"
    of the, 124; perfume, 125; salvation
    by, 111, 115, 142

"breakthrough into integral comprehension," 193

Brebner, J. B., 12

Bryson, Lyman, 1

Buddha: Amida, 249; manifestations of, 113, 116, 125; miracles of, 121; new concepts of, 115. See also Śākyamuni

Buddha-land: Abhirati, 125–26; perfections of, 121–22; "pure," 126

Buddha nature, 139

Buddha Sugandhakūta of the Perfume Universe, 125

Buddha Wonder Sound, 113

Buddha-worlds, 111, 112

Buddhism: Confucianism versus, 47; Esoteric, 3, 234–35; Essays in Idleness (Tsurezuregusa) and, 259–60; Laozi and, 73; "last days of the Law" (mappō), 242–43; Murasaki Shikibu, condemnation of, 210–11; Pure Land Buddhism, salvation by, 249; superstitions, 319–20; The Tale of Genji and, 225–26. See also Mahāyāna Buddhism; Theravāda Buddhism

"Buddhist Law," last days of. See mappō ("last days of the Buddhist Law")

Buddhist monks, education of, 2. See also monastic life

Buke-giri monogatari (The Warrior's Sense of Duty), 316–17

bu-ren (pain), 185

bushidō ("way of the warrior"), 254, 310

businessmen as aristocrats, 316

Butler, Nicholas Murray, 5

The Calculating World (Seken mune-zanyo), 315

"canons," description of, 38

Cao Xüeqin: biographical information, 174–75; works as Asian classics, 25

Carman, Harry J., 13, 39–40

"central wisdom" (prajñāpāramitā), 162

Chan Buddhism. See Zen Buddhism

Chan, Wing-tsit, 73

Chan yuan qinggui ("Pure Rules for Chan Cloisters"), 146

Chang, H. C., 172

Chang Rong, 110

chastity, 383

checks and balances, system of, 205

Chen Liang, 207

Cheng Weiyüan, 175

Cheng Yi, 188

Chikamatsu Monzaemon: The Battles of Coxinga, 302–304; domestic plays, 304–309; European playwrights versus, 302; history plays, 302–304; isolation of, 301; as "Japanese Shakespeare," 301; The Love Suicides at Sonezaki, 304–309; puppet theater, 302–304

Chikamatsu, works of, 26

"child of Heaven," 45

childhood in literature, 355

China: education in, 202; literary portrayal, 302–304; religions in, 16; Three Teachings, 17

Chinese literature, 17; classics, suggested list of, 24–25. See also specific titles; Tang poetry

"Chinese Socialism," 51, 208

Chŏngjo, King, 359

chōnin-dō ("way of the townspeople"), 310

Chosŏn society, 353–54. *See also The Song of the Faithful Wife Ch'unhyang*

Chronicle of Tsuo, 137

Ch'unhyang (fictional character), 371–72

Chūshingura, 26

Chuzi (Songs of the South), 174

cicadas, 278–79

civil-service examinations: control of education through, 202; in *Ten Diagrams on Sage Learning*, 339

"classic," "sūtra" versus, 136

Classic of Changes, 58, 331, 344

"Classic of Dao and De." *See Laozi*

Classic of Documents, 346

Classic of Filial Piety, 110

Classic of History, 52–53, 137, 330

Classic of Odes, 149–51

classics: decline in study of, xiii–xiv; enjoyment of, 10–11; etymology of term, 57–58; learned elite, for the, 2; memorization and recitation of, 11; reappropriation of, xii; terminology for, 12, 35; universal consensus on, xv. *See also* humanities; translations

"Classics for an Emerging World," xv

"Classics of the Western World," xv; audience, intended, 9–10; development, 12

"clearly manifesting" (ming), 188

cold (hie), 256

colloquialisms as barrier to classics education, 3

"The Colloquium on Important Books" (seminar), 12, 39

Columbia University: classics in translation, 5–6; "Classics of the Western World." xv; core

curriculum, 34–38; general education requirements at, 34; "The Great Conversation" and, 1; "Humanities A" course, 8, 12

"combination" (toriawase) haiku, 279–80; cutting words in, 282–83

comic fantasy. *See Journey to the West*

"Commanderies and Prefectures" (jun xian lun), 207

common good (gong), 196

common humanity, 64

common people (min), 206

compassion, 68; bodhisattvas and, 115; Guan-yin as embodiment of, 116; personal salvation and, 183; suffering needed to develop, 125; as virtue, 331

"Complete Library in Four Branches of Learning and Literature" (Siku quanshu), 175

The Conference of the Birds, 22

Confucian Five Classics, 5

Confucian Four Books, 4, 5

Confucian Tradition and Global Education, xiii

Confucianism: Buddhism versus, 47; classics, 2; family, view of, 62; Five Relationships, 339; the *Laozi* versus, 78; Mahāyāna Buddhism versus, 188–89; surviving texts of, 188; *The Tale of Genji* and, 225–26; virtues, 47, 50, 51; Western exploration of, xiii. *See also* Neo-Confucianism

Confucius: character of, 51–55; disciples of, 47, 48, 55, 88; life experience, summary of, 53;

Mencius and, 70; mission of, 58; modesty, 52; Old Testament prophet, compared to, 46; public office, refusal to take, 54; as Sage, 52, 58; wu-wei, development of, 90; Zhu Xi versus, 93–96

consciousness, source of, 95–96

consensual rule, 201

consumerism, 340

Contemporary Civilization (course), 34; characteristics, 37–38; description, 35–36

convenient means, doctrine of, 116

core curriculum: changes in, controversy over, 30; "core" described, 38; definition, 36–37; extending, 38–43; nature of, 31–38; Songs of the Five Moral Relations, 366. See also general education requirements

cosmology, 322

court ladies: Confucian classics, education in, 2; life of, 356–57

court precedents and ceremony, 263

courtesans, 305–306

courtesy, 68

"courtliness" (miyabi), 215

creation myths, 178

Crossen, John Dominick, 87

Crow-Cock Kingdom, 170

"crown prince of wisdom." See Mañjuśri

Crucible of the Eight Trigrams, 167

Csikszentmihalyi, Mikhail, 88

cuckoo (hototogisu), 286n

cultural imperialism, liberal humanism as, 13

cultural relativism, traditionalism versus, 30

culture: globalization of, 40; religion and, 16; self-awareness in, 19

"cut-off lines" poetry, 155–56

"cutting word" (kireji), 282–83

Da ("the Great"), 74

Da-Tang San-zang qü-jing shi-hua, 160

Dao. See "The Way" (Dao)

dao tong ("The Reconstruction or Reconstitution of the Way"), 189

Daodejing. See Laozi

Daoism: literature, 2; Mahāyāna Buddhism and, 79; overview, 76–78. See also Zhuangzi

"Daoist" (daojia), 76

Daxue. See Great Learning

de. See virtue (de)

Deane, Herbert, 13

death and love, 229–30

"Death of Atsumori," 253–54

Deliverance from Error, 22

democratic education, 35

desire, 340; advertising and, 340; nature of, 225–26; nurturing, 102–103; religion and, 228

destiny versus talent, 384–85

detachment (Gellassenheit), 91

devotion, salvation through, 116

dharma (truth), 104; eternal, 235

Dharma of Sudden Enlightenment, transmission of, 140–41

Diagram of the Elementary Learning, 339

Diagram of the Rules of [Zhu Xi's] White Deer Hollow Academy, 339

Diagram of the Study of the Heart-and-Mind, 346–47

Diagram of the Supreme Ultimate, 336–37

Diamond Sūtra, 132, 134, 137–38

"diary literature," 295

differentiation of function, principle of, 107–108

diglossia, Korean, 354

ding. *See* meditation (ding)

disasters, natural, 243–44

discernment, 330

"*The Discipline of the Mind-and-Heart*" (*shinjutsu*), 324

discipline, spiritual. *See Precepts for Daily Life in Japan (Yamato Zokkun)*

discussion method, 5–6

"distant combination" haiku, 280–82

"distribution requirements," 32

diurnal realism, 178

The Documents, 52–53

domestic plays, 304–309

Dong-lin movement, 207

doro (mud), 280

double suicides, 304–309

drama. *See* plays

A Dream of Red Mansions (Honglou meng), 17; as Asian classic, 25; composition and publication, 175–76, 209; creation myths, 178; description, 174; diurnal realism in, 178; love and suffering in, 185; plot, 176–77; preferred title, 185–86n

Dream of the Red Chamber (novel), 17

"dressing the heroes" as narrative device, 253

drunkenness, 267

Drury, John, 59

Du Fu, 152, 156, 298

Duke of She, 48

duty. *See* rightness (yi)

Duyvendak, J. J. L., 73

dynamic pattern, 344

"early winter showers" (shigure), 275

"The East," perception of, 14, 18

Edman, Irwin, 12

education: in China, 202–204; choices in, xv–xvi; civil-service examinations and, 202; crisis in East Asian, 18–19, xiii, xiv; democratic, 35; "distribution requirements," 32; general education requirements, classics in, xv; multicultural learning, 2–3; "openness" in, 32; traditionalism versus cultural relativism, 30; universal, 202–204, xiv; utilitarian goals and, 10

educational reform, 35; in *Waiting for the Dawn (Mingyi daifanglu)*, 202–204

ego, 83–85; dangers of the, 81

Eight Items (Ba tiao mu), 191

Eitai-gura (Treasury for the Ages), 315

Ekken. *See* Kaibara Ekken

electives, educational, xv

elegies, 174

Elementary Learning (Xiao xue), 5, 327–28

Eliot, T. S., xii

Eliot, William, xv

emotions. *See* feelings (ninjō)

emptiness (xu): absolute, 123; as form, 163; in the *Laozi*, 74; mutual interpenetration and nonobstruction and, 124

enfeoffment system, 204

English language as lingua franca, xiv

enlightenment: feelings as means to, 226–28; nature of, 123

environmental crisis: Confucianism and, 338, 339–40; industrial versus agricultural vision and, 345–46

epic poetry. *See The Tale of Kieu*

epistles, 354

epithets, 285*n*

Erskine, John, xi; classics in translation, 5–6; Honors course, 8–9, 34

Esoteric Buddhism, 3, 234–35

essays, assumptions about, 265–66

Essays in Idleness (Tsurezuregusa): as Asian classic, 26; Buddhist influences, 259–60; impact of, 259; provenance, 258; title, source of, 257; translations, 254*n*. *See also* Kenkō

"The Essentials of Learning", 193–94

Essentials of Salvation, 243

eternal truth (tathatā), 235

ethical practice, 322

ethicoreligious treatises (kunmomo), 322

"Everyman" concept, 194; in *Journey to the West*, 162; in the *Platform Sūtra*, 138

exemplary actions (xian fa), 105

exile, 244–45

existence, nature of, 336–37

exoticism, 316

expectations, 87

"expedient means" (hōben), 234

Extending One's Knowledge (zhi zhi), 192, 195, 328–29

fa. *See* "model" (fa)

Fa-hai, 128, 133

The Faerie Queene, 172

faith, salvation through, 116

fajia. *See* Legalism (fajia)

fame, best not to seek, 268

family: Mencius versus Plato on, 62; in *Ten Diagrams on Sage Learning*, 337–38

Fan Zhongyan, 147

Farber, Leslie, 82

"fasting of the mind," 82, 88–89

fate (unmei), 250

feelings (ninjō): control of, 330–31; Kenkō versus Montaigne on, 273–74; as means to enlightenment, 226–28; obligation versus, 307; proper ordering of, 340; Seven Feelings, 329–30, 341, 350

feminism in core curriculum, 30

Feng-yü bao-chian (A Mirror for the Romantic), 176

Fenollosa, Ernest, 198; on the *Analects*, 55–56

filiality (xiao), 46; Confucianism, virtue of, 47; "fate" of, 89; government and, 52–53; reciprocity and, 47–48; in *The Tale of Kieu*, 386; in *Ten Diagrams on Sage Learning*, 337–38

filicide of Prince Sado, 352, 357–58, 359–63

Five Classics, 329

Five Relationships, 323–24, 339

Five Women Who Loved Love: impetuosity in, 318; karma in, 319–20; money in, 315; sin and, 319; women, boldness of, 318. *See also* Ihara Saikaku

"The Floating Bridge of Dreams," 218

Floating World (ukiyo-zoshi), 314

"floodlike qi," 69

"flow," 88

folk narratives, 210

folksong poetry, 153

"following the brush" (zuihitsu), 257

form as emptiness, 163

Formless Precepts, 129

Four Beginnings of virtue, 68–69, 343

Four Books: in extension of knowledge,
    329; Huang Zongxi and, 200; as
    "neoclassical", 187–88; priority
    of, 187; Xunzi excluded from, 93.
    *See also Analects of Confucius; Great
    Learning (Daxue); Mean
    (Zhongyong); The Mencius*

"four crazies" (samang), 369

"four heavenly kings" of poetry, 258

fragrance (nioi), 281, 282

"fragrant links" (nioi-zuke), 280–81

Frankel, Charles, 13

Franklin, Benjamin, xii

free speech in education, 203

friendship, 156–57

"frog in the caved-in well" story,
    83–85

"frog poem": effect of, 278;
    interpretation, 289–90

frogs (kawazu), symbolism of, 276–78,
    280

Fu-she movement, 207

Fujiwara Kamatari, 226

Fujiwara no Yoshitsune, 284

"functionality" (yong), 79

furu ("old"), 289

Future Buddha, 116

Fuwa Barrier as utamakura, 284

ga ("high"), 285

Gandhi, Mohandas, 23

Gao Ê, 175

Gao Pien, 155

*Gao-seng juan (Biographies of Eminent
    Monks)*, 110

Gaozi, Mencius versus, 69

Gargantua and Pantagruel, 172

Garland scriptures, 126

Gellassenheit (detachment), 91

Gempei War of 1180–1185, 248

"General Education in a Free
    Society," 33

general education requirements:
    classics in, xv; evolution of, 33–34.
    See also core curriculum

Genji clan. *See* Minamoto clan

Genji (fictional character). *See The Tale
    of Genji*

*Genji Monogatari. See The Tale of Genji
    (Genji Monogatari)*

Genshin, 243

gentlemanly conduct, 262–63

"gentlemanly learning," 10–11

"getting it for oneself" (zide), 327

giri (obligation), 307

"globalization" of culture, 40, 41–43

gnosis, 76

Go-Daigo, Emperor, 258

Golden Lotus (Jinpingmei), 25, 174

gong (common good), 196

gong-lun (public opinion), 205

good and evil, emotions and, 329

"good books." *See* classics

"good knowing" (liangzhi), 48, 325

governance (matsurigoto), 235

government: filiality and, 52–53;
    good, requirements for, 50–51;

humaneness and, 63; laissez-faire, 77; representative, 206

Graham, A. C., 27

"Great Books" programs, xi; challenges, 42; discussion method, 6–7; East, of the, 8, 14–15

"The Great Conversation," xi–xii; Asia, extension to, xii–xiii; Islam in, 1–2

"The Great" (Da), 74

Great Learning (Daxue), xiii, 55, 327–28; Confucianism, as surviving text of, 188; Four Books, as one of the, 187; "key to the pursuit of learning," 188; self-cultivation and, 195; table of contents, 190

"Great Understanding," 89

Great Vehicle, 115

grief: absence of, 242, 247; passage of spring and, 297; restrictions on, 357. *See also* sorrow

Gu Yan-wu, 207

Guan-yin, 113–14, 116–17

Gutmann, James, 13

Hadas, Moses, 12, 13

haecceatis ("thisness"), 87

haibun (poetic prose), 283

haigon, 284–85

haikai poetry, 275; "awakening to the high" and, 284–85; defined, 313; "haikai," meaning of, 279; history, 278; structure, 278; "the unexpected," element of, 279, 280, 286n. *See also* haiku poetry; Matsuo Bashō

haiku poetry, 15; allusion in, 288–89; difficulty of, 287–88; interpretation, 289–90; meaning, sources of, 283, 287, 288; origin of, 275; puns, use of, 294; revisions, 291–92; seasonal words in, 275–76; selective juxtaposition, 282; sensory techniques, 290–92; simplicity in, 294–95; syllables, restriction on, 287; types of, 279–82; unique to Japan, 15. *See also* haikai poetry; Matsuo Bashō

Hakuin, 26

han, 365–66

Han Feizi, 24, 72

Han Feizi (philosopher), 64, 203

Han Yü, 188–89

Hanjung mallok. See The Memoirs of Lady Hyegyŏng

Hanjungnok. See The Memoirs of Lady Hyegyŏng

Hanshan, 154–55

"Hardships of Life in the World," 244

harmony, 332–33; in Confucianism, 51; of man and nature, 192

harusame ("spring rain"), 275

Harvard University: "Five Foot Shelf of Classics," xv; general education requirements, changes in, 30

"having utmost refinement," 330

heart, mind not separate from, 69

Heart Classic, 321, 330

Heart Sūtra, transmission of, 162–63

Heaven: in the *Analects*, 53–54; and Earth, gratitude to, 323–24; mandate of, 104; as nature, 70; self-knowing and, 70; self-sufficiency of, 107

Heian period: Esoteric Buddhism and, 234–35; literature, 2–3, 25; women's role in, 213

Heike clan. *See* Taira clan

Heptameron, 271

hie (cold), 256

"high" (ga), 285

Highest Perfect Wisdom (prajñā paramita), 137

Hīnayāna Buddhism, 115; as "lesser vehicle," 145

Hinduism: claims, evaluating, 16; sacred literature, 2

historiographies, 353, 359, 363

history plays, 302–304

Ho Xuan, 377

hōben ("expedient means"), 234

Hōjō family, revolt against the, 258

Hōjōki. See "An Account of My Hut" (Hōjōki)

hokku poetry, 275; independent versus linked verse, 283. *See also* haiku poetry

"holding fast to the Mean," 330

Holland Saikaku (Oranda Saikaku), 316. *See also* Ihara Saikaku

"Holy Scripture of the Universal Vehicle," 120

homosexuality, 314

Hong Nagim, 358

Honglou meng. See A Dream of Red Mansions (Honglou meng)

Hongzhou School, 135

hon'i (poetic essence), 277, 284

Honors course, 8–9; transformation of, 34–35

honzon (object of worship), 237

hototogisu (cuckoo), 286n

Hsia, C. T., 17

hsin ("mind" and "heart"), 69

Hu Shi, 160

Huang-Lao, doctrine of, 77

Huang Zongxi: biographical information, 199; consensual rule,

201; constitutional order, advocacy for, 205; influences, 206–207; interests, 199–200; self-cultivation and, 200; works, 25, 199. *See also Waiting for the Dawn (Mingyi daifanglu)*

Hui of Liang, King, 59

Huineng, the Sixth Patriarch, 128: autobiography as fabrication, 130; Dharma transmission, 140–41; parting message, 147. *See also Platform Sūtra of the Sixth Chan Patriarch*

"human desires," 196

human mind versus "the Way" mind, 330, 346–47

human nature: as evil, 93–94; Mencius on, 61, 62, 67–71; wood likened to, 96–97; in *Xunzi*, 94–95

humaneness (ren): burden of, 50; compassion as beginning of, 68; government and, 63; importance disputed, 78; Mencius on, 62–63, 66; profit versus, 59, 63–64; singlemindedness and, 197; as virtue, 47, 323–24, 331; the "Way" and, 70

humanities: education, crisis in, xiii–xiv. *See also* classics

"Humanities A" course, 8, 12; characteristics, 37–38

humanity: common, 64, 197; explanation of, 344–46; life-giving quality of, 344; model of, 105

humans: environment, differences based on, 66–67; "four beginnings" of, 68–69; learning, need for, 96; nature and, 58, 341–44; responsibilities of, 324; as "thing among other things," 81 humility, 87

humor: in haikai, 276, 279; in haiku, 294–95; of Tripitaka, 169

"Hundred Great Books," 35, xii

"Hundred Great Ideas," xii

Hung-jen, the Fifth Patriarch, 131

husband-wife relationship, 375n. *See also The Song of the Faithful Wife Ch'unhyang*

Hutchins, Robert, 7

huts, symbolism of: "An Account of My Hut," 241, 244–45; deprivation, aesthetics of, 256; *The Tale of the Heike*, 255–56

Huyn Sanh Thong, 377

Hyegyŏng, Lady: arranged marriage, 355–56; biographical information, 352; court life, 356–57; suicidal thoughts, 357. *See also The Memoirs of Lady Hyegyŏng*

"I bow" (namo), 111

Ibn Khaldūn, 2; histories, 15; Qur'ān and, 16; works as Asian classics, 22

ichimotsu shitate ("single-topic") haiku, 279–80

ideal nature, 194–95

idleness, 266

Ihara Saikaku: biographical information, 313; *The Calculating World*, 315; chōnin-dō and, 310; inconsistencies, 317; lifestyle, 310; nickname, 316; other genres, 313–14; *Treasury for the Ages*, 315; works as Asian classics, 26. *See also Five Women Who Loved Love*

Imagawa Ryōshun, 258

imagery, 383–84

immigrants: at Columbia University, 35; education of, 7

imperfection, love of, 261

"Imperial Law," decline in, 249

impermanence (mujō), 249, 259–61; Montaigne on, 267–68

"inconceivable liberation," 124

India, religions in, 16

Indian literature, 23. *See also* specific titles

industrial versus agricultural vision, 345–46

infidelity, marital, 224–25

inga. *See* karma

"The Initiates' Chapter," 254–56

inner power (de), 101

insecurity, personal, 223

Inside Academe, xiii–xiv

"inside the circumference" haiku, 280

intellectual illumination, 333

interpretations, translations versus, 27

investigation in extension of knowledge, 328–29

"Invitation to Learning" (radio series), 1

Ise Taira, 256n

Islam: as Asian and Western tradition, 28–29n; geographic coverage, 15–16; "The Great Conversation" and, 1–2

Islamic literature, 22. *See also* specific titles

Japan: Heian period, 2–3, 25; religions in, 16

Japanese literature, 17: classics of, 25–26; influences, 210; Nō drama, 15, 26; waka poetry, 210. *See also* haiku poetry; specific titles

Jayadeva, 23

jealousy, 223

Jewel Heap scriptures, 126

Jia Baoyü (fictional character), 178–85

jie-tan tu jing ("platform precept
 book"), 129

jin. *See* humaneness (ren)

Jin ping mei, 178

jing: applications, 136, 137; etymology,
 57–58

*Jinpingmei. See Golden Lotus
 (Jinpingmei)*

jinsi, meanings of, 189

Jinsilu, 189, 190; "The Essentials of
 Learning," 193–94; jitoku. *See*
 "getting it for oneself" (zide)

Journey to the West: as Asian classic, 17,
 25; authorship, questionable, 160;
 Communist perspective, 168–69;
 Gargantua and Pantagruel and, 172;
 mythical aspects, 169–70; ridicule
 in, 170–71; translations, 159. *See also*
 Monkey (fictional character); Pigsy
 (fictional character); Tripitaka

"Jue jü," 156

jueju poetry, 155–56

jun xian lun ("Commanderies and
 Prefectures"), 207

junzi. *See* Noble Person (junzi)

ka (questioning note), 220

Kālidāsa, 23

Kagami Shikō, 289

Kagerō Nikki, 212

Kaibara Ekken: human beings, unique
 status of, 323; influences, 321; *Record
 of Great Doubts*, 333. *See also*
 "learning of the mind-and-heart"
 (xinxue); Neo-Confucianism;

*Precepts for Daily Life in Japan
 (Yamato Zokkun)*

Kakuichi, 248

Kaltenmark, Max, 73

kami-gata-mono, 315

Kamo no Chōmei: portrayal of,
 246–47; works as Asian classics,
 25–26. *See also* "An Account of
 My Hut" (Hōjōki)

kanbun prose, 322

Kannon. *See* Bodhisattva Kannon

kare (withered), 256

Karlgren, Bernhard, 73

karma, 319–20

karumi ("lightness"), 294

*Kashima mōde (A Visit to Kashima
 Shrine)*, 283

Kautilya, 23

kawazu (frogs), symbolism of, 276–78,
 280

Keats, John, 81

Kenkō: biographical information,
 257–58; Confucian classics, education
 in, 2; on drunkenness, 267; on
 feelings, 274; "four heavenly kings,"
 one of the, 258; on idleness, 266;
 insights of, 263–64; on nature, 273;
 "passing the time," 269; on pleasure
 and fame, 268; on politics, 273; on
 sensual pleasure, 271–73; on
 uncertainty, 267–68. *See also Essays
 in Idleness (Tsurezuregusa)*;
 Montaigne, Michel de

Kenreimon'in, 254–56

kerria (yamabuki), symbolism of, 277,
 280

ki. *See* qi (life force)

kidai (seasonal topics), 278

kigo, 275, 278

King Wonderful Splendor, 114

Kinne, Burdette, 13

kireji ("cutting word"), 282–83, 286n

kisaeng, 362–63

Kiyomori: death, 250; regret, 254

knowledge, 192; and action, integrating, 326–28; "good knowing" (liangzhi), 48, 325; principle and, 192–93; "subjective" and "objective," 324–26. *See also* Extending One's Knowledge (zhi zhi); learning

kōan, 124, 146; no evidence for, 130

Kokinshū: as Asian classic, 26; frogs in, 277; loneliness in, 213–14

Korea: diglossic culture of, 354; language in, 3

Koremori, portrayal of, 251–52

Kōshoku ichidai otoko (A Man Who Loved Love), 314

Kūkai: on Confucian classics, 2; Esoteric Buddhism and, 234; public schooling advocacy, 3; works as Asian classics, 26

Kumārajiva, 117–18

kunmono (ethicoreligious treatises), 322

Kuzu no Matsubara, 277

kwŏnsŏn ching'ak ("to encourage virtue and shun evil"), 367

laissez-faire government, 77

lament (aishō), 218

language as barrier to classics education, 3, 5

Lankāvatāra Sūtra, 131

Lao Dan. *See* Laozi (philosopher)

Laozi, 2; alternative names, 73, 74; as Asian classic, 24; as civil service exam text, 79; commentary, 72; Confucianism versus, 78; division of, 74; history, 72; major concepts, 74; in medieval thought and religion, 78–79; on military operations, 77–78; paradoxical discourse, 76; Sages, rejection of, 78. *See also* Daoism

Laozi (deity), 167

Laozi (philosopher): legend of, 73; as Master, 46; as "Most High Lord Lao," 78; as mystic, 75–76; real name, 73; Xunzi versus, 98

"last days of the Buddhist Law." *See* mappō ("last days of the Buddhist Law")

Lau, D. C., 73

law: as "model," 106; reconception of, 201–202

laymen, scholars versus, 11

Le-Xuan Thuy, 377

leaders: characteristics of skillful, 77; moral responsibilities of, 201

learning: goals of, 99–100; human need for, 96; methods, 326–28; necessity of, 344; in *Ten Diagrams on Sage Learning*, 339–340. *See also* knowledge

learning imperative, 324–29

"learning of the mind-and-heart" (xinxue): description, 321; framework, Ekken's, 322; origin, 322. *See also* self-cultivation; xin (Mind-and-Heart)

"leaving the world," 227–28

Lee (fictional character), 372–73

Legalism (fajia): description of, 104; filiality and, 47; free speech and, 203; policies, 77; profit and, 64; "lets go" (tsukihanasu), 281

li. *See* principle (li); ritual (li)

Li Bo, 153–54, 157

Li Dan. *See* Laozi

Li Er. *See* Laozi

Li Gou, 207

Li Si, 203

liangzhi ("good knowing"), 48, 325

Liberal Education, 12, 42–43

liberal humanism, 7–8; as cultural imperialism, 13

liberation through literature, 228–29

"liberative art," 126

licensed quarters, 305

life: aesthetic response to, 226–27; impermanence of, poignancy in the, 260; lotus flower as symbol of, 114–15; pace of, 348–50

life force. *See* qi (life force)

"Light Furs, Fat Horses," 151–52

"lightness" (karumi), 294–95

Liji (Record of Rites), 55

lingua franca, English as, xiv

linked verse (renga), 211, 214

Literary Guide to the Bible, 59

literate discourse (wen), 49

literature, liberating function of, 228–29

Little Clay Cart, 23

"little understanding," 83, 89

Liu Yüxi, 150

living systems, 342

Locke, John, 208

loneliness (sabi), 214, 256; in haiku, 278–79, 291–92

loss, 221. *See also* death

lotus flower, symbolism of, 114–15

The Lotus of the Wonderful Law, or The Lotus Gospel, 117

The Lotus Sūtra: as Asian classic, 24; believers, blessings bestowed upon, 113; critique, 114; as drama, 111; reverence of, salvation and, 112; symbolism, 114; teaching, ways of, 113; translations, 117–18, 119*n*; women and, 113. *See also* Mahāyāna Buddhism

love (qing): death and, 229–30; diversity in, 310–20; in *A Dream of Red Mansions*, 185; happiness in, 311; lust versus, 179; of money, 315; "perfect," 224; in *The Tale of Genji*, 221

love stories, 370

The Love Suicides at Sonezaki, 304–309

Low, Seth, 5

low tide (shiohi), 280

"low" (zoku), 284

loyalty (zhong), 49, 50. *See also* filiality (xiao)

Lü Liu-liang, 207

Lu-Wang School of the Mind, 324

"luck running out," 254

"luminous virtue" (mingde), 188, 192

Luo Qinshun, 321

lust (yin), love versus, 179

Magic Flute , 372

Mahābhārata, 23

Mahākāśyapa, 112

Mahāyāna Buddhism: basic concepts, 117; "central wisdom" texts of, 162; Confucianism versus, 188–89;

Daoism and, 79; expedient means (hōben), 234; Hīnayāna Buddhism versus, 115; scriptures, 2, 23, 24, 120–21; syncretism, allegories of, 25. *See also The Lotus Sūtra; Vimalakīrti Sūtra*

Making One's Intentions Sincere, 195

"man of service" (shi), 50

A Man Who Loved Love (Koshoku ichidai otoko), 314

"The Mandate," 337

"Mandate of Heaven" (tian ming), 53, 54

Mang Wu Bo, 47

Mañjuśri, 113, 122–24

Manyōshū, 17; as Asian classic, 25; poets, 218; *The Tale of Genji* and, 226–27

mappō ("last days of the Buddhist Law"), 242–43, 249

marital infidelity, 224–25

marital residences, succession to, 213

marriage: arranged, 355–56; chastity in, 383

Martin, Everett Dean, 10–11

Masaoka Shiki, 299–300

Master of Cold Mountain, 154–55

"Master" (zi), 46

"Mastering Life," 86–88

Matsunaga Teitoku, 259

Matsuo Bashō, 275–76: "combination" haiku, 280; criticism of, 299–300; death, nearing, 294–95; "diary literature," 295; "distant combination" haiku, 282; "fragrant links," 281; impact of, 284–85; output, surviving, 287; poetic prose, 283, 295–99; "saint of haiku," 298–99; "single-topic"

haiku, 280; works, 26, 276–77, 283, 288. *See also* haiku poetry; *The Narrow Road to the Deep North*

matsurigoto (governance), 235

McCullough, Helen, 248

McKeon, Richard, 12

"The Mean," holding fast to the, 330

Mean (Zhongyong): feelings, proper ordering of, 340; Four Books, as one of the, 187; knowledge and action, integrating, 326; Mind-and-Heart, direction and control of, 195–96; Medieval period, the *Laozi* during, 78–79; meditation (ding); monastic setting and, 145–46; "no-thought" and, 141–42; in the *Platform Sūtra*, 134; wisdom as, 141

The Memoirs of Lady Hyegyŏng, 352; genres of, 353; structure, 354. *See also* Hyegyŏng, Lady; Sado, Prince

Memoirs Written in Silence. See The Memoirs of Lady Hyegyŏng

memorials, 358–59

memorization of classics, 11

The Mencius: Four Books, as one of the, 187; influence of, 57; "midreading," 59–61; parent-child relationship, 48–49; Thirteen Classics, as one of the, 57

Mencius (philosopher): antagonists, 65, 69; on basic needs, 61; family, view of, 62; on human nature, 61, 62, 67–71; on humaneness, 66; impact of, 70; profit rejected by, 66; "public" and "private" spheres, continuity of, 61–62; sagehood, self-doubt regarding, 60; warfare, response to, 58–59; works as Asian classics, 24

Meng Hao-ran, 157

"Meng-cheng Hollow," 153

Mengzi. See Mencius

merchant guilds (za), 315–16

Merton, Thomas, 27

Message of the Mind (xinfa), 196–97

Miao-fa lien-hua jing, 117

"midreading," 59–61

military: in the Analects, 50, 51; in the Laozi, 77–78

min (common people), 206

Minamoto clan, 248, 256n; "way of the warrior" and, 254. See also The Tale of the Heike

Mind-and-Heart (xin), 195–96

mind, heart not separate from, 69

"mind to mind" transmission, 143, 144

mindfulness: admonition on, 347–48; mastery of, 349; reverent, 332

ming ("clearly manifesting"), 188

Ming dynansty literature, 199

mingde ("luminous virtue"), 188, 192

Mingru xuean, 199

Mingyi daifanglu. See Waiting for the Dawn (Mingyi daifanglu)

A Mirror for the Romantic (Feng-yü bao-chian), 176

Mirror of Manly Love (Nanshoku ōkagami), 314

miyabi ("courtliness"), 215

Mo Di. See Mozi

"model" (fa), 104, 105; of a king, 106; laws, 106, 201

modesty, 68

Moemon (fictional character), 317, 318–19

Mohists, 66

monastic life, 247n; as exile, 244–45; as "leaving the world," 227–28; in the Platform Sūtra, 145

money, love of, 315

Monkey, 159

Monkey (fictional character): detachment, 164; devotion, 167–68; magic, 165–66; as monster, 167; superior understanding, 163–64. See also Journey to the West

The Monkey's Raincoat, 281

mono no aware ("poignancy of things"), 227, 255, 256

monogatari (vernacular tales), 211

Montaigne, Michel de: on drunkenness, 267; feelings, elusive, 273–74; on idleness, 266; on impermanence, 267–68; on nature, 273; on "passing the time," 268–69; on politics, 273; on sensual pleasure, 269–71. See also Kenkō

moon, symbolism of, 380

moral commitment, 59–61; of leaders, 201

moral purification, 330–31

Morris, Ivan, 233–34

"Most High Lord Lao" (Taishang laojun), 78

Motoori Norinaga, 2

"Mountain Pavilion, Summer Day," 155

"mountain temple" (yamadera), 291

Mozart, 372

Mozi: filiality and, 47; Mencius versus, 65–66; works as Asian classics, 24

mud (doro), 280

Muhammad, 1, 16

mujō (impermanence), 249, 259–61

multitasking, 348

Mumyōshō (Notes Without a Name), 245

Murasaki (fictional character), 224–25

Murasaki Shikibu, 25; Buddhism, condemnation by, 210–11; corpus, 214; education, 2; Sei Shōnagon, comments on, 231–32. *See also The Tale of Genji (Genji Monogatari)*

Murray, Gilbert, 7–8, 12

mutual constraint, 342

mutual interpenetration and nonobstruction, 124

"mysterious" (xuan), 75

myth, 169–70

namo ("I bow"), 111

Nanshoku ōkagami (Mirror of Manly Love), 314

narrative devices, 253

"narrative verse" (truyen), 378

The Narrow Road to the Deep North (Oku no hosomichi), 295–99; Matsushima, description of, 293; poetic techniques, 278–79; themes, 276; utamakura, search for, 283. *See also* Matsuo Bashō

natural disasters, 243–44

natural knowledge (liang zhi), 48

nature: in "An Account of My Hut," 246; as "Heaven," 70; humans and, 58, 341–44; Kenkō versus Montaigne, 273; man and, harmony of, 192; in Tang poetry, 154–56

nebu ("to sleep"), 294

"negative capability," 81

Neo-Confucianism: *Analects*, reading of the, 55–56; influence of, 206, 321; public schooling advocacy, 3–4;

"quiet sitting," 147; "recorded conversations," 3; terminology, justification for, 187–88; translation of classics and, 11. *See also* Kaibara Ekken; *Ten Diagrams on Sage Learning (Seonghak sipdo)*; Yi T'oegye

neoclassicism, 189

New Asia College, xiii

New England Transcendentalists, xii

"newborn baby," heart of a, 184–85

"newness" (atarashimi), 279

Ngyuen Du, 378. *See also The Tale of Kieu*

Ngyuen Dynasty, founding of, 378

Nichiren School, 110

nikkō (sunlight), 299

ninjō. *See* feelings (ninjō)

nioi (fragrance), 281, 282

nioi-zuke ("fragrant links"), 280–81

Nirvāṇa, 123

Nirvāṇa Sūtra, 134

Nō drama, 15, 26

"no-thought," 134; meditation and, 141–42

"Noble Eightfold Path" of Theravada, 143

Noble Person (junzi), 105; defined, 45; in governance, 105; humaneness, as model of, 49; "man of service" (shi), equivalence to, 50; as model, 106–107; path to becoming, 46–47; recognition and, 45, 53; roles of, 108

Nom (writing script), 376–77

nondualism: in the *Platform Sūtra* , 141; in the *Vimalakīrti Sūtra*, 123, 124

Northern Chan, 132

nostalgia, 242

Notes Without a Name (Mumyōshō), 245

nothingness (wu): in the *Laozi*, 74–75; "mysterious," part of, 75; refinement of, 79

Nozarashi kikō . See Record of a Weather-Exposed Skeleton (Nozarashi kikō)

Nozawa Bonchō, 281

Nukada, Princess, 226–27

object of worship (honzon), 237

"objective" and "subjective," 223

obligation (giri), 307

Ohatsu (fictional character), 308

Oi no kobumi (Record of a Travel-Worn Satchel), 283

Oku no hosomichi. See The Narrow Road to the Deep North (Oku no hosomichi)

"old" (furu), 289

"On Old Age, to Send to Mengde (Liu Yüxi)," 150–51

One Vehicle, 111, 112, 116

"openness" in education, 32

operas. *See The Tale of Kieu*

Oranda Saikaku (Holland Saikaku), 316. *See also* Ihara Saikaku

Orientalism, 13–14

Osaka society, portrayal of. *See* Ihara Saikaku

Outline and Details of the Comprehensive Mirror (Tongjiangangmu), 329

"outside the circumference" haiku, 280

overtones (yojō), 217

"overwhelming energy," 69

Ox-head School of Chan, 133–34

pain (bu-ren), 185

Pañcatantra, 23

p'ansori tradition, 368–69, 374n; flaws of, 373

paradise, 125–26

paradoxical discourse, 76

parent-child relationship, 47–49, 355, 360–61. *See also* filiality

"parity of treatment," 19–20

participation, 88

"the passing of spring" (yuku haru), 276

"passing the time," 268–69

passion. *See* feelings

"patriarch" (zu), 144

peace, 242

pedophilia, 314

The Peony Pavilion, 174

"people of the book," 1

People's Institute of New York, 10

"people's institutes," 35

"perfect" women, 222–23

"perfect world," 121–22

Perfection of Wisdom, 134

personal integration, 329–31

Pervading Fragrance (fictional character), 183

petitions, 358–59

phenomenal existence (you): in the *Laozi*, 74; "mysterious," part of, 75; refinement of, 79

Pigsy (fictional character), 164, 171–72; characterization, 173. *See also Journey to the West*

The Pillow Book (Makura no sōshi), 17; as Asian classic, 25; beauty more important than virtue, 233–34; genre, lack of, 232; zuihitsu, as model of, 232. *See also* Sei Shōnagon

"platform precept book" (jie-tan tu
jing), 129
*Platform Sūtra of the Sixth Chan
Patriarch*: as Asian classic, 24;
background, 131–33; Buddhism,
elements common to all, 129;
compiler of the, 128, 133; "Everyman"
concept in, 138; formal title of, 136;
Formless Precepts, 129; lineage,
claimed, 143–45; major concepts,
134; monastic life in the, 145;
nondualism, 141; provenance, 128,
133–34; public versus private life in,
146; "Recorded Sayings," 130;
scripture, status as, 15; *The Tale of
Kieu* and, 385. *See also* Huineng, the
Sixth Patriarch
Plato: family, view of, 62; "public" and
"private" spheres, 61
plays: Nō drama, 15, 26; puppet,
302–304. *See also* Chikamatsu
Monzaemon
pleasure, best not to seek, 268
Poems of Rūmī, 22
poetic essence (hon'i), 277, 284
"poetic places" (utamakura), 217,
283–84
poetic prose (haibun), 283, 295–99
poetic techniques: allusion, 288–89;
sound, 290–91, 300*n*
poetic themes, 154–57
poetry: folksong, 153; "four heavenly
kings" of, 258; Japanese, 25, 26,
226–27; jueju poetry, 155–56; renga,
211, 214, 275; shi, 151; waka, 210, 214,
275; yūgen, 245. *See also* haiku
poetry; Tang poetry
poignancy, 260

political philosophy, 77
politics: as a "bird cage," 89; Kenkō
versus Montaigne, 273; literature
and, 378–79
"popularization," 10
Pound, Ezra, xii–xiii, 149–50; Four
Books and, 198; trustworthiness and,
49–50
prajñā intuition, 139
prajñā paramita (Highest Perfect
Wisdom), 137
prajñāpāramitā ("central wisdom"), 162
Prajñāpāramitā, manifestation of, 124
pre-Islamic poetry, 22
*Precepts for Daily Life in Japan (Yamato
zokkun)*: "five relationships," 323–24;
humaneness (ren), 323–24; influences,
322; learning imperative, 324–29;
modes of practice, 331–33; personal
integration, 329–31; "Pursuit of
Learning," 324; religious impetus,
323–24; spiritual harmony and
intellectual illumination, 333;
"subjective" and "objective"
knowledge, balancing, 324–26;
themes and principal components,
322; virtues, 331–333. *See also*
Kaibara Ekken
Precious Clasp (fictional character),
177, 181–85
Primer for Youth, 366
"The Prince" (Yuan jun), 200
principle (li), 192; qi and, 328
private and public spheres, continuity
of, 61–62
profit: humaneness versus, 59, 63–64;
Legalism and, 64; Mencius, rejected
by, 66

The Prolegomena to World History, 22

propriety, modesty as beginning of, 68

prose, kanbun, 322

prostitution, 305–306, 380–81

psychological novels. *See The Tale of Genji*

psychophysical energy. *See* qi (life force)

psychophysical energy (qi), ideal nature and, 194–95

pu ("raw substance"), 94–96

Pu-ji, attack on, 132–33

public and private spheres, continuity of, 61–62

"public cases" of Zen Buddhism, 124, 146

public opinion (gong-lun), 205

public schooling, advocacy for, 3–5

puns, use of, 294, 369

puppet plays, 302–304; women in, 306

Pure Land Buddhism, 249

Pure Land of Bliss scriptures, 126

"Pure Rules for Chan Cloisters" (Chanyuan qinggui), 146

"Pursuit of Learning," 324

qi (life force), 69–70; clarity of, 341; depletion of, 81; philosophy of, 321; principle and, 328; in *Ten Diagrams on Sage Learning*, 335

Qian-liang ("Taxes in Money"), 207

Qilüe, 76–77

qing. *See* love (qing)

quan-ji, 165

Queen of Navarre, 271

questioning note (ka), 220

quiet and activity, rhythm of, 349

"quiet sitting," 147

The Qur'ān: as Asian classic, 22; claims, evaluating, 16

Rāmānuja, 23

Rāmāyana: as Asian classic, 23; influence of, 165

"raw substance" (pu), 94–96; consciousness versus, 95–96

realism, diurnal, 178

"realm of origin," 114

"realm of traces," 114

Realpolitik, 64

receptivity, 87

reciprocity: filiality and, 47–48; importance of, 331

recitation of classics, 11

The Recognition of Things (ge-wu), 191–92

"reconciliation of dichotomies," 124

"The Reconstruction or Reconstitution of the Way" (dao tong), 189

Record of a Travel-Worn Satchel (Oi no kabumi), 283

Record of a Weather-Exposed Skeleton (Nozarashi kikō), 283, 284, 288

Record of Great Doubts (Taigiroku), 333

"Record of Music" (Yueji), 196

Record of Rites (Liji), 4, 55, 196, 254, 326

"recorded conversations," 3

"Recorded Sayings" (yü-lu), 130

Records of the Grand Historian (Shiji), 24, 329

Records Written in Silence. See The Memoirs of Lady Hyegyŏng

Rectification of the Mind-and-Heart, 195

Red Inkstone (Zhihyan chai), 175

"refined discrimination," 196–97

"reflection" as human quality, 69
Reflections on Things at Hand (Jin-si-lu), 4
The Reforming of General Education, 34
Regulations of the King, 108
relationships: human-to-nonhuman, 343–44. *See also* husband-wife relationship; parent-child relationship
relativity, 124
religion: culture and, 16; desire and, 228; in Heian society, 234–35
religiosity of ritual, 102
religious impetus, 323–24
ren. *See* humaneness (ren)
renga (linked verse), 211, 214; hokku in, 275–76
representative government, 206
The Republic, 61, 62
resolution, 330
respectful conduct, 46
reverent mindfulness, 332
Rhodes, Alexandre de, 377
ridicule, 170–71
Rig Veda, 23
rightness (yi), 49, 64; qi and, 69–70; shame as beginning of, 68; Zhuangzi on, 81
"rising early and retiring late," 348–50
ritual (li): aesthetic importance of, 235–38; in the *Analects*, 51; as beauty, 102; dismissed by Zhuangzi, 81; purpose of, 102–103; religiosity of, 102; self-fulfillment and, 101; in *Ten Diagrams on Sage Learning*, 335
Rizhi lu, 207
The Romance of the Three Kingdoms, 173

The Romance of the Western Chamber, 174
ru-lai quan-shen ("Total Body of the Buddha"), 118
rulers: education and, 203; humaneness of, 62; moral standards for, 65; qualities of successful, 66; "transforming influence of morality," 66. *See also specific names*
Rulin waishi. See The Scholars (Rulin waishi)
Rūmī, 22
ryōchi. *See* "good knowing" (liangzhi)
Ryūsaku Tsunoda, 221

sabi (loneliness), 214
"Sacred Books of the East," 14
Sado, Prince, 352; filicide of, 357–58, 359–63; mental illness, 361–62. *See also The Memoirs of Lady Hyegyŏng*
The Saga Diary (Saga nikki), 283
Saga nikki (The Saga Diary), 283
sage-kings, 105
Sages (shengren): anyone becoming, 194; becoming, ultimate goal of, 325–26; Confucius, 52; Mencius, 60; qualities of, 83; rejection of, 78; "transforming influence of morality" as mark of, 66
Sahā Universe, 125
Saichō, 2
Saikaku. *See* Ihara Saikaku
"saint of haiku," 298–99
St. Augustine, 1
St. Thomas, 1
Śakuntalā, 23

Śākyamuni, 110; Buddha as, 116; discourse by, 111–13; teachings of, 120–21

salvation: in "An Account of My Hut," 244; by bodhisattvas, 115, 142; personal, compassion and, 183; by Pure Land Buddhism, 249; through faith and devotion, 116; universal, doctrine of, 115

"samādhi of oneness," 141, 142

samang ("four crazies"), 369

samidare ("summer rain"), 275

saṃsāric life, 123

samurai class: plays, 307; values of, 252. *See also The Tale of the Heike*

San guo (Three Kingdoms), 159

Sandy (fictional character), 164

Śaṅkārācārya, 23

Sarashina kikō (A Visit to Sarashina Village), 283, 292

Śāriputra, 111–12

Sarumino, 281

"scholar and beauty novels," 376

scholar-bureaucrats (shi): position of the, 205–206; Tang poetry as product of, 152

scholarly expertise, importance of, 202

scholars, laymen versus, 11

The Scholars (Rulin waishi), 25

scholarship, "gentlemanly learning" versus, 10–11

school and state, separation of, 203–204

"School of Law" (Fajia), 64, 104

school systems, universal, 197–98

Scotus, John Duns, 87

seasonal topics (kidai), 278

seasons, 344–45

secrecy, 140

secret censors (amhaeng ŏsa), 367

"The Secret of Caring for Life," 85–86

Sei Shōnagon: commentary on, 231–32; Confucian classics, education in, 2; contributions, overlooked, 239; religiosity of, true, 235–38; self-liberation of, 213; works as Asian classics, 25. *See also The Pillow Book (Makura no sōshi)*

Seidensticker, Edward, 219n

Seken mune-zanyo (The Calculating World), 315

selective juxtaposition, 282

self-centeredness, 341

self-cultivation, 195; *Great Learning (Daxue)* and, 195; Huang Zongxi and, 200; as human right and responsibility, 372. *See also* "learning of the mind-and-heart" (xinxue)

"Self-cultivation for the Governance of Humankind" (xiuji zhiren), 55

self-discipline. *See* self-cultivation

self-fulfillment, 100–101

self-interests, legitimacy of, 200

self-knowing, 70

self-liberation, 182, 213

self-respect, shame and, 51

"selfish gene" theory, 345

selflessness, subjective and objective, 123

sensual pleasure, 269 73

separation: sorrow of, 276; in Tang poetry, 156–57

service, "man of" (shi), 50

Seven Feelings, 329–30, 341, 350

sexuality, 179

Shakespeare, decline in study of, xiv

shame, 68

shame, self-respect and, 51

shared humanity. *See* humaneness (ren)

Sharing in the Good Books (essay), 10

Shen-hui, Pu-ji, attack on, 132–33

Shen-xiu, 132

shengren. *See* Sages (shengren)

shi ("man of service"), 50

shi poetry, 151

shigure ("early winter showers"), 275

Shih-ching, 149

Shiji (*Records of the Grand Historian*), 329

Shijing. See Book of Odes (Shijing)

shimitsuku, 291

shina no sadame, 221–22

shingaku. *See* "learning of the mind-and-heart" (xinxue)

shinjutsu (*The Discipline of the Mind-and-Heart*"), 324

Shinkokinshū, 26, 284

Shintoism, 210

shiohi (low tide), 280

Shōtetsu, 259

Shōtoku, Prince, 51

shrine rituals, 236

Shui hu. See Water Margin (Shui hu)

shushin, 319–20

Siku quanshu ("*Complete Library in Four Branches of Learning and Literature*"), 175

Sima Qian, 15, 24

simplicity: in haiku, 294–95; preference for, 261–62

sin, 319

"single-mindedness," 197, 330

"Single Origin," 337

"single-topic" (ichimotsu shitate) haiku, 279–80

"sitting in meditation" (zuo-chan), 141–42

Sixteen-Word Formula, 196–97

Sixth Patriarch. *See* Huineng, the Sixth Patriarch

social order, upholding, 363–64

social status: "classics" and, 57; classics education and, 2–4; in *The Song of the Faithful Wife Ch'unhyang*, 371

Socialism, "Chinese," 51, 208

"son of Heaven," 45

"*The Song of Sorrow*," 218

"Song of the Bowman of Shu," 149–50

The Song of the Faithful Wife Ch'unhyang: Ch'unhyang, 371–73; goodness of the Universe, 372; young Lee, 372–73; p'ansori tradition, 368–69, 373, 374n; plot, 366–67; social status in, 371; Songs of the Five Moral Relations, one of the, 366; themes, 365

Song Zhiwen, 153

Songs of the Five Moral Relations, 366, 374n

Songs of the South (Chuzi), 174

Soothill, W. E., 117

Sora, diary of, 298–99

sorrow, 276. *See also* grief

"soul," Mencius and the, 69

"soul of creation" (banbutsu no rei), 323

sound as poetic technique, 290–91, 300n

Southern School of Huineng, 132

spells, 114

spiritual discipline. *See Precepts for Daily Life in Japan (Yamato zokkun)*

spiritual harmony, 333
spirituality, dimensions of, 87
spontaneity (ziran), 75; wu-wei and, 98
"spring rain" (harusame), 275
Stanford University, 30
stereotypes, 252
Stern, Fritz, 12
stillness, 88, 92
The Story of the Stone, 175
"Story of the Virtuous Mouse," 378
storytellers, 248
Study of Mysteries movement, 79
"subjective" and "objective," 223; knowledge, balancing, 324–26
Subodhi, 167
"substantiality" (ti), 79
Śudraka, King, 23
suffering: in "An Account of My Hut," 241–42; compassion, needed to develop, 125; in *A Dream of Red Mansions*, 185; of others, man cannot bear, 67–68
Sufi poets, 22
suicide: attempts, 382; double, 304–309; thoughts of, 357
"summer rain" (samidare), 275
Sun Aware of Vacuity. *See* Monkey (fictional character)
Sun Wu-kong. *See* Monkey (fictional character)
"superlative forms," perceiving, 87
Supreme Being, concept of, 115
"Supreme Swindle," 89
Supreme Ultimate, 336–37, 341
Śurangama Sūtra, 25
surrogate figures, 215
sustainability. *See* environmental crisis

"sūtra": "classic" versus, 136; meaning of, 129
Sūtra of the Humane King, 147
symbolism: in haiku, 275–79, 282, 288; in the *Lotus Sūtra*, 114–15; in the *Platform Sūtra*, 140; in *The Tale of Kieu*, 380; in The *Tale of Genji*, 216–17. *See also* huts, symbolism of
syncretism, 25
systems, living, 342

Tae hak, 340
Tagore, Rabindranath: "East," perception of the, 18; works as Asian classics, 23
Taigiroku (Record of Great Doubts), 333
Taira clan: courtiers, portrayal as, 250–52; fate, subject of, 250; Ise Taira, 256n; "luck running out," 254. *See also The Tale of the Heike*
Taishang laojun ("Most High Lord Lao"), 78
Taketori monogatari (The tale of the Bamboo Cutter), 212
The Tale of Genji (Genji Monogatari), 17; aesthetics in, 216–17; as Asian classic, 25; as bildungsroman, 215–16; Buddhism, condemnation by, 210–11; "The Floating Bridge of Dreams," 218; historical cast, reason for, 211; jealousy and insecurity in, 223; literature, liberating function of, 228–29; *A Man Who Loved Love*, likened to, 314; *Manyōshū* and, 226–27; marital infidelity, 224–25; opening line, 220; philosophical undertones, 225–26; poetry, as sourcebook for, 211; "poignancy of

things," 220, 227; provenance, 209; as psychological novel, 209, 214; romantic love in, 213; shina no sadame in, 221–23; significance of, altered, 214–15; summary, 209; surrogate figures in, 215; themes, 221; translations, 218–219n; vernacular tales (monogatari) in, 211, 212. *See also* Murasaki Shikibu

The Tale of Kieu: background, 376; final words and reflections, 384–86; imagery, 383–84; politics in, 378–79; shape of, 379–83; text and context, 377–79; texture of, 383–84; translations, 377, 385–86. *See also* Ngyuen Du

The Tale of the Bamboo Cutter (Taketori monogatari), 212

The Tale of the Heike, 243–44; as Asian classic, 26; "Death of Atsumori," 253–54; impermanence in, 249; "The Initiates' Chapter," 254–56; mappō in, 249; narrative devices, 253; provenance, 248; stereotypes in, 252; structure, 250; symbolism, 255–56; themes, 253–54; translations, 248, 256n; "way of the warrior," 254; women in, 252. *See also* Taira clan

talent versus destiny, 384–85

tan-jing. *See Platform Sūtra of the Sixth Chan Patriarch*

Tang Buddhism, *Platform Sūtra* and, 129

Tang dynasty, 79

Tang poetry: as Asian classic, 24; folksong form, 153; nature in, 154–56; overview, 149; scholar-bureaucrats, product of, 152; shi form, 151; themes,

154–57; tone of, 152; verbal parallelism, 151

Tang San-zang. *See* Tripitaka

Tang Zhen, 207

Tathāgata, Buddha as, 116

tathāgataśarīra, 118

tathatā (eternal truth), 235

"Taxes in Money" (Qian-liang), 207

tayū, 305

temple schools (terakoya), 197

Ten Diagrams on Sage Learning (Seonghak sipdo): civil-service examinations in, 339; concepts, 335; environmental crisis and, 338, 339–40, 345–46; *Learning*, 339–40; mindfulness, 347–48; relevance of, 335–36; "rising early and retiring late," 348–50; *Study of the Heart-and-Mind*, 346–47; Supreme Ultimate, 336–37; *Tae hak*, 340; tranquility, world, 340; *Western Inscription*, 337–338. *See also* Neo-Confucianism; Yi T'oegye

Tendai School, 110

Tenji, Emperor, 226

terakoya (temple schools), 197

Theravāda Buddhism, 23, 111; "Noble Eightfold Path" of, 143

"thinking" as human quality, 69

Thirteen Classics, 57

"thisness" (haecceitas), 87

Thousand and One Nights, 22

Three-fold Body of the Buddha (Trikāya), 142

Three Kingdoms (San guo), 159

Three Teachings, 17

Three Treasures, 142

Three Vehicles, 111, 112

ti ("substantiality"), 79

tian ming ("Mandate of Heaven"), 53, 104; "noble person" and, 54

Tian-pin miao-fa lien-hua jing, 117

tian-ren he yi (harmony of man and nature), 192

Tian-tai School, 110

tianzi, 45

"to encourage virtue and shun evil" (kwŏnsŏn ching'ak), 367

Tō no Chūjō, 221–23

"to sleep" (nebu), 294

tohak, 339

Tōhō Gakkai of Japan, 239

Tokubei (fictional character), 308

tonal patterns, 156–57

Tongjiangangmu (Outline and Details of the Comprehensive Mirror), 329

toriawase ("combination") haiku, 279–80; cutting words in, 282–83

"Total Body of the Buddha" (*ru-lai quan-shen*), 118

tradition, recovery of, 189, 263

traditionalism, cultural relativism versus, 30

tranquility, world, 340

Transcendent Wisdom scriptures, 126

"transforming influence of morality," 66

translations: interpretations versus, 27; multiple, selecting from, 27, study of, 5–6, 11, 34

Treasury for the Ages (Eitai-gura), 315

Trikāya (Three-fold Body of the Buddha), 142

Trilling, Diana, 7

Trilling, Lionel, 7, 12

Tripitaka (fictional character): aspects of, 161; compassion, 164; as Everyman, 162; humor, 169; spiritual progress, lack of, 162. *See also Journey to the West*

trust: family versus public, 48; in government, 50–51

trustworthiness (xin), 49–50

truth. *See* dharma (truth)

truyen ("narrative verse"), 378

tsukihanasu ("lets go"), 281

tsurezure naru mama ni ("with nothing better to do"), 257

Tsurezuregusa. See Essays in Idleness (Tsurezuregusa)

Tugwell, Rexford Guy, 12

"two great decrees," 89

ukiyo, 311–12

ukiyo-e, 305

ukiyo-zoshi (Floating World), 314

Uma no Kami (ficitonal character), 222, 223

uncertainty, 267–68

"the unexpected," element of, 279, 280, 286n

United Nations, xv

unity, 75–76, 336

Universal Declaration of 1948 (United Nations), xv

universal education, 202–204, xiv

universal love, 65

universal salvation, doctrine of, 115

Universal Virtue, bodhisattva, 114

unmei (fate), 250

Upanishads, 23

"uplift enterprise," 10

Urabe no Kaneyoshi. *See* Kenkō

utamakura ("poetic places"), 217, 283–84
utilitarianism, 10

Vālmīki, 23
Van Doren, John, 40–41
Van Doren, Mark, 1, 42, xi; "The Colloquium on Important Books," 12; Orientalism, 13; publications, 12
"The Vanishing Bard" (survey), xiii–xiv
Vedānta Sūtra, 23
verbal parallelism, 151
vernacular literature, 211, 212, 377
Vietnamese literature. See The Tale of Kieu
Vimalakīrti: alternate names, 125; Mañjuśrī, conversations with, 122–24; silence of, 124
Vimalakīrti Sūtra: as Ārya Mahāyāna Sūtra, 120; as analogy of Mahāyāna scriptures, 126; as Asian classic, 24; provenance, 121; themes, 126
virtue (de), 101: in the Analects, 51; beauty more important than, 233–34; Confucianism, 47; in Elementary Learning, 327; "four beginnings" of, 68–69; hidden, 332; "luminous," 188, 192; of not contending, 77; reverent mindfulness, 332; "The Way" (dao) and, 74, 75
A Visit to Kashima Shrine (Kashima mōde), 283
A Visit to Sarashina Village (Sarashina kikō), 283, 292

Waiting for the Dawn (Mingyi daifanglu): as Asian classic, 25; checks and balances, system of, 205; as "early modern classic," 207–208; educational reform, 202–204; enfeoffment system, 204; future applications, 208; "Laws" in, 201; meaning of title, 201. See also Huang Zongxi
waka poetry, 210, 214, 275
Waley, Arthur, 73, 159; The Tale of Genji and, 214; translations, 218–19n
Wang Bi, 78–79; the Laozi, commentary on, 72
Wang Wei, 152–53
Wang Yang-ming: Huang Zongxi, influence on, 206; translation of classics and, 11; works as Asian classics, 24–25
war tales. See The Tale of the Heike
Warring States Period (463–222 B.C.E.): Confucius during, 58–59; political philosophy schools, 77; Zhuangzi during, 81
warrior class, 316–17. See also The Tale of the Heike
The Warrior's Sense of Duty (Buke-giri monogatari), 316–17
WASPs, core curriculum and, 30
Water Margin (Shui hu), 25, 159, 173
Watson, Burton: interpretations, 86; translations, 27, 80
"The Way" (Dao), 47, 70; nothingness of, 74–75; reconstitution of, 189; in Ten Diagrams on Sage Learning, 335; Unity and, 75–76; virtue (de) and, 74, 75; will and, 82; as Yin/Yang, 82; Zhuangzi and, 89
"The Way" mind versus human mind, 330, 346–47
"The Way of Humaneness," 49
"way of the human," 324

"way of the townspeople" (chōnin-dō), 310

"way of the warrior" (bushidō), 254, 310

"Ways of Knowing," xv

Ways of the Will, 82

wealth, how to acquire, 315

Weaver, Raymond: "The Colloquium on Important Books," 12; Orientalism, 13

Weil, Simone, 80

Wen, King, 105

wen (literate discourse), 49

Western Inscription, 337–38

"Where's the Bard?" (essay), xiii–xiv

White Deer Grotto Academy, 4

White Lotus of Holy Truth, 126

wife-husband relationship, 375n. See also *The Song of the Faithful Wife Ch'unhyang*

will: assertion of, 81–82, 96–98; realms of, 82; the Way and, 82

willow (aoyagi), 280

wisdom (zhi), 68; "central," 162; as guiding force, 86; meditation as, 141; in the *Platform Sūtra*, 134; Zhuangzi on, 81

"with nothing better to do" (tsurezure naru mama ni), 257

withered (kare), 256

women: autobiographers, 363; boldness, 318; courtesans, 305–306; as dutiful wives, 224–25; judging of, 221–23; Kenkō on, 271–73; *The Lotus Sūtra* and, 113; love of, weakness in, 314; Montaigne on, 269–71; narration by, 353; "perfect," 222–23; prostitution of, 305–306, 380–81; in puppet plays, 306; roles of, 213,

305–307; in *The Tale of the Heike*, 252; vernacular prose and, 212. See also Hyegyŏng, Lady; Murasaki Shikibu; Sei Shōnagon

"Women in Japanese Buddhism," 239

Woodberry, George, 5

Woodside, Alexander, 377

words: meaning more important than, 80–81; understanding and, 89

worship, object of (honzon), 237

wu. See nothingness (wu)

Wu Cheng-en, 25, 159, 160

Wu-qian wen. See Laozi

wu-wei ("absence of [purposeful] action"), 75; in the *Analects*, 90; Gellassenheit and, 91; as laissez-faire government, 77; practice of, 85; receptivity and, 87; spontaneity and, 98; will and, 82; you-wei and, 86

Xi yu ji. See Journey to the West

xian fa (exemplary actions), 105

xiang yue (community assembly), 201

xiao. See filiality (xiao)

xin (Mind-and-Heart), 195–96. See also "learning of the mind-and-heart" (xinxue)

xinfa (Message of the Mind), 196–97

xing, 94

"Xing-e," 94

xinxue. See "learning of the mind-and-heart" (xinxue)

xiuji zhiren ("Self-cultivation for the Governance of Humankind"), 55

xu. See emptiness (xu)

xuan ("mysterious"), 75

Xuan of Qi, King, 65

Xuan-Phuc, 377, 385

Xuan-Viet, 377

Xuan-zang, 25

Xuanxue school, 78–79

Xuanzang. *See* Tripitaka

Xuanzong, Emperor, 72, 79

Xunzi: as Asian classic, 24; on governance, 103–108; "Xing-e," 94

Xunzi (philosopher): Confucius versus, 93–96; Laozi versus, 98

yamabuki (kerria), symbolism of, 277, 280

yamadera ("mountain temple"), 291

Yamaga Sokō, 2

Yamato Zokkun. See Precepts for Daily Life in Japan (Yamato Zokkun)

Yang Guifei, 218

Yang Zhu, Mencius versus, 65–66

yangban families, 355

Ye Shi, 207

Yeats, W. B., xii

Yen Hui, 88–89

yi. *See* rightness (yi)

Yi T'oegye: on mindfulness, 347; relevance of work, 335–36; on "the Way," 349. *See also* Neo-Confucianism; *Ten Diagrams on Sage Learning (Seonghak sipdo)*

yin (lust), love versus, 179

Yin Xi, Laozi and, 73

Yin/Yang images, 82

Yoga Sūtras of Patañjali, 23

yojō (overtones), 217–18

yoki, 233

yong ("functionality"), 79

Yŏngjo, King, 352

yosei. *See* yojō

Yoshida no Kenkō, 26

Yoshitsune, 250, 251

you. *See* phenomenal existence (you)

you-wei actions: alternatives to, 82; wu-wei and, 86

yü-lu ("Recorded Sayings"), 130

Yuan jun ("The Prince"), 200

Yueji ("Record of Music"), 196

yujŏng ("affectionate"), 369

Yukinaga, 248

yuku aki ("the passing of autumn"), 276

yuku haru ("the passing of spring"), 276

za (merchant guilds), 315–16

Zai Wo, 48

Zen Buddhism: anti-scripture advocacy, 4; dominance of, 134–35, 143; history, questionable, 130; human nature and, 61; influences, 79; literature, 24; origin of, 17; "public cases" of, 124; public life, concessions to, 146–47. *See also* *Platform Sūtra of the Sixth Chan Patriarch*

Zengzi, 55

Zhen Dexiu, 321, 330

zhi. *See* wisdom (zhi)

zhi zhi. *See* Extending One's Knowledge (zhi zhi)

zhong (loyalty), 49

Zhongyong. See Mean (Zhongyong)

Zhou, Duke of: leadership of, 108; as sage-king, 105

Zhou Dunyi, 114, 336–37

Zhu Xi, 55; Huang Zongxi, influence on, 206; public schooling advocacy, 3–5; on reading the *Analects*, 55; self-control and, 200; subjectivity in knowing, 325; translation of classics

Zhu (*continued*)
  and, 11; works as Asian classics, 24.
  See also Four Books
Zhuangzi, 2; as Asian classic, 24;
  "Autumn Floods," 83–85; "inner"
  chapters, 83; "Mastering Life,"
  86–88; "outer" chapters, 83–88; "The
  Secret of Caring for Life," 85–86;
  transformative potential of, 82–83;
  translations and interpretations, 27;
  understanding, 80–81
Zhuangzi (philosopher): humor of, 80,
  81; as master, 46; as "perspectival
  realist," 89

zi. *See* "Master" (zi)
"Zi-ye Song," 153–54
zide ("getting it for oneself"). *See*
  "getting it for oneself" (zide)
Zihyan chai (Red Inkstone), 175
ziran ("spontaneous"), 75; wu-wei and,
  98
zoku ("low"), 284, 285
zu ("patriarch"), 144
zuihitsu ("following the brush"), 232,
  257
zuo-chan ("sitting in meditation"),
  141–42
Zuozhuan, chronicle of Zuo, 329